Theater and

the Politics

of Culture in

Contemporary

Singapore

Theater and

the Politics

of Culture in

Contemporary

Singapore

WILLIAM PETERSON

Middletown, Connecticut   WESLEYAN UNIVERSITY PRESS

Published by Wesleyan University Press,
Middletown CT 06459
© 2001 by William Peterson

ISBN 0-8195-6471-0 cloth
ISBN 0-8195-6472-9 paper
Printed in the United States of America
Design and composition by
    B. Williams & Associates

5   4   3   2   1

CIP data appear at the end
    of the book

To my partner Dane
for nearly two decades of
love, support, laughter,
encouragement, and
mental stimulation.

Contents

Acknowledgments ix

Introduction 1

1 Setting the Stage 9

2 The Culture of Crisis 33

3 Staging Identity and Nationhood 51

4 Commodifying and Subduing the Body 83

5 Constructing Gender 103

6 Queering the Stage 129

7 Festival Culture 161

8 The Great Singaporean Musical 181

9 Interculturalism and the Big, Bad Other 203

10 Conclusion 219

Notes 237

Works Cited 261

Index 277

Acknowledgments

This book would not have been possible without the opportunity to live and work in Singapore provided by the National University of Singapore, which hired me in 1992 to help create the country's first university-level Theatre Studies program. I wish to thank K. K. Seet and Ban Kah Choon for giving me a job and for supporting my research interests as they shifted from Sumatra to Singapore. The institutional support of NUS enabled me to travel around the region and attend conferences and symposia in Asia, Australia, and the United States. The warm and welcoming manner of Singapore's theater artists offered me an early entry into their community and the opportunity to have my perceptions challenged, stretched, and altered. Among the many artists who have supported my research and inspired me are playwrights Kuo Pao Kun and Robert Yeo, directors Ong Keng Sen and Krishen Jit, performance artist and playwright Chin Woon Ping, and Alvin Tan and Haresh Sharma, stalwarts of Singapore's The Necessary Stage. Finally, my own students in Singapore taught me the greatest lessons, and I continue to learn from their experiences via e-mail and the now less frequent human contacts. Additional credit must be given to Lim Eng Beng, a former student who served as my Singapore-based research assistant and without whose diligence this project would not have been possible. The materials he assembled for me bridged the gap between my personal stay in Singapore and my years living outside the country.

The visual dimension of the book owes its life to contributions from the Singapore Tourism Board; Saatchi and Saatchi

(Singapore); Music and Movements (Pte.) Ltd.; theater artists Robert Yeo, Chin Woon Ping, and K. K. Seet; TheatreWorks (Singapore) Ltd.; and the Singapore Repertory Theatre. Without the diligence of TheatreWorks's administrator, Traslin Ong, this book would not possess many of its most striking images. The assistance of Michele Lim at TheatreWorks has also been invaluable in the development of this work.

In 1995, I moved to New Zealand, where the support of the Humanities Research Committee at the University of Waikato supplied me with the funds to move this project further toward an actual book-length study, something that I would have considered impossible just a few years earlier. In particular, Jan Pilditch and Alan Riach in the English Department at Waikato helped encourage me to apply for these funds and showed flexibility and understanding when the focus of my research was altered. My current employer, the California State University at San Bernardino, provided the final institutional support in the form of a grant that enabled me to fully update the book and rewrite sections that needed additional work.

Some of the threads contained within this book were initially developed in other publications. Specifically, an earlier, scaled-down draft of chapter 9 appeared as "Interculturalism Derailed: The Case of Singapore" in *Disorientations: Intercultural Theatre from an Australian Perspective* (Melbourne: Centre for Drama and Theatre Studies, Monash University, 1999). Segments of chapter 4 are contained in the article "Commodifying and Subduing the Body on the Singaporean Stage," *SPAN Journal* 42/43 (April/October 1996), while an analysis of Singapore's festival of the arts in the early 1990s appears in "Singapore's Festival of the Arts," *Asian Theatre Journal* 13.1 (Spring 1996). Finally, portions of chapter 6 appear in "Sexual Minorities on the Singaporean Stage," *Australasian Drama Studies* 25 (October 1994), and in a forthcoming publication devoted to sexual minorities that is being disseminated by Singapore's Millennium Project.

The Australasian Drama Studies Association and the Association for Asian Performance at ATHE (Association for Theatre in Higher Education) have furnished a stimulating and supportive group of peers who have helped to refine this book. While the individuals connected with those organizations who have contributed to the climate for this book are too numerous to list, two individuals, Helen Gilbert of the University of Queensland and Craig Latrell of Hamilton College, offered detailed and thorough responses to the first draft of this work, making the book clearer, better organized, and deeper in its analysis.

Finding a publisher for this work met with some initial setbacks, as the process of blind review meant that individuals with a strong stake in Singaporean theater sometimes found fault with the book's failure to set out a complete and comprehensive account of the history of theater in Singapore. As I argue in the introduction, this book serves another function, one that enlarges the field beyond Singapore to look at a particular developmental model through the lens of culture and, more specifically, through theater. Thus I wish to thank the editors at Wesleyan, particularly Suzanna Tamminen, for seeing past the minutiae of theater in Singapore and recognizing that the territory for this book extends beyond the boundaries of the relatively small field of theater in a small island nation. I also want to commend the entire editorial staff at Wesleyan for their professionalism and their speedy replies to each and every inquiry directed at them, no matter how seemingly trivial or inconsequential.

The road which led to the creation of this book started in graduate school, where I had the privilege of working with faculty, staff and students in possession of fine minds and good hearts. In particular, I would like to thank Anne-Charlotte Harvey of San Diego State University and Oscar G. Brockett of the University of Texas at Austin for mentoring me not just in graduate school, but throughout the years which have followed.

Finally, I wish to thank Singapore, its citizens, and yes, even its government, for creating a complex and fascinating country in which I had the privilege of spending three exciting and interesting years.

Theater and

the Politics

of Culture in

Contemporary

Singapore

Introduction

Singapore's small size and population belie its importance in world affairs.[1] One of the most geopolitically blessed of nations, this multiethnic city-state lies virtually on the equator and at the crossroads for trade moving to and from Europe, Africa, and the Middle East to the rest of Asia, the Pacific, and the West Coast of the Americas. Singapore's ultramodern port, the world's busiest in terms of shipping tonnage, serves as a major transshipment point for goods originating throughout Asia. The country's level of material prosperity is the highest in Asia and on par with many European nations, and its glitziest shopping malls are filled with affluent, cell-phone-toting yuppies wearing fashionable clothing who appear to be just as harried, brusque, stylish, and sophisticated as any Manhattanite.[2] Long touted as Ross Perot's "favorite country," Singapore has for over a decade been held up as a model for other developing nations, with its unique blend of "authoritarianism lite,"[3] which combines elements of state capitalism with socialism. Given the considerable political, economic, and social chaos that so many developing nations in the region have experienced in the postcolonial era, it is hardly surprising that Singapore's material success and relative social stability have come to be so envied by other nations. Singapore's seat aboard the bandwagon of global market capitalism no doubt looks very attractive to other nations wishing to leapfrog over regional economic rivals, as Singapore has done.

Supporting the export of the "Singapore model" is the rhetoric of Singapore's ur-politician, Lee Kuan Yew, the country's first post-independence prime minister, who tenaciously held on to power for thirty-one years and who continues to travel the globe articulating a set of "Asian values" in his capacity as senior minister. Lee's persuasiveness, wit, and ferocious intellect have won over, worn down, and antagonized many, both within the region and on the world stage. If a formula were invented to determine the importance of a politician weighted to factor in the size of a nation, then Lee Kuan Yew would no doubt rise to the top as the most important politician on the world stage over the last forty years. Lee's ruling party, the People's Action Party (or PAP), has been the sole party in power throughout virtually the entire postcolonial era and has taken the lion's share of the credit for the country's material success. Because the politics of the party and the man have until recently been virtually inseparable, the so-called Singapore model continues to find its public and international voice in Lee's impassioned defense of what he and other PAP functionaries have come to identify as "Asian values."

The Western visitor to Singapore cannot fail to be impressed by the relative safety of the city's streets and public spaces, even at night. I only have to recall my first night in the city, where, after wandering down Orchard Road, the major shopping thoroughfare, I ended up at a park that skirts the waterfront in the virtual center of the city's urban core; there I saw hundreds of men, women, and children of all ages playing, talking, and just milling about. The freedom from fear was so overwhelming that it took my breath away, providing me with a powerful positive image of urban life that was unforgettable in its clarity and intensity. Given Singapore's many visible achievements — not the least of which are safe and clean streets — it is hardly surprising that Lee's "Singapore model" has become increasingly attractive even outside Asia at a time when Western society, with its habit of navel-gazing and its tradition of self-criticism, has shown itself fractured and beset by a now well recited litany of ills, including any or all of the following: crime, the breakdown of the family, loss of core religious values, and good old-fashioned selfishness.[4] In seemingly dangerous, uncertain times, when many argue that the moral compass of Western society is out-of-kilter, the easy promise of *any* other system of values has proven incredibly enticing. In such a world, the "Singapore model" assumes an importance far greater than its tiny size might suggest.

While Singapore's significant and impressive successes on the economic front have been much touted by politicians, journalists, and economists, very little attention has been paid to the cultural context of the nation's achievements. If we ignore culture and the process of cultural creation in which Singapore's government has had such a strong hand, we learn little about the full price the populace pays for this economic and material success. It is my hope that this work will at least partially remedy that situation by providing insights into the territory on which politics and culture collide in this much-admired Asian nation-state. The title of the book, *Theater and the Politics of Culture in Contemporary Singapore*, was chosen because my own experience in Singapore taught me that theater cannot be divorced from politics just as culture in Singapore cannot be seen apart from the political apparatus that seeks to contain and shape it. Thus, this book must necessarily be as much "about" politics in contemporary Singapore as "about" the creation of a national culture. Because Singapore possessed no unified past and no defining national myths at its moment of independence from England, the Singaporean government in the postcolonial era has sought to create a sense of national identity and a culture that brings together the ethnically and culturally diverse people of this tiny, resource-deprived city-state. Thus the construction of a common past and a shared culture has become as important to the nation-builders of contemporary Singapore as economic development.

English-language theater has been chosen as the primary lens through which to view the politics of culture in Singapore, not just because it is a field in which I am trained but also because throughout the 1990s, theater in English showed itself to be the single most dynamic and volatile form of cultural expression. The visual arts, music, or — most likely — film may someday supplant English-language theater as the form that provides the sharpest insights into the effect of government policies on emerging cultural formations, but for the moment, theater reigns supreme. I would argue that it is English-language theater more than any other form that was the most actively and consistently engaged with and controlled by Singapore's political culture throughout the 1990s. It merits detailed consideration also because it was the first largely indigenous theater to become professional, and by this I mean simply that a significant number of Singaporeans now make a full-time living creating it. Finally, it is clearly English-language theater that the government is "banking on" in terms of developing cultural institutions at home and promoting Singapore's brand of the "New Asia" overseas. In this last capacity, Singaporean theater in English is also the form that most aggressively promotes interculturalism, a force that has emerged during the last two decades as one of the most significant cross-currents in world theater.

The practice of an English-language theater is relatively new in Singapore, resulting from the intersection of numerous politically driven factors, such as language and cultural policy, along with the continuing push for sustainable economic growth and development. Singapore is a young nation, now in its fourth decade of independent existence, so it is hardly surprising that the country's theater practice is correspondingly youthful; many key practitioners are in their thirties, while the established theater companies and most of the plays performed are also of recent vintage. Only in the late 1980s did companies with professional standards begin to emerge offering programs and seasons of plays by Singaporean playwrights that dealt with Singaporean issues. Because those with the best command of English tend to occupy the apex of the educational and economic pyramid, Singaporean theater in English is in many ways a relatively elitist institution. Though some companies in Singapore have made great strides in bringing theater to communities that are economically and educationally disadvantaged, the fact remains that much English-language theater in Singapore is written and experienced by those who have made it into the top 10 percent in terms of education and economic power. Yet ironically, it is because of its relatively privileged position within the culture that Singaporean theater in English offers so much potential to demonstrate how the intersecting grids of politics, economics, and culture function in that nation. Using theater as a lens, I will hold the larger political and cultural field up for examination, hopefully making this work of interest to readers in a range of disciplines stretching from politics to cultural studies.

Readers looking for a detailed history of the development of theater in Singapore will not find it here; it is not my intention to provide an overview of this vast territory. Because Singapore is a country that is Asian, postcolonial, multiethnic, *and* multicultural, the field of performance encompasses a wide range of Chinese, Malay, Indian, and European traditions. Southern Chinese forms in various dialect groups are well represented, running the gamut from Hokkien hand puppetry to Chinese opera in Cantonese, Hokkien, Teochew, and Mandarin. Among ethnic Malay Singaporeans, the popular melodramatic form of *bangsawan* is still staged at some local community centers, while a variety of dance and musical traditions continue to be popular. More recently, there has been a surge of text-based dramatic activity in the Malay language—a number of new groups have emerged. Similarly, the performance traditions represented in the Indian community are vast indeed, ranging from theater in the Tamil and Malayalam languages to a rich array of dance traditions, including the North Indian form of *kathak* and the ancient south Indian dance tradition of *bharata natyam*. Clearly, dissertations could be written on any one of these forms. That this book focuses primarily on the exchange between politics and English-language theater will no doubt disappoint some who are looking for a broader picture of the entire spectrum of Singaporean theater. Apart from the reasons already noted for giving primacy to English-language theater, my relative lack of linguistic competence in Malay, Mandarin and Tamil inevitably makes it impossible for me to explore the *entire* range of theater, a task that would be better suited to a Singaporean fluent in these tongues. Nevertheless, I would argue that like it or not, it is English-language theater, with its direct and immediate connection to the dominant, English-language-speaking and largely ethnic Chinese elites in Singapore, whose culture, is *the* culture being offered up for export overseas.

Most chapters begin with an analysis of the political, social, and cultural forces that coalesce around a particular area of inquiry, followed by a more extended analysis of specific plays and productions. Because the Singaporean government has so much direct control over the ways in which the arts are perceived by its citizens and developed by its artists, the book starts with an examination of various fixed frames of reference established by the ruling elite that have contributed to the articulation of a national arts policy. The second chapter looks at theater against the backdrop of what David Birch refers to as the "discourse of crisis" ("Staging Crises" 72), a phenomenon that has become a recurring trope in the country's political life. By continuing to stir up the rhetoric of crisis, the government of Singapore has quite effectively stage-managed the "debate" over a seemingly endless proliferation of internal and external threats as a means of uniting its populace; whereas the threat to domestic stability was once the danger of cultural and linguistic fragmentation, in more recent times it has been variously configured as the bogeymen of communism, drugs, Western decadence, and liberal values. The third chapter focuses on three related strands that have contributed to the development of a nation and a Singaporean citizenry: language policies that have encouraged each citizen to claim a single cultural orientation; the use of the country's two great human symbols of nationhood, Sir Thomas Stamford Raffles and Lee Kuan Yew, the English and indigenous "founding fathers" of Singapore; and the cultural forces that coalesce under the aegis of Singapore's National Day, the nation's largest and most elaborate paratheatrical spectacle, which provides the nation with the opportunity to stage itself.

The subsequent three chapters deal with related but discrete issues relating to the position of the body on the Singaporean stage and, by extension, in the culture at large. Chapter 4 looks at the sexualized body as an object of consumption, not only in theater but also at street level, where advertising everywhere reinforces its power. Where the Caucasian body serves a similar function, the body may be met with ambivalence, or even occasional hostility. Yet another paradigm explored in the chapter offers the body as a metaphor for oppression, as citizens exchange power over their bodies for social advancement. Chapter 5 examines the ways in which the gender marked female is socially constructed both on and off the Singaporean stage, looking at the discourse of the state with regard to the generic category "woman." The third "body" chapter—chapter 6, "Queering the Stage"—focuses primarily on gay male life in Singapore and its coded expressions, subtle and overt, both within the culture and onstage. Also explored is the theater of the culturally invisible lesbian as well as the visibility of transsexuals and transvestites both on- and offstage.

Chapters 7 through 9 also constitute a related unit in that each chapter is based on a single piece of terrain that is determined more by theater and the demands of the international marketplace than by forces that emerge organically from within the culture. "Festival Culture," the focus of chapter 5, 7 examines the seemingly endless proliferation of festivals through which Singapore markets its goods to both its citizens and foreign tourists. The scale, scope, and content of the government-run Singapore Arts Festival is analyzed on the basis of the government's own goals and objectives for this event, revealing an approach to arts development that is radical in its unerring pragmatism. Musical theater, the form most identified with Western culture, is explored in chapter 8. Here Singaporean artists have displayed varying degrees of success in adapting the form to speak with a uniquely Singaporean voice, while the government has actively supported this project in ways that at times have undermined its potential for success. Chapter 9 focuses on interculturalism, a significant force in Western theater for the last two decades that has rarely been examined in "reverse," which is to say when Asian artists borrow Western techniques or rely on the traditions of other Asian cultures. During the 1990s, Singaporean theater artists began to work increasingly aggressively across cultural boundaries, and in ways that suggest that the Western model of interculturalism may need refinement as this cultural practice takes hold in wealthy Asian nations such as Singapore. The concluding chapter endeavors to pull together the major strands of the book by using the flogging of American Michael Fay in 1994 and the theater associated with it as the basis for some final ruminations on the past, present, and future of theater, culture, and politics in Singapore.

Throughout this book, no one piece of the playing field will be examined in isolation for the same reasons that theater has proved itself such a rich source of raw material for the semiotician: theater is the most collaborative of all of the arts, while the conditions that govern its reception before an audience are variable and complex. Because the individual play script represents only one contributor to the process by which theatrical meaning is conferred on the spectator, this study will look more to the conditions of theatrical production and the social, political, and economic forces that inform a particular production of a play than to the text itself. This more open-ended reading of the play in production is especially important in a Singaporean context, given that the meanings generated by a performance often extend far beyond those that might be openly acknowledged by the audience or the critics, a situation that brings the act of performance quite squarely back into realm of politics. As Edward Said observes: "Texts are protean things; they are tied to circumstances and to politics large and small, and these require attention and criticism. . . . But reading and writing texts are never neutral activities: there are interests, powers, passions, pleasures entailed no matter how aesthetic or entertaining the work. Media, political economy, mass institutions — in fine, the tracings of secular power and the influence of the state — are part of what we call literature" (*Culture and Imperialism* 318). What interests me is the process of identifying those non-neutral activities that, as Said argues, are essential ingredients of literature, and, by extension, any artistic endeavor.

The invocation of Said's name brings up the question of theory, the mere mention of which is guaranteed to vex as many readers as it delights. While greatly informed by the writings of feminists, cultural critics, political scientists, postcolonialists and — gasp — yes, even Marxists, this work is not driven by a single theoretical approach, in large measure because I do not believe that any single theory is adequate to the task of explicating the interrelated fields of politics, culture, and theater in Singapore.[5] While the academy increasingly asks us to become card-carrying members of a particular theoretical position, my own interests are just too wide-ranging and my mind too analytical, questioning, and pragmatic for that to be possible. The most radical deconstruction of the subject found in much contemporary theorizing in the humanities carries within it a kind of unity far more oppressive than any that could be imposed from the outside, especially inasmuch as once you accept the premise that meaning is always "deferred" as "signifiers" endlessly chase the "signified," you have in effect created a closed system, possibly elegant and "theoretically sophisticated," but hermetically sealed, making rebuttal an impossibility. At times I make extensive use of theory, but I categorically refuse to put theory—especially deconstruction in its many manifestations—in the driver's seat; I believe this would be especially dangerous in a book that cuts through so many disciplinary boundaries. I have enough experience reading across disciplines and talking to colleagues in other fields to know that academic subtribes often have very different and competing claims with respect to what a particular theoretical position means. Thus I feel that to speak only to one subtribe, using the closed language of that group, would be counter to my desire for this book to break through barriers, not impose them. Like Said, I take the possibly "theoretically unsophisticated" view that the field of inquiry must suggest its own internal coherence, and I believe the task of attempting to uncover this coherence is far more difficult and potentially satisfying than relying exclusively on theory to create the semblance of analysis.

My perceptions of Singapore's complex and interwoven fields of politics, culture, and performance were initially formed and continue to be colored by my experience working as an expatriate lecturer teaching theater studies at the National University of Singapore from 1992 to 1995. Because I had the privilege and pleasure of teaching students of theater and bearing witness to their intellectual and ethical bravery in a country where pursuing certain lines of inquiry meant carefully negotiating one's way through a political minefield, there is a sense in which I cannot stand on the sidelines and keep my mouth firmly shut. Because I have seen others persecuted in the courts and driven from Singapore for expressing their opinions openly, I cannot pretend to be neutral when it comes to the intersection between politics and the process of artistic creation. Yet I do not have an agenda, as some involved in the governing of Singapore might contend; I saw and felt the profound yearning many young Singaporeans have to speak out, write about, and place their lives onstage for themselves and others to see and can only hope that this work, regardless of how it is judged by the powers that be in Singapore, has the effect of supporting that very basic human desire.

Setting the Stage

I

Singapore's phenomenal economic success is attributed by many to its adherence to a form of state capitalism where civil liberties are curtailed for the sake of economic development. Some have argued that this model, known variously as "soft authoritarianism," "corporatism," or "neo-Confucianism," has the potential to become *the* new hegemonic political discourse over the next few decades, replacing the older models of Western-style democracy advocated by European nations, and, more aggressively, by the United States.[1] Francis Fukuyama has argued that this model represents an increasingly attractive "potential competitor to Western liberal democracy" throughout Asia as it combines an adherence to market capitalism with a more "paternalistic authoritarianism that persuades rather than coerces" ("Asia's Soft-Authoritarian Alternative" 60–61).

Lee Kuan Yew, Singapore's former prime minister, has emerged as one of the world's most respected and articulate advocates of this position as he travels the world representing Singapore at international forums in his capacity as senior minister. Perhaps the most contentious element of this model is its willingness to sacrifice democratic principles for stability, an issue that Lee addressed head-on in a 1992 interview with the *Manila Chronicle*: "Contrary to what American political commentators say, I do not believe that democracy necessarily leads to development. I believe that what a country needs to develop is discipline more than democracy. The exuberance of democracy leads to undisciplined and disorderly conditions" (qtd. in Neher 961). As a country well positioned to take advantage of the emerging Chinese and Southeast Asian markets due to many of the same economic, political, cultural, and linguistic factors that first made it attractive to multinational corporations as a base for their operations in the 1970s, Singapore stands poised to engage in the wholesale exportation of its political ideology and the structures of state and economic organization on a scale never before undertaken by a small Asian nation. The island nation of 3.2 million has already established Singapore-style townships in China, India, and Vietnam, with many more soon to follow, while the media at home in Singapore regularly extols the virtues of pan-Asian and particularly Chinese-Singaporean joint ventures.[2] From this perspective, one can argue that Singapore is in a position to influence the internal affairs of a country like China far more profoundly than China is likely to affect Singapore over the next few decades. Given that Singapore was the first country in the region to recover from the Asian economic crisis of the late 1990s, their model of economic, social and political development is likely to receive continued interest.[3]

The Singaporean government's control over the creation and dissemination of this narrative of success brings to mind Edward Said's observation that "the power to narrate, or to block other narratives from forming and emerging, is very important to culture and imperialism, and constitutes one of the main connections between them" (*Culture and Imperialism* xiii). Singapore's positioning of itself as the repository of Asian values suggests the possibility of a neo-imperialist expression for this master narrative, while on the home front the government clearly has the power to "block other narratives from forming and emerging." In his reexamination of Franz Fanon's classic study on the effects of colonialism, *The Wretched of the Earth*, Said argues, "Fanon was the first major theorist of anti-imperialism to realize that orthodox nationalism followed along the same track hewn out by imperialism, which while it appeared to be conceding authority to the nationalist bourgeoisie was really extending its hegemony" (*Culture and Imperialism* 273). The only way to avoid the perpetuation of a new domestically replicated imperialism, he argues, is by taking a "rapid step . . . from national consciousness to political and social consciousness." Said observes that this "means first of all that needs based on identitarian (i.e., nationalist) consciousness must be overridden" (*Culture and Imperialism* 273). Rather than working toward the development of "political consciousness," the Singaporean government under the PAP has sought to manufacture a sense of national consciousness that is manifested at all levels of society.

Through the examination of one manifestation of cultural expression—namely theater—this political model of a kinder, gentler authoritarianism can be examined from a culturally based perspective. Before examining how this model plays itself out through theater in subsequent chapters, however, one needs a clearer understanding of the narrative frames established by the government that set the stage for theater in Singapore. Thus the rest of this chapter will be devoted to four key areas in which the government maintains control over that narrative, moving from the larger circle of the government's master plan for Singapore, to the smaller frames that determine how cultural and arts policy is articulated and implemented.

National Development and Culture

The People's Action Party, or PAP, has governed Singapore since 1959, shepherding it through the years following independence from England, followed by the brief union with Malaysia from 1963 to 1965, and continuing through the period of fully independent nationhood that began in 1965. Under the commanding presence of former prime minister Lee Kuan Yew, the PAP is credited with playing a key role in the successful economic transformation of this tiny, densely populated island nation with no natural resources into a thriving, cosmopolitan, international city with the world's busiest containerized shipping facilities. The former mangrove swamp obtained for the British crown in 1819 by Thomas Stamford Raffles is now the wealthiest nation in the region, enjoying a higher standard of living than many European nations, including its former colonizer.[4] When the PAP came to power, it faced the challenge of bringing together a multiethnic, multicultural population with nothing to link them to one another apart from the fact that they were largely descendants either of people who came to Singapore to make a better life for themselves or of workers or convict laborers imported by the British to develop the colony. During the 1960s and 1970s, while the government focused on the country's economic development and its citizens concerned themselves with ensuring that their proverbial rice bowls remained full, Singapore was not known as a country with its own distinct national traditions in the arts. Given the multiethnicity of the country and the sheer number of languages spoken by its inhabitants, which included English and a number of southern Chinese dialects as well as Tamil and Malay, cultural expressions that reflected a pan-Singaporean identity were largely nonexistent.[5] Generally speaking, Singaporeans supported a wide range of traditional performance activities largely associated with their own ethnic and cultural groups. Largely absent were cultural artifacts and a cultural practice that crossed cultural and ethnic lines.

Throughout Lee's thirty-one-year tenure as Singapore's prime minister, his political rhetoric rarely strayed from the realm of economic development and pragmatic politics. Indeed, it is precisely Lee's fierce pragmatism and bread-and-butter approach to economic development and international politics that has won him so many friends and admirers in the international arena. In a 1996 address on the future of Singapore entitled "Will Singapore Survive after Lee Kuan Yew," Lee's own enumeration of PAP achievements made no mention of cultural matters and instead focused entirely on the country's rapid economic advances, which enabled it to "leap-frog the region." He notes that at the time Singapore gained independence from the Malaysian Federation in 1965,

> our neighbors were out to reduce their economic links with us. So we linked up with the developed world. MNCs became a driving force in manufacturing and we exported our products to them. . . . Now this strategy has proved so successful that all our neighbors, and the whole of Asia, are doing likewise. . . . We created First World conditions in what was then a Third World region. We succeeded in establishing First World standards in public and personal security, health, education, telecommunications, transportation, both sea and air, and in social services. (*Straits Times*, 13 June 1996)[6]

Lee's vision of Singapore's future promises economic growth, not cultural development: "To the young and the not-too-old, I say, look at the horizon, find that rainbow ,o ride it. Not all will be rich; quite a few will find a vein of gold; but all who ̣ursue that rainbow will have a joyous and exhilarating ride and some profit." Singapore is painted as the proverbial pot of gold at the end of the rainbow, a place where state capitalism ensures that some will become rich, while everyone will at least enjoy "some profit." Even Singapore's most famous domestic critic, the late statesman David Marshall, while calling Lee Kuan Yew "at base a fascist," remarks that he is "in awe, genuine awe, of what they [the PAP] have achieved pragmatically. . . . There is no unemployment, there is no homelessness, there is an overflowing rice bowl"

(Gray). In the age of global capitalism, where the ends are seen to justify the means, Lee has become an icon for the kind of "benign authoritarianism" that supposedly makes rapid economic growth possible.

In 1981 the issue of Lee's political succession was raised for the first time in Singapore, and a significant portion of the country's political life over the course of the rest of the decade revolved around preparing a younger genera-tion of leaders to take the reigns of power from the elder generation of PAP stalwarts. By the decade's end, the two front-runners for the nation's top job were Lee's own son, BG (Brigadier General) Lee Hsien Loong, and Deputy Prime Minister Goh Chok Tong.[7] Both had been thoroughly tested and given tough jobs, with the younger Lee responsible for creating a strategy for deal-ing with the 1985 economic recession while also presiding over the PAP's Youth Wing. When Goh became prime minister in 1990, many expected him to serve as a mere "seat-warmer" for Lee's son, assuming that dynastic succession was in the cards.[8] Goh's ability to gradually distance himself from Lee, while simultaneously claiming the mantle of power and legitimacy from the master elder statesman, enabled him to consolidate his hold on power to the point where Goh ruled unchallenged throughout the 1990s. The younger Lee has been carefully groomed to become prime minister in 2007, and Goh has made it abundantly clear that his plan for succession will be followed, observing, "I don't expect factions to break out. I don't expect ri-valries or personality conflicts" (*Straits Times*, 24 January 2001).[9]

Critical to Goh's success with the public has been a decade of political rhetoric that repeatedly stresses his interest in developing a more gracious, gentler, more culturally vibrant nation. Lee's nuts-and-bolts approach to the business of government has been much contrasted with the rhetoric of his successor. Indeed, Goh himself likens Lee's relationship to his people as that of a "stern father," while characterizing his own position as that of "elder brother" (*Straits Times*, 20 October 1994). Even Goh's inaugural speech was marked by a significant shift in tone: "My mission is clear: to ensure that Sin-gapore thrives and grows after Lee Kuan Yew; to find a new group of men and women to help me carry on where he and his colleagues left off; and to build a nation of character and grace where people live lives of dignity, ful-fillment and care for one another" (qtd. in Shee, "Singapore in 1990" 173). It would have been almost unthinkable for Lee to emphasize the building of a nation based on intangibles such as "character" or "grace," much less a soci-ety in which people are "fulfilled" and "care for one another." Throughout the early 1990s, the political rhetoric found almost daily in Singapore's English-language newspaper, the *Straits Times*, reinforced the idea that Goh was ushering in a era of more "gracious" living in a nation that was finally in a position to allow some of the finer things in life to flourish now that it had entered the select club of First World nations. Though Goh's "kinder, gentler style" has sometimes been at odds with his dogged pursuit of political foes and his unwillingness to allow dissenting views to have a voice, there is a sense in which the development of the performing arts would have seemed anathema to a Singapore under Lee Kuan Yew's direction.[10] In fact, during Lee's tenure two well-known performing artists who have now achieved the status of cultural treasures spent the late 1970s under arrest, while as late as 1987 actors connected with a socially conscious theater company were detained and forced to publicly admit their involvement in a "conspiracy" to overthrow the government. Set against Lee's record of relative hostility with respect to the performing arts, this new discourse stressing both continued economic growth *and* the development of culture is one of the most significant ways in which the second generation of leaders under Goh have distinguished themselves from their predecessors.

Indeed, the development of culture and the articulation of a national cultural policy emerged as one of the master narratives in Singapore's social and political life in the 1990s. Allied with cultural development has been a range of social policies designed to change outmoded or socially undesirable behaviors. Goh's 1996 New Year's address to his compatriots reinscribed the ruling party's commitment to economic growth and prosperity, while at the same time encouraging Singaporeans to help build a culture and, in the process, a more "gracious society": "In one generation, we have moved from attap- and zinc-roofed wooden huts in kampongs to four- and five-room HDB flats in new towns.[11] But some Singaporeans still behave as if they were in the stone age. . . . Let us now complement our economic achievements with social, cultural and spiritual development. Then, by the 21st century, Singapore will be a truly successful, mature country with a developed economy and a gracious society" (*Singapore Bulletin*, July 1996). While Goh's concluding statement suggests a broadening of priorities, the language he uses when chastising those citizens who behave "as if they were in the stone age" echoes the "stern father" rhetoric of his predecessor. Even as Goh distances himself from Lee in terms of style, he continues his political mentor's policy of trying to educate an unruly citizenry. Throughout the senior statesman's tenure, organized campaigns were waged to alter a bewildering array of social and cultural behaviors ranging from procreation to urinating in elevators; in each instance, the tone used in the campaign was very much that of the stern father telling his offspring how to behave. Goh's discourse, though softer than Lee's, takes the senior politician's master plan one step further by broadening social correctives to include the realm of culture.

Specifically, what Goh is referring to when he derides his fellow citizens for "stone age behavior" is a streak of selfishness that has virtually become a defining feature of what it means to be Singaporean. The press, which has frequently exposed and ridiculed this kind of behavior, in 1995 carried a report of Mercedes-driving parents in a wealthy area who trampled over each other to carry away the free books that were being offered for the benefit of needy schoolchildren. Indeed, this kind of "me first" behavior has become so widespread that a new word—*kiasu*—has officially entered the lexicon in Singapore and increasingly throughout Australasia. The term *kiasu*, based on a Hokkien word meaning "fear of losing out," is used to characterize a wide range of behaviors that fail to take into account the needs of others.[12] Specific examples of "kiasuism" reported in the press include the practice of loading up on expensive items such as shellfish at a buffet table, hiding library books in obscure places because you may need them at a later date, or driving in a less than courteous manner. This phenomenon is so much a part of Singaporean culture that a popular cartoon character is known as "Kiasu Man," while McDonald's at one point in the mid-1990s even went so far as to introduce a "kiasu burger." There is a sense in which kiasu behavior is regarded by many as a negative but necessary aspect of Singaporean life. In a small country with limited resources, the kiasu mentality would seem to play into the scarcity model.

To counter this kind of behavior, annual "courtesy campaigns" are devised and carried out. The 1994 courtesy campaign, for example, was entitled "Let's Be More Considerate" and focused "on promoting thoughtfulness and consideration, moving beyond persuading Singaporeans to say "please" and "thank you." Spearheaded by the Ministry of Community Development, the sixteen-year-old campaign undertook activities such as the creation of a comic book to "encourage Singaporeans to look at courtesy from a lighter side"; launching a campaign to promote courtesy in the workplace "as a means to improve productivity"; and "giving awards to courteous passengers and tour managers" (*Straits Times*, 29 June 1994). The link between "courtesy" and "productivity" reflects a position frequently articulated by the dominant PAP state discourse, which connects gracious social behavior with future economic prosperity; the ubiquity of this theme suggests that generosity in the social sphere is valued not as an end in itself but as a means of contributing to Singapore's economic development.

Six years later, in April 2000, Prime Minister Goh was still hammering away on this issue when he appeared at a two-day "carnival" at a shopping center to promote "Kindness Week," an event created to support the Singapore Kindness Movement (or SKM), which he launched earlier in the year to promote small acts of kindness (*Straits Times*, 9 April 2000). Given that two decades of courtesy campaigns have apparently failed to achieve the desired effects, it is hardly surprising that Goh would chide his country's citizens for behaving "as if they were in the stone age." His choice of words suggests that bad or uncivil behavior is related to the citizenry's lack of development, the unspoken implication being that in an "advanced" nation such as Singapore, such retrograde behavior is shameful.

The development of culture goes hand in hand with the creation of a gentler, better-mannered citizenry; together they form key building blocks that will support the creation of a gracious and sophisticated nation as Singapore enters the next leg in a "race" to become the "Switzerland of Asia." In a December 1996 speech before an audience of university students, Prime Minister Goh outlined his vision of Singapore in the twenty-first century as an "outstanding, refreshing cosmopolitan society [with a] vibrant economy. Good jobs. Cultural liveliness. Artistic creativity. Social innovation. Good schools. World class universities. Technological advances. Intellectual discussion. Museums. Nightclubs and theatres. Good food. Fun places. Efficient public transport. Safe streets. Happy people." In closing, he added, "We can do with more spontaneity and creativity" (*Straits Times*, 21 December 1996). Goh's tantalizing list of big-city attributes once again links cultural vitality with economic success, and his demand for "more spontaneity and creativity" reflects the PAP penchant for calling forth intangibles such as creativity with the voice of a cool pragmatism; here Goh sounds very much like the stern elder brother standing over his siblings, ordering them to be creative on command.

As proof that the country was well on its way toward achieving this vision, Goh cited an article in *Fortune* magazine that rated Singapore as the third best city in the world in which to work and live, after Toronto and London. The *Fortune* article proclaimed, "Clean, green, orderly, and efficient, Singapore runs like clockwork under the watchful eyes of a government that leaves nothing to chance. . . . It may sound like a police state, but in fact this small island is an exceptionally pleasant place to do business and raise a family" (Precourt and Faircloth). Adding validity to the findings, the *Straits Times* noted that the survey was conducted by the prestigious firm Arthur Andersen, which "surveyed executives worldwide, sought feedback from ambassadors and governors, carried out a survey of economic development organizations of major cities and relied on research done by Andersen's offices around the world" (21 December 1996). Positive external evaluations of Singapore's achievements frequently appear in the state-controlled media, and they not only rely on Western models but also use, by and large, the standards of the international business community, reflecting Singapore's status as a hub for multinational operations in Southeast Asia.[13] Thus it should come as no surprise as we turn toward the issue of government support for culture and the performing arts to find that the government's vision of an artistically vibrant Singapore owes much to what it believes are Western standards; in fact, the fixed markers are frequently those set by the international business community, making Singapore a model society in terms of its ability to enshrine the values of global capitalism.

National Arts Policy

According to Singapore's National Arts Council, "In 1985, the Singapore government announced its intention to create a culturally vibrant society by 1999" (Lau 2). Three years later, as Lee was preparing to step down as prime minister, a government committee was created and charged with the task of making recommendations concerning the future of the performing arts in Singapore. In November 1988, a final report articulated the following role for the arts in the country's future development:

> With a relatively small population, strategizing for a potentially vibrant performing arts environment in Singapore is no different from the strategies successfully applied to Singapore's high-tech economic activities. In many respects, performing arts in Singapore [sic], apart from being an enrichment experience for the people, will form an integral part of the Singapore lifestyle no different from its greenness and cleanliness which together will affirm its position as a center of excellence and an attractive place in which to invest. (Singapore Government "Report on the Performing Arts")

With the same remarkable pragmatism that has come to characterize so many aspects of life in Singapore, the government came to the conclusion that the performing arts were just as essential to the country's image as its "greenness" and "cleanliness," recognizing that a vibrant arts scene would help cement its position as "a center for excellence" and "an attractive place in which to invest." A syllogism seems to be at work here that runs something like this: Developed countries have a vibrant arts scene. We are a developed country. Therefore we must create a vibrant arts scene.

One local satirist observed that "foreigners and returnees from overseas universities tended to judge Singapore by what they saw in London, New York or Paris. Hence when they could not find the kind of entertainment they were used to, they felt bored and proclaimed Singapore a cultural desert." Now, he notes, thanks to its commitment to developing the arts along Western lines, "Singapore has been transformed from a cultural desert into a cultural dessert. We now have something nice and sweet to offer our people as well as tourists after dinner" (Macaw). As we shall see in subsequent chapters, the brazenly commercial justification behind the government's support for the arts has not changed over time. The current minister for information and the arts, Lee Yock Suan, justified the doubling of the arts budget over the five years beginning in 2000 with an argument both pragmatic and familiar: "A vibrant arts scene can give us that creative buzz and stimulate our minds to think outside the box. At the same time, it enlarges our leisure options and makes Singapore an attractive place for talent" (L. Lim). Not surprisingly, the moral dimension to art is never mentioned as one of its values.

In 1991, the government created the National Arts Council (NAC) by an act of Parliament, entrusting them with the following mission: to "help nurture the arts and develop Singapore into a vibrant global city for the arts" (Lau 3). The same language of economic development that runs through the earlier "Report on the Performing Arts" is repeated here, with no sense that the arts have any real contribution beyond that of making Singapore a more attractive place. The NAC has subsequently become involved in a wide range of activities, including the distribution of training and grant money, sponsorship of local theater companies, running the country's major performance venues, and overseeing the growing Singapore Arts Festival. Many of the original objectives for the NAC are focused on raising the profile of the arts and developing a more sophisticated arts audience.[14]

Not content with merely creating a "vibrant culture," as the millennium approached, the ministry responsible for the arts called for the creation of "a renaissance city of information, culture and the arts in the 21st century"

(*Straits Times*, 1 June 1997), a remarkable goal that will be explored in greater detail in chapter 7. Of course, creating a "vibrant culture by 1999" or starting a "renaissance" is not simply a matter of turning on a spigot and letting the money and the cultural lubricants flow. Nevertheless, the centerpiece of the government's cultural policy since the mid-1990s has been the construction of the largest and most expensive performing arts center in the region: a S$595 million[15] complex to be known as "The Esplanade—Theatres on the Bay,"[16] located on a prime site along Marina Bay near the mouth of the Singapore River. At the formal groundbreaking ceremony for the center, Tony Tan, then deputy prime minister, picked up on Goh's "gracious living" theme, remarking that the Esplanade "marks a new milestone for our nation, a new phase of national development with an emphasis on culture and gracious living," adding that "the Esplanade will set a new standard for concert and theatre-going and will be a launching pad to help bring Singapore to the forefront of the international arts scene" (Tsang, "20 Year Arts Dream"). As with so many achievements touted by Singaporean politicians, the value of the undertaking is related to its ability to bring the country international recognition. Tan's remarks suggest that "launching" Singaporean work before an international audience is more important than providing a "landing pad" for Singaporean work to be seen by Singaporeans.

Tan's rhetoric at the groundbreaking merits further examination. Using the language of computer technology, Tan observed that while the new theaters will constitute the hardware, "what's necessary to make this hardware come alive is the software" (Tsang, "20 Year Arts Dream").[17] Tan's relegation of the artist to "software" status harks back to the language used in the original 1988 policy paper, which suggested that creating a vibrant performing arts environment "is no different from the strategies successfully applied to Singapore's high-tech economic activities." Mindful of the fact that Singapore is a money-driven society, Tan also used the occasion to assure aspiring young artists that they need not make financial sacrifices by pursuing a career in the arts:

When asked by reporters whether choosing art and other "soft" subjects[18] in Singapore meant that students would not be able to attain the five Cs — career, cash, credit card, car and condominium — Dr. Tan replied: "I'm not sure that if you choose the "soft option" in Singapore, you won't achieve the five Cs. You become an artist, or an author or a composer or a musician or a dancer because this is what you want to do. This is what you are and if you are very good at it and you are successful then all the other things will follow." (Tsang, "20 Year Arts Dream")

Of the artists associated with even the longest-running and most established companies in Singapore, one would be hard-pressed to find any in possession of all of the "five Cs." In a country where a new Honda Accord costs in excess of S$125,000 and private flats in well-heeled neighborhoods cost more than S$500,000, the modest income of theater artists would appear to be completely inadequate to attain the great Singaporean financial dream.[19] Perhaps Tan is thinking about the potential financial resources of the arts administrators who will be running the center, or the few Singaporean artists, such as pop singer Dick Lee, who have met with international success. Just a few months before the groundbreaking for the arts center, in a move that generated much publicity, T. Sasitharan, a well-known arts journalist, took a "five figure pay cut" when he left his secure and comfortable job as an arts editor for the *Straits Times* to take over the operation of the Substation, an established but relatively modest arts center (*Straits Times*, 4 April 1996).[20] There is a sense in which Tan's comments reflect his "market"; in a country where the top civil servants command the world's highest salaries — salaries that,, according to Prime Minister Goh, provide "a visible demonstration of the sacrifice involved in becoming a minister" (Wallace, "Pay Raise Plan") — it may not occur to Tan that anyone would choose a career that did not lead directly to the "five Cs."[21]

"Asian Values," "Western Values"

No discussion of the parameters of culture in contemporary Singapore would be complete without revisiting the longest-running and most carefully stage-managed "debate" that continues to "rage" in Singapore's state-controlled media: namely the extent to which Singaporeans should accept or reject so-called Western values, a topic that is inevitably linked with the government's attempts to articulate a set of pan-Asian values. Given Singapore's status as a multiethnic, multicultural country in which expressions of Asianness include the entire range of Chinese, Indian, and Malay cultures, it is obviously quite a tricky thing to put forth a monolithic set of Asia values. The debate between value systems is frequently framed in terms of its political dimension: many Western commentators condemn Singapore's "soft authoritarianism," while Singapore argues for the necessity of curtailing individual rights for the greater good of society. In the interests of creating a safer, more harmonious Singapore, a range of policies have been justified, among them the rights to detain people suspected of criminal activity without cause, to stifle or carefully manage political debate, and to maintain tight controls over the broadcasting and print media. One of the chief defenders of the Singaporean government's position is Kishore Mahbubani, whose views have been widely circulated in the West.[22]

Contemporary Western urban society in many ways presents an easy target for criticism, given the astronomical crime rates compared to those of Asian cities, the decaying inner-city neighborhoods, the alcohol- and drug-related problems, the out-of-wedlock births, and the racial tensions, there is no shortage of social ills to enumerate. Frequently cited as reasons for these problems by Singaporean observers are the social policies of earlier decades, state welfarism, liberalism and—most of all—faulty values that place too much emphasis on individual actions and rights at the expense of the group. The 1994 caning of American teenager Michael Fay for spray-painting automobiles and stealing road signs gave the debate an international dimension as the American media largely excoriated Singapore for such a "barbaric" practice, while the Singaporean press countered with statements by Americans who supported the country's harsh penalties and argued that they constituted an effective deterrent against crime. By September 1994, as reactions to the Michael Fay affair hit a fever pitch, the government was apparently so concerned that they had painted such an overwhelmingly bleak portrait of the United States that a number of personal testimonials by prominent Singaporeans suddenly appeared in the *Straits Times*, with headlines such as "Many little things endear the US to me" (Tan Bah Bah) or "Why the US is not dying—yet" (Devan). Given the size of the Western expatriate community in Singapore and the large number of people whose livelihoods depend directly and indirectly on multinational corporations, to some extent press-generated criticism of the West routinely becomes less strident almost as soon as it reaches its peak.

In spite of the numerical majority of the ethnic Chinese in Singapore and the danger that any articulation of "Asian values" by Singapore's Chinese-dominated ruling elite might not reflect the values of the Malay and Indian minorities,[23] the values that have been articulated by the government are proudly hailed as Confucian. In a 1994 speech before the inaugural meeting of the International Confucian Association in Beijing, Lee Kuan Yew credited Confucian values as being central to Singapore's success. Lee, himself the honorary chairman of the association, noted in Mandarin that Singaporeans did not believe in the "unlimited individualism of the Americans," adding that "as long as the leaders take care of their people, they will obey their leaders. This reciprocity is basic. It was the people's respect for their leader which made them accept tough government policies" (Fernandez, "Confucian Values"). David Brown argues that the articulation of a set of Confucian values is largely directed at the Chinese community anyway, perhaps because they are perceived as being the most "at risk" where "Western values" are concerned:

> There have been sustained campaigns, beginning in 1978 and 1982 respectively, to promote Confucian values and the Mandarin language. Both campaigns have been implemented through changes in the school curriculum and through media advertising. "Chineseness" is portrayed as a traditional culture encapsulated in Confucianism and Mandarin, which embodies the values of discipline, respect for authority and commitment to the community. Confucianism is not associated with a backward China, but with and conducive to economic development, political stability, national unity and, potentially, democracy. Given the numerical and socioeconomic dominance of the Chinese in Singaporean society, this image of Chinese culture inevitably provides the major building-block for the creation of the consensual national culture. Moreover, the argument that Confucianism should not be associated specifically or solely with the Chinese, but also with Japanese and Korean societies, engenders the claim that it constitutes the core component of a truly "Asian" culture. ("Corporatist Management" 24)

Tied to these so-called Confucian principles is the model of "soft authoritarianism"; taken together, they are heralded by Singapore's politicians as the basic ingredients for successful economic development in emerging Asian nations. Jan Pieterse and Bhikhu Parekh observe that "in East Asia, neo-Confucianism and the 'Confucian ethic' serves as an ideology to explain the economic success of the East Asian Newly Industrialized Countries, as an Asian equivalent to Weber's Protestant ethic as the spirit of modern capitalism. Promoted from Singapore to Japan, it serves well as a state ideology of civil obedience and collective conformity in the name of economic prosperity" (7). David Marshall, Singapore's last remaining old-guard opposition voice until his death in 1996, articulated his strong disapproval of this practice of linking Singapore's prosperity with Confucian values in a speech at the UN Day Dinner in 1992. His remarks were met with stunned silence by the assembled PAP dignitaries seated in the front tables, who were no doubt mortified that such criticism could be articulated at a forum that included so many prominent figures from the international diplomatic community resident in Singapore.

Outside of Singapore, other Asians are hardly in complete agreement as to what constitutes Asian or even Confucian values. South Korean dissident Kim Dae Jung asserts that Lee Kuan Yew's "view of Asian cultures is not only unsupportable but self-serving" when he argues for the superiority of so-called Confucian values (190). Kim notes that "almost two millennia" before English political philosopher John Locke laid the foundation for modern democracy, "Chinese philosopher Meng-tzu preached similar ideas" when he articulated "the ancient Chinese philosophy of *Minben Zhengchi*, or "people-based politics," [which] teaches that "the will of the people is the will of heaven" and that one should "respect the people as heaven" itself" (191). He notes that "when Western societies were still being ruled by a succession of feudal lords" (191–92), the sons of Chinese peasants were able to join the ranks of the civil service and even advance to the top, concluding that "the biggest obstacle is not its [Asia's] cultural heritage, but the resistance of authoritarian rulers and their apologists" (194).

Initial attempts to fashion a set of core Singaporean values that would counter Western values began in 1988, when Goh—then under the watchful eye of Lee Kuan Yew—argued that "such a National Ideology, setting out society's guiding principles, will help Singaporeans keep their Asian bearings as they approach the twenty-first century" (Brown, "Corporatist Management" 25). Ultimately, a 1991 White Paper articulated five core values that have since become the standard for a "national ideology." The following core "national values," supposedly based on Confucian teachings, are now widely circulated throughout Singapore, published in newspapers, and posted on bulletin boards in the communal areas situated on the ground floor of Singapore's vast public housing blocks: "(1) nation before community and society before self; (2) family as the basic unit of society; (3) regard and community support for the individual; (4) consensus instead of contention; (5) racial and religious harmony" (Clammer 35). Throughout the 1990s, many political scientists have argued that these communitarian[24] values are also consistent with old-fashioned, Western Protestant work-ethic values and, furthermore, that they bear a strong resemblance to Indonesia's state ideology, enshrined in the "five pillars" of *Pancasila*.[25] John Clammer argues that these values are in fact "universal" and takes Singapore to task for proposing such an essentialist framework, noting that in this paradigm, the West is "characterized by individualism, selfishness, materialism, and decadence, the latter [Asia] by a sense of community, spirituality and family" (40).

In the seventeenth century, when John Locke wrote of the reasons that led man to accept limits on his behavior by entering into a civil contract, he was proposing a model virtually indistinguishable from the first "Confucian" value of "nation before community and society before self." Rather than the principle itself being the point of contention between Singapore and a "West" seen as uniform and monolithic, differences arise over the degree to which individuals can still retain their autonomy in the face of the strictures of the state. In the "soft authoritarian" model adhered to by Singapore, the government, under the umbrella of safeguarding community and national interests, has vast and sweeping powers over the individual that would not be deemed acceptable in many democratic societies, both Asian and Western. Clearly these practices do not necessary follow from the value itself.

Similarly, most societies value "family," though many differ radically as to what constitutes that basic unit: Does it include lesbian and gay families? People unrelated to one another by blood who have a special bond? Unmarried couples? Certainly in a Singaporean context the term *family* is interpreted to mean not only husband, wife, and children but also the respect and care given to extended family members and parents, who would be far more likely to live with their offspring in Asia than they would be in a Western context.

Where the third value, "community support for the individual," is concerned, again the application of that value depends on what definition of "community" one uses; in a Singaporean context, self-help organizations based on ethnicity define one expression of community. Yet some argue that these "self-help" organizations merely perpetuate divisions within society and neutralize the possibility of political action to agitate for social change. Tania Li argues that these organizations promote a "Malay cultural-weakness orthodoxy" (168), while David Brown notes that this underdog ethos encourages Malays "to see their internal cultural attributes as responsible for their socioeconomic problems, instead of blaming the Chinese or the government" ("Corporatist Management" 24). As for volunteerism, most Singaporeans have shown very little willingness to give of their time and money to support volunteer work, a phenomenon that has been much commented upon in the Singaporean press.

The fourth value, "consensus instead of contention," is enshrined as a key national value in neighboring Indonesia as well. Yet most cultures could be said to value consensus over contention, and this simple statement affirming its worth begs the question of how much contentiousness is permitted. Whereas writing articles and speaking out against one's government is considered acceptable in a democracy, in Singapore opposition views can be expressed only in approved forums. Even under Goh, the Singaporean government has made it abundantly clear that political criticism can only take place in the context of government itself, effectively meaning that openly criticizing PAP policies requires one to form a political party, as novelist and short story writer Catherine Lim was instructed to do in 1994 when she suggested that Goh's liberalization of Singapore had been derailed (*Straits Times*, 24 January 1995). Given the fact that over the last two decades virtually every politician who has spoken out openly and forcefully against PAP policies in existing political forums has been tried and convicted by the Singaporean courts for a range of illegal activities — among the most popular of which are tax evasion and libel — one would have to be brave indeed to enter the realm of politics as a member of the opposition.

With religious disharmony continuing to threaten the stability of the nations and the lives of individuals around the globe, the final value of "racial and religious harmony" would also appear to be an exemplary one. However, what happens when a religious organization concerns itself with social issues? As we shall see in the following chapter, in 1987 the Singaporean government ruthlessly suppressed a Catholic Opus Dei–style group lobbying for social justice, detaining some of its participants and reputedly subjecting a number of them to torture in an attempt to extract public confessions. In this instance, an exemplary "value" would also appear to constitute a convenient and effective means of stifling dissent.

In *Culture and Imperialism*, Said warns of the dangers associated with a one-to-one correspondence between state and culture, a situation that I will argue that the PAP is largely responsible for creating in Singapore:

In time, culture comes to be associated, often aggressively, with the nation or the state; this differentiates "us" from "them," almost always with some degree of xenophobia. Culture in this sense is a source of identity, and a rather combative one at that, as we see in "returns" to culture and tradition. These "returns" accompany rigorous codes of intellectual and moral behavior that are opposed to the permissiveness associated with such relatively liberal philosophies as multiculturalism and hybridity. In the formerly colonized world, these "returns" have produced varieties of religious and nationalist fundamentalism. (xiii)

Ironically, while Singapore carefully guards against fundamentalist expressions of Islam and has a history of quashing Opus Dei–style demands for social justice, its political leaders have fostered a kind of state-defined or "nationalist fundamentalism" largely based on the distinction between "us" and "them." Accompanying this distinction is a corresponding degree of xenophobia that, in Singapore's case, is directed against the monolithic construction of "Western values," which are equated with decay, decline, and all manner of social ills. The rhetoric of the state repeatedly hammers home its opposition to the "permissiveness" associated with those "liberal" values.

At the height of one such "Asian values versus Western values" campaign waged by the Singaporean media in 1992, a survey conducted in people's homes on a range of moral issues was used to demonstrate that most Singaporeans, unlike their Western counterparts, were morally and socially quite conservative. Given the general and understandable reticence of Singaporeans to speak about government policies, the presence of government survey-takers at people's front doors no doubt ensured that the response would provide a resoundingly strong show of support for government policies. The results of the survey were then held up as a justification for the continuation of censorship controls over the media and the arts. The end result was that a state-created discourse became effectively internalized by the masses through the use of a compliant, state-controlled media.

In another exercise justified by "Asian values," in 1997 Prime Minister Goh and virtually the entire top leadership of the PAP sued opposition Worker's Party (WP) leader and Non-Constituency MP [26] J. B. Jeyaretnam for libel a few months after they had succeeded in virtually bankrupting former WP candidate Tang Liang Hong in an earlier libel suit.[27] In the months prior to the trial, Jeyaretnam had strongly criticized the government in Parliament, on one occasion charging the PAP with running a "Mafia government" that relied on fear to cower its citizens into submission (*Straits Times*, 5 June 1997). His "libelous" offense however, was not his "Mafia government" slur but rather a seemingly innocuous public reference to police reports filed by opposition colleague Tang Liang Hong immediately prior to the election. Tang had asked for police protection at his political rallies, noting that Prime Minister Goh and other PAP leaders had painted him as an "anti-Christian

Chinese chauvinist" (*Straits Times*, 3 January 1997). Because Jeyaretnam had been a thorn in the side of the PAP for almost two decades, his trial was monitored by international organizations, including Amnesty International and the International Commission of Jurists. Since no Singaporean lawyer in their right mind would defend Jeyaretnam against the country's ruling elite in the High Court, Queen's Counsel George Carman, an eminent jurist from the United Kingdom, was engaged to face off against fellow Queen's Counsel and countryman Thomas Shields, who represented the prime minister, Lee, and the government. Jeyaretnam, whose modest assets were nowhere near those of millionaire Tang, noted immediately before the trial, "[Lee's] out to bankrupt me so that I have to give up my seat in Parliament" (*Straits Times*, 16 August 1997)—a well-known tactic used to permanently silence political opponents.

Needless to say, Jeyaretnam lost the case, though initially a mere S$20,000 in damages was awarded to the prime minister, 10 percent of the S$200,000 he had asked for (*Straits Times*, 10 October 1997).[28] Miraculously, Jeyaretnam was able to keep his parliamentary seat, though the fact that the United States and other nations condemned the Singaporean government's actions that year may well have been responsible for its decision to scale back its pursuit of the politician through the courts. Perhaps the greatest irony in the entire sequence of events is that when testifying against Jeyaretnam in August 1997, the prime minister chose to use Confucian values as a defense for the libel proceedings, which stemmed, at least in part, from the claim that the PAP had painted opposition candidate Tang as an "anti-Christian Chinese chauvinist." Goh, representing a ruling party that includes a large number of Chinese Christians, used the rhetoric of Confucianism to justify his silencing of Jeyaretnam: "We are a different society. In Singapore, we believe that leaders must be honorable men, gentlemen or *jinzi*, and if our integrity is attacked, we defend it." He noted that unlike in the West, where leaders do not feel compelled to defend their integrity, "here, if leaders and politicians do not defend their integrity, they are finished" (*Straits Times*, 20 August 1997). Goh's conflation of Confucian with Asian values in a multicultural society such as Singapore would no doubt seem offensive to the nearly quarter of the population that is not Chinese, a point that seems to be lost on both him and the elder statesman, Lee. In an attempt to justify PAP rule, Goh and Lee have repeatedly returned to the "Confucian values" defense, creating a kind of chauvinism or nativism of the type Said warns against when he writes that in many formerly colonized countries, the post-independence scenario moves as follows: "Nationality, nationalism, nativism: The progression is, I believe, more and more constraining" (*Culture and Imperialism* 229). The irony is that in condemning Tang for "anti-Chinese chauvinism," Goh's defense relies on rhetoric that would strike many non-Chinese as nothing if not chauvinistic.

Censorship: Preserving Values

Inextricably linked to state values is the issue of censorship, the final factor that sets the parameters for theater in Singapore. Given Singapore's status as a major business hub for Southeast Asia in the information age, the country's rulers have chosen not to completely restrict the free flow of information, recognizing that to do so would jeopardize Singapore's ability to compete in the global marketplace. The explosive growth of the Internet makes it impossible for even the largest army of government censors to completely cancel out objectionable or dangerous materials. During the 1990s, Brigadier-General George Yeo, Singapore's first minister for information and the arts,[29] emerged as the point man for the government's position on the matter: "In reality, censorship is very difficult and it is an endless game. So, on the one hand, we must not give up the idea of censorship, of holding up standards; and, on the other, [we must have] a realistic assessment that there are limits to what we can do" (*Straits Times*, 27 August 1994). Even though Yeo would appear to be articulating a middle course, it bears noting that the government has a long history of restricting the circulation of major international publications—including the *Far Eastern Economic Review, The Economist, Time, Asian Wall Street Journal*, and *Asiaweek*—when they have published materials deemed objectionable by the government.

In a case that received considerable international attention, a 1994 article by writer/academic Christopher Lingle published in the *International Herald Tribune* which suggested that there were nations in Southeast Asia where a "compliant judiciary" has been used to "bankrupt opposition politicians" (7 October 1994) resulted in a swift and harsh response from the government; Lingle, then a lecturer in political economy at the National University of Singapore, was questioned in his office, his private papers were confiscated, and a libel action was initiated against not only Lingle but also the *International Herald Tribune* and its editors, as well as Singapore Press Holdings, the company that printed the paper locally. Huge judgments were levied against the paper and Lingle; even Lee Kuan Yew filed a private suit against the writer. The irony, of course, is that the government pursued Lingle and the *International Herald Tribune* using the very same methods that Lingle had suggested that unnamed Asian nations used to silence political opposition; thus Singapore had to demonstrate that in fact it *was* the country to which Lingle referred. According to Stephen Wrage, in his defense, Senior Minister "Lee adduced 12 cases in which he had in fact successfully used the judiciary to bankrupt political adversaries" (44). In spite of the apparent lunacy behind publicly proclaiming your own lack of integrity in a court of law, the suit had the intended effect; Lingle promptly left the country to avoid prosecution and a possible jail term, while the *International Herald Tribune*, no doubt mindful of the importance of holding on to Singapore as base for their operations in the region, has subsequently avoided offending the sensibilities of the government.[30]

Where theatrical censorship is concerned, prior to 1992 approval for all plays to be staged in Singapore was completely in the hands of the Public Entertainment Licensing Unit (PELU), an arm of the police that was not noted for its sensitivity to the nuances of the dramatic text. The policy was altered in September 1992 after the publication of a set of recommendations by the government-appointed Censorship Review Committee. While PELU was to continue to decide whether or not to grant licenses to produce plays on the basis of "public order considerations" (Yeo, "Theatre and Censorship" 51), the newly created National Arts Council was given the authority to vet incoming scripts first. The larger, established groups with a proven track record were exempted from the NAC vetting requirements, though they were encouraged to "exercise self-regulation" and were called upon to deny entry to children where the content or language of the play was not suitable for youth. Scripts were still to be submitted, however, even if they were not to be formally evaluated.

In addition, plays were prohibited if they had the potential to (a) erode the core moral values of society; (b) subvert the nation's security and stability; or (c) create misunderstanding or conflict in Singapore's multiracial and multireligious society (Yeo, "Theatre and Censorship" 51). Given the broadness of these classifications, the apparent liberalization of the censorship review process was regarded by many theater practitioners at the time as a double-edged proposition; while the extent to which a play infringes upon any of these strictures was left to established companies to determine themselves, the possibility of a kind of overly rigorous self-censorship was created. Indeed, the track record of theater companies throughout the remainder of the decade suggests that playwrights and theater practitioners often impose more rigid limitations on their work than any external censor might call for.

Established theater companies, which have the most to lose, have generally become more politically and socially conservative in their programming than many of the smaller companies, while at the same time there has been a notable absence of new playwrights joining the field. In fact, well-known Singaporean playwrights were actually fewer in number at the end of the decade, as some of the most promising writers either scaled back on the volume of writing, or quit playwriting altogether.

In an age in which the free flow of information has become increasingly difficult to impede, the government of Singapore has taken the tack of attempting to influence values from the ground up rather than denying its citizenry access to Western culture and its so-called liberal values. Though Singapore's theater is subject to censorship, as subsequent chapters will demonstrate, there remains a remarkable amount of social and even pointed political criticism that manages to find its way onto the Singaporean stage, especially where viewers are capable of reading between the lines; because an ironic sensibility is not particularly well developed among those who assess the plays for objectionable elements, only the most obviously offending tropes — such as the sympathetic depiction of openly gay males or direct attacks on identifiable politicians — are ripe for censoring. Given the ubiquity of government policies in all aspects of life and the ever-present reality of surveillance in such a small state, the potential for self-censorship is far more alarming than overt methods that might be used to silence dissenting voices. Nevertheless, even under the "liberalizing" influence of Goh, the government has repeatedly demonstrated that there is a limit to what is tolerable in a performance context; clearly out of bounds are any overt and serious-minded jabs at government policies.

Because Singapore's government is so obsessed with fulfilling material concerns, the official rhetoric of the policy makers overseeing the arts is often at odds with the more human-focused concerns of individual theater artists. By way of providing a concluding frame, we return again to the observations of BG Yeo, the former minister for information and the arts. Yeo's ministerial brief links two fields that some might see as only tangentially related; yet in Singapore the arts constitute an important element in the flow of information to be regulated by the government. Yeo, a brigadier-general like Lee's son, represents one of the rising stars who has made it to the top of the political hierarchy at a relatively young age. He currently serves as minister for trade and industry, placing him in line for the top job at some point in the future. He is a frequent speaker at various forums, and his pronouncements on the arts throughout the 1990s can be viewed as a reflection of government views on the intersection between the arts and politics.

In a 1993 speech before a dinner for 1,000 that marked the official opening of the vast Takashimaya Shopping Centre on fashionable Orchard Road, Yeo made it clear that the arts are essential to the future economic growth of the nation, echoing the rhetoric of the 1988 government report: "In the new world we are entering, it is important to be good at science and mathematics but it is not enough. . . . We must also have artistic sense. With science and mathematics, we can produce accurately and efficiently. But to create high value, we must also produce artistically" (*Straits Times*, 9 October 1993). He went on to assert that "we have to be in the business of creating lifestyles and total experiences," citing the example of a popular Chinese dish known as "Chicken Rice" that is widely available throughout the island at open-air eating establishments known as hawker centers. "The $2 chicken rice in the coffeeshop is not the same product as the $12 chicken rice in a coffeehouse. Aesthetics has become an inseparable part of production and consumption," he observes (*Straits Times*, 9 October 1993). Put another way, whereas it was once perfectly acceptable for Singaporeans to put up with the heat and less than pristine conditions of a hawker center, many are now willing to pay six times as much to eat the same food in the air-conditioned comfort of a coffeehouse that features paintings on the walls and offers a more contained ambience.

Yeo went on to praise the Japanese retail giant Takashimaya for creating a complex where "space is set aside for art exhibitions" and "cultural programs are a regular feature," adding, "These things don't come cheap. They cost money. Yet they make good business sense."[31] Yeo concluded his remarks with a call for taking the middle ground: "Balance is very important. . . . The more yang we want, the more yin we must have. Thus, to reach higher levels of economic development, we need higher levels of cultural development." Though one attempting to interpret such remarks might risk being slapped with a defamation suit in a Singaporean court, at the very least it seems clear that Yeo's comments can be seen as furthering the dominant political discourse, which envisions the arts as working reciprocally toward the larger goal of continued economic prosperity. It is precisely the tension between this mindset—which seems to prevail among the younger, more "liberal-minded" second generation of Singapore's political leaders, such as Yeo— and the more specifically human-centered concerns of theater artists that propels theater and culture in Singapore toward an uncertain future.

Perhaps the most frequently invoked trope in Singaporean political and cultural life is what David Birch has termed the "discourse of crisis." The maintenance of this discourse, he argues, is "one of the main strategies adopted by the Singapore government to maintain its ideology of control, anchor its people to the nation and create a climate of domestic uncertainty about the fragility of the state and the economy" ("Staging Crises" 75). Using this paradigm, the history of the ruling People's Action Party (PAP) and their ultimate lock on political power can be seen as the unfolding of a series of carefully stage-managed "crises" that have been used to justify their political and social policies. Raised on this steady diet of crises trumpeted in the newspapers of the country's state-controlled press, the citizens of Singapore are routinely called upon to help eradicate threats both internal and external. In spite of the fact that contemporary Singaporean theater companies vigorously eschew politics, theater has been at the center of a number of significant controversies.

The first national crisis was that of nationhood itself, a process that began during the mid-1950s as England granted Singapore limited self-rule. One can argue that Singapore's first indigenous leader was not Lee Kuan Yew but rather David Marshall, a distinguished lawyer who became Singapore's chief minister in April 1955 when his Labour Front coalition won an election that gave the country its first period of limited self-government. When the votes were counted, Marshall's Labour Front had trounced the PAP, a party that at that time relied upon the support of students and procommunist groups. The year 1955 was a turbulent one for Singapore, with the domestic calm shattered by strikes, riots, and the communist-organized seizure of secondary school buildings, events that seriously undermined the strength of Marshall's government. Because Marshall was still ruling for the British, who maintained control over internal security, he found himself in the impossible situation of being forced by the British to order military action to quell a domestic disturbance. Marshall resigned in June the following year and was replaced with a caretaker government under Lim Yew Hock, which faced the continuing occupation of Chinese middle schools by communists, as well as a series of strikes. Lim's government responded to the situation with arrests, detentions, and physical occupation of the contested schools.

During these transition years, communist support was vital to the success of the PAP. At this time Lee believed that "any man in Singapore who wants to carry the Chinese-speaking people with him cannot afford to be anticommunist" (Lee Kuan Yew 207). This was so because the balance of power in the late 1950s was held by the Chinese-educated, a group that was considerably more radical than the English-educated and had control over well-organized groups of communist-leaning students and workers. Lee Kuan Yew emerged as the clear leader of the PAP in 1957 after a number of left-leaning members of the party's Central Executive Committee (CEC) were arrested by Lim's government, leaving Lee, supported by moderates, effectively in control of the party's leadership. Ironically, in the early years of the PAP, opposition parties painted it as the radical, Chinese-language dominated group (Ong Chit Chung 83).[1] In the 1959 election, the first election in which all fifty-one seats of the Legislative Assembly were contestable, the PAP, with Lee leading the party, won forty-three seats with 53 percent of the vote (Ong Chit Chung 81). Following its brief and unsuccessful merger with Malaysia, which ended in 1965, Singapore became a sovereign, independent nation.

At the same time that the PAP was cementing its hold on power during the 1960s and early 1970s, a tradition of radical theater aligned with workers' and students' movements that began in the 1950s continued to find an audience. In a 1992 interview, Singapore's senior playwright and theater practitioner Kuo Pao Kun recalled the politicized nature of theater during this period: "The involvement of the theatre with politics, not necessarily party politics, but politics, ideological debate, was quite inevitable, arising from the volatile situation in the sixties when Singapore first became independent. It was a time of strife—there was the pressure to succeed, particularly economically, on the part of the government which was expressed in radical economic and social changes like the evacuation of people, of farmers from their land for new development" (Lo 139). Indeed, during the course of the fifteen years up to the mid-1970s, Singapore was radically transformed from a city of colonial dwellings, shop houses, and outlying kampongs into an advanced, high-rise metropolis with a bustling containerized port. These changes, wrought by a government that embraced both capitalism and socialism, involved leveling entire neighborhoods while bringing many people into an urban way of life for which they were psychologically unprepared.[2] The scale and the speed of the social transformation was astonishingly rapid, and naturally not everyone was happy with the changes taking place. According to Kuo, it was the Chinese-language theater that was the most "socially committed" and "politically sensitive," due to its ongoing connection "with the student movement, the labour movement, teachers, [and] the intellectual movement" (Lo 139).

Kuo himself was swept up in a wholesale purge of left-leaning students, artists, and intellectuals in the mid-1970s and spent four years (from 1976 to 1980) detained under the Internal Security Act.[3] During the years immediately prior to his arrest, Kuo was involved with a socially committed company at the Practice Performing Arts School. Under the group's "Go Into Life" campaign, "young artists and intellectuals would spend time experiencing the life of the masses in Singapore and Malaysia" (Lo 139). As part of their training, artists "spent days, some weeks, some months; some in the end spent years, working in construction, working in factories and even going to the rice fields, the pineapple farms up in Peninsula Malaysia and in the fishing villages. At the time the guiding ideology was [that] art comes from life" (Lo 139–40). Upon returning to Singapore, artists fashioned theater based on their experiences. One such work, a ballet entitled *The Stormy Season* or *The Fishing Village*, was created by Kuo's wife, Goh Lay Kuan, and dealt with life in a traditional fishing village. According to Kuo, it represented "the first ballet that confronted the life of the masses, and of the fishing village" (Lo 140). Kuo recalls that "people came to our productions in buses, lorries, and cars, and some people even came down from Johor, and even Kuala Lumpur or Penang" (Lo 141). The history of this socially committed worker's theater is virtually unknown among Singaporeans under forty years old; because of its perceived oppositional stance in relation to government policy, no one in Singapore has attempted to document this phenomenon.

Kuo's comments need to be placed against the social and political back-drop of the time. While Singapore's rulers were rapidly modernizing the country, the war in Vietnam was at its height, providing a visible, regional ex-ample of the dangers of communism. Meanwhile, in China, the Cultural Revolution (1966–76), under the leadership of Mao's wife, Jiang Qing, her-self a former actress, put theater at the forefront of the class struggle. Jiang Qing proposed a new model in which "every action, every word and every bar of music must dramatize the class struggle, taking the side of the proletariat against the bourgeoisie" (MacKerras 167). One of the eight models of dra-matic performance deemed adequately proletarian for public performance was the well-known story *The White-Haired Girl*, rewritten during the Cul-tural Revolution as a ballet in which "the white-haired girl's ballet move-ments are designed to be aggressive and defiant to show her revolutionary qualities" (MacKerras 169). Clearly theater had become a handmaiden to communist ideology in mainland China by the mid-1970s, a fact that would not have gone unnoticed by Singapore's ruling PAP. The party's own histori-cal alliance with Chinese-speaking communists throughout the 1950s would still have been a fresh memory among many PAP leaders, who no doubt had little interest in repeating the power-sharing that characterized their rise to power in the years leading up to the 1959 general election. Thus by the mid-1970s, theater focusing on working-class concerns began to be seen by the PAP as having the potential to undermine the security of the state.

In addition to worker's theater, other manifestations of popular dissent also came to a head in late 1975. One of the most widely publicized incidents of the time was the 1975 "disappearance" of former University of Singapore Students' Union (USSU) leader Tan Wah Piow. Tan had served a year in prison on a charge of "rioting" with others at a building occupied by the PAP's trade union organization (*Far Eastern Economic Review*, 10 December 1976: 38). During the course of his forty-seven-day trial, Tan represented himself with considerable skill and forcefulness, ultimately becoming a hero to the stu-dent movement. An excerpt from one of his 1975 speeches reflects this com-mitment to social justice:

> I was conditioned to have my eyes blinded so that I see no social evils; my
> ears plugged so that I heard no cries of the people; and in case I did see
> or hear some evil, my mouth was to be gagged so that I speak no protest.
> I broke the rules altogether. I ripped the blindfold and saw the pathetic
> living conditions of neglected old pioneers of Chinatown and the exploited

workers of Jurong; I dug out the ear plugs and heard the voice of Said
Zahari [a journalist under detention without trial for 13 years] coming
from behind the prison walls. Finally I took the decisive step to liberate
myself—I spoke up. (Senkuttuvan, "A Student's Disappearance" 24)

Tan's comments are contemporaneous with the "Go Into Life" aesthetic of
Kuo's theater and were seen as a threat to the dominant order. Upon his release from prison, Tan was given three days of freedom prior to being called
up for national service. According to the *Far Eastern Economic Review*, Tan,
who is severely myopic, "should have been exempted or drafted into the service side of the military" (10 December 1976: 38). Instead, he was drafted into
the artillery, which is considered one of the military's toughest units and or-
dinarily conscripts only "tall and well-built soldiers" (ibid.). Fearing that he
would not survive his stint in the military, Tan fled to England, where he re-
surfaced a year later.

Rather than serving as a warning to other students who dared to buck the
system, Tan's trial and subsequent prison term resulted in the election of
eleven of his supporters to the twelve USSU counselor positions that were
contested in the next student election (Senkuttuvan, "Singapore Tightens"
13). Not only were the PAP candidates put forth by the on-campus Democratic
Socialist Club (DSC) soundly defeated, but a record number of students voted
in the election, a sign that student opinion and government policy were on a
collision course. The student election results prompted Singapore's Parliament to pass a law requiring that henceforth leaders of the student union
would be appointed by the university administration instead of being elected
by the student body (Senkuttuvan, "Singapore Tightens" 12), an antidemo-
cratic tradition that continues to this day.

Those perceived to be enemies of the state were arrested and detained in
large numbers from late 1975 and well into 1976, with dance teacher and
performer Goh Lay Kuan and theater artist Kuo Pao Kun swelling their ranks.
Goh was given the moniker "The Red Ballerina" by the Singaporean press
and forced to make a television confession in which she revealed her admiration for communism by noting that "artistes and dancers were given ample
opportunities to develop their talents in a communist socio-political system"
(Stockwin 13). She also went on to describe her visit to a communist guerrilla
camp on the Malaysian-Thai border where "more than half" of the guerrillas
were women, observing that "about 50% of the communist terrorists in the
camp were about 20 years old" (Stockwin 13). The scripted quality of such

statements, combined with Goh's dazzling display of statistics, no doubt contributed to the *Far Eastern Economic Review*'s wry observation that she had revealed "how she had sought to combine fancy ideological footwork together with the steps of classical ballet" (Stockwin 12). Government press statements at the time linked Goh's arrest with others who were charged as communist agitators.[4] Clearly "Go Into Life" had backfired for both Goh and Kuo, as it placed them in a situation in which they could easily be tainted with the communist brush.

At the time, Amnesty International slammed Singapore for the detentions, noting that "the Internal Security Act has frequently been employed as a means of repressing and discouraging legitimate, non-violent political opposition in Singapore" (Ho Kwon Ping, "Countering" 22). The release of eight political detainees in December 1975 resulted in allegations of torture, which was reported to have taken place at the Whitley Detention Center (Ho Kwon Ping, "Allegations of Torture" 13), the main Internal Security Department (ISD) holding and interrogation center, constructed in the mid-1960s to hold suspected communists or subversives. The description of the torture is quoted here because it bears a striking resemblance to more recent claims of brutality by the ISD.[5] According to the *Far Eastern Economic Review,* ex-prisoner Tan Ek was held in "a specially built airconditioned room for the first three days and nights with only a bare pyjama trouser by way of protection against extreme cold. On the fourth day, he was removed to a still colder cell with the same pyjama trousers for three more days and nights. Through the six-day period he was kept standing. He was not allowed to sleep. A spotlight was so fixed that he had to face it throughout the period. In addition, he was hit with fists and kicked many times" (Ho Kwon Ping, "Allegations of Torture" 13). Stories of torture and inhumane methods of extracting confessions by the ISD over the course of the last three decades have been well documented by a range of sources.[6]

For his part, Kuo does not seem at all bitter about the four years he spent in detention, characterizing that period as "a very, very deep education process" (Lo 141). He asserts that "on a very fundamental level, detention strips away one's vanities and pretensions. It forces one to either look reality straight in the face and be humbled by it, or take sanctuary in insanity. The purging effect was deep and total. Fantasies burst, and reality began to take on a kind of simplicity which only honesty could help me negotiate" (Interview with Janadas Devan). In 1989, less than a decade after his rehabilitation, Kuo was awarded the national Cultural Medallion for his contributions to theater in Singapore, an honor that was also bestowed on his wife, Goh Lay Kuan, the former "Red Ballerina," in 1995. The Cultural Medallion is given out annually to Singaporeans who have achieved excellence in a particular field. Today Kuo is widely regarded as Singapore's finest playwright, with a significant body of work in Chinese and English.

A decade after the "Go Into Life" campaign and the mass arrests of the mid-1970s, the communist threat was once again linked to theater, only this time with the supposed complicity of radical elements within the Catholic Church. Claiming that a group of young people in Singapore were receiving orders from 1970s student leader Tan Wah Piow in London, the government ruthlessly crushed this so-called Marxist conspiracy, which was allegedly plotting to overthrow Lee Kuan Yew's government and replace it with a communist state. Given the rapid economic development of the country during this period and the correspondingly huge increase in the number of people who could be classified as middle class, many looked upon Lee's dogged pursuit of these young people with amazement. In fact, some Singaporeans privately speculate that Lee's mishandling of this situation contributed to his decision to step down as prime minister in 1990. Though the evidence suggests that Lee instead decided to hand over the reigns of power at the precise moment when he felt he had groomed successors who would not retreat from his policies, it is certainly true that Lee's reputation was seriously tarnished by this incident.[7]

To understand the basis of the 1987 "Marxist conspiracy" and its relationship to both theater and the Catholic Church, it is necessary to view what happened in Singapore in the context of other developing nations. Catholic "liberation theology," perceived as one of the key villains in this affair, dates back to 1968, when the Medellín Bishop's Conference of the Latin American Church "took a radical stance in solidarity with the poor and explicitly identified colonialism and neocolonialism as the causes of wide-spread poverty in the developing world" (van Erven 12). Rather than calling for armed insurrection against the forces of neocolonialism, which were seen as complicitous with the old colonial masters, the church called into being a form of social organization known as "Basic Christian Communities," or BCs. These BCs were to be responsible for the spiritual and development of members of the group. Clodovis Boff outlines the organizational structure and potential functions of these units:

BC's are made up of small groups of an average of ten people; it is most usually a number of these groups — usually ten, usually one parish, that is known as a BC. . . . The overwhelming majority of members of the BC's are poor people. They come from the lowest strata of society, the peasants and the workers — those who suffer. . . . The basic group usually meets once a week, in a set place, usually a family house, but it might be any room available, in a chapel or simply the shade of a tree. And what do they do? They pray, they listen to the word of God, and they discuss problems affecting their lives. . . . The atmosphere in a BC is full of human worth and greatness of heart, but never the ingenious happiness of those who know nothing of the contradictions and hardships of life. No, it goes with a fairly critical outlook on reality, a very sharp class feeling, and an extremely committed and dangerous struggle. . . . This is a real exercise in participatory democracy. (Qtd. in van Erven 12).

One of the problems that BCs encounter under authoritarian regimes, observes Eugène van Erven, is that they are frequently seen as "potential Communist cells" (12). Indeed, in a Singaporean context any group that engages in a "critical outlook on reality" with a "sharp class feeling" and that ventures into the terrain of "participatory democracy" is on an automatic collision course with the ruling party. Throughout its history, the PAP has made it abundantly clear that they alone must control the terms of political debate.

The ringmaster of the Singaporean group supposedly receiving instructions from "foreign agent" Tan was Vincent Cheng, a Catholic Church social worker. All of the twenty-two English-educated activists arrested in May and June 1987 under the guise of the Internal Security Act were accused of associating with Cheng to overthrow the PAP government. Specifically, "it was alleged that the detainees had infiltrated the opposition Workers' Party (WP), politicized the Law Society, and worked with a theater group known as the Third Stage" (Lee Lai To, "Singapore in 1987" 202). The arrest of the activists met with strong criticism outside Singapore, and by the end of the year, all detainees except Cheng had been released, though eight of them were re-arrested the following year when they recanted their confessions, alleging that they had been tortured and that their statements were obtained under duress.[8] In a theme that would be picked up repeatedly in the future, Lee made it clear in a June 1987 meeting with church representatives that what was unacceptable in his view was that this group was using the church as a cover for "building up a mass base and pressure points for political action" (Lee Lai To "Singapore in 1987" 202).

Of those arrested and allegedly tortured, a number were members of the amateur theater group Third Stage (van Erven 234). Third Stage was influenced by the socially conscious Filipino theater group PETA (Philippines Educational Theatre Association), and a number of company members had participated in the group's summer courses (van Erven 233).[9] During its five years of existence, Third Stage took on a number of trenchant social issues in productions that were generally well received by the public and the Singaporean press. Their musical comedy *Corabella* poked fun at government policies designed to encourage university-educated women to have more children. The so-called problem of the "lopsided pattern of procreation" identified by Lee Kuan Yew in his 1983 National Day Speech resulted in legislation that year that gave graduate mothers with three or more children top priority in registering their children for Primary One classes in schools of their choice (Quah 220). From the government's point of view, Third Stage's open criticism of an unpopular policy may well have set them up for future repression. What is so remarkable is that Third Stage managed to criticize other controversial policies, including the widespread regulation of all aspects of civic life for which Singapore is so famous (in their satire *Oh Singapore!*), as well as the exploitation of Filipina maids (in their play *Esperanza*). Given the importance of cheap imported domestic help for the nation's economy — a state of affairs that is by no means unique to Singapore — their final production stepped into very dangerous territory indeed. In the 1990s, under Goh's leadership, it should be noted that many of these same themes have been tackled by theater groups, though often under the guise of settings in "fictional" Asian countries.

In spite of Third Stage's history of social criticism, there is no evidence to suggest that they were trying to prepare the general public for a future Marxist state. Ironically, their activities were subsidized by the Ministry of Community Development, the government entity that was then charged with developing the arts. Francis Seow notes that "the minister himself attended as an official guest on one occasion, and, by most accounts, enjoyed immensely the satire" (78). Furthermore, Seow adds, "there was not the slightest whisper of Marx or Marxism echoing through the auditorium; nor were there any hints that Singapore and its quality of life were being lampooned by these Marxists for evil political ends!" (78). Having subsequently met a number of the detainees in an informal context a few years after these events, my overall impression of them was that they were gentle, intelligent, modest individuals, hardly personalities capable of inspiring or leading a mass political movement!

Why, then, was this group of young professionals and amateur dramatists persecuted? Francis Seow suggests that the reasons are far less complicated than the government wanted to admit:

> The plain unvarnished truth was the prime minister had marked this group of sixteen young professionals, augmented by the later arrest of another six persons, for retributive action because of their effective assistance to opposition MP J. B. Jeyaretnam and the Workers' Party in snatching [his] victory in the 1981 by-election and the 1984 general election. They helped him to print and distribute WP pamphlets during the elections. They also helped to brighten the editorial contents and pages of *The Hammer*, the WP's stodgy official publication, an important source of the party's news and funds. (79)

In a truly remarkable coincidence, Singaporean writer Gopal Baratham's novel *A Candle or the Sun*, reputedly penned four years prior to the arrests, recounts the story of a writer who comes into contact with a group of young evangelical Christians who run afoul of the authorities. In Baratham's novel, members of the group clandestinely distribute copies of a street paper meant for the general public, one that articulates a position that would be too risky for anyone to voice publicly in Singapore:

> You are unhappy and you dare not admit this to anyone. Certainly not to your masters in the government. After all you have no right to be unhappy. Your masters provide you with good housing, safe streets, good hospitals, schools for your children and pay you enough for three square meals a day and a colour TV. . . . Ask yourself why this streetpaper is necessary. Because, my friend, our masters control every newspaper and every magazine on this, our wonderful island paradise. And every movie, TV show and tape-recording is censored before it gets to you. But why should this make you unhappy? After all, you've got all you really need. Because, my friend, you are a man, not a dog. And men must be free to talk, to write, to contact other men, to organize themselves into groups. Groups they choose themselves, not groups ordained by our masters like the Peoples Consultative Committees and other Residents Committees.

Men who are not free to do this are no more than animals. You have been
made into dogs. Your masters kennel you in neat boxes, doctor your females, control litter size according to pedigree and tell you what names
you can give your pups. It is no wonder you are unhappy and ashamed.
In your own eyes you have become animals. (56)

There is no doubt that distributing such "subversive" material in Singapore
would meet with a strong and swift response from the government.

In *A Candle or the Sun*, a writer named Hernie Perera has an affair with a
young woman who belongs to the "unorthodox Christian group" known as
the "Children of the Book" (Baratham 9), which distributes these missives.
Circumstances and his love for the young woman eventually implicate him in
the group's activities. Upon discovering the "secret" of the group, he voices a
position that is essentially the same as the one articulated by Lee Kuan Yew
just a few years later when he quashed the Catholic-affiliated group: "You're
not really a religious group. You're what the government calls a clandestine
political organization" (131). Echoing the ideology of liberation theology, the
group's spokesperson responds, "You know the Bible so well, you should
know how Christians have always been looked upon as subversives. Well,
they still are. Here and everywhere. In the Philippines, in South America,
priests resist tyrants, fight new Herods backed by legions in helicopter gun-
ships" (131). After initially wavering, Hernie assists his lover, Su-May, and
Peter, the group's leader, as they flee Singapore. Of course Hernie has been
under constant surveillance and is arrested and imprisoned on the very day
they escape. Predictably, he is tortured in a manner that sounds strangely
familiar: "I have lost all sense of time. Day and night have ceased to exist.
Blinding lights alternate, meaninglessly, with pitch blackness; freezing cold
follows scalding heat" (194).

Not surprisingly, Baratham was unable to find a publisher in Singapore for
the novel, though it was eventually picked up in 1991 by a small British publisher that distributed the book in Singapore. Just like the writer in the novel,
Baratham himself was questioned at the time of the arrests by a Special
Branch officer (Elegant 47). When I taught at Singapore's National University,
Baratham's novel was required reading in the first-year English literature
course. In lectures, both Baratham himself and one of the course lecturers
strenuously denied that there was any connection between his novel and
events that had taken place just a few years earlier. Even in tutorials, my students never even hinted at the possibility that the book had any parallels

with Singapore, past or present. By teaching the novel in such a highly visible forum and denying its connection with contemporary life, educators, including myself, were complicit with a system that actually exceeded Orwellian proportions; rather than banning such a book, those in power decided to defuse its power by teaching it strictly as fiction.

Long after the total breakdown of communism virtually everywhere in the world, and at a time when even China was moving increasingly toward capitalism, the specter of a "Marxist conspiracy" was again revisited in 1994 when the Straits Times published an article that provocatively declared, "Two Pioneers of Forum Theatre Trained at Marxist Workshops." The article, by editor Felix Soh, charged the eight-year-old company The Necessary Stage (TNS) with having a "political agenda" by virtue of their use of Forum Theatre, a form in which two key members of the company received brief training the previous year when they attended a New York workshop led by Brazilian theater practitioner Augusto Boal. Alvin Tan, the founder and artistic director of TNS, and Haresh Sharma, the group's resident playwright, had attended workshops sponsored by the Brecht Forum in which Boal himself taught his "Theatre of the Oppressed" techniques. The underlying commitment of both the Brecht Forum and Boal to the use of theater as an instrument for promoting social change raised the red flag and made two of Singapore's most dynamic theater practitioners suddenly appear to be guilty by association. Soh had spent months researching the article; he blew the whistle after interviewing and obtaining juicy quotes from a member of the Brecht Forum's board of directors as well as several school principals at institutions in which TNS had practiced Forum Theatre. Tellingly, both school principals quoted in the Soh's article were so frightened of being identified with any attempt to promote social change that their comments were printed anonymously.

Boal's Forum Theatre, just one of many techniques he has developed, has been widely used by theater practitioners all over the world for over twenty years and has been taught, discussed, and/or demonstrated at virtually all international theater conferences. The process begins with improvisational work involving a group of individuals who wish to explore the sources of oppression in their lives. Boal makes it very clear in his writings that "oppressions" manifest themselves in different ways in each new cultural context; thus the subject matter dealt with by each group changes depending on their specific needs. The leader of the group, or "joker," guides participants in a range of exercises designed to free them of tension and make them more aware of themselves as individuals whose choices and reactions are determined by their sociocultural conditioning. After working with a group for quite some time — possibly a week or more — eventually themes emerge that are explored in a series of improvisations. Ultimately, a short theater piece is created around a particular issue that invites a number of possible outcomes; points at which interventions could occur to change the outcome are identified, and ultimately the work is performed before an audience. The skit is first performed in its entirety with an outcome that the group identifies as one that is not necessarily acceptable.

Mixed Blessings, one of TNS's 1993 Forum Theatre pieces that was much discussed privately, dealt with a cross-cultural relationship between an Indian man and a Chinese woman. When the piece was first presented to the audience, the parents opposed the relationship, and the work ended in conflict. Using Boal's framework, the piece would then be repeated, with the audience invited to intervene (by simply calling out "stop") at any point in the action where they felt the protagonist was making a mistake; the spectator — who at this point assumes the role of what Boal terms the "spect-actor" — then enters into the action herself or himself and attempts to alter the outcome by following a different course of action. The remaining actors in turn typically renew their efforts to pursue the undesirable outcome, and the "spect-actor" is forced to respond flexibly as new obstacles are put forth. The spect-actor may well be thwarted by the other actors and is free to drop out; the action may then continue from that point, with other spect-actors free to intervene. If, alternately, the spect-actor begins to break the oppression, additional spect-actors are free to enter the game as the supporting actors and put forth new, possibly unforeseen obstacles. As Boal explains, "The knowledge which results from this investigation will, of necessity, be the best that that particular human social group can attain at that particular moment in time" (21). An audience member I spoke to who had attended one of the TNS Forum Theatre sessions remembered that on the night she went, the group disbanded only after being prompted to leave by the cleaning crew, so engrossed were they in the process. In a country like Singapore, where feelings that grow out of a set of socially determined constraints are not the subject of private, much less public scrutiny, the potential therapeutic value of such a technique is enormous.

TNS, with funding from the NAC (National Arts Council), also brought Forum Theatre to a number of secondary schools, creating a piece that focused on the pressures facing Singaporean teenagers. The principal of one of the schools where the work was presented recalled that "the students really shed their inhibitions during the performance," adding ominously that the evaluation of the action, "led by the director, was slanted. It could lead to slanted views." Another principal asserted, "We were quite happy. Our students gave positive feedback and we, in turn, saw that the students were involved. . . . It did not occur to us that they were doing anything wrong," especially given that the group was "sponsored by the National Arts Council." The same speaker, now fearing the subversive potential of the form after inquiries from the press, added that in the future, "I will study their activities more closely and we will have closer monitoring. . . . We will ask the company for a proposal. Only when we are satisfied that the material is not subversive will we allow them to perform at our school" (*Straits Times*, 5 February 1994). Apparently the open exploration of feelings that came from placing teenagers in situations they could openly identify with was now deemed subversive.

In addition to the charge that the form itself contained the seeds of subversion, the two young practitioners who attended Boal's workshop were painted as Marxist sympathizers by virtue of Boal's political persuasion. Cited in the *Straits Times* article was the *Cambridge Guide to Theatre*'s characterization of Boal as "a Marxist ideologue who encountered problems with his country's political situation and was imprisoned for a period of time" (Soh). Most theater practitioners and scholars would recognize the *Cambridge Guide* entry as seriously flawed, emphasizing as it does Boal's political orientation instead of his contributions to theater, which are widely regarded as among the most significant made by a practitioner in the last quarter of the twentieth century.[10] What Soh in his crusade against TNS failed to understand is that Boal's politics have little to do with the practice of Forum Theatre, as the comments of Boal's translator in the foreword to one of his recent books make clear:

> In his working practice as a teacher of the Theatre of the Oppressed,
> he eschews labels, carefully dodging questions which might pin down
> his current ideology or pigeon-hole it in a category of, say, "Marxist," or
> "Brechtian," or whatever; such limiting categorizations are inimical to
> the whole spirit of the Theatre of the Oppressed, involving as they do the
> mechanization of actions and reactions, and eliminating the possibility of
> change or individuality. . . . Whatever Boal's current political views, they
> never infringe on this work, beyond the basic philosophy of being in sym-

pathy with the oppressed in any situation and the belief in humanity's
ability to change. (Jackson xxiii)

From a Singaporean perspective the real danger was the potential the form
had for creating an engagement with social issues. Soh's article suggested
that TNS had "targeted" schools and wished to bring the technique to factories, something that was ultimately deemed unworkable because of the lack
of English-language skills among factory workers. Since acknowledging social problems necessarily involves entering into the political realm and politics is off-limits except through the officially sanctioned discourse that comes
from the top, then it follows that depictions of the human being in an actual
Singaporean social situation involving conflict are necessarily suspect. The
real culprit in the Forum Theatre "controversy" was the potential the form
had for demonstrating that alternative outcomes were possible. In a state
that seeks to dictate single outcomes for each social situation, the notion that
individuals have the power to change a particular social situation is quite
dangerous.

While the subsequent reaction to Soh's article in the press suggested that
the state apparatus realized that the writer had gone too far in his condemnation of TNS and Forum Theatre, the ultimate outcome of the "controversy"
was a prompt banning of the form. A few days after Soh's bombshell, a more
moderate article without a by-line appeared in the *Straits Times* that contextu-
alized Tan and Sharma's New York trip. It pointed out that Sharma was in
New York on a one-month United States Information Service–sponsored
tour of American theaters and noted that Tan met him at the end of that trip
for one week in New York, during which time they happened to see a newspaper announcement about Boal's workshops and decided to attend. Kok
Heng Leun, TNS's business manager at the time, observed that the two decided to attend because Boal's "experience and contribution to theatre have
been rated as high as Brecht, Grotowski and Stanislavski — all major figures
in theatre. Not wanting to miss out on this once-in-a-lifetime opportunity, we
decided to go for the workshops" (*Straits Times*, 8 February 1994). The effect
of this and subsequent articles was to somewhat soften Soh's initial attack on
the group.

It was probably Tommy Koh, then head of the NAC and a relatively liberal
voice within the hierarchy of the PAP, who did the most to quickly "rehabili-
tate" the group and make it clear that neither Tan nor Sharma would be penalized for their advocacy of this form. His letter to the editor of the *Straits*

Times in support of the group, which appeared just two days after the "controversy" was first raised, signaled that a less shrill response to the group would ultimately prevail. It is typical of all such press "debates" in Singapore for a person at the top of the party apparatus with expertise in a particular area to moderate or strengthen the initial position and articulate the government's final stand. Typically, Koh took a middle ground, noting that "TNS has a good track record and is one of the most promising theatre groups in Singapore" and concluding, "The NAC will continue to support TNS as long as it keeps up its good work. The only exception is that the NAC will not provide assistance to TNS to stage forum theatre" (*Straits Times*, 7 February 1994). Though another lengthy letter condemning the incendiary tone of Soh's initial article was published a week later, the editor's defensive and guarded reply to that letter[11] made it abundantly clear that Soh's brand of journalism would prevail, regardless of the pain it inflicted on many of us who were active in the theater community at the time.[12] For his part, Soh did not seem to be penalized for his lack of professionalism as a journalist; indeed, he had been promoted to foreign editor even before the story appeared.

Tan and Sharma, speaking indirectly through the comments of their business manager that were printed in the *Straits Times*, were forced to distance themselves completely from any political or socially committed motives in choosing to bring Forum Theatre to Singapore. Using the language of economic development parroted daily by the country's leading politicians, TNS Business Manager Kok asserted that Tan and Sharma's "intentions were to improve their skills as theatre practitioners and to learn new theatre techniques, thereby supporting the Government's vision of promoting arts activities in Singapore" (*Straits Times*, 7 February 1994). Thus their decision to attend the workshop was framed as something that would have tangible and concrete benefits for the country. Furthermore, he stated unequivocally that "Mr. Tan, Mr. Sharma and The Necessary Stage have no interest whatsoever in using theatre for political purpose," adding that "the intention of The Necessary Stage is not to effect social change as espoused by Boal" (*Straits Times*, 7 February 1994). Ultimately, this disavowal of any concern with social change would appear to have been enough for the government at the time; ten years earlier, under the Lee regime, their activities would have probably met with a far harsher response, culminating in public confessions on television. Of course, it might strike many theater artists and practitioners as ludicrous that any theater company could successfully distance itself from political or social change, but this is precisely what theater practitioners in Singapore are required to do if they wish to survive.

Like the rehabilitated Kuo Pao Kun and Madame Goh, TNS continues to thrive, and it still receives support from the NAC, though the ban on Forum Theatre remains in effect. The company remains Singapore's most socially committed group, as they are the only professional company that routinely stages work that deals with Singaporean social realities in a direct, no-non-sense manner. They also have the distinction of being the only company with an extensive touring schedule of shows for both adults and youth, performed in nontraditional and outdoor theater venues all around the island. Along with TheatreWorks, they are probably the best-known Singaporean theater company internationally due to overseas tours and the high profile of the company leaders.[13]

The ripples from the Forum Theatre "controversy" extended beyond the-ater into the realm of freedom of speech. Sadly, the one institution that could have raised its voice to protest the loss of the form silenced itself out of fear that the government would clamp down on it as well. In October 1994 the National University of Singapore Society (NUSS) announced its plans to scrap the publication of its midyear issue of *Commentary*, a journal that in 1994 brought together some of Singapore's brightest and most talented young writers to contribute to a special issue entitled "Looking at Culture." Fearing that the contents of the journal would offend the government, the society withdrew the completed publication, which contained, among other writ-ings, a deeply insightful analysis by Sanjay Krishnan into the implications of the loss of Forum Theatre:

> Whereas Forum Theatre sought to draw artistic experience out of the
> private and into the public realm, the state's response suggested its dis-
> comfort with an art that failed to remain within the agreed-upon bounds
> of the private. The discovery of a form which had the potential to enable
> an autonomous relationship between artist and audience was the very
> reason for Forum Theatre's eventual proscription. Failing to recognize
> that this form represented a renegotiation of artistic initiatives *within*
> the state-sponsored civic society project, the government deemed Forum
> Theatre to have violated the unwritten compact between state and artist,
> to have used art to meddle in politics: Forum Theatre failed to respect
> the division between public and private where it mattered. (93)

By banning the form, the government was also effectively proscribing the process through which Forum Theatre is created. In this manner, Singaporean theater artists have been deprived of the opportunity to use a highly promising technique of dramatic construction that is widely practiced throughout the world. The inability of the country's theater artists to defend Forum Theatre marks a kind of triumph of the PAP's political apparatus over Singaporean artists and intellectuals; while in the early 1970s audiences of up to 20,000 witnessed highly political *huaju* Chinese-language plays that took a strong oppositional stance toward the ruling PAP, by the mid-1990s the country's intellectual elite were afraid to even publicly discuss culture.

As the government's response to theater's forays into the realm of politics demonstrate, controlling the outcomes of theater has become a key element in maintaining the state-sanctioned public discourse dominated by the ruling party. Beginning with the 1976 detentions and continuing on into the 1980s, with the Third Stage arrests, and the 1990s, with the ban on Forum Theatre, the government has responded to "political" theater with strong-arm tactics ranging from wholesale purges followed by televised, public confessions, to the apparently softer and more benign tactic of merely banning a form. While the strategy employed by the government in the 1990s might appear to be "kinder" and "gentler," it should be remembered that the targeted artists were initially branded as "Marxists," an epithet with dark and sinister tones in Singapore. Thus the power of the public denunciation of the Necessary Stage in the state-controlled press cannot be understated, even though the artists involved were quickly "rehabilitated" and brought back into the fold. That the government has felt the need to intervene so forcefully and directly against theater on the three occasions chronicled in this chapter reaffirms the enormous power of the form and its potential for laying the groundwork for social change.

Singapore is unusual among postcolonial nations in that it possessed no sizable indigenous population prior to the arrival of the colonizer. As the only country in Asia where the population came to be constituted almost entirely of a largely immigrant population representing a wide range of Asian cultures that originated elsewhere, Singaporeans have no natural cultural cohesiveness that comes from shared traditions. Many of the earliest Singaporeans were doubly removed from their ancestral homes, as they were colonized either directly (as was the case in India and British Malaya) or indirectly (consider the effects of the opium wars in southern China) before they ended up in Singapore. Even Singapore's seemingly unified Chinese community is naturally fractured in that the vast majority of them do not share the same cultural and linguistic traditions, unlike the relatively homogeneous Cantonese that came to predominate in Hong Kong. The absence of a strong group identity prior to independence, when combined with the country's rich linguistic and cultural mix, have made it difficult for the country's leaders to create a sense that all Singaporeans share core elements that constitute a common, national identity.

The ruling party has devoted considerable energy to creating and identifying the common ground on which all Singaporeans stand. While on the one hand the government wants to encourage its citizens to continue to identify with their cultural roots, it also seeks to articulate a sense of what it means to be Singaporean that transcends ethnic, cultural, and linguistic borders. In a young, ethnically diverse country, even national symbols can be difficult to come by, as former president Ong Teng Cheong's comments in a 1994 broadcast of the Singapore Broadcasting Corporation (SBC) television show *Face to Face* suggest. Echoing the rhetoric of other PAP leaders, notably the prime minister, Cheong observed that while it is "better" to have a country with a single culture, Singapore was faced with the difficult task of creating a single country out of many cultures. One problem, he observed, is that Singaporeans, unlike other Asians, cannot be identified by their attire; he noted that the sari communicated Indianness, while the *cheongsam* was clearly Chinese and the Malay *sarong* and *kebaya* made it very easy to spot Malays. As a solution, he suggested that Singaporeans should begin wearing clothes bearing an orchid motif, something that would immediately mark them as Singaporean, especially while traveling overseas. Interviewing him was a woman in a orchid-patterned *cheongsam*, as if to suggest that his personal "campaign" already had adherents.

As Jan Nederveen Pieterse and Bhikhu Parekh point out in their work *The Decolonization of Imagination*, a tension exists in many postcolonial settings between civic and national demands to move toward the creation of a national culture, and the reality of multiple identity: "This is a matter of viewing cultural pluralism not as a 'social problem,' from the point of view of a static 'national culture,' nor as a transitional stage towards some other end state (as in 'melting pot'), but as a condition in itself of complex multiple identities—a situation which increasingly reflects the global human condition" (15). While the country's leaders fret over fragmented identity and seek to create a unified national discourse, it seems clear that multiple identity is increasingly becoming the norm throughout much of the developed world. Even though the world is still rife with interethnic tensions and outright warfare, the overall pattern of the last few decades, especially among the nations aspiring to First World status, has been toward a greater willingness to come to terms with diversity in both the cultural and personal spheres. Rather than recognizing that capitalism, consumerism, and an increasingly globalized media make this phenomenon inevitable among countries like Singapore, which are an integral part of the new economic order, the country's leaders continue to invoke the specter of past cultural collisions as a reason for remaining wary about the future.

Prime Minister Goh has spearheaded the movement toward infusing the citizenry with a heightened sense of what it means to be Singaporean, devoting considerable verbiage to the task in very visible forums such parliamentary "debates" and his National Day speech, which traditionally sets out the major issues facing the both government and the general public. In his 1997 National Day speech he urged continued vigilance on the part of Singaporeans, especially inasmuch as many of the country's younger citizens have known nothing but relative peace and prosperity: "There is a danger that after 31 years of peace, stability and growth, we sometimes forget that Singapore is totally man-made, the result of human organization and human ingenuity, and that it requires special effort to maintain its position and its regional and global role. We have to make sure that all Singaporeans, especially those born after 1965, are conscious of our limitations and will make that extra effort" (*Straits Times*, 18 August 1997). If anything, Goh's rhetoric on the subject has become increasingly strident over time, no doubt a reflection of his genuine concern that Singaporean national identity is still not coalescing to an adequate degree. In a 1999 parliamentary debate, he created an even more alarmist picture of a complacent citizenry, arguing, "A strong dose of realism is necessary. A nation is not built in one generation, much less a country made up of different races and religions, who until recently, were living in different racial enclaves" (*Straits Times*, 6 May 1999). Goh thus raises the specter of interethnic conflict; like President Ong, he seems to be suggesting that Singapore's diversity is a negative force rather than a source of strength. He continues: "For Singapore is not yet a nation. It is only a state, a sovereign entity. . . . But whether it [Singapore] will last the next 100 years will depend on whether the different races can gel as one people, feel as one people and pulsate with the same Singapore heartbeat" (*Straits Times*, 6 May 1999). Goh's remarks flag his continuing concern with the lack of an emotional investment that many Singaporeans have in their own country.

Though Goh's invocation of an ongoing crisis may well serve the long-term institutional interests of the ruling PAP, there is a sense in which many Singaporeans do indeed lack a strong commitment to the future of their country. The relative absence of a personal identification with the nation runs deep and has its roots in the country's history. As playwright Kuo Pao Kun has observed: "Singapore is unique among postcolonial countries in that it had no nation to revive and no national identity to invoke after gaining independence because modern Singapore began as a colony; practically its entire population were new immigrants (or their descendants) to the island" ("Evolving an Identity" 2). Instead of creating a country out of a range of existing cultural, political, and social units that were brought under a single administrative center, in Singapore the British expropriated a sparsely inhabited island from the indigenous Malays and effectively created a kind of *terra nullis* that quickly became peopled by immigrants and convict labor from countries both within and outside the region. From the beginning, Singapore was a place where people came to make money or give of their labor rather than to settle permanently and create a new culture or nation. The original urban grid laid out by the British in the last century was designed to ensure that each immigrant community retained its uniqueness, isolated in its own enclave, complete with its own shops and educational facilities. The remnants of some of Singapore's old ethnic neighborhoods can still be found, and for the most part, they still retain much of the distinct flavor of the cultures they originally housed and contained: Little India, Geylang Serai, and Chinatown continue to fulfill important functions among the Indian, Malay, and Chinese communities. Singapore's identity as a commercial entrepôt where people are driven by economic considerations was thus reinforced by city planning from the earliest days of nationhood.

Given this history, it is perhaps not surprising that at the dawn of the twenty-first century the PAP government continues to work to "create the Singapore tribe," to borrow a newly minted phrase coined by the prime minister (*Straits Times*, 6 May 1999). To counter these "crises," the government has taken the leading role in manufacturing a sense of national identity using two equally important strategies: through policies that have resulted in English becoming the language designed to cut through ethnic, cultural, and linguistic divisions; and through the manipulation of public opinion using government-instigated social campaigns and large-scale events, the most significant of which is the mammoth National Day celebration held in August every year. The remainder of this chapter will examine the ways in which Singaporean identity has been shaped by language policies, using theater as the primary lens, followed by an analysis of *The Eye of History*, a work by Singaporean playwright Robert Yeo that restages the country's great foundation myths. A fitting concluding frame for this topic is the vast public theater that is National Day, scripted and staged by the government and reflecting the values desired for the nation.

Finding a Language

Perhaps because of the county's multiethnicity, Singaporeans seem to have a passion for acronyms that cut through linguistic boundaries. Not surprisingly, one has recently emerged that denotes the country's ethnic mix: CMIO, or "Chinese, Malay, Indian, Other." Of these four, the Chinese constitute the numerical majority, with slightly more than 77 percent of the population. They are followed by Malays (14 percent) and Indians (7 percent), with a very small Eurasian, Arab, and European population accounting for the rest.[1] The Chinese themselves are divided linguistically; because most are descended from immigrants that came from southern China, many older Chinese Singaporeans grew up speaking the distinct Chinese dialects of Hokkien, Teochew, Cantonese, or Hakka rather than the Mandarin of the North. Though these dialects share the same characters with Mandarin, the sounds of the words and their shades of meaning can be radically different. In this sense, one could argue that in some respects Mandarin, as the lingua franca of the capital rather than the South, is culturally foreign to most Chinese Singaporeans.

In the years immediately following independence, Singapore was very much divided linguistically, with the Chinese dialects (Hokkien was the dominant one) competing against Malay, Tamil (the South Indian dialect most commonly used in the Indian community), and the English bequeathed by the colonizer. During these years, apart from the theater associated with colonial groups and expatriate organizations, the real Singaporean theater was based on ethnicity and culture and was therefore performed in a language other than English. Traditional forms of theater in other languages are still widely presented in Singapore, though audiences for some forms — such as Chinese operas in Teochew, Hokkien, or Cantonese — are struggling to survive as the number of fluent speakers of dialect diminishes every year. With the exception of Indian dance, which is still well supported by the Indian community, the future of many of the traditional performing arts in Singapore appears uncertain, in spite of the many attempts to pass these forms on to a younger generation.

Given the country's linguistic complexity, it is hardly surprising that the government's policies with regard to language education and use have driven Singapore's postcolonial identity. During the 1970s, the PAP government began to aggressively promote English-language education rather than stressing Malay — which remains Singapore's official "national language" — or Chinese, which was linguistically divided and perceived as radicalized by virtue of its association with communism and leftist causes. Of course there were economic motivations behind this decision as well; by encouraging the educated elite to speak English fluently, Singapore has been able to transform itself into a regional magnet for overseas investment as well as a major center for multinational business and international finance.[2] Today, briefcase-toting yuppies scampering in and out of the high-rise office buildings along Shenton Way—Singapore's Wall Street—are more likely to be answering their cell phones in English than any other language. By pushing English-language education, the government has also caused Singapore's tourist sector to prosper; indeed, the Western tourist who spends a few days in the pricey, gleaming hotels of central Singapore often leaves the country impressed by the relative ease with which they have been able to communicate with Singaporeans in English, not only in their hotels but also at virtually any shop in the areas frequented by tourists. With the exception of educated East Asians, tertiary-educated Singaporeans arguably lead the rest of Asia in their fluency and command of the English language.

Singaporean theater in English dates back to the mid-1960s, when a generation of university-educated playwrights began writing naturalistic, Western-influenced plays on Singaporean themes.[3] Lim Chor Pee, the best-known playwright from this period, wrote an article on the state of Singaporean theater in the mid-1960s that was grimly entitled "Is Drama Non-Existent in Singapore?" For many educated women and men of his generation, the problem, he argues, was one of language: "English is English as written by the British and no one else could really write English creatively" (42). Because Lim and his contemporaries grew up under British rule, it is hardly surprising that for many of them speaking the language correctly meant adopting the plummy sounds and full vowels of an Oxbridge graduate, while models for the written word were taken entirely from high-culture English sources. Singaporean theater in English during the 1960s and 1970s was largely by and for the English-speaking university-educated and featured cultural imports rather than indigenous plays, many of them performed by expatriates in the context of amateur drama clubs.

Even as Singaporean theater in English entered the 1980s with Robert Yeo's then controversial "political" play *One Year Back Home*, the use of English onstage remained problematic.[4] In an influential 1986 article on theater in Singapore, Max Le Blond, the director of Yeo's play, commented on the unnaturalness of some of the play's language to support his assertion that even the best Singaporeans writers had not yet found their English-speaking voice onstage. As an example, Le Blond cites a moment in which the play's protagonist, Reginald Fernandez, takes leave of a fellow Singaporean's London flat with the words, "Bye Hua, and say *selamat malam* to little Lisa for me" (Yeo, *One Year Back Home* 19). The Malay *selamat malam*—loosely translated as

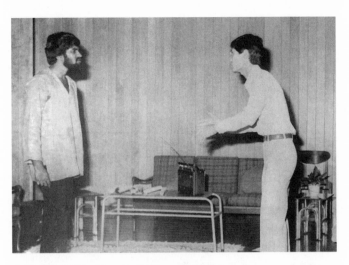

Robert Yeo's One Year Back Home, *staged in 1980, was a land-mark play in the development of an English-language theater in Singapore. Directed by Max Le Blond for the University of Singapore Society. Left to right: T. Sasitharan as Reggie and Chia Chor Leong as Chye. Photo courtesy of Robert Yeo.*

"goodnight" — seems unnatural and forced, as if tossed into the middle of a very English sentence simply in order to make a point about Singapore's multicultural identity. That neither party is Malay makes the intrusion seem even odder, especially as *selamat malam* is not really the equivalent of "goodnight" and it is highly unlikely that anyone who uses the term would invoke it to be uttered both after the fact and in their absence. Le Blond faults himself as well, however, noting that while in rehearsal, "blatantly against the facts and demands of the script, the tendency was to shift up through the gears of accent and settle at a level tangibly closer to the norms of received pronunciation" (117). According to Le Blond, even as late as the early 1980s, English-educated playwrights were still finding it difficult to write in a way that captured the authentic idioms and multilingualism of Singaporean speech, shackled as they were by deeply ingrained ideas about the kinds of behaviors and accents that were appropriate for the stage. Thus language represented a barrier to the representation of Singaporean identity onstage, rather than the means through which identity would be articulated.

As Singapore grew increasingly wealthy and international throughout the 1970s and 1980s, the PAP government became concerned that an over-reliance on the English language had the potential to undermine what they began to define as "traditional Asian values." In the interest of "preserving" those values, the government launched a "Speak Mandarin" campaign that was—and still is—aggressively promoted to the Chinese community. Over the course of the 1990s, as Chinese-stream students have matured and entered universities and the workforce, increasingly larger numbers of young people have become speakers of both English and Mandarin. Nevertheless, most Singaporean Chinese are far from being completely bilingual, and many Mandarin-speaking mainland Chinese living in Singapore complain of the difficulty they have being understood by Singaporean Chinese speakers who claim to speak Mandarin. In spite of the "Speak Mandarin" policy, which is promoted through advertisements and a range of free educational schemes, the vast majority of Chinese Singaporeans—especially those who do not have the benefit of secondary or tertiary education—continue speaking some combination of dialect and English at home.

Even though Mandarin-language theater began to blossom somewhat in the 1990s, it is English-language theater that has been the most successful in projecting a trendy, hip image, a factor that is largely responsible for the relative youth of Singapore's theatergoing public. Audiences witnessing productions by TheatreWorks, The Necessary Stage, and Action Theatre—three well-established companies that are largely devoted to Singapore-themed plays —are almost always uniformly young; unlike the typical Western theatergoer, whose profile is that of a college-educated woman in her fifties, the typical Singaporean audience member watching an English-language play is likely to be a young, working professional in his or her twenties or early thirties. What these theatergoers have in common with their Western counterpart is education; unlike the audience for the traditional performing arts, which tended to be predominantly non-tertiary-educated and non-English-speaking, the audience for theater is largely tuned in to English due to the country's language policies.

Over the course of the last few decades, Singaporeans have become increasingly comfortable asserting their own brand of English, which, like Englishes everywhere, has its own idioms, diction, and idiosyncrasies. Though educated Singaporeans speak an English that is understood by most native speakers of the language from overseas, there is yet another English spoken in Singapore: that ubiquitous form known as Singlish. Singlish consists of a largely English-based vocabulary peppered with Malay and dialect, but with syntax closer to Chinese or Malay than English. Though Singlish is the closest thing to a truly indigenous, national language, it is considered too collo-quial for use in business or education, and it is often virtually unintelligible to native speakers of English from other countries. The balance between the use of Singlish, English received pronunciation (or "RP"), and American-accented English continues to be a hotly contested subject in Singapore.

Even though English predominates in Singapore's thriving business and tourist hubs, there are still many neighborhoods where Singapore's older citizens speak a Chinese dialect as a first language and where Hokkien, Malay, or Tamil are more freely and widely spoken than English both at home and in the workplace. There remain very palpable cultural and economic divisions between dialect speakers and the better-educated professional class, which can communicate in English and Mandarin. Because English is now virtually a requirement to make it to the top of the social and economic pyramid, those who express themselves most articulately in dialect are often not represented onstage. Perhaps because Singaporean film is still more marginal than its theater, it is the former medium that has been responsible for perhaps the most stirring and eloquent evocation of a linguistic community that is otherwise largely absent in the country's cultural sphere. The films of Eric Khoo, notably his *Mee Pok Man* (1995) and *12 Storeys* (1997), and the Singaporean blockbuster *Money No Enough* (1998) have been particularly significant in this regard, as all three have relied heavily on the use of Hokkien rather than English or Mandarin.[5]

Peopled with types other than Shenton Way yuppies and high achievers, Khoo's *Mee Pok Man* focuses on a young, lonely food stall operator who specializes in a particular kind of noodle dish known as *mee pok*. The hapless, underachieving young man, played with understated realism by Joe Ng, develops an obsession for a prostitute (portrayed by Michelle Goh) who is hit by a speeding car and seriously injured. The "mee pok man" brings her broken body home to his grim, spartan two-room flat in an ill-fated attempt to nurse her back to health. Khoo's film was unlike anything that preceded it in any artistic medium with its gritty sense of reality and its trenchant but subtle social criticism. Instead of showing us the sanitized images of Singapore seen by most tourists, Khoo provided glimpses into the poverty, spiritual and economic privation, and lack of opportunities for advancement that prevail among some segments of the dialect-only community. The only intrusions of the dominant English-speaking professional class into the hermetically sealed world of the film were from a radio occasionally heard in the background. At the moment in the film's narrative structure when it becomes clear that the "mee pok man" has fallen into a tragic, downward spiral from which escape is no longer possible, the filmmaker shows the young man sitting silently in his grimy kitchen, while a news story on the radio exhorts Singaporeans to work harder to make it to the top of the economic heap. The juxtaposition of the dynamic, external world driven by money and education against his bleak, hopeless reality provided a moving counterpoint to the young man's poverty, cultural dislocation, and spiritual emptiness.

Perhaps the fact that Khoo expressed this relatively radical statement in such a moving, simple, and unaffected manner is what made it possible for the film to be shown in Singapore. Unfortunately, Khoo's vision of Singapore's underclass has not penetrated the theater. In 1986, when Max Le Blond wrote that "Singapore has yet to produce its own analogue to [English playwright John Osborne's] Look Back in Anger" (120), he probably could not have imagined that it would have taken place first not in theater but in film. As the Singaporean film industry is still in its infancy, it is too early to predict the course it will take.

Given the country's linguistic complexity, it is hardly surprising that Singaporeans are renowned for what linguists refer to as "code switching" and "code mixing." This is to say that many Singaporeans not only freely switch from one language to another but also mix words from different languages within the same sentence.[6] As Mary Tay observes, "The typical code switcher or mixer is usually not aware of why he/she switches codes at certain points of the discourse" (412). Altering the mix of words used in an exchange can be driven by the perceived age, ethnic, cultural, and class identity of the other speaker as well as such factors as what the speaker wishes to accomplish in the exchange. Many who teach in Singapore comment on how lively and animated the students are in the student canteens and hallways outside the classrooms as they chat with their peers in Singlish and dialect and how they suddenly clam up and become stiff and uncomfortable once they enter the lecture hall or tutorial room. In the teaching of drama this shift is even more apparent: the expressive range in the exchanges taking place outside the classroom often does not cross the threshold of the rehearsal room door. Students who were marvelously fluid and comfortable with their friends moments before could appear tongue-tied and taciturn when given English words with which to express themselves.

Perhaps no Singaporean play has more skillfully captured these distinctly Singaporean shifts in syntax and vocabulary than Stella Kon's 1985 work,

Emily of Emerald Hill. The play's protagonist is Emily, a middle-aged woman of Peranakan (or mixed Chinese and Malay) heritage, who is capable of shifting from the Queen's English, to the Chinese and Malay syntax that characterizes Singlish, to a blend of Malay, Hokkien, and English that she uses in the marketplace.[7] In the following exchange with a range of different characters, all of whom are unseen, Emily, originally played by actress Margaret Chan,[8] moves freely from one linguistic and cultural territory to another as she navigates between the stalls of an outdoor market before eventually moving indoors to continue her shopping in an adjacent, Western-style supermarket:[9]

> *Low lights on auxiliary acting area. We hear Emily bawling, offstage.*
>
> Ah Hoon! Ah Hoon![10] Open the door! Bring the basket! Call the driver! Tell him Nonya Besar want go to market!
>
> *Lights up on auxiliary acting area. Emily enters, with marketing basket. Approaches fishmonger and harangues him.*
>
> Hei, Botak![11] What are you doing ah! What kind of fish you sent to me yesterday? All rotten ones lah! Yes! How to eat ah? You want my family all go to hospital die ah? Mmmh! You don't know ah, how can you don't know—all right. You give me good ones today. If not all right I bring back I throw at your head . . .
>
> *She goes on to the next stall.*
>
> Ah Soh! How are you, chiak pah boey?[12] Ya I'm fine, family is fine, chin ho, chin ho.[13] I want to buy sixteen cucumbers today, half a kati of long beans, half a kati of French beans. Yes, you guessed correctly, I'm making achar[14] for the New Year. . . .
>
> *She moves on to the next stall.*
>
> Ai, tambi![15] Give me sesame seed please, dried chilli, peanuts. Thank you, thank you.
>
> Hai Mat, put all the marketing into the car and wait for me, I am just popping in to Cold Storage.
>
> *She enters Cold Storage and assumes a posh accent.*

Good morning Mr. Chai. I would like to order one honey-baked ham for the Chinese New Year. Eleven pounds will be excellent, please deliver it to Emerald Hill.

Oh, good morning Mrs. Schneider, how nice to run into you! Yes indeed, I shall send you some orchids for the Church Bazaar as usual. Not at all, with my sons at the Anglo-Chinese School I'm very glad to make my little contribution. Do give the Bishop my best wishes won't you? (27–28).

In the first exchange, Emily shouts unceremoniously from some distance at her Chinese servant to summon her Malay driver. She uses the Malay term *Nonya Besar* to refer to herself from the driver's point of view. *Nonya* is the term for married woman, or in her case the matriarch of a Peranakan household, while *besar* is the Malay word for large, important, or, in her case, chief. Thus to the Malay man who drives her car, she is the one whose nickname clearly marks her as being in charge.

When speaking with the fishmonger, Emily employs some of the most masterfully written Singlish ever created for the Singaporean stage. Her use of the emphatic *ah* and the more and open-ended *lah* at the end of certain phrases marks it as Singaporean and Straits Chinese speech, while the inflection, syntax, and grammatical structure of each barb she tosses out to the fishmonger is classic Singlish market-speak. Koh also conveys the sense in which the one-way exchange is rooted in a comfortable, familiar relationship based on many years of trading, which gives her the liberty to harangue the seller in a manner more playful than actually harsh. Even her parting threat to return to throw fish at his head—though a serious threat in Emily's case, as she is an imminently formidable woman—would only be uttered to someone with whom one had a relationship of long standing. Her choice of words throughout the exchange and the final jab also serve to express her disappointment in a vendor with whom she has obviously developed a good working relationship. By now the vendor has an obligation to ensure that Emily is looked after, as she has presumably patronized his business for years. Her comments also serve to drive home the point that she feels let down by his lack of special consideration for her.

In her exchange with the vegetable stall holder she switches to dialect-peppered English; then, moving on to a spice stall, she acknowledges the Tamil/Indian ethnicity of the stall holder with the mildly derisive *Ai tambi*.

She refers to her Malay driver simply as *Mat,* a colloquial title for a Malay male, as she instructs him to put the groceries in the car and wait for her there. Her final stop is the English-only world of an air-conditioned Western-style supermarket, where she adopts the Queen's English to place her order with an English-speaking Chinese man (whose name is Anglicized as *Mr. Chai*) behind the meat counter. On running into an expatriate woman (Mrs. Schneider) whom she knows from a well-heeled Christian church, she not only assumes a posh accent but also structures her sentences as if she were an upper-class English lady. Kon's writing does not heighten these exchanges for theatrical effect. If anything she softens them somewhat: her play, apart from a few words in Malay or a Chinese dialect, is written almost entirely in English. In real life, the code-switching and mixing might be even more pronounced.

While the social and language policies of the ruling PAP have encouraged Singaporeans to choose a culture and stick with it, the reality of multiple identity has become expressed with growing strength and conviction on-stage. The stress on English in education and the attempt to sell Mandarin as *the* language of one's culture for Singaporean Chinese has meant that many younger people's ability to speak in dialect has been greatly diminished. Many educated young Singaporeans inhabit a cultural zone radically different from the zones inhabited by their parents or their grandparents; it is not uncommon for grandchildren not even to share a common language with their grandparents, or for children to have a parent who speaks a dialect they themselves are not capable of speaking. When individuals in a culture straddle cultural zones that range from the traditional values of their grandparents to the consumer-driven multiracial model of contemporary Singapore espoused by the government, it becomes especially difficult for a theater restricted by the demands of one language to reflect more than one small facet of the larger multicultural prism that individual inhabits.

In fact, much contemporary Singaporean theater increasingly takes place in the zone that crosses the boundaries of education, class, ethnicity, and culture. The 1990s witnessed a proliferation of plays by Singaporean playwrights that reflected the rhythms of Singaporean English with increasing accuracy. Kuo Pao Kun, whose own work has moved across linguistic and cultural borders more freely than any other Singaporean playwright's, has long been the most forceful and articulate proponent of a kind of theater that explores the intersections of cultural identity in a sensitive, honest manner:

Rediscovering the ethnic cultures is essential, but it is inadequate to just dig into one's own ethnicity. Confronted by a 4-civilization reality in Singapore where practically the whole world is actively present, the enlightened option seems to be embracing all ethnicities. Not in a superficial way, but accessing in-depth into the diverse cultures which Singapore's diverse population suggests. . . . Placed in a situation where ethnic character, national history, and indigenous aesthetics are wanting, the way to transcend is to take in the world. . . . Deprivation can be turned into advantage. While the lack of ethnic loyalty deprives one of spontaneous affinity to ethnic energies, it also frees one from ethnic bias. ("Evolving an Identity" 3–4)

Many of Kuo's works have been performed in both English and Mandarin (*The Silly Little Girl and the Funny Old Tree, Lao Jiu, Descendants of the Eunuch Admiral, The Spirits Play*), while his 1988 play, *Mama Looking for Her Cat*, created in a workshop setting with a team of eleven, was Singapore's first aggressively multilingual play, with segments in Hokkien, Teochew, Cantonese, Mandarin, Tamil, and English. The structure and action of the play help make it comprehensible to most Singaporean English-only speakers, and the potentially bewildering multilingualism comes across as very necessary, not as a gimmick. Kuo has subsequently penned and produced two other multiethnic, multilingual plays, *Geylang People in the Net* (1997) and *Sunset Rise* (1999). The integrity in Kuo's multilingual work may be partly due to his age and his memory of a Singapore that existed before nationhood; the educational system has made it difficult, if not impossible, for most young people to be able to cross this intracultural terrain as easily as he does.[16]

Mindful of the potential his suggested artistic program has to become an artificial formula for expressing an authentically Singaporean vision, Kuo cautions that this intraculturalism "means, at least for the artists and writers, an unavoidable long period of study and reflection into the history, philosophy, art and literature and folklore. Not doing it risks permanent myopia" ("Evolving an Identity" 3). Even though the 1990s saw an explosion in the number of plays that crossed linguistic and cultural boundaries, many of these works — some of which were created in workshop settings — fell into a kind of formulaic trap; many of them presented representatives of each of the country's major groups (CMIO) who proceeded to tell their stories, often addressing the audience directly at points along the way. By mid-decade, this structural device had become something of a theatrical cliché in Singapore,

TheatreWorks's 1993 English-language production of Kuo Pao Kun's Lao Jiu *(The Ninth Child). Codirected by Casey Lim and Ong Keng Sen. Kuo's play focuses on a boy whose insistence upon pursuing a career in the dying art of hand puppetry is met with parental disapproval, providing a backdrop for the larger issue of the loss of traditional culture as money values are elevated over all others. Photo courtesy of TheatreWorks.*

as too often the characterizations served to reinforce racial or cultural stereotypes: the obligatory professional Indian woman having difficulty finding a man, or the young, materialistic, highly successful, English-speaking overseas-educated Chinese professional began to reappear in play after play.

The expanded linguistic complexity of Singaporean plays also corresponded with an increasing reliance on historical and archival sources as the raw material from which to craft the stories of the past. As Kuo Pao Kun observes, "We talk about the corrosive effects of foreign cultures. The government is best at doing this for its own defense. But it never goes on to properly contribute to creating our own culture. If you don't have your own culture, how can you defend yourself? We need to study ourselves and our complex, multicultured pasts" ("Between Two Worlds" 140). For Kuo, the process of restoring memory is essential in order to decolonize the mind. He argues, "Every country which was colonized will undergo a de-colonization process and recall memories that belong to the nation" (Ho Sheo Be). Ong Keng Sen, artistic director of TheatreWorks, echoes Kuo's comments: "Theatre practitioners are now moving closer to the theatre of memories. They want to re-connect themselves to their roots. We are reaching back to the past because of the insufficiency of the present. We are eking out our own theatre and his-tory" (Ho Sheo Be). Kuo and Ong, along with Alvin Tan and Haresh Sharma of The Necessary Stage, have been leaders in putting before the public a range of plays that excavate the past while also reflecting the linguistic com-plexity that is still a part of daily life for many in Singapore. While Singa-pore's leaders have relied on the "discourse of crisis" to divide and conquer, stressing the inherent dangers in a country that comprises so many discrete cultural identities, many of Singapore's theater artists are suggesting that multiple identity is instead a source of both personal and cultural strength.

Staging the Founding Fathers

The government is not alone, however, in proposing a unified discourse that articulates a common history or sense of nationhood. While the playwrights and practitioners noted above have invoked difference as a key to identity, at least one playwright, Robert Yeo, has attempted to stage national identity in a way that suggests a more unified vision of Singapore's past and present. Yeo's 1992 work, *The Eye of History*, has the distinction of being the only play that has simultaneously brought to life Singapore's two great political icons: Sir Thomas Stamford Raffles, the British colonial administrator responsible for setting Singapore up as a trading center in 1819, and Lee Kuan Yew, uni-versally acknowledged as the most influential figure in the shaping of post-colonial Singapore. The playwright chooses 1981 as the year for this fictional meeting of the minds, as it represents both the two hundredth anniversary of Raffles's birth and the year in which the issue of Lee's political succession was first publicly discussed in Singapore. The two men are conflated in both the dramatic text as well as the production text, with Raffles, the ur-colonizer at the height of his power and influence, ultimately conferring legitimacy on his rightful successor, "Harry" Lee Kuan Yew.[17]

Yeo's play illustrates Homi Bhabha's contention that "nations, like narra-tives, lose their origins in the myths of time and only fully realize their hori-zons in the mind's eye" (1). By staging the meeting of two of Singapore's greatest minds, Yeo combines historical "fact" with the great foundation myth that constitutes a cornerstone in the edifice of a unified national identity. In fact, by linking the two icons of national identity and tying them simultane-ously to Singapore's past and present, the play takes the process a step further by articulating a nationalist discourse that Bhabha identifies as one that "produces the idea of the national as a continuous narrative of national progress, the narcissism of self-generation, the primeval present of the *Volk*" (1). Yeo's play proposes a "continuous narrative of national progress," collapsing the past into the present, while creating a link between the actions and the personality characteristics of Singapore's two most famous men. Interestingly enough, the play ends ambivalently, closing on a note that suggests the ultimate unrecoverability of both the past and the present, as it too quickly fades from what Yeo terms the "eye of history."

In the 1992 production directed by K. K. Seet and staged at Singapore's Victoria Theatre, our first image of Raffles is in the form of the famous statue of the man on a pedestal in the center of the stage.[18] Raffles, a character of mythic proportions who is virtually synonymous with Singapore, is reduced to his most potent signifying icon: that of a huge, very hard and very dead white male in his classic power stance, with his legs apart, his feet planted firmly on the ground, his arms folded guardedly across his chest, and his heroic profile turned slightly outward and upward, displaying just a hint of the requisite arrogance as he gazes out over his rightful domain. In Yeo's play, the occasion depicted onstage is the placement of a replica of the original Raffles statue (which is situated outside the Victoria Theatre) to a more historically appropriate site on the banks of the Singapore River and next to Parliament House, where in fact Raffles landed with Colonel R. J. Farquhar in 1819.

Significantly, playwright Yeo entrusts the task of erecting Raffles's image to three workmen of different ethnicities — an Indian, a Malay, and a Chinese — thus providing us with a microcosm of Singapore by including represetatives from each of the country's major ethnic groups. After positioning the statue while it is still draped in fabric, the trio together recites the inscription on its base: "On this historic site Sir Thomas Stamford Raffles first landed in Singapore on 28th January 1819 and with genius and perception changed the destiny of Singapore from an obscure fishing village to a great seaport and modern metropolis" (*Eye of History* ms. 10).[19] In the 1992 production, the three workers surrounded the statue as they recited these lines, underscoring the message that all Singaporeans were not only united around this potent signifier but were also in agreement with the sentiments expressed in the inscription. The words *genius* and *perception*, which are literally set in stone, serve to link Raffles and Lee even before their first meeting in the next act; these are the same qualities most frequently ascribed to Lee by the Singa-

The famous statue of Sir Thomas Stamford Raffles, the British colonial administrator who established Singapore as a trading center in 1819. Photo courtesy of Singapore Tourism Board.

porean media, and, to a large extent, by the Western press as well. A sense of equivalence between the two men is further underscored earlier in the act, before the statue's identity is even revealed, when the Chinese workman positioning the statue expresses surprise upon learning that the statue is of Raffles rather than Lee (*Eye of History* ms. 8). Though this moment is diffused by comedy and the idea that Lee would erect a statue of himself is later dismissed, it serves to reinforce the notion that there is a profound connection between the two men, a sense in which they are on equal terms.

The veneration of Raffles continues with a paean to the man offered by Abdullah bin Abdul Kadir, author of the *Hikayat Abdullah*, a Malay work that chronicles the early years of Singapore. Appearing as one of the characters in the play, Abdullah uses his own written words to describe Raffles:

> He was broad of brow, a sign of his care and thoroughness; round-headed with a projecting forehead, showing his intelligence. He had light brown hair, indicative of bravery; large ears, the mark of a ready listener. . . . His lips were thin, denoting his skill in speech. . . . As to his character, I noticed that he always looked thoughtful. He was very good at paying due respect to people in a friendly manner. . . . Moreover, he was extremely tactful in ending a difficult conversation. . . . Whatever he found to do he adopted no half-measures, but saw it through to the finish. (*Eye of History* ms. 15)

Once again, Singapore's founder is portrayed as a model of rectitude and intelligence, possessing the same qualities that would be admired in a statesman today. He shares with Lee his intelligence, his skill in speech, and his willingness to see things through to completion. These components of Abdullah's description of Raffles could almost serve as a description of Lee, so closely does the rhetoric follow that which Singapore's press uses to highlight the personal qualities of the Singapore's most famous statesman.

The 1992 production included two additional phrases absent from the original manuscript of the play that went even further toward suggesting that contemporary Singapore represents the successful realization of Raffles's vision. Immediately before the historic fictional meeting of the two men at the heart of the play, Abdullah solemnly states, "Tuan [a title of respect in Malay] Raffles had intended Singapore to be a commercial enterprise," adding, "I know that he would be as adamant about his vision two centuries from now" (*Eye of History* video). Here Abdullah conveys the sense that Singapore is merely fulfilling its destiny as a successful "commercial enterprise," anticipating the pride Raffles will feel when he returns to 1980s Singapore in the next act and sees how the immigrant populations that followed him built upon his dream. By demonstrating that Lee has fulfilled a sacred, national dream, Yeo upholds one of the great myths that provide a foundation for the nation of Singapore.

Thus even before we are introduced to Prime Minister Lee in act 2, our image of him is already more than a little conflated with that of Raffles. In the 1992 stage production, the second act began as Lee practiced his golf strokes in his office with his back to the audience. Just as our first view of

Raffles in statue form was obscured by a drop cloth, so too Lee is not fully re-vealed to the audience when we first glimpse him. In both cases, there is an extent to which the stage representations of these two icons is held back, a device that creates a sense of anticipation and heightened audience tension. Even Lee's physical environment in the 1992 production served to under-score the connection between the two men; the colonial architectural fea-tures found in the earlier scenes set outside Singapore's Parliament House were carried forth into the set design for Lee's office. Significantly, there was only one non-Anglo element in Lee's office: a small work of Chinese calligra-phy hung in an awkward and inconspicuous position, as if added as an after-thought. Thus, the visual introduction to Lee Kuan Yew and his working en-vironment in the 1992 production reinforced the sense that he is in many ways a Chinese mirror of the perfect Anglo leader. When the act opens, we see only the back of a man of indeterminate ethnicity playing golf, the game that itself is a symbol of having arrived in a white man's world.

Finally, the meeting of the minds takes place. The prime minister's nerv-ous press secretary announces the arrival of an unexpected visitor who seems to have "materialized out of thin air" (*Eye of History* ms. 17), as we come face to face with the Raffles statue made incarnate. Bearing a reasonable resem-blance to the stone icon, actor Christopher Townsend's Raffles enters Lee's office and immediately strikes both his characteristic pose and correspon-ding attitude. He conveys a sense of Raffles's haughtiness, addressing the prime minister in a posh, plummy accent. His visit to Lee's office corresponds with his own two hundredth birthday on 5 July 1981 and is in part dedicated to the task of convincing the prime minister to declare the day a public holi-day. Raffles notes, "You have installed my statue in front of the Victoria Con-cert Hall, you allowed a replica by the river close to the Parliament Building, you have numerous institutions named after me, your history books credit me as the founder of modern Singapore, but on this matter of sentimental importance . . . you have all but forgotten me" (*Eye of History* ms. 20). Quite characteristically, Lee replies bluntly, "We are not a sentimental people, Sir Stamford," and Raffles proceeds to upbraid Lee for being sentimental only when it suits him (*Eye of History* ms. 20). The brusque nature of the ex-change is a bit surprising at times, especially given the unlikelihood that anyone would address Lee that way in real life. In a country where political opponents are likely to be bankrupted by a "compliant judiciary," to borrow the infamous phrase coined by a former colleague at NUS who fled the coun-try in November 1994 to avoid prosecution,[20] it seems appropriate that only a

After a considerable buildup, Sir Stamford Raffles (on left, played by Christopher Townsend) finally meets Lee Kuan Yew (Leslie Koh) in Robert Yeo's The Eye of History. *Here Raffles uses Lee's putting iron to show off his golfing skills, the sport being one of the actual Lee's great passions. Directed by K. K. Seet for the National University of Singapore Society at the Victoria Theatre, 1992. Photo courtesy of Robert Yeo.*

dead white Englishman identified both with the greatness of Singapore and with the prime minister himself could be given the license to address the Lee Kuan Yew in such an honest and direct fashion.

Ultimately, Raffles seems to be won over by Lee as the latter defends himself by listing his achievements, pointing out to Raffles that "the multi-racial harmony you tried to create I have now created" (*Eye of History* ms. 22). Raffles responds graciously to Lee's almost unbelievably arrogant claim that he was personally responsible for this transformation: "Quite so, Prime Minister, and History will remember that as one of your crowning achievements, among many others" (*Eye of History* ms. 22). It seems ironic indeed that a man who refused to recognize the marriage between his historical peer Colonel Farquhar and a Malay woman would congratulate the prime minister for his accomplishments in achieving racial harmony. But national myth is also about forgetting the past, as Ernest Renan observed in his classic work on nationhood over a hundred years ago: "Forgetting, I would even go so far as to say historical error, is a crucial factor in the creation of a nation, which is why progress in historical studies often constitutes a danger for [the principle of] nationality" (11).

As the scene continues, Raffles proceeds to praise Lee for recognizing the contributions of the colonizer to Singapore's development: "I am ever grateful that I have in you a ruler who takes a long and enlightened view of history and places the contributions of people like myself in perspective. Who knows what will happen if someone else should come along, some anti-history, anti-British demagogue and altogether denies my part in the founding of Singapore" (*Eye of History* ms. 29). Once again, Raffles applauds Lee for not turning his back on Singapore's colonial past, for acknowledging the contributions of the colonizer, and for being able to see that Raffles, for all his faults, was merely a product of a particular historical era. There is a sense in which Raffles is granting legitimacy upon Lee, especially as Lee himself is a product of the colonial system. A Cambridge-educated lawyer who knows the history of the colonizer better than virtually any Englishman, "Harry" Lee was praised by his peers in England for his deep understanding of all things English in the years before Singapore's independence.

This discussion of the need for a proper historical perspective serves as a segue into a discussion of the issue of Lee's political succession—a hot topic in 1981, as it had not been broached before. At that time Lee articulated the vision that has subsequently been carried out; over the course of the 1980s and early 1990s, the "old guard" of the ruling PAP—that is to say, individuals in key posts who were active during the years when Singapore forged its identity as an independent nation—were gradually phased out and replaced with younger cadres handpicked by Lee and carefully groomed for the top spots. Yeo gives Lee his own rhetoric when he tells Raffles, "I'd like to be around to groom the next generation. If I may use the image of the relay runner, I am passing the baton and I'd like to know to who I'm doing that. I'm the manager and the first runner, you know, and if I see one of the new members of my team falter, I shall have time to check him, make changes in the team or form a new team" (*Eye of History* ms. 31). This rhetoric of the race is one that is still frequently invoked by Prime Minister Goh, who often speaks of Singapore's economy as though it were part of a larger global race to make it to the top of the pack. That Lee took up the newly created post of senior minister when he stepped down as prime minister serves as a constant reminder that there is a stern father figure waiting in the wings if the team he assembled fails to perform in ways he deems appropriate. Raffles listens dutifully to Lee's plans concerning his political succession and serves to affirm them. The former departs, somewhat humbled by being in the presence of such greatness, excusing himself by saying, "I am terribly sorry to have kept you, Prime Minister" (*Eye of History* ms. 31). Thus the once cocky and arrogant arch-imperialist is ultimately tamed by Lee and leaves his office reverently, knowing that he has finally met his equal.

In a scene that bridges the first and last meetings between Lee and Raffles, another fictional meeting of the minds takes place, this time between Lee and the Malay historical chronicler Abdullah. Here Lee is again linked with Raffles as Abdullah enthuses, "And if I may say so, we are now living in a remarkable time with remarkable people under your exemplary leadership" (*Eye of History* ms. 38). And finally, as if to dispel any doubts as to the relative status of the two, Abdullah states, "It is a very great privilege to be able to meet you, a man the equal of Tuan Raffles in vision" (*Eye of History* ms. 41). Once again, contemporary times are seen as equal to the greatness of Singapore's historical past under the illustrious visionary Sir Thomas Stamford Raffles.

In the play's final scene, Raffles returns to Lee's office, this time even more humbled—indeed, even apologetic. Lee accuses the Englishman of becoming "almost confrontational" (*Eye of History* ms. 46) during their previous encounter, and of course, as we have seen, confrontation is politically dangerous in Singapore. Raffles adds, "I regret my behavior, Prime Minister, but you must admit that I was speaking to you as an equal" (*Eye of History* ms. 47). In his parting speech, he unapologetically observes, "I've never pretended to be other than what I was, an imperialist, a representative of my time, but I would like to think that I was an enlightened imperialist" (*Eye of History* ms. 50). Thus we have in Raffles an "enlightened imperialist," one who may have been (in hindsight) racist and Anglocentric in this dealings with real people during his own historical epoch but who is rehabilitated both because of his position as an important signifying icon for Singapore and due to his obvious links to the other great man of Singapore's history: Lee Kuan Yew.

Raffles has virtually all of the last words in the play, as he places the two men in history, side by side. "But in the end, the eye of history will focus on us clearly, like the sun on a cloudless day. Sir, history has an eye, not always objective, but in the long run it will, through ups and downs, be unerring in its judgment of people and their deeds. I left a Singapore to those who will realize my vision, albeit an imperialist one, but will expand it, modify it, deepening it, making it their own, as you have" (*Eye of History* ms. 50). While on the one hand Raffles asserts that history is "not always objective," he affirms that ultimately it will be "unerring in its judgment of people and their deeds," a fascinating contradiction but one that is wholly necessary for him to be able to legitimize his successor, "Harry Lee." One wonders what Raffles might have in mind when he suggests that Lee has expanded his own imperialist vision; could he be referring to the use of inexpensive imported labor from Thailand and Indonesia, which has built Singapore's gleaming skyscrapers? Or perhaps he means the Singapore-style townships being created today in China's special economic zones. It is no accident that the final adjective Raffles uses to characterize Lee's performance is "remarkable" (*Eye of History* ms. 50). As the curtain falls, the audience is left with the image of these two "remarkable" men clasping hands, two partners in a single shared vision.

In spite of the inherent risk in staging a living icon such as Lee, there can be little doubt that Yeo's play constitutes no threat to the current regime, valorizing, as it does, the great foundation myths of colonial and postcolonial Singapore. The fundamental conservatism of Yeo's play also illustrates Stephen Slemon's observation that much postcolonial theory is fundamentally misguided in its persistent use of the "center-periphery" model in characterizing all relationships between the colonizer and colonized in the postcolonial era. He writes:

> I am afraid that a postcolonial theory which creates a unitary postcolonial subject by erasing the differences between and within diverse postcolonial societies, and replaces it with the difference between the "center" and the "margin," is as problematic to me as the postmodernist theory that it critiques. Instead of making us aware of these significant differences, both across and within national boundaries, the theory locks us into the binary oppositions of colonizer/colonized, domination/resistance. This interpretive framework then homogenizes and standardizes postcolonial literature through its assumption of endless substitutability and comparability of postcolonial texts. (37)

Indeed, there is virtually no room for these limiting and irrelevant categories in a reading of Yeo's drama, as the colonizer *is* the colonized and those who once resisted now identify seemingly completely with the colonizer. In fact, there would appear to be no binary opposition operating within the play at all.

In spite of Singapore's success in the economic sphere and its willingness to face off against the West on matters of ideology and politics, to a significant extent Singapore continues to rely upon external—and sometimes even colonial—standards to legitimize decisions and policies. In the educational sphere, O- and A-level examinations are still sent to Cambridge for marking, even though this practice ceased long ago in most other former colonies. At the university level, external examiners evaluate not only graduate work but also honors-level[21] work. English educators are often surprised to find that the Singaporean educational system contains many idiosyncrasies from an earlier era, making it in some ways "more English" than the English system. Even though the media in Singapore frequently runs stories warning of the dangers of a wholesale adoption of "Western values," as noted earlier, newspapers in the country frequently judge Singapore's performance in a wide range of areas using standards that are essentially Western-defined.

Thus the reincarnation and elevation of the long-dead but still-potent ur-colonizer, Sir Thomas Stamford Raffles, at Yeo's behest begins to take on an expanded meaning: in a country that was initially the artificial creation of the British, an economic zone to which disparate peoples brought diverse cultures, Raffles not only serves as a vital symbol for the greatness of Singapore but also provides the nation with a much needed sense of continuity with the past, while reinforcing the belief that the country is fulfilling its historical destiny as an economically successful city-state. As we have seen, the equation "Raffles equals Singapore" could be extended to "Raffles equals Lee Kuan Yew equals Singapore"; just as Raffles was imbued with wisdom, insight, and ambition, so too are Lee and, by extension, the PAP stalwarts who have succeeded him. Thus Raffles the man functions outside of history; it is only because he inhabits the realm of the mythic that he can remain a colonizer while conferring both legitimacy and strength on an independent former colony. Once again, this formation is classic nation-building, as Renan observed a century ago: "A nation is a soul, a spiritual principle. Two things, which in truth are but one, constitute this soul or spiritual principle. One lies in the past, one in the present. One is the possession in common of a rich legacy of memories; the other is present-day consent, the desire to live together, the will to perpetuate the value of the heritage that one has received in an undivided form. . . . A heroic past, great men, glory (by which I understand genuine glory), this is the social capital upon which one bases a national idea" (19). Because Singapore lacks a collective history capable of embracing all difference, the imagined heroic past reflected in the glory accorded to these two "great men" becomes the sacred ground on which a key element of national identity rests.

Staging Nationhood

Creating that "desire to live together, the will to perpetuate the value of the heritage that one has received in an undivided form," is the project embodied in the country's most massive and carefully orchestrated theatrical enterprise, namely the annual National Day celebrations. In fact, to refer to the event simply as "National Day" is a bit misleading; though the big day itself falls on 9 August, the whole process of speeches, parades, celebrations, rallies, musicals, and fireworks extends for two weeks. Extensive speechifying on the part of the prime minister includes his massive English-language speech on a huge range of issues — its length makes the U.S. president's State of the Union address look like a collection of brief sound bites — as well as shorter speeches in Mandarin and Malay that are more specifically geared for the Chinese and ethnic Malay communities.[22]

Goh's speeches, like those of his predecessor, fulfill an educative function and often speak to a particular group of people, as the following extract from his 1997 address demonstrates:

> To today's young, I say: I understand your preoccupation with careers and families. You can fulfill your aspirations, your Singapore Dream, but only if you keep Singapore strong and socially cohesive. Our basic constraints and vulnerabilities have not changed. We are not a natural country like Japan with a homogeneous population, one race, one language, and one culture. We are of different races, with different languages and culture. We have to put in that extra effort to stay together to build on our common experiences in life together in schools, polytechnics, universities, National Service, at work and at play, and in our HDB new towns. Gradually, we will create common reference points which can rally us to protect and uphold our national interests. (*Straits Times*, 18 August 1997)

Goh's vision of Singapore as a fundamentally fragile country, one whose weakness rather than its strength comes from its diversity, is a constant theme in the country's political discourse, as I noted earlier.[23]

Throughout all of the events associated with National Day, efforts are made to hammer home the point that civic duties override personal desires through song, a large-scale musical production, and the orchestration of a National Day parade and rally. In the weeks before National Day, new "national" songs are released and aired on television. This program, originally carried out by the Psychological Defense Division of the Ministry of Communication and Information, has subsequently been taken over by the Publicity Section of the Ministry of Information and the Arts; the shift itself is noteworthy, as it suggests that while overt propagandizing for reasons of "psychological defense" was once acceptable, today it is modern "publicists" who are responsible for presenting a positive image of Singapore, even if the end result is the same. In an article on the function of ideology in Singaporean popular music, Phua Siew Chye and Lily Kong observe that "these songs arouse a frenzy of patriotic emotions in the participant as well as the spectator" (221). One such song, *Stand Up for Singapore*, calls upon citizens to pledge their loyalty to the state:

> Recognise you can play a part,
> Let it come right from your heart;
> Be prepared to give a little more.
> Stand up, stand up for Singapore.
> (Phua and Kong 221)

While the music and lyrics of these songs are now available on the Internet,[24] most Singaporeans encounter these works on television, where they are disseminated to the masses in the form of music videos. Phua Siew Chye and Lily Kong note that these videos "invariably contain images of smiling people, the intermixing of ethnic groups, and happy family groups with young children, as well as national landmarks and national symbols such as the Merlion, City Hall, the container port, Benjamin Sheares Bridge, Changi Airport and Singapore Airlines" (221). Each of these symbols embodies a different aspect of the country's collective achievements: in 1945, Admiral Lord Louis Mountbatten accepted the Japanese surrender on the steps of the City Hall, and today that site provides the stage from which PAP luminaries view the National Day parade (E. Lee 40); Sheares Bridge represents an engineering triumph; Changi Airport is a highly visible example of the standards of international excellence achieved by Singapore's services industry; and Singapore Airlines and the ubiquitous "Singapore Girl" project a positive international image of the country. Indeed, the "Singapore Girl"—aptly named because air hostesses on the country's national carrier until recently were

The Merlion, a mythical half-lion, half–sea creature, is the official national symbol of Singapore, the "Lion City." The statue is located on Singapore's Boat Quay. Photo courtesy of Singapore Tourism Board.

forced to resign or take on administrative duties at thirty-five — is now an icon herself: she has earned a place at Madame Tussaud's as a perpetually young wax figure (Catherall).

The official national symbol of Singapore, however, is the Merlion, the mythical half-lion, half–sea creature reflected in the country's original Sanskrit-derived name, Singa Pura, or "Lion City." Legend has it that a Sumatran prince landed on the island in a storm and stumbled across a strange creature that resembled a lion. He defeated the Malay inhabitants of the original settlement known as Temasek (or "sea town") and gave it the name Singa Pura, Anglicized as Singapore. A creature equally adept both on land and sea would seem to be a highly appropriate symbol for a country that has generated so much of its wealth by virtue of its role as a transshipment center. As a symbol of Singapore, the Merlion is seen everywhere and of course figures prominently in the ubiquitous keychains that are invariably popular with foreign tourists. A statue of the Merlion along the waterfront in downtown Singapore stands as a guardian of the city, and tourists routinely line up to have their photos taken beside it.

The Merlion was incarnated as a central character in the 1997 National Day musical, *My Singapore, Our Future*. Staged in Singapore's cavernous indoor stadium and featuring a cast of 10,000, the musical depicted the development of Singapore from its origins to the present. In the musical, Singapore's own "Mer-li" the Merlion is one of only five mythical creatures that settle on earth, suggesting that Singapore has a sacred mission and linking the present with a higher reality. As Malinowski observes, "Myth acts as a charter for the present-day social order; it supplies a retrospective pattern of moral values, sociological order, and magical belief, the function of which is to strengthen tradition and endow it with a greater value and prestige by tracing it back to a higher, better, more supernatural reality of initial events" (qtd. in Worsley 5). Thus the sacred mission of Raffles and Lee goes back to another, higher power: a supernatural occurrence linked to the present by the country's most widely recognized symbol, the Merlion.

The 1994 National Day musical, *A River in Time*, also endeavored to present a history of Singapore, only this time a bit more modestly, by focusing on the story of a poor Chinese immigrant named Boon Leong who arrived in Singapore in the 1930s. Boon marries and fathers a child, only to lose his wife during the Japanese occupation. The child, Kim Seng, now separated from his father, is raised by a stepmother and matures without knowing who his real father is. Meanwhile Boon Leong becomes financially rich but spiritually poor, throwing himself fully into his business while ignoring the emotional needs of those around him. One night his wife appears to him in a dream and reminds him that the key to the identity of their son is a locket that she bequeathed to the boy as she lay dying. Recognizing his long-dead wife's locket on one of his employees, he realizes that the other man is in fact his long-lost son. Reunited with his son, he is transformed from a slave-driving boss into a kind, warm-hearted employer and father.

Much like Prime Minister Goh, who reminded the "post-independence generation" of the struggles of their forebears in his 1997 National Day address, this musical stressed the sacrifices of Singapore's early immigrants that made today's prosperity possible. Kim Seng's foster mother, struggling to raise a child alone after the war, laments:

> Times are very hard
> Look at all this rationing
> How to live like this
> How can we survive.

Not enough to eat
Very hard on children
My adopted son
He is my light.

So much to be done
No time for pleasure
Got to start again
Try to build a life.

Working every day
Never stop for leisure
Seven days a week
From dawn till night.
            (Singapore Government, *A River in Time*)[25]

The foster mother's cry of despair reflects another key element in the formation of a national culture, namely the articulation of a set of shared griefs and sacrifices that brought formerly disparate peoples together. As Ernest Renan puts it, "More valuable by far than common customs posts and frontiers conforming to strategic ideas is the fact of sharing, in the past, a glorious heritage and regrets, and of having, in the future, [a shared] program to put into effect, or the fact of having suffered, enjoyed, and hoped together. . . . Where national memories are concerned, griefs are of more value than triumphs, for they impose duties, and require a common effort" (19). Indeed, Renan carries this position a step further, arguing that "a nation is therefore a large-scale solidarity, constituted by the feeling of the sacrifices that one has made in the past and of those that one is prepared to make in the future" (19).

This sense of having a shared past that includes tremendous sacrifices is precisely what Prime Minister Goh sought to invoke in his 1997 National Day speech. Of special concern were the young, those born after 1965, who "have known only peace and growing prosperity." For them, he notes, life "has been an exhilarating ride along an expressway." By way of contrast he notes, "I remember the numerous strikes, the Hock Lee Bus riots,[26] the Chinese Middle School students' examination boycott, the bomb that went off at MacDonald House during Soekarno's campaign of Confrontation, killing two innocent office workers, the 1964 racial riots, the tension, the curfews, the announcement of Separation from Malaysia on 9 August 1965" (*Straits Times*, 18 August 1997). Thus the themes present in the National Day musi-

cals are strangely consistent with those articulated by Singapore's top politician. Goh's 1997 speech, like the 1994 musical, sought to rekindle the memory of past sacrifices in order to fuel a sense of collective identity, while ultimately concluding with a glorious vision for the future of Singapore.[27] As
Said observes, "Appeals to the past are among the commonest of strategies in
interpretations of the present" (*Culture and Imperialism* 3).

Ironically, the shapers of Singapore's masterfully nationalistic musicals
have not always been Singaporeans. The composer, lyricist, orchestrator, and
musical director for the 1994 musical was Eric Watson, an Englishman, who,
according to the program for the event, "is directly influenced by the sights
and sounds of South East Asia" (Singapore Government, *River in Time*). The
program notes are presumably meant to assure Singaporeans that there really are Asian influences behind this work about their own shared experiences. Consciously multicultural, Watson's *River in Time* opened with a lus-
cious cavalcade of representatives of each of Singapore's major ethnic groups
attired in colorful, wildly exaggerated traditional costuming, suggesting nothing so much as a large-budget "Instant Asia" cultural show staged for foreign
tourists. The non-multicultural focus on a Chinese immigrant's story was
balanced by adding the music of an onstage Javanese gamelan to a recorded
symphonic score by the Shanghai Philharmonic, while the vocals provided
by singers with noticeably Anglo-Saxon names were lip-synched by the Singaporean actors who played the principal adult roles. As a consciously nationalist Singaporean musical written and composed by an Englishman and
sung by unseen Caucasians, *A River in Time* represents a strangely hybrid
form of intercultural work that was created to advance the interests of the
state, providing a vivid illustration of Said's statement that "far from being
unitary or monolithic autonomous things, cultures actually assume more
'foreign' elements, alterities, differences, than they consciously exclude" (*Culture and Imperialism* 15). Indeed, the Singapore experience suggests that the
notion that all postcolonial societies necessarily set themselves up in opposition to the metropole is clearly a false one, as so many of Singapore's cultural
products continue to be greatly influenced by the former colonizer.

In *Culture and Imperialism* Said asserts, "The concept of the national language is central, but without the practice of a national culture—from slogans
to pamphlets and newspapers, from folktales and heroes to epic poetry, novels, and drama—the language is inert; national culture organizes and sus-
tains communal memory" (215). In this chapter we have seen how Singaporean artists and politicians have sought to create and sustain a national

culture. The recurring challenge in the articulation of that culture, however, was outlined at the outset by veteran playwright Kuo Pao Kun, who observed that because Singapore was created wholly as a commercial entrepôt, there was no unitary culture to revive upon independence. Franz Fanon, one of the first to theorize about the postcolonial condition vis-à-vis cultural formations, argued, "A national culture is not a folklore, nor an abstract populism that believes it can discover the people's true nature. It is not made up of the inert dregs of gratuitous actions, that is to say actions which are less and less attached to the ever-present reality of the people. A national culture is the whole body of efforts made by a people in the sphere of thought to describe, justify and praise the action through which that people has created itself and keeps itself in existence" (188). Folklore, Fanon is suggesting, can too often be reduced to something static, as is the case with any kind of populism that seeks to make pronouncements on a people's "true nature." What interests the cultural theorist are not the "dregs" of actions that apply only to a few individuals but rather the entire dynamic web of relationships that determine not only how a people came to create themselves but also how they continue to define their existence. In this sense, Singapore's national culture lies somewhere quite outside the parameters of the work discussed here, while it is also enclosed and constrained by it: the complexity of Singapore's cultural web is something that cannot be acknowledged by any artist or politician who seeks to reduce it to a few potent signifiers or aphorisms.

Commodifying and Subduing the Body

4

In the last few decades of the twentieth century, the field of semiotics, originally the province of linguists, was applied with increasing frequency and success to the theater. Theorists enthused that theater was the most complex of all sign systems, especially given the multiple layerings of dramatic and performance texts, as well as the multiplicity of interpretations possible on the part of the spectator as they responded to visual and aural cues, both intentional and accidental. If nothing else, the collective insights of this continuing inquiry have demonstrated quite clearly that the diverse readings of the performer's body onstage are far more complex and numerous than anything that could be foreseen by an individual playwright, director, or actor. This analysis will pick up on that strand of inquiry by focusing on the act of reading the bodies of both Singaporeans and Caucasians on the Singaporean stage, while also articulating a series of strategies for looking at how the body functions on its home territory. As Arun Mukherjee observes, "Postcolonial critics, with their centre-margin framework, have overlooked the cultural work that a post-colonial text does on its home ground" (6). Using observations drawn from four performance texts created by Singaporean playwrights and theater practitioners during the 1990s, this analysis will suggest four possible models for conceptualizing the body both on and off the Singaporean stage: (1) the body configured as a site of sexuality; (2) the body as an object of consumption; (3) the body as a site of ambivalence or even hostility; and (4) the body as a metaphor for oppression or confinement. While these readings are by no means exhaustive, they represent a few of the general categories in which the performer's body was presented and packaged to Singapore's theatergoing public during the 1990s.

As we saw in chapter 3, Singapore's two great national symbols are a mythical creature harnessing the combined strengths of both the land and the sea, embodied by the Merlion, and Raffles, the ultimate ur-colonizer, whose image and name are inscribed everywhere on the country's physical and psychic landscape. Given Singapore's complex, ambivalent, but still key relationship with the former colonizer, it is appropriate that Sir Stamford Raffles, the deadest, whitest, and most clearly male of all men, continues to provide a potent symbol that lies at the core of national identity. In Robert Yeo's *The Eye of History*, the linking of Raffles with Lee served as a powerful demonstration of how identity can be manipulated in ways that reinforce the values of the state. As Said notes, "'Identity' does not necessarily imply ontologically given and eternally determined stability, or uniqueness, or irreducible character, or privileged status as something total complete in and of itself" (*Culture and Imperialism* 315). Indeed, Raffles has power precisely because Lee and the ruling elite grant him power and wrap themselves in his re-created imaginary image.

The distance from Raffles — the ultimate privileged icon of power personified — to sex is perhaps very short indeed, especially given that sex continues to be the human impulse most strongly and consistently associated with the exercise of power. While this relationship may be problematic and troubling to many, it shows no sign of diminishing. The now publicly discussed and much judged sex lives of U.S. presidents Kennedy and Clinton would seem to prove the veracity of former secretary of state Henry Kissinger's observation that "power is the ultimate aphrodisiac." Indeed, as any famous or influential person will tell you, there is a long line of people who want to have sex with famous or influential people, regardless of the possible consequences. As the ever-incendiary Camille Paglia observed in the trendy, Web-based *Salon Magazine* shortly after the story of President Clinton's involvement with young intern Monica Lewinsky made headline news around the world, "A man of power is going to be a man of very high sexual energy. I want that kind of a man. . . . I want someone in the White House who would love to have sex with 10 different people in three days" ("Animal House"). In spite of the best efforts of theoreticians and sex puritans within the academy to unchain sex from power, the connection continues to rear its ugly head everywhere from popular culture to politics.

Singapore, like the West, has no shortage of sex puritans, while on the stage, it is clear that "sex sells" here just as it does everywhere else in the world. At the same time that Singapore's press has added irresponsible sex to the list of ills causing the decline of the West, the culture at large is inundated with sexual images that are used to market products. This ambivalence toward sex and its acceptance as a tool so powerful that it can be used to sell anything to consumers has also been manifested onstage. The dramatic text provides only a partial or incomplete account of this dynamic; of greater use is the stage text created by the actors, the director, and the designers.

The linkage between power, sex, and desire was visibly concretized in the stage text of TheatreWorks's 1994 Arts Festival production of Lloyd Fernando's adaptation of his novel *Scorpion Orchid*.[1] Staged at the Victoria Theatre under the direction of Krishen Jit, this "history play" was set amid the backdrop of the turbulent mid-1950s as the country was moving toward full independence from England. The bulk of the play's action unfolds relatively sequentially, focusing on the friendship between four male students at the University of Malaya in Singapore and a young working-class woman. All five are swept up by the events of the time as race riots and strikes disrupt Singapore's first period of limited self-rule, forcing the young people to make difficult life decisions.

Though the presence of the colonizer in the play is relatively small, it is significant, especially inasmuch as this is the period of time when the British are quite literally on their way off the stage of public life in Singapore. Now stripped of his power to dominate, the British male is portrayed as morally and intellectually bankrupt. Our first glimpse of the colonizer is at the top of the play's second act in the context of that most admired and ubiquitous of English cultural institutions, the tea party. As the stage action begins, the audience sees Ellman, a British philosophy lecturer at the university, engaged in a spirited exchange with four of his students over British contributions to the emerging nation. Interestingly enough, Ellman is portrayed by Christopher Townsend, the very same actor who gave life to Raffles in Yeo's play *The Eye of History*. The haughtiness and arrogance that Townsend brought to bear on his re-creation of the appropriated Singaporean icon was mirrored in his portrayal of this less-admired colonizer, who ultimately embodies all of the possible negative characteristics one could attribute to the English. In addition to the many cultural clichés piled on the character of Ellman is the one most frequently attributed to white males: an out-of-control libido. In the tea-party scene where we first meet him, Ellman plays the role of the "civilizer" to the hilt: we hear him arguing with his students, recapitulating many of the standard arguments articulated by colonial powers everywhere in order to justify their rule. His opening shot, "If we had never come you would still be living in your kampung huts," certainly has a familiar ring to it, as does his claim "We brought you law and order" (Fernando, *Scorpion Orchid* unpublished ms. 37).[2] When his first volleys fail, he puts forth the standard line of defense used to justify colonialism: "You have too little in common. You need us" (*Scorpion Orchid* unpublished ms. 37). Of course, the irony is that it is precisely because the British treated Singapore solely as an economic entity that the major ethnic groups were faced with the specter of interethnic conflict upon independence.

This scene articulating the standard colonialist discourse is interrupted by an apparent flashback featuring Ellman and his Indian lover, Neela, who is now pregnant with his child. He offers to send her to London for an abortion, and she refuses his offer of "help," leaving him dejected, confused, and powerless. The exchange between the two subverts our expectations; while he, like Pinkerton, falls for the classic "flower of the East" (*Scorpion Orchid* unpublished ms. 40), to use his own words, he is ultimately abandoned by the stronger woman, just as England is about to lose its control over Singapore as the country moves toward independence. Through Neela, Ellman comes to see himself more clearly; without an Orient to fetishize, his identity as a breed apart, so to speak, has no reality. Cultural critic Rey Chow has ingeniously argued that without the "native," the colonizer lacks complete self-consciousness:

> Contrary to the model of western hegemony in which the colonizer is
> seen as a primary, active "gaze" subjugating the native as passive "object,"
> I want to argue that it is actually the colonizer who feels looked at by the
> native's gaze. This gaze, which is neither a threat nor a retaliation, makes
> the colonizer "conscious" of himself, leading to his need to turn this gaze
> around and look at himself, henceforth "reflected" in the native-subject. It
> is the self-reflection of the colonizer that produces the colonizer as subject
> (potent gaze, source of meaning and action) and the native as his image,
> with all the pejorative meanings of "lack" attached to the word "image."
> ("Where Have All the Natives Gone?" 139)

Indeed, the rhetoric between Ellman and the "natives," combined with staging that reinforces his position as the object upon which the gaze rests, suggests that the natives are continually creating the colonizer in a way that makes him fully conscious.

In the third and final scene featuring Townsend (and the former Raffles) as Ellman, the lights come up to reveal the actor sprawled languidly across a planter's chair with his legs wide apart. The planter's chair is itself a potent symbol of the ease of colonial life; the simple but elegant design of these wooden chairs enabled the "planter"—presumably an Englishman or the Dutchman—to stretch his legs on the chair's wooden extensions while overseeing his plantation workers. Ellman wakes from what had presumably been a dream to find his British lover Ethel massaging him and proceeding to take off his shirt, creating a stage picture of pure colonial decadence. Especially given Townsend's conventionally attractive looks, his seductive pose in the planter's chair provided a visual echo of the images of young, attractive, Caucasian men who appear in Singaporean print advertisements, notably those selling underwear or alcohol. Under Jit's direction, Ellman and Ethel became increasingly passionate while exchanging colonial platitudes as if they were aphrodisiacs, a choice that underlines their total lack of concern for the hardships being faced by ordinary Singaporeans at a time when the city was breaking out in violence. Ethel suggests casually that they'll "have to grin and bear" the riots, adding that it's part of "the white man's burden" (*Scorpion Orchid* unpublished ms. 39). While Singaporeans are risking their lives to travel from one neighborhood to the next, the sex-obsessed colonizers are making love, knowing that whatever happens they will be safely insulated from the dangers faced by the natives. The effect of this scene is to connect the colonizer's sexuality with aggression; as Ellman and Ethel near a mock climax, they speak of troops rolling in to quell the public disorder.

In the 1994 production, this entire scene seemed awkward and oddly out of place. Ellman's initial stage position, which had him napping in the planter's chair, was difficult to fathom, as there was little to alert the audience that the prior exchanges involving his students or his lover Neela were intended to be seen as manifestations of his dream life. Curiously enough, in the novel, the highly charged and sexual verbal exchange between Ellman and Ethel is entirely chaste, with only the hint of a possible future sexual encounter between the two (*Scorpion Orchid* 79–80), something which would suggest that the sexual content in the scene was added later for unknown reasons. In fact, only the Caucasians in the play are shown as sexually active, even though the primary action of the play centers around the rivalry between a number of the Singaporean university students for the affections of a young, uneducated Malay woman; while it is abundantly clear that some of the Singaporean men are having a sexual relationship with the woman, their sexual activity is never made explicit onstage. Thus even though sex between Asians is much discussed in the play, it is never shown. This pattern of foregrounding the Caucasian as a sexually active figure is also reflected in Singapore print and movie advertisements; one ad that appeared in the city's public spaces in the early 1990s featured the caption "We give you the world" underneath a hunky, bikini-clad Caucasian male. In these ads, power and sex are tied up in the same package; the naked corpus of the Other bequeaths "the world" to Singaporeans. Given the position of the Caucasian as a site of sexual desire through advertising in popular culture, one could argue that Jit's staging of Fernando's play reflects this dynamic at work, though perhaps not in an altogether conscious fashion.

Significantly, Townsend brought many of the same mannerisms from his enactment of Raffles to his portrayal of the languid and lecherous lecturer; the multiple uses of the same Caucasian actor's body underscores the ambivalence with which the (male) colonizer is viewed in contemporary Singapore, suggesting that while he is valued in one context for being haughty and arrogant, he is later dismissed when it is discovered that underneath that arrogance there is no core, only a poseur enslaved to a libidinous nature. Ellman, like many Caucasian expatriate men in Singapore, also serves as a symbol for sexuality, a sort of signifier for a phallus. Caucasian expatriate men frequently remark that they are considered "hot" commodities in Singapore, often because they are perceived as being somehow more sexually available than non-Caucasian Singaporeans. To some Caucasian men this makes Singapore a kind of sexual paradise; whereas at home a particular man might be considered unattractive or lacking in social skills, in Singapore the color of his skin somehow makes him desirable to young and attractive women and men. Thus I would argue that Ellman's potent posturing in a planter's chair reflects the role in which many "successful" expatriate males find themselves cast in Singapore today: as a cipher for sexuality, as libido run amok, as power and sexuality combined into one highly desirable and marketable package.

The colonizer was embodied in a radically different manner in the 1993 production of Kaylene Tan's *Children of the Pear Garden*, staged at the World

Trade Centre by Eusoff Hall, a hall of residence at the National University of Singapore.[3] Deriving its name from a designation given to actors during China's Tang dynasty (A.D. 618–904), Tan's play touches on the standing of actors in Chinese culture and, equally, on the reactions of the colonizer to Chinese opera during the early period of colonial rule. The staging of street operas so disturbed the (in)sensitive ears of the colonizer that they had the form banned in 1857, a legal move that resulted in protests and strikes on the part of the Chinese community until the ban was eventually rescinded. This event provides a historical backdrop for a play that was also about contemporary and inherited views of acting and actors.

In Tan's work, directed by Tang Fu Kuen, the Caucasian body appears as a series of grotesque and clichéd figures, reduced in form to cardboard cutout images manipulated by the actors from behind. The effigies used in the production presented the Europeans with stereotyped physical characteristics: large girth, red hair, huge, round eyes, and bulbous noses. In the text, the offending Europeans are referred to collectively as "red-haired devils," a term related to one still in common use in Singapore. Caucasians are routinely called *ang mo* in Hokkien, the dialect indigenous to the greatest number of Chinese Singaporeans. *Ang mo* translates literally as "orange hair," a label that is used to denote all Caucasians, regardless of their actual hair color. There appears to be no sense whatsoever that the use of this kind of physical marker as a substitute for "Caucasian" is a fundamentally racist term little different from phrases that reduce Asians or any other group to certain physical characteristics.

In one of the play's key scenes, which is staged as a demented tea party, the Europeans make their entrances denouncing Chinese opera while waltzing clumsily across the stage as an electric guitar belches forth strains of "The Blue Danube."[4] Each of the three adults is reduced to a caricature of Victorian prudery: the first one, a male, introduces himself as the "President of the Society of Moral Correctness," followed by a Mrs. Butterworth, who professes to "hold a master's degree in early childhood development," while the remaining adult male proudly declares that he's a novelist who "writes for the betterment of the human spirit." Following these Brechtian-style character introductions, the three engage in the "Dance of the Red-Haired Devils" along with a fourth actor, who plays the role of a child. Like the others, he hides behind a cardboard cutout that exaggerates Caucasian physical features. As the four dance, a jarring, discordant tune punctuates their jerky, awkward movements. The first actor proclaims, "I am the one and only red-haired devil," followed by the other two adults, who repeat the refrain. A portion of the exchange, all of which is sung, follows:

> *Actor 1:* Look at my great big eyes, oh so huge.
> *Actor 2:* Look!
> *Actor 3:* Look!
> *Actor 1:* The size of eggs.
> *Actors 2 & 3:* Eggs!
> *Actor 2:* My nose big like the evil crow's beak.
> *Actors 1 & 3:* The evil crow's beak.
> *Actor 1:* My funny hair
> *Actor 2:* twisting
> *Actor 3:* turning, curly whirly
> *Actor 1:* like snakes telling lies (snake hissing sound).
> *Actor 2:* I stink of horse shit.
> *Actors 1 & 3:* Yelch!
> *Actor 2:* I do not wash.
> *Actor 3:* Listen to my stupid language
> *All:* Fee ffff fi fye (K. Tan 9)

Though clearly intended to be taken in a comic vein, this image of the colonizer plays into virtually every imaginable racist stereotype of the European: their hair is twisted and funny-colored; their noses are large and beaklike; they smell bad; and even their language is stupid-sounding, characterized by flat, unmusical sounds foreign to the Chinese ear. The contrast between these ugly, coarse cardboard cutouts and the refined legitimacy-conferring Raffles of Yeo's play could not be greater.

A complex sort of cultural schizophrenia may be at work here; while on the one hand Singaporeans need to feel that their country has a sense of history and rootedness that is at least in part Anglo-Saxon, there may also be a residue of unconscious resentment over the false, reductive, and racist views of Asians that were perpetuated by the British during their period of dominance. The images of the generic Caucasian in *Children of the Pear Garden*, offensive as they seem when taken out of their performance context, mirror the ways in which Asians were reduced to physical characteristics when they were represented by Westerners. Of course, images of Asians in English drama are virtually nonexistent; when the Asian appeared at all, it was generally as an exotic Other or as a generic "coolie" or servant. More recognizable examples come from the Hollywood films of the 1930s and 1940s, in which the rarely depicted Asian was reduced to a caricature that collapsed racial and cultural difference among Asians. Rey Chow's comments about the seductive power of extracting "revenge" from the colonizer have direct relevance here: "The desire for revenge—to do to the enemy *exactly* what the enemy did to him, so that colonizer and colonized would meet eye to eye—is the fantasy of envy and violence that has been running throughout masculinist anti-imperialist discourse since Fanon" ("Where Have All the Natives Gone?" 131). When I witnessed the 1992 production of *Children of the Pear Garden*, the audience found the "Red-Haired Devils" scene uproariously funny. The audience may have been responding on some level to the fact that they now have control over representations of the Other and that the Other is no longer themselves but their former British masters. But were they laughing *at* racism, or were they laughing because they were *themselves* racist?

The answers are perhaps to be found on the streets of prosperous Singapore's shopping districts, where only recently have Asian mannequins come to model the latest fashions in storefront windows. Similarly, subway station walls are full of advertisements showing scantily clad Caucasian men and women in seductive and even blatantly sexual poses. To the Caucasian in Singapore, it may even seem that white men and women have become objectified as sites of sexuality and physical beauty; sometimes one wonders where the Asian bodies are in this consumerist metanarrative of desire. With the Singaporean social and sexual context in mind, the hostile, racist images presented in the *Children of the Pear Garden* begin to take on new meaning; perhaps precisely because the Asian body is only beginning to become a site of desire in Singapore's postcolonial environment, laughing at the "otherness" of Caucasians" physical attributes may provide an antidote to the ubiquity of the Caucasian body in the sale of consumer goods. *Children of the Pear Garden* would appear to be a vivid illustration of Freud's assertion that at least one strain of comedy is funny to the viewer because it helps individuals deal with their underlying hostility.

In such an environment, it is hardly surprising that Singaporean audiences found the "Dance of the Red Haired Devils" in *Children of the Pear Garden* so funny. When the media and all forms of advertising seemingly conspire to reinforce the notions that only Caucasians have sex and that only Caucasians can set the standard for physical beauty, an opportunity to laugh at the former colonizer may fulfill a useful social function, acting as an escape valve for hostile feelings. Like the colonizer, the Caucasian expatriate in Singapore today is alternately venerated and viewed with latent hostility; thus the audience reaction to the play's 1993 production of the play reflected this dynamic, as many Singaporeans laughed wildly at the "Dance of the Red-Haired Devils," while expatriate Caucasians in the audience tittered nervously and looked at their (big) feet. Nevertheless, setting aside the issue of social correctives, the fact remains that the cardboard cutout images of white people with big noses, red hair, and round eyes were fundamentally racist in the sense that they reduced a class of people to exaggerated physical characteristics; they erased difference between members of that class just as effectively as Hollywood films once did by conflating all Asians into a few limited stereotypes. Some might argue that the limited possibilities for public expression combined with the lack of power experienced by the colonized during the lengthy period of colonial rule necessitate this turning of the tables when it comes to racist iconography. Yet is not the reduction of difference always dangerous, regardless of where one sits on the power continuum at a given moment in history? At the very least, these issues should be acknowledged and publicly discussed, something that is not happening in Singapore, as the country is presumed to be a multicultural paradise where racism has been eradicated.

In spite of the frequency with which Caucasians continue to be used to sell products, Singaporeans have witnessed a relative increase in the number of overtly sexed Asian bodies in commercial settings ranging from store windows to print advertisements in MRT (rapid transit) stations and in women's and men's magazines. Arguably no work staged in Singapore during the 1990s presented the sexed Asian body as an object to be commodified, fetishized, and consumed in a manner more overtly calculated and market-driven than the 1995 National University of Singapore Society production of Christopher Hampton's play Les Liaisons Dangereuses. The director, K. K. Seet, had originally intended to find a Chinese equivalent for the world of eighteenth-century France, which provides the backdrop for Hampton's deliciously wicked exploration into the interwoven discourses of sex, power, and confession. He initially identified the Tang dynasty as the most appropriate period, as during that era women at court possessed some of the more visible trappings of power and had a relatively high degree of freedom to move about outside the domestic sphere. Somewhere along the line, he scrapped that concept and decided to mount a "beautiful people production" that would unfold "like a series of Vogue fashion spreads" (Chin Soo Fang). An ardent and unapologetic fan of the television series *Models, Inc.* for its unrelentingly trashy qualities, the director wanted a production that would titillate and even provoke with its raw sexual energy. Thus, as a substitute for the Tang dynasty or eighteenth-century France he proposed a glamorous, contemporary world peopled with good-looking men and women. Audition notices made it very clear that "only those under thirty who considered themselves beautiful need apply" (Chin Soo Fang).

That Hampton is English makes the cross-cultural adaptation of his play even more interesting from a postcolonial perspective, just as the site of the encounter between East and West, the Jubilee Hall in the posh and historic Raffles Hotel, is itself a potent symbol of Singapore's colonial past. In fact, the refurbished Raffles Hotel and adjacent public areas have a kind of overwhelming whiteness and immaculateness that they never had when Raffles functioned as a slightly tattered, grand old hotel for white colonials. Jubilee Hall, the venue for the work, is a small, intimate eighteenth-century-style proscenium arch theater seating around 500 people. Independent productions, frequently sponsored by credit card companies such as American Express, are often mounted in this space, perhaps because it has a slightly classier and more elegant feel than any other similar-sized venue in the country. A sense of high drama comes from merely walking into Raffles and its adjacent areas, priming an audience for an experience that puts distance between themselves and postcolonial Singapore.

The press buildup prior to the event was significant, in part because Seet was bucking a discernible trend among Singaporean directors in the early and mid-1990s to stage only plays written by their compatriots. Adding to the ambitiousness of his project was the fact that many Singaporeans had recently seen the filmed version of the story, with famous American movie stars Glenn Close, John Malkovich, and Michelle Pfeiffer, creating the likelihood that many would compare the stage play with the movie. Advance press was largely devoted to the concept behind Seet's staging of the play. Indeed, the preshow publicity stressed the sexual dimension of the work, and the graphics advertising the production featured a scantily clad couple assuming a suggestive pose in bed; all of this may have been responsible for the fact that this otherwise fairly restrained playscript was given an R(A) rating, which restricted entry to individuals over twenty-one years of age. Some in the theater community suggested that Seet foregrounded the sexual in order to guarantee that the play was granted an R(A) rating, a designation that,

Advertising for the 1995 production of Les Liaisons Dangereuses, *adapted from a play by Christopher Hampton, stressed the sexual dimension of the play. Conceived and directed by K. K. Seet for the National University of Singapore Society at the Jubilee Hall. Audrey Lum as Lady Lydia and Kenneth Quek as Sir Lionel de Martinez. Photo courtesy of K. K. Seet.*

with plays as with movies, often ensures sell-out houses. In a country that prohibits pornography, an R(A) movie or play is a signal to the consumers that they can expect to see some exposed flesh. It is not unusual to attend an R(A)-rated movie in Singapore that might be designated an art-house film in the West and discover, when the lights come up at the end of the movie, that one was surrounded by single, middle-aged men in trench coats—or rather long, oversized singlets, the Singaporean equivalent.

Nevertheless, a *Vogue* magazine–like unfolding of a succession of pretty people packaged as a play is an accurate reflection of the Singapore that is marketed to the world and its people as a capitalist, consumer paradise. Vast sections of the country seem to be devoted to shopping, and the centerpiece of it all, Orchard Road, features thousands of shops housed in gigantic air-conditioned shopping centers—any one of which would seem to be sufficient to satisfy the shopping habits of a medium-sized city. Every famous brand name known to global consumers is represented somewhere, while the store windows and posters in the underground passageways between the centers bombard the shopper with images of thin, beautiful, young women and well-toned, handsome men. While it is easy to rejoice in the director's decision to mount this "sexy" production using Asian actors in order to disrupt the hegemony of the Caucasian body in favor of the sexed Asian body, as Pieterse and Parekh point out, what is really at work may be the substitution of one oppressive system with another:

> If, however, we view images as, in the words of Maffesoli, "vectors of communication," it follows that liberation means the substitution of one vector of communion—imported and imposed by the colonial power—by the other, presumably self-generated vectors. Emancipation involves communion, and communion cannot exist without binding images. The distinction between image and reality, falsity and truth, merges, then, with the boundary between dominator and subaltern, and, in turn, with other and self. In the process, the other of colonialism becomes the self of decolonization: the roles are reversed, but the logic of image and power, which is also the power of communion, has not necessarily changed. (6)

Thus the sudden appearance of Asian bodies both onstage and in the print media in Singapore could be seen as a reversal in the roles of dominator and subaltern—Other and self—as the sexed Other of colonialism becomes the self in an era of decolonization, while throughout the process the image of the sexed body continues to function as it always has in a consumerist society: as a means of encouraging consumption of goods or as an entertainment product. As Pieterse and Parekh suggest, Singaporeans may have produced self-generated "vectors of communication," but they continue to function in the same manner as the vectors imposed by the colonizer.

For the theatrical consumer, Koh Boon Pin's review of the production in the *Straits Times* ("What Was Delivered") served as a kind of tongue-in-cheek guide to the lovely objects onstage, commenting as he did not so much on their acting—which he found appalling—but rather upon their looks, even going so far as to assign a numerical rating on a scale of one to ten for the key players in the drama. Koh assigned a two out of ten to actress Farhana Sharmeen, noting that "the poor woman needed an education in personal grooming more urgently than she needed one in the birds and the bees as Cecile." Of the male lead, Kenneth Quek, who played the Valmont character under the potentially Eurasian name Sir Lionel de Martinez, Koh wrote: "Reminded one of Omar Sharif, but spoke like he had been given a shot of female hormones. Having a photogenic face was about the only thing he had going for him." He received a three out of ten. Though the reviewer jeopardizes his credibility by engaging in deeply personal and even hurtful attacks on the actors, there may be an extent to which Koh's poison ink was a response to the director's preshow comments that the play would unfold "like a series of *Vogue* fashion spreads."

As the history of this production suggests, Singapore is an uneasy site of postcolonial discourse: while on the one hand the rulers of the country have taken a firm rhetorical stand against the encroachment of perceived Western liberal values, to some extent the country is rapidly becoming the globe's foremost example of what happens when consumerist values are elevated above all others. Both the production itself and critical response to the unabashedly consumerist play serves as a kind of metaphor for Singapore in the 1990s; here we find that a Western play is repackaged and "sold" to a largely ethnic Chinese audience by foregrounding the sexual dimension, which is largely suggested rather than shown in the original stage play, while trading on the play's overseas critical reputation. The play seemingly reclaims the Asian body, but the bodies shown are presented merely as if they were consumable items. Is it any wonder, then, that the reviewer responded in the spirit of the production by rating the onstage bodies from a consumer's point of view?

If Seet's production of *Les Liaisons Dangereuses* was unapologetic in its commodification of the body, then playwright Kuo Pao Kun's *Descendants of the Eunuch Admiral* was remarkable for asserting an inverse relationship between sex and power. Staged in the vast colonial Victoria Theatre in June 1995 and directed by Ong Keng Sen, *Descendants of the Eunuch Admiral* was TheatreWorks's submission to the 1995 Festival of Asian Performing Arts. Using a well-known historical figure, the powerful Eunuch Admiral Zhenghe (also known as Cheng Ho) who served the Ming dynasty Emperor Chudi in the early fifteenth century, Kuo wove a narrative that moved between recitation of historical fact and strands of dreams recounted by four young Shenton Way yuppies.[5] Kuo's national allegory relies on a historically significant figure whose stature in the region's history is roughly equivalent to that of Sir Stamford Raffles, and it uses his journey from poverty to power and his sacrifice as a metaphor for the losses of his compatriots. As with Zhenghe, who lost the full use of his ultimate signifier, each of the yuppies depicted in the play gave up some sacred or personal part of themselves in order to ascend the corporate ladder. As one of the characters in the play observes, "We were related. . . . I was a descendent of the Eunuch Admiral" (TheatreWorks, video of *Descendants of the Eunuch Admiral*).[6]

Early in the play, an inverse relationship between sex and power is established, using a potent and grim description of the interior of a special chamber in the Imperial Palace in Beijing where the dried and cut penises of the eunuchs were kept during the Ming dynasty. The narrator describes their storage:

> What is interesting about this chamber is that the boxes of penises, or
> treasures or *au bei* as they were called, were not stacked or stored. No,
> they were not stacked in rows, or locked in cupboards. Instead, they were
> hung up, suspended in the air from the ceiling. . . . The most junior eu-
> nuchs get their penises suspended at ground level, then as you get a pro-
> motion, your position goes higher. Your penis box, commensurate with
> the higher stages, will also get to a higher level. As you get promoted, your
> penis box also gets higher and higher, higher and higher until it reaches
> up to the top of the ceiling. . . . Of course every time you get a promotion,
> you have to show your *au bei*, just as every time we get a promotion, we
> have to show our degrees, diplomas, and testimonial letters. (Theatre-
> Works, video of *Descendants of the Eunuch Admiral*)

Kuo Jian Hong's[7] set underscored this sense of loss by creating an environment in which the power-suited clad actors were isolated from one other as they gave up items of clothing, beginning with the surrender of their dressed-for-success shoes, the loss of which suggested a symbolic castration that linked them with Zhenghe in word as well as deed. As with the penis boxes, the loss of power experienced by the yuppies onstage was underlined by the presence of discarded items of clothing, potent symbols of power that were freely forsaken. As the clothing was abandoned, a solemn, robe-clad character disappeared into the wings with their apparel, suggesting that it was not enough merely to cast off the trappings of power—that the vestments would be preserved, in the same manner that the dried and cut penises of the eunuchs were stored. Just as the penis needed to be preserved in order to confer power through sacrifice and submission, the clothing would be saved in order to remind the subject of his loss and of the power that came from that sacrifice.

One of the recurring narrative features of the play were detailed descriptions of different methods of castration. Perhaps the most chilling one is contained in this passage from the end of the play, which describes "the most sophisticated and ultimate castration":

> You have to do it when the boy is very young. The operation is usually handled by a specially trained nanny employed when the boy is still an infant. When the nanny has won the confidence of the boy, she would begin to massage his testicles, softly, very softly at the beginning, after bath, before bedtime, softly, softly, so that there is not only no pain, there is actually comfort and pleasure. As time goes by, the nanny would have increased the pressure of the massage to such a degree that although the boy still finds it pleasurable, she would have started to crush the testicles so hard that the impact begins to damage the inside of the organ. Of course by this time the pain tolerance of the child would have risen so high that he would still perceive the massage as benign and pleasurable. Very soon, the function of the testicles would have been completely destroyed and the job is done. Apart from the absence of perceived pain, the greatest merit of the method is that no part of the organ gets cut off. In fact, externally everything looks the same. Nothing is missing; everything looks normal and untouched. (TheatreWorks, video of *Descendants of the Eunuch Admiral*)

Given the placement of this passage at the end of the work, it seems clear that this description could be seen as a metaphor not only for the lives of the four Shenton Way yuppies in the play but also, by extension, for the lives of other Singaporeans who feel as though they have sacrificed something essential of themselves in order to obtain material success.

Kuo's criticism can also be seen to extend beyond the boundaries of individual choice and into the realm of external social and political controls, which function as the larger vessel that fashions the individual; like the proverbial frog slowly cooked to death unknowingly, one could argue that the Singaporean populace has been made powerless by submitting to external forces and pressures that seem comforting and pleasurable but are in fact destroyers of the spirit. The firm hold over the country exerted by the ruling PAP makes it risky for playwrights and theater practitioners to step too far outside the realm of allegory and dish up pointed social or political criticism; given that Kuo, the country's most highly regarded and most senior practicing playwright, himself spent many years in detainment, it is unlikely that he would ever be willing to actually put a name to the source of the oppression

In Descendants of the Eunuch Admiral, *by Kuo Pao Kun, actors exchange their modern power suits for traditional robes, while invented rituals convey a sense of loss and longing. Directed by Ong Keng Sen for TheatreWorks at the Victoria Theatre, Singapore, 1995. Set and lighting design: Kuo Jian Hong. Left to right: Tang Fu Kuen and Janice Koh. Photo by Lawrence Siow.*

in the play's final allegory. As in Czechoslovakia prior to the fall of communism, where a moment in a play in which someone was inadvertently locked in a closet could be construed by the audience as a powerful statement about political oppression or simply as farce, the Singaporean audience member is free to arrange the signifiers that constitute *Descendants of the Eunuch Admiral* to create a variety of interpretations. The play is just open enough textually and visually to be perceived as a dream, as a statement about power and loss of self-worth, as a historical document, as social or even (indirect) political criticism, or as all of these.

The reception of the play in the press focused on its apparent criticism of corporate life, as the headline of the review that appeared in the *Straits Times* would suggest: "Castration and Corporate Ladder. Parallels are drawn between power struggles of court eunuchs and today's office workers in Kuo's new play." The same reviewer who had savaged Seet's production of *Les Liaisons Dangereuses* lauded Kuo's play for having "brought Singapore theatre to the next millennium by taking the audience on a trip into a new world," heaping further praise on director Ong, who, in his view, "succeeded in extending the Asian identity beyond that of silk and satin costumes, and painted, instead, a richer picture though his actors, who perform against a backdrop of computer projections and an eclectic soundtrack ranging from Meredith Monk to Faure's Requiem, creating a cohesive assault on the senses that was spell-binding" (Koh Boon Pin, "Castration"). By ignoring the social and political criticism embedded in the play and focusing on the marketable externals communicated through the outer trappings of the production, the reviewer is to some extent complicit with the system the play comments upon.

Kuo's play demonstrates oppressive institutions's power to erase the category of gender on the body; indeed, the yuppies in his play become increasingly androgynous as they buy into the Singaporean corporate system, mirroring the progress of the court eunuchs in the Ming dynasty. Standing in stark contrast to the virtual obliteration of gender is Seet's adaptation of Hampton's play, placing the sexed, Asian body center stage as an object of both desire and commodification, "liberating" the sexual voyeur from the fixed gaze on the Caucasian subject. To return to the culture that prevails on the street, however, one has to look no further than the marketing of Tiger and Anchor beers, the region's two signature alcoholic libations, which are consumed by and marketed to middle- and working-class Singaporean males. Like Budweiser in the United States or Foster's in Australia, both beers are uncomplicated and unpretentious, relatively inexpensive, and sold everywhere. Tellingly, many of the ads for Tiger and Anchor feature not the largely Chinese males who would presumably represent the largest consumers of the beer but, rather, reasonably attractive and often rugged-looking Caucasian males with whom the Chinese male is expected to identify.

One Tiger ad that seemed to precede every movie shown in Singapore for a while in the 1990s showed a couple of fairly conventional-looking, fully clad Caucasian men on a boat sport-fishing in the company of bevy of curvaceous, attractive, and apparently mute young women in tiny bikinis. After successfully pulling in a huge fish with his large rod while the women look on with expressions that suggest the near attainment of orgasm, one of his male buddies, in a strong Australian accent remarks, "Give that man a Tiger!" The final tableau shows the blondest of the women, in a gold bikini, standing with her left breast pressed into the chest of the successful fisherman, both with foaming glasses of Tiger, as a gigantic marlin pierces the frame from

Tiger Beer ad from the "Marlin Campaign." While Chinese bodies are selling American financial services for Citibank, Caucasians hawk underwear and Singaporean beer. Photo courtesy of Saatchi and Saatchi Singapore.

above, its long, pointy snout inevitably drawing the viewer's focus back down to the golden beer and the golden blond. Another often-seen beer ad shows a classic, towering "blond bombshell" wending her way through a dark, crowded bar, while an overawed man of indeterminate ethnicity pops his beer and the bubbles foam bountifully from the bottle. Many of the ads regularly shown in Singapore's movie theaters featured Caucasian actors in physical settings far removed from Singapore, as if to suggest that if the beer was good enough for white people, it was good enough for Singaporeans.

One of the few major advertising campaign of the 1990s that consistently featured Asian models was that of the "Citibank Yuppie," which effectively linked young, attractive, ethnic Chinese men and women with economic rather than sexual power. So remarkable was this achievement that at the end of the decade a prominent Singaporean newspaper columnist praised this campaign for having "captured the heady capitalist spirit of the 90s," concluding that "the Citibank Yuppie did more than any advertiser to introduce the idea of Asian Cool: urbane and at home in the modern Western world, always knowing what he wanted, and always able to get it, with the confident flash of a card and the flourish of a signature" (C. George). The exclusion of non-Chinese Asian actors in multiracial Singapore goes unre-marked by the writer, as does the obvious implication that the Chinese alone are associated with wealth, sophistication, and style. Where are the Asian (read Chinese) bodies in Singapore's consumer-driven metanarrative of de-sire? They are selling American financial services, while the Caucasians use their "sexy" bodies to hawk underwear and Singaporean beer.

The word *feminism* is virtually never used in Singapore, a phenomenon that increasingly seems to be the case throughout the developed world. Contributing to the distaste for the term is the relative absence of a generation of Singaporean women who were linked personally and ideologically to that first wave of populist, liberal feminism that emerged in Europe and North America in the 1970s. Lacking that older generation of self-proclaimed feminists, even highly educated Singaporean women avoid the "F word" like the plague. Indeed, the country's most visible proto-feminist group, AWARE (Association of Women for Action and Research), not only shuns the term *feminism* but also resists the notion that the issues they are concerned with are solely the province of women. According to Kanwaljit Soin, former head of the group, "There are no women's issues. I don't like that labelling. If there is violence against a woman, that is an ethical issue. If a woman goes out into the workforce, it is an economic issue. If it is childcare, it is a family issue. Many national issues have been conveniently marginalized and compartmentalised as women's issues" (Charlotte Lim). One of Singapore's most visible women, Soin served until 1997 as a Nominated Member of Parliament, a position that gave her the right to participate in parliamentary debates without full voting rights, making her well situated to understand the politics of social action where women are concerned.

Soin's unwillingness to "compartmentalize" women's issues is shared by other educated and professional women in

Singapore. When I taught a seminar on feminism and theater to a group of thirty-something, predominantly female graduate students at the country's national university, I found few women willing to embrace any of the feminist models put forth by theorists in the West; most of them argued that feminism was largely irrelevant in Singapore. Students routinely pointed to the degree of autonomy women had in the household sphere, noting that in traditional Peranakan and Malay families the eldest woman (generally the husband's mother) ruled the roost with unquestioned authority. In terms of education, Singaporean women excel both numerically and in terms of most markers of academic achievement, while they have become increasingly well represented in the workforce. In such an environment, argued my students, the value of feminism was questionable, especially given that the movement was also associated with the perceived excesses of so-called liberal Western values. As a coup de grace, students would frequently compare their situations with those of women in Malaysia, Indonesia, and Thailand, pointing out that they enjoyed greater autonomy than any of their Asian sisters.

Even though my students failed to identify with the theoretical precepts of Western-style feminism, the PAP government from its earliest days has been committed, in word if not in deed, to the egalitarian agenda of the "liberal" model of feminism. Indeed, the ruling PAP placed itself firmly behind the rights of women as early as 1959, when Lee Kuan Yew's wife Choo delivered the party's policy on women over the radio: "Our society is still built on the assumption that women are the social, political and economic inferiors of men. This myth has been made the excuse for the exploitation of female labor" (Lee Kuan Yew 325). The PAP election manifesto, *The Tasks Ahead: PAP's Five Year Plan, 1959–1964*, made their commitment to furthering the rights of women even more explicit: "In a full socialist society which the PAP will work for, all people will have equal rights and opportunities, irrespective of sex, race and religion. There is no place in the socialist society for the exploitation of women. The PAP believes in the principle of equal pay for equal work" (V. Wee 6). As the party that sat on the left in 1959, it was quite natural that the then socialist-identified PAP would advance the cause of women. Other specifics that the party committed itself to included encouraging women to participate in politics; helping to create a unified women's movement; opening up employment possibilities for women; granting maternity leave; looking after the care of widows and orphans; providing day care for the children of working mothers; and passing a monogamous marriage law (V. Wee 6).

Two years later, in 1961, the government made good on its promise to out-law polygamy with the passage of the Women's Charter, an act that, in spite of its far-reaching title, was directed at providing women with rights in the context of marriage (PuruShotam 323–24). Equal pay for equal work was granted in the civil service in 1962, while employment opportunities have in fact been extended to women throughout the last four decades, to the point where now over half of all women participate in the formal workforce. Never-theless, their advances in terms of these traditional markers of liberal femi-nism need to be tempered by other factors. For instance, even as women were granted equal pay in the civil service, in 1967 a pay scale was intro-duced to compensate men for the loss of two years of work experience that results from compulsory military service; essentially, this new scheme en-abled men who had completed their National Service to leapfrog over all low-ranking women by starting them at a two-increment-higher salary. As Singa-porean sociologist Vivienne Wee notes, this has had the effect of creating "two gender-based salary scales: a higher one for males who have completed NS and a lower one for all females since they have no access to NS" (7). In ad-dition, even women in the civil service do not enjoy all of the same employ-ment benefits accorded to men; in spite of a carefully managed "debate" on the issue in the newspapers in 1993, married female civil servants, unlike their male counterparts, still do not possess medical benefits that extend to other family members.

In a 1975 speech to mark International Women's Year, Prime Minister Lee Kuan Yew noted that while the government was committed to ensuring that women advance in the public sphere, social attitudes at home are more difficult to change:

The only differences between men and women workers are the physical and biological ones. Women are equal to men, in intellectual capacity. . . . On the whole, we have been fortunate in educating our women, opening up jobs for them, and having them more independent, without too great an upset in traditional family relationships. . . . However, what has not yet taken place in traditional male-dominant Asian societies is helping in household work by husbands — the marketing, cooking, cleaning up. This change in social attitudes cannot come by legislation. Such adjust-ments should be allowed to develop naturally. Our primary concern is to ensure that, whilst all our women become equal to men in education, getting employment and promotions, the family framework in bringing up the next generation does not suffer as a result of high divorce rates, or, equally damaging, neglect of the children, with both parents working. (V. Wee 8–9)

Ever the pragmatist, Lee recognizes the necessity of women's contributions in the economic sphere, noting that "societies which do not educate and use half their potential because they are women, are those which will be worse off" (V. Wee 9). Thus one could argue, as some have, that Lee is interested only in increasing the productive capacity of the country, not in changing social attitudes; given that the PAP has a long history of engineering campaigns to address a whole host of social concerns, there is no reason that the government could not throw its ideological weight behind a program that was geared toward changing retrograde "social attitudes." While Lee asserts that "change" in this area "cannot come by legislation" and must be "allowed to develop naturally," the government historically has induced change not merely through the use of legislation but rather through the mobilization of its many resources, including the press.

While the number of women in the workforce mushroomed from 17.5 percent in 1957 to 50.3 percent in 1990, much of the growth was in labor-intensive unskilled and semiskilled positions in the electronics and textile industries (PuruShotam 325). Thus the apparent advances were really about fueling Singapore's economy, not necessarily about creating more fulfilling opportunities for women. As Chan Heng Chee notes, "The mobilization of women into the economy is a conscious government policy . . . to relieve the labour shortage to reduce the dependence on immigrant labour. It is by no means clear that the participation of women in labour is a commitment (to the) principle of belief in emancipation, that women are entitled to the equal right as men to work" (qtd. in PuruShotam 326). Though these comments were made in 1975, they are equally true today, as Singaporean women have been able to advance in the professional sphere largely because of the existence of a significant pool of inexpensive imported female domestic workers who can relieve them of many of their household responsibilities. In 1978, at a time when the number of women entering the workforce was skyrocketing, the government introduced the Foreign Maids Scheme, which made it possible for women from foreign countries to live with Singaporean families. By the early 1990s there were an estimated 50,000 foreign maids in Singapore, most of whom came from the Philippines (approximately 30,000), Sri Lanka (approximately 10,000), and Indonesia (approximately 5,000) (PuruShotam

348). The more affluent dual-income households can easily afford the monthly fees required to hire a maid, and it is certainly true that many women in high-powered positions could not be where they are without this relatively inexpensive labor on the home front.[1]

With such a large community of foreign maids living in Singapore, it is not surprising that some employers have been accused of abusing or taking unfair advantage of their domestic servants. The treatment of foreign maids by Singaporean employers was at the center of one of the most serious diplomatic incidents of the 1990s, which placed Singapore at odds with another Asian country. In March 1995 Filipino maid Flor Contemplacion was convicted in a Singaporean court and hung for the 1991 killing of her friend Della Maga, also a maid, and Nicholas Huang, a child under the latter's care. The following month, the government of the Philippines came close to breaking diplomatic relations with Singapore after a Philippine presidential fact-finding commission concluded that Contemplacion had been "a victim of grave injustice," proposing the theory that Mr. Wong Sing Keong, Nicholas's father and Della Maga's employer, "must have killed her." Among the assertions advanced by the commission was their belief that "only a very strong woman, if not a man, could have committed the offence." The commission called for a reopening of the case, noting, "It is said that Singapore is a police state which tolerates, if not allows, the use of intimidation and torture in order to compel an accused individual to confess and incriminate himself" (*Straits Times*, 10 April 1995). The controversy died down only after an autopsy conducted by U.S. experts confirmed the Singaporean government's assertion that Contemplacion was Maga's killer. Nevertheless, the press in the Philippines continued to pay attention to the story long after the autopsy findings were released (Mauzy, "Singapore in 1995" 122) and Contemplacion came to represent the plight of "legions of Filipino overseas workers" who, according to the report, "being similarly placed in foreign shores, suffered the denial of their human rights, indignities, oppression, torture, maltreatment, sexual harassment and the deprivation of their right to due process" (*Straits Times*, 10 April 1995).[2] Thus, while engaged in a campaign to assert the Singaporean interpretation of "Asian values" both at home and abroad, Singapore was strongly rebuked by another Asian nation for its failure to affirm basic human rights.

Interestingly enough, one of the sins that linked the theater group Third Stage with the so-called Marxist conspiracy of 1987 was the staging of a play that criticized the way foreign maids were treated in Singapore. Two members of this group, which was said to be ideologically in tune with the left-leaning liberation theology of the Catholic Church, were imprisoned for masterminding a "Marxist plot to overthrow the government." Their play *Esperanza*, along with other socially relevant works, was singled out by the press at the time as evidence of their tendency to show Singapore in a negative light. According to the *Straits Times*, censors felt that in *Esperanza*, "the idea was to show that this conflict between the maids and the employers was not just a matter of cultural differences, but more of a class difference" (30 June 1987). Sharaad Kuttan's unpublished thesis examines the effects that the government's actions against the group have had on the practice of self-censorship by theater practitioners; one of his respondents noted that in the wake of the Third Stage arrests, "it was unlikely that any group would venture to perform another, as he coined it, 'maids play'" (31). Indeed, for many in theater *Esperanza* served as a flash point for work that strays too far into the realm of politics to be politically acceptable to the state. Tellingly, in the subsequent decade, no group has created or staged a full-length play that deals with the issue of foreign maids living in Singapore,[3] although stories about the ill treatment of domestics continue to feature prominently in the news.[4]

Regardless of the treatment accorded foreign maids in Singapore, the bottom line is that their continued presence in the republic enables a certain class of largely educated and upper-middle-class women to pursue career opportunities that would otherwise be closed to them. As PuruShotam observes, "On the one hand, there are classes of women for whom feminism appears immediately irrelevant: they have the best of both worlds. They work outside the home, but they can also retain, should they wish to, some amount of work within the home. The latter is a matter of choice: the boring and the dreary can be eliminated or alleviated by its transference to other women more willing, more capable, and more chained to it. The skilful and the creative can be kept back for themselves, as is the respect, admiration, and related status given to these tasks" (348). The existence of this inexpensive and compliant labor force—which is mirrored in the male domain by low-paid laborers from nearby Thailand and Indonesia who have built so many of the country's gleaming steel and glass towers of commerce—is a necessity for continued economic prosperity. In this respect Singapore is not unlike other developed countries, such as the United States, where consumers enjoy access to inexpensive, domestically grown produce thanks to legions of Mexican farmworkers who are willing to work for wages that are a fraction of what would be paid to a U.S. citizen or any northern European, English-speaking illegal alien.

By the early 1980s, as increasing numbers of women entered the workforce and began to occupy positions that had previously been reserved for men, it became evident that professional, educated Singaporean women were not procreating at a rate anywhere near that of their less-educated counterparts. Thus a concerned Lee Kuan Yew, an impassioned believer in eugenics, announced the beginnings of a policy shift to combat this worrisome tendency in his August 1983 National Day speech: "We must further amend our policies, and try to reshape our demographic configuration so that our better-educated women will have more children to be adequately represented in the next generation. . . . Equal employment opportunities yes, but we shouldn't get our women into jobs where they cannot, at the same time, be mothers. . . .You just can't be doing a full-time heavy job like that of a doctor or engineer and run a home and bring up children" (V. Wee 9). The following year, the government introduced two new policies designed to encourage graduate mothers to have more children. The first policy announcement was that henceforth graduate mothers with three or more children would be given top priority in registering their children for Primary One in the schools of their choice (Quah 221). Given the fact that being from the "right school" is extremely important to a child's future success in Singapore, this was a significant gift to both graduate parents and their children. In a way it also ensures that those who have found their way to the top of society will be assured that their children will be able to follow in their footsteps. Later in the year, a second policy was announced to combat the "problem" of low-income, nongraduate mothers with four or more children: the government would provide a cash grant of $10,000 to mothers under thirty with little or no education who consented to being sterilized or ligated after their first or second child (Quah 222). Both schemes proved so unpopular with the public that they were quickly abandoned.

A further measure was instituted in 1984 to encourage graduate men and women to meet each other on equal terms. Concerned with the tendency for graduate men to marry "down" while graduate women remained unmarried at an unacceptably high rate, the government created the Social Development Unit (SDU), which was designed to fulfill a matchmaking function between single graduates of the opposite sex. The SDU sponsors social events, "cruises to nowhere," and other functions at which eligible men and women are to mingle, meet, and eventually marry. Given the relative youth of most

Singaporean playwrights and the fact that so many of them come from the very group that the SDU aims to reach, it is perhaps not surprising that a number of plays in the late 1980s and early 1990s have dealt with the strong social pressure on graduates to marry. Cynthia, a successful, unmarried woman in Moh Hon Meng's play *Single*, provides an outline of a character type that was often seen on the Singaporean stage throughout the 1990s:

> I'm only 29 years old, and I am already a general manager. I earn more than 4,000 dollars a month, I have my own apartment, my own car. I enjoy my single life. I can take a trip to Malaysia over the weekend to do some shopping, or just stay at home and read. I can stay late at work, and I can just take off on a business trip on a moment's notice. I can go to the theatre, if I feel like it, or play on my piano, or just hang out and gossip with my girlfriends. The point is: I'm carefree! I do what I want! I don't have to worry about another person; what he feels about my doing this or my doing that . . . And God knows I don't need kids to bug me right now! *(pause)* Don't get me wrong. I . . . do want to have a baby. I'm just not sure I'm willing to exchange my present lifestyle, and all that I've achieved, for it. Not right now. (8)

Though penned by a male playwright, the character of Cynthia contains many features found in other, similar stage personae: though outwardly successful, she is perhaps a bit too self-absorbed, and, when she speaks of her choice not to have a child, there is more than a hint of regret in her voice. Not surprisingly, Cynthia is last seen onstage as an old woman with a "sad disposition" (44) who clearly regrets her choice not to marry and have children, as she is left with "dreams" rather than "memories." Her male counterpart, the equally successful Mark, ends his days more happily: although he too is childless, he spends much of his free time in the company of a friend whose "whole place is crawling with kids" (46). The unmistakable moral of the story is that while women have a biological imperative to have children, men merely need to be around them to feel their lives have been complete.

Another SDU-inspired play, also by a male playwright, is Robert Yeo's *Second Chance*, a work about a young woman who seeks advice from a male university lecturer on how to make herself more desirable after being jilted by her boyfriend. The boyfriend, "a graduate from a Canadian university" who's "quite handsome and charming" (Yeo and Sherborne, *Second Chance* 82), has fallen in love with a woman who is not only half his age, but who also, notes the jilted woman with horror, only has "A levels and he's a graduate" (*Second*

When Robert Yeo's Second Chance *was restaged by Guy Sherborne in 1992, it was reenvisioned as a fundamentally absurdist play, with the reconstructed woman in a Madonna-style breastplate. Remesh Panicker as the lecturer and Christine Lim as Helen, his former student. Presented by the National University of Singapore Society at the Substation. Photo courtesy of Robert Yeo.*

Chance 83). After a long conversation with the young woman in which the lecturer attempts to console, placate, and offer helpful suggestions, he finally blurts out that she might consider changing her appearance. Six months later, the same woman, now totally unrecognizable, returns after a considerable amount of beauty-enhancing plastic surgery and turns the tables on the somewhat rumpled and nerdy lecturer, suggesting that he is the one now in serious need of a makeover. When the one-act play was originally presented in 1988 just a few years after the SDU was created, it was done in a straightforward, realistic manner, a style that was abandoned when the play was reworked in 1992 by Australian director Guy Sherborne as a fundamentally absurdist play. Yeo and Sherborne's decision to rewrite the play reflects the fact that by 1992 a realistic production of the play would have been seen as theatrically passé and possibly even sexist.[5] That Yeo's play was again revived in 1999 by a university drama group[6] suggests that while young people might express cynicism about the aims and methods of the SDU in private, they still have to reckon with its implications in the public sphere on a daily basis.

When revived in 1999, Yeo's Second Chance *returned to its original, naturalist impulses. Directed by Corrine Yeo for the National University of Singapore Society at the Guild House. Ahmed Ali Khan as the lecturer, Tan Bee Leng as Helen, his former student. Photo courtesy of Robert Yeo.*

Indeed, Lee Kuan Yew's desire to ensure that the talented and educated pass their genetic material on has not abated one iota since the mid-1980s. In a speech to university students in July 1994 he spoke of the benefits of having a well-educated wife, noting that he himself had made certain that his wife was even smarter than he, "just in case." Dismissing the Singaporean male who marries down as "a duffer, a fool," he argued that many of them possessed "an outmoded set of values which makes him want to marry or have a wife who is seen to be his subordinate, or at least does not challenge him" (S. Tan). Lee's comments were followed by a campaign in the English-language press that picked up on Harvard professor R. J. Herrnstein's thesis that the average I.Q. of Americans was facing a sharp decline due to the fact that childbearing was being redistributed toward the lower social strata. Herrnstein's article, which first appeared in the *Atlantic Monthly*, was re-printed in the *Straits Times*, contained the following warning, which was meant to have implications for Singapore's situation: "Because parents and children tend to have comparable levels of measurable intelligence, the average intelligence of the population will decline across generations to the extent that reproduction shifts towards the lower end of the scale" (Herrnstein).

The Harvard professor quotes Lee Kuan Yew, who warns that "levels of competence will decline, our economy will falter, our administration will suffer, and society will decline" unless educated men marry equally well educated women. Lee's thesis was thus scientifically verified by one of the most elite institutions in the West, as accompanying articles were meant to illustrate.

An article, published in the same paper on the same day featured the headline "Latest Figures Show Children of Grads Do Better in Exams" and observed, "Those whose mothers and fathers were graduates were 170 times more likely to make it to the Gifted Education Programme (GEP) at Primary 4 than children whose fathers were non-graduates and mothers had primary education" (Fernandez, "Latest Figures"). Given the staggering advantage educated parents bequeath to their children in competitive Singapore, what parent in their right mind would marry down? Another article by a regular columnist contained the ominous headline "When Smart Parents Lead to Smart Kids—And Fewer Smart People" (Han Fook Kwang), while an article on the facing page contained the disturbing confessions of three single mothers who presented a very stark and desperate picture of single parenthood in Singapore. The article, produced by the *Straits Times* Political Desk, claimed, "In the past two weeks, many Singaporeans interviewed have come out to support the Government's strong stand against single motherhood, agreeing that it can lead to all sorts of moral, social and economic problems for the mother, child and society in the future" (Ibrahim). In fact, two related issues had been conflated in the press that day: Prime Minister Goh's move to prohibit unmarried mothers from buying flats directly from the Housing Board in order to further discourage single motherhood, and the related issue of the "dumbing down" of the population that was ostensibly furthered by single motherhood.

Miraculously, a mere two weeks later, the *Straits Times* in its top front-page news story, declared triumphantly, "Well-educated men changing marriage attitudes," noting that now 59 percent of all male graduates marry equally educated women, up from 40.7 percent in 1984, the year the SDU was instituted (S. Tan). Interestingly enough, there had been virtually no change in the percentage of women who chose graduate husbands, a figure that held steady at approximately 75 percent over the same ten-year period. The reasons for this shift were put forth in pragmatic terms that the paper's largely educated readership could relate to. One sociologist was quoted as observing that "in order to maintain a certain life-style, you now need dual incomes in a family," adding, "In most cases, if it is just the male and his salary, it will be quite difficult for couples to own a car and their dream house. So marrying someone who is also a graduate and earns a high income makes practical sense" (S. Tan). Thus in order to achieve the great Singaporean dream of the "five Cs" (career, cash, credit cards, car, and condominium), marrying at your own level was now an absolute imperative.

Though the press campaign reached a crescendo on this particular issue in the mid-1990s, advertisements and television commercials continue to target well-off, educated Chinese in their bid to encourage them to meet, marry, and procreate. Print ads appearing in newspapers and in public spaces depict good-looking, well-dressed ethnic Chinese Singaporeans and are clearly aimed directed at those who speak English and identify with a high-consumption lifestyle. One ad, which appeared frequently in the mid-1990s, featured a twenty-something ethnic Chinese man singing karaoke-style to an attractive, pregnant ethnic Chinese woman who playfully covers her ears, while another couple of the same ethnicity looks on with good cheer. Accompanying photos included shots of the mother/wife on a city street; of her leaving the passenger side of the vehicle, presumably being dropped off for work; of the happy couple in a romantic pose; of them clowning around while painting their home; and finally of the man painting an empty crib, presumably for the child who would soon arrive to complete the family. As if the photos were not directive enough, the corresponding text makes the agenda of the advertisement even more explicit: "When it comes to love and marriage, it's all too easy to spend our lives waiting for somebody who's just too good to be true to appear and whisk us off our feet. That's why it's so important to remember that it's not money or status that brings real happiness, but genuine, lasting, love and companionship, which will stay with us throughout the years. Qualities that don't cost a cent, and can be found all around us—if we only care to look." While the text of the ad is directed at *both* men and women, the text seems to target the educated woman, urging her not to wait for her Prince Charming but to pay attention to the shy guy with the bad voice.

In a case of art imitating government policy, Moh Hon Meng's play *Single* also expresses many of the same themes reflected in the ad. His character Cynthia, the archetypal successful single Singaporean yuppie described earlier, talks confessionally about the one that got away in a manner that reflects the tone of the government's ad campaign: "I was in love once, with this guy named Tiong Boon. He may not have the most exciting name in the world, but he is really the sweetest, most romantic man that I've ever known. We met in the University when were staying in the Hostel. Initially, I didn't even notice him. He was a quiet, unassuming guy, loved to read, watch plays. I was a busy Student Union vice president sitting on seven subcommittees at one time" (Moh 19–20). As in the ad, Cynthia falls for Tiong Boon while he performs a hackneyed imitation of the Bee Gees' hit song "Stayin' Alive" that, in her words, "sounded like somebody choking a cat!" (20). Just like the English-speaking, university-educated, ethnic-Chinese woman featured in the ad, Cynthia learned to appreciate a man with an old-fashioned Chinese name, unassuming manners, and no singing talent. Unlike the mother-to-be, however, Cynthia allowed her beloved to get away, and she ended up an un-happy, barren woman with a "sad disposition" (44). Thus the state's hege-monic discourse with regard to procreation practices has in this instance been reinscribed in the theater, without any apparent awareness of the racial dimension of the campaign; though there are certainly plenty of educated Malays and Indians to target, they are invisible in the government's campaign — only ethnic Chinese are pictured in the ads. To even raise the issue publicly and suggest that there might be a racially motivated element to this long-running battle over Singapore's gene pool would result in being branded a danger to the state intent upon stirring up racial disharmony.

In contrast to the clichéd cutouts of womanhood found in Moh's *Single* stand the more complex, fluid images of women that have emerged in a body of work by four of the most promising women writing for the Singaporean stage: Stella Kon, Ovidia Yu, Leow Puay Tin, and Chin Woon Ping. Though Leow and Chin are not Singaporean, they have both spent a great deal of time in the country, and they have created their most significant works with a Singaporean audience in mind. Apart from Kon, whose best-known work, *Emily of Emerald Hill*, was written as a series of realistic monologues by the same character extending over time,[7] the three remaining writers have worked largely outside the boundaries of realism, creating characters that embody many of the features of feminist playwriting in the West. Though Singaporean theater from the late 1980s has been characterized by a move-ment away from realism toward styles that are Brechtian, non-naturalistic, and often aggressively postmodern and intercultural, Yu, Leow, and Chin have further expanded theater's aesthetic boundaries by creating work that challenges the notion of fixed identity, while situating the socially constructed identity of women back into a distinctly Singaporean and largely Straits Chinese context.[8]

Among feminists in the West, theatrical realism has historically been at the centre of controversy, with theorists such as Jeanie Forte advancing the now widely circulated argument that "classic realism, always a reinscription of the dominant order, could not be useful for feminists interested in sub-version of a patriarchal social structure" (116). Because realism relies upon a "narrative of enigmas and mysteries which are revealed gradually until the final scene of (dis)closure" (117), it presents a world in which meanings and identities are stable and fixed, leading to a final moment in the play that is characterized by "closure," a state that, following this argument, also implies the powerlessness of the spectator. Once the events offered onstage have un-folded and been resolved, there is no room for the agency on the part of the spectator, a situation that many feminists have argued is mirrored by the structure and operation of the patriarchy itself.

Many feminists have positioned themselves in opposition to realism, argu-ing, as Forte does, that only by departing from realism can writers restore agency to all categories of women: "A subversive text would not provide the detached viewpoint, the illusion of seamlessness, the narrative closure, but instead would open up the negotiation of meaning to contradictions, circu-larity, multiple viewpoints; for feminists, this would relate particularly to gender, but also to issues of class, race, age, sexuality, and the insistence on an alternative articulation of female subjectivity" (117). While many realistic plays undoubtedly reinscribe the dominant order, it does not necessarily fol-low that plays which depart from realism are all subversive. While many Sin-gaporean works that would seem to be most fully support and advance the discourse of the state are written in the realistic mode (e.g., Robert Yeo's *The Eye of History*, Moh Hon Meng's *Single*), it hardly follows that to write in a form other than realism implies a subversive view.[9] What departing from realism does allow for is a fluidity of identity, an important element in the work of Yu, Leow, and Chin.

Ovidia Yu's two-character play *A Woman in a Tree on the Hill* features the character "Woman," who doffs and dons female identities at will from her perch in a tree. The other character, a male, functions as narrator and adopts a range of voices associated with the more repressive aspects of the patri-archy. Significantly, Yu starts with one of the first in a long line of silent women, Noah's wife, who, prior to climbing the tree, was called upon to do her husband's "dirty work," which, she informs us, once included the dis-tasteful task of carving up a female unicorn and turning her into dinner after the animal was attacked and killed on the boat by mountain lions. Yu's plays are laced with a delightfully absurdist sense of humor, a factor that may have

Rosita Ng as the female character with multiple identities in Ovidia Yu's A Woman in a Tree on the Hill, *staged by TheatreWorks at the Theatre Carnival on the Hill, 1992. Photo courtesy of TheatreWorks.*

accounted for some of the popularity of this particular play with audiences at the 1993 Edinburgh Arts Festival, where the TheatreWorks production won the Festival First Award. From the character of Noah's wife, the woman then shifts into the persona of a modern married woman who climbs a tree and refuses to descend after her husband suddenly announces that he's leaving her. The woman's next transformation is into the androgynous legendary Chinese character Nu Wa, who simultaneously embodies both the sister and brother of the human race. Nu Wa, the goddess of marriage and the patroness of matchmakers, sagely observes that "what too few women realise too late is that marriage is best considered as a business adventure" (Yu 15). What Yu's variously incarnated women ultimately all have in common is a desire to reclaim the "person I lost when I was growing up. The person I was meant to be" (25). The woman's refusal to vacate the tree in spite of the protestations of a string of men arises from the fact that "women need trees because they need to know that they can stretch out into the sky while keeping their roots in the ground" (34). Unlike a boy, who "climbs a tree to conquer it, . . . a girl climbs a tree to become part of it" (35).

Yu's play recalls the work of African American playwright Adrienne Kennedy, who relies on the absence of a fixed identity to demonstrate the constructedness of both gender and race. Sydné Mahone's observations about Kennedy's poetic, densely packed work could also be applied to *The Woman in a Tree on the Hill*: "Linear time gives way to psychological time in which memory collides with the present or an imagined time is delivered up in the urgency of now. A multi-layered, often fractured time/space reality hosts the recurrent themes of . . . woman struggling through the crisis of identity" (xxiv). As with Kennedy and other feminist playwrights, Yu here manages to provide a critique of inherited patriarchal structures by playfully engaging with categories of time and space that would be rigid and unchangeable in the context of a realistic work.

The shifting boundaries of Yu's women perform gender in much the same way that Judith Butler suggests gender is constantly being performed in life: "In this sense, gender is in no way a stable identity or locus of agency from which various acts proceed; rather, it is an identity tenuously constituted in time—an identity instituted through a *stylized repetition of acts*. Further, gender is instituted through the stylization of the body and, hence, must be understood as the mundane way in which bodily gestures, movements, and enactment of various kinds constitute the illusion of an abiding gendered self" ("Performative Acts" 270). The actions of each of the variously constituted women in Yu's play create their social identity as women throughout time. At the end of the play all of the women again merge into the character of Noah's wife as the skies darken and Noah worries that once again God is bringing down the heavens to destroy the earth. The woman observes, "What is happening now, Man has brought upon himself" (36). When Man asks for a spot in the tree to avoid the imminent flood, Woman replies,

No.
Plant your own future.
Trees grow.
If you let them. (36)

Through the form and content of her work, Yu provides a trenchant social critique of both the past and the present, while ultimately empowering spectators by restoring agency.

Leow Puay Tin's Three Children *features three actors in multiple roles as well as
a narrator that both comments upon the action and interacts with the characters.
Directed by Krishen Jit and Ong Keng Sen for TheatreWorks at The Drama Centre,
1988.*

Identity is also fluid in the plays of Malaysian Leow Puay Tin, whose major
works, *Three Children* and *Family*, have also been staged by TheatreWorks. In
Three Children, the four actors who take on the roles of Girl #1, Girl #2, Boy,
and Narrator each adopt a range of characters who are only loosely connected
to one another by virtue of similar temperaments and the mirroring of relationships between the three principal characters. Even the narrator violates
his role as a single, detached subject by interacting directly with the actors
at various points during the play. Leow's work evokes the past of Malacca, a
richly historic, predominantly ethnic-Chinese city on the west coast of peninsular Malaysia, at a time when on one street named Kappan Road, "there
were butchers and blacksmiths; coffin makers and cobblers; goldsmiths; tai-
lors, shit, gunnysack and bottle collectors; people who owned coffee shops, tea
shops, opium dens" (*Three Children* 5). The play is no mere re-creation of the
past, however: the three principal characters move in and out of historical
time and pass through the realms of imagination and legend while shifting
identities.

Krishen Jit and Ong Keng Sen, the directors of the 1992 production, combined performance styles ranging from Chinese opera and martial arts to the full-frontal, white-light, sparse staging associated with the Berliner Ensemble's productions of Bertolt Brecht's plays in the early 1950s. As the directors observe, their "aim was to fuse past, present, and the future, into a singular event, better to shape a timeless zone for the play" (K. Jit and Ong Keng Sen, "Director's Notes" xiii). While this fusion of performance traditions has at times become something of a trap for TheatreWorks, as it has virtually become their "house style," their production of Leow's play benefited enormously from a stylistic approach that allowed for fluid movement through a range of characters and historical periods.

One of Leow's principal thematic concerns in both *Three Children* and her more recent *Family* (1996) is the way in which traditional concepts of womanhood continue to play themselves out through successive generations. The latter play begins with an extended quote from the *I Ching* that articulates the role of women in a traditional, Confucian context:

A good wife is persevering and loyal. [author's italics]

The foundation of the family is the relationship between husband and wife.

Within the family a strong authority is needed. This is vested in the parents. But the tie that holds the family together is the loyalty and perseverance of the wife.

Her place is within whilst that of the husband is without. It is in accord with the great laws of nature that husband and wife take their proper places

In the family we see the three basic social relationships: between father and son, love; between husband and wife, chaste conduct; and, between two brothers, correctness.

When the family is in order, all mankind's social relationship will be in order; the reverence of the son reflects a prince's faithfulness to duty; the affection and correctness between two brothers reflects, firstly, loyalty to a friend and secondly, deference to a person of superior rank.

(*Family* 169)

Much like the "Great Chain of Being," this schema is a set of building blocks, each one of which must be in its correct position relative to the other

in order to ensure the proper and harmonious functioning of society. Without the "foundation" relationship between husband and wife, the rest of the
social order cannot follow. Thus, it is the duty of the wife to be both "loyal"
and "persevering" while occupying her rightful place "within" the house; to
assert herself "outside" in the traditionally male domain is to invoke disharmony. Duty and "chaste conduct" characterize the relationship between
husband and wife, while "love" is reserved for the father's relationship with
his son, as the necessary continuation of the male line is presumably the
only real basis for male love. Appropriately enough, the relationship between
sisters is not even commented upon: women are assigned a lesser value than
men and are not thought to be fully capable of the noble sentiments of "correctness" and "loyalty"; women also ultimately serve as objects of exchange
in the traditional, Confucian, male-dominated paradigm in that when they
leave the family to marry they become property of the husband and, by extension, the husband's family.

Leow's plays subvert and challenge this traditional paradigm even as it
continues to be enshrined within many Straits Chinese families and reinforced by many of the government's social policies. In her epic play *Family*,
Leow chronicles the history of the fictional Yang family, which, despite all of
the social prescriptions that have made it difficult for women to have a
strong, independent life, effectively functions as a matriarchy, as it is dominated by the focused and determined matriarch Tan Neo, whose life spans
the entire twentieth century. Even though men are supposed to take care of
matters "outside" the household in a traditional Confucian context, the reality is that they often die first, leaving the women behind to fend for themselves. Tan Neo's husband not only proves himself incapable of providing for
his family materially, but he also dies young, leaving his wife with a mountain of debts, an unprofitable gunnysack business, and children she could
not afford to feed. Yet through determination and hard work, Tan Neo manages to slowly pull the family out of poverty, initially by enlisting the aid of
her children to sell her traditional sweet cakes to food stalls. As the generations unfold, a food stall business becomes a diversified business empire,
with the aged matriarch still at the center of it all. Because the Yang men either die prematurely or lack leadership skills, the entire extended family remains more a matriarchy than a patriarchy.

Thus Leow's invocation of the principles of Confucianism at the beginning of the play ultimately serves as an ironic counterpoint to a portrait of a
family that would seem to have turned most of these principles upside

down; Tan Neo is forced through both nature and circumstances to venture into the outside world to provide for her family. While her sons possess loyalty toward one another, this sense of duty ultimately becomes the key to their own undoing, as one brother follows the other to join a logging operation in Sabah, where the brothers survive the ravages of tropical diseases only to die tragically in a forest fire. Yu avoids blaming the patriarchy for the plight of women by demonstrating that the men too were victimized by a system that used them as cheap labor and robbed them of a future. Given the relative absence of men in the Yang family, it is left to the daughters to hold the family together. Even though necessity ultimately requires Tan Neo to venture out in order to support her family, she remains loyal to the family and to the memory of her husband, thus in her own way ultimately living up to the dictum "A good wife is persevering and loyal."

In both plays Leow provides images of strong women who persevere and do what they have to in order to survive. In *Three Children*, a young mother struggling to feed her family attempts to give one of her children away to the nuns and, after being refused, sees no alternative but to sell her daughter to a childless widow for a mere five dollars. The mother later observes matter-of-factly, "That night we had a good dinner. Then the children went to sleep" (13). In the context in which the story unfolds, it is hard to judge the young woman. To sell one's child might seem morally wrong, yet is it not preferable to permitting the entire family to slowly starve to death? Leow carries out an important social function by reminding her audience of the harshness of life in the recent past, and the inherited values that must, by necessity, still remain embedded somewhere within the culture. She leaves the judgments to the audience, choosing to present characters who are all deeply flawed because they live in a world where moral choices are not always clear-cut.

Leow brings up issues that are still current, framing them in a way that invites the audience first to laugh and ultimately to question the extent to which inherited values remain prevalent. One of the Yang daughters-in-law in *Family* recites an English translation of a Hokkien chant, "Song of the Daughter-in-Law":

> A daughter-in-law gets it tough
> Wake up groggy but can't look rough
> Last one to sleep, but first one to rise
> So wash your face and open your eyes!

Dust and sweep, mop and rinse
And don't forget the most important thing
To praise his family day and night
"What a good family, such a delight!"

(243)

Though humorous in the context of the play, the chant would seem to describe the way some Singaporean and Straits Chinese daughters-in-law are still treated in their husband's homes. In many traditional households it is not uncommon for the eldest son and his wife to live with his parents in a situation that for many daughters-in-law can be nothing short of oppressive. Everyone in Singapore knows someone who can tell hair-raising stories about sisters, neighbors, or female cousins whose lives are virtually held hostage by the whims of their husband's parents. This is clearly the downside to the value of filial piety. Where mutual respect is present, filial piety does indeed fulfill the valuable societal function of ensuring that people are looked after in their old age; without mutual respect, however, the bonds that link members of the extended family can become ones of servitude and forced obligation.

In *Three Children*, Leow uses also ironic humor to make a statement about aspects of colonial culture that were accepted without question in an earlier era. At one point in their travels across time and space, the children recount the adventures of the "Famous Five," characters from a series of children's books by English author Enid Blyton. Like their American counterparts, Dick and Jane, the Famous Five inhabited a middle-class white world in which everyone looked and spoke as they did; just as Dick and Jane were "typically" American, the Famous Five were quintessentially and stereotypically British, capable of solving all of the problems of the world with their stiff upper lips and their jolly attitudes. The adventure Leow's actors recount is one in which the five spend a night outdoors next to the "Green Pool." After dark, they built a campfire while "Anne cooked sausages and fried bacon and bread and drank ginger ale" (*Three Children* 7). Later, "Anne washed up and curled up in her sleeping bag" while George counted the stars and Anne recognized the North Star. Timothy the dog let out a grunt and fell asleep. "He dreamt of chasing rabbits" (8). The Narrator interrupts the tale, making abundantly clear the total lack of relevance these stories have for the lives of three impoverished Chinese Malaysian children growing up on Kappan Road in Malacca: "Test! What is bacon? *(Silence)* What's a sleeping bag? *(Silence)* What's a grunt? *(Pause)* Where is the North Star? Where is the Green Pool? Where is Brighton?" (8). In a playful and entertaining way, Leow's juxtaposition of the adventures of the Famous Five with the lives of these children living on the equator drive home one of the fundamental legacies of colonialism: the inherited stories, myths, and cultural practices that fail to connect on any level with the actual culture of the colonized.

Fanon has written of how, even after independence, "the national bourgeoisie identifies itself with the Western bourgeoisie, from whom it has learnt its lessons" (124). The system of education and the values of cultural and civic life come together to create a citizen that identifies more strongly with the colonial center than with the traditions and values that predate the colonial era. Thus even the impoverished children of Kappan Road come to know the stories of other cultures better than their own. The intrusion of the Narrator in Leow's play could be seen as marking the onset of the postcolonial condition, for if, as Elleke Boehmer asserts, postcoloniality is that "condition in which colonized peoples seek to take their place, forcibly or otherwise, as historical subjects" (3), then the three children become independent historical subjects from the moment they begin to realize that the adventures of the Famous Five are not *their* adventures.

While the plays of Ovidia Yu and Leow Puay Tin express the link between identity and identity politics in a postcolonial context, the work of performance artist/poet/singer Chin Woon Ping carries that linkage one step further by asserting the feminist dictum "The personal is the political." Chin grew up in Malacca, like Leow, and took a degree in English at the University of Malaya, where she was exposed to Absurdism and the plays of Strindberg, Ionesco, and Pinter. Unlike Leow and Yu, however, Chin spent over twenty years living in the United States, where she admits to having been "subconsciously influenced" by the work of her friend, performance artist Carolee Schneemann, as well as the performance work she witnessed over the years at Philadelphia's Painted Bride Art Centre. Chin's 1992 work, *Details Cannot Body Wants*, may well have been Singapore's first performance art piece that exemplified characteristics that would have been marked as "feminist" in a Western context. Presented at the Substation as part of a double bill that included Robert Yeo's *Second Chance*, Chin's play also had the distinction of being "Singapore's First R-rated Play," a designation heralded by the press that virtually ensured that the work would sell out (Ong Soh Chin, "Singapore's First R-Rated Play" 1992). The Public Entertainment Licensing Unit

(PELU), the body that grants performance licenses, had found sections of Chin's work "offensive," owing to its "adult language" and "taboo gestures" such as the grabbing and scratching of crotches. Thus the work was produced with a disclaimer that cautioned the audience regarding its use of language and "discouraged" anyone under eighteen from seeing the piece.

Under the direction of K. K. Seet, Chin herself enacted multiple personae in a four-part journey through the female landscape as she alternately danced, sang, rapped, and shared intimacies with the audience. Accompanying her was a black-clad chorus of two women and one man who punctuated the performance text with sounds, whistles, claps, intonations, and a series of ingenious sound effects. Throughout the duration of the piece, the chorus sat impassively on the floor near the central acting area, while a musician playing the *ku-chén*, a traditional Chinese lute, underlined both Chin and the chorus with an occasional musical phrase.

The piece was structured like a poem, with four sections, each of which dealt with differing though interrelated concerns. "Details," the first segment, underscored the minutiae in women's lives that provide a subtle and often overlooked foundation for the continuing repression of women across cultures. Chin made her initial entrance into the space laboriously crawling across the floor in a flesh-colored body suit, trailed by a bulky, clanging mass of pots, pans, and household paraphernalia. A woman's first lesson, she noted, is that of learning to first internalize and then to disguise shame behind various socially acceptable masks; a distinctly Asian "scintillating, provocative laugh," she noted, is just one of many lines of defense. Ultimately, she added, as she grew older, "I learned to make my shame beautiful." In "Cannot," the performer went through an extensive catalog of culturally determined "cannots," such as "cannot fart, cannot fly, cannot cry," ending with a rap song instructing men on how to treat women with respect. The "Body" section explored the landscape of the female body as well as the Orientalist stereotype of the perpetually horny and eager-to-please "China Doll," created by and available for the sexual consumption of the straight Caucasian male. Domestic violence, a topic rarely discussed in Singapore in the early 1990s, was addressed courageously and poignantly with the most highly charged of all the props used, an inflatable female sex doll. "Wants," the final section, traced the cycle of a woman's wants through her life, building up to her desire to have children, and ending with self-acceptance.

The press response to Chin's piece demonstrated how unprepared critics and arts writers were to deal with work that fell outside existing categories of

Chin Woon Ping explores the landscape of the female body in her four-part performance piece Details Cannot Body Wants. *Directed by K. K. Seet for the National University of Singapore Society at the Substation, 1992. Photo courtesy of Chin Woon Ping.*

performance. Even the producer, playwright Robert Yeo, referred to Chin's work as a "play," while the country's leading theater critic at the time summarily dismissed the piece as a "rather formless mishmash of all things woman-oriented" (Pandian, review of *Renewable Women*). The fundamental problem in terms of reception was that while Chin's work reflected local content, it was presented in a form with which many in the arts community were unfamiliar. Because it was packaged as a "play," expectations were raised that the work would possess a kind of structure that was not wholly associative and internally driven.

Chin's shifting identities and her ability to step outside of her skin and comment on herself reflect the double alienation that comes being a woman in a male-dominated society. Lacan argues, after Freud, that language develops during the so-called mirror phase, in which the (male) child begins to distinguish itself as an independent subject. Sue-Ellen Case, anticipating Judith Butler's complete destabilization of Lacan's "symbolic phallus,"[10] overturns the sexism in the Freudian and Lacanian models while clearing a space for the female gender in a way that has direct application to the work of Chin and other feminist performance artists: "If I might expand Lacan's metaphor in order to include the possibility of the female subject, "she" also sees in that mirror that she is a woman. At that moment she further fractures, split once as the male-identified subject and his subjectivity, and split once more as the woman who observes her own subject position as both male-identified and female" ("From Split Subject to Split Britches" 130–31). Thus women in a society where the images of themselves are primarily generated by men must necessarily view her subject position in a way that is identified with *both* the male and the female. Case concludes that as a result the female subject "cannot appear as a whole, continuous subject as the male can because she senses that his story is not her story"; thus, from the beginning, she enters "the doors of discourse in male drag" ("From Split Subject to Split Britches" 131). Indeed, Chin's performance was marked by a succession of characters in various forms of actual drag, who also adopt an incredible range of linguistic drag, among them the language of an inner-city African American woman who at one point takes over Chin's body to offer linguistic ammunition in order to reclaim female space:

> we yo sistahs and yo mothas and yo lovahs one an all
> you see us in the kitchen, you see us in the hall
>
> you think you got us figured out maybe you think you do
> want a taste of womanpower or a taste of our voodoo?
>
> we teach you how to clean yo butt
> we teach you how to sing
>
> you never pay attention
> cause you think you are the king
>
> we're all alike and different
> all doin equal time
>
> whats mine is yours is mine is yours
> is mine is yours is mine

so haul yo skinny ass down here and get to work you all
we yo sistahs and yo mothas and yo lovahs one an all
(*Details Cannot Body Wants* 10)

Chin aggressively disrupts stable categories of identity by adopting both the language and mannerisms of a "sister," who is marked as visibly different from the ethnicity and culture inscribed on her own body.

While *feminism* may be a word that is not in the current Singaporean lexicon, the actual practice of a number of women theater artists working in the country suggests that it is alive and well, even as it hides its true colors under safer, more politically acceptable terms. The fluidity of gender and the efforts of these practitioners to point to its fundamental constructedness evoke this observation by Judith Butler: "Because there is neither an 'essence' that gender expresses or externalizes nor an objective ideal to which gender aspires; because gender is not a fact, the various acts of gender creates the idea of gender, and without those acts, there would be no gender at all. Gender is, thus, a construction that regularly conceals its genesis" ("Performative Acts" 273). The playful fluidity of Yu's single female of multiple identities in *The Woman in a Tree on the Hill* (Noah's Wife, the androgynous Nu Wa, the Singaporean married woman) express an idea of gender as a construct created through actions that are not generally acknowledged because of the way the construct itself is normalized within the culture as "the way things are." Leow's play, *Family*, contrasts the socially approved construct of womanhood validated by Confucian teachings with the reality of the actual behavior of women in the world. Finally, Chin's unpacking of stereotypes using a fractured but connected four-part structure that breaks down a woman's life into "details/cannot/body/wants" shows how these "various acts of gender" in turn create the "idea of gender," as Butler argues. While gender is variously enacted by women every day on the streets of Singapore, a number of women theater artists have created a body of performance work that mirrors the refracted personae of Singaporean women.

As the country counted down to the year 2000, Prime Minister Goh announced the creation of a Singapore 21 Committee "to identify new ideas to make Singapore the place of choice to live a fulfilling life, make a good living and raise a happy family" (*Straits Times*, 25 August 1997). The final recommendations of the governmental committee, widely circulated throughout the country and available in both abbreviated and full-length versions on the Internet,[1] identified five areas in which Singaporeans needed to make advances over the next century.[2] The backbone of the document, and the theme most directly relevant to the lives of Singapore's gay, lesbian, and bisexual communities, was the first tenet, which asserts, "Every Singaporean Matters." In order to realize this ideal, the report specifically calls on Singaporeans to "be more broad-minded." Taking this statement at face value, one caller in a live interview with Lee Kuan Yew that was broadcast worldwide on CNN in December 1998 asked a daring and unexpected question:

> *Caller:* I am a gay man in Singapore. I do not feel that my country has acknowledged my presence. As we move into a more tolerant millennium, what do you think is the future for gay people in Singapore, if there is a future at all?
>
> *Lee Kuan Yew:* Well, it's not a matter which I can decide or any government can decide. It's a question of what a society considers acceptable. And as you know,

Singaporeans are by and large a very conservative, orthodox society, . . . completely different from, say the United States and I don't think an aggressive gay rights movement would help. But what we are doing as a government is to leave people to live their own lives so long as they don't impinge on other people. I mean, we don't harass anybody. (Utopia)

Many in the West might be surprised that the venerable senior minister did not rise in righteous indignation at being asked such a question. Unlike right-wing American politicians who have used religion as a justification for failing to grant gays and lesbians equal protection under the law, Lee places the ball entirely in society's lap, avoiding moral imperatives and holier-than-thou invectives, suggesting that these social values must be determined by the people, not by the government. Of course the irony, as noted in previous chapters, is that the PAP under Lee has been utterly devoted to the notion that social values can be controlled and even created from above. That the caller's question mirrored the government's own stated commitment to creating a "more broad-minded" citizenry further undermines the power of Lee's argument in that the caller was merely asking for a commitment from the government to its own objectives, circulated in the most widely publicized values campaign of the new millennium.

Lee's decision to hide behind the smokescreen of Singapore's social conservatism on the subject of gay rights reflects the government's ambivalent position on the subject, which is something akin to the "don't ask, don't tell" policy now enforced in the American military. In spite of Lee's belief that his countrymen and -women are conservative on this issue, one recent poll of almost five hundred Singaporeans showed that 73 percent of those questioned on the street "agreed or strongly agreed" with the statement "Companies should not discriminate against homosexuals in employment and promotion."[3] Perhaps surprisingly, only a minority said they would be unable to accept a brother or sister who is homosexual (26 percent; 9 percent of those responding via the Internet) or a son or daughter who is homosexual (35 percent, 13 percent on the Internet). While this survey may well have been flawed to the extent that only younger people seemed willing to respond to these questions, the results suggest a far greater openness to gay and lesbian life than one might expect to find in "conservative" Singapore.

Yet gay life in Singapore, at least for men, would appear to be anything but conservative, especially subsequent to the advent of the Internet revolution of the 1990s, which by the end of the decade made it possible for a significant and growing group of educated, relatively affluent, and predominantly ethnic-Chinese gay men to create increasingly cohesive communities while completely circumventing any of Singapore's onshore resources.[4] Indeed, anyone in the world with an Internet connection now has immediate online access to a wide range of resources for gay male Singaporeans, including a complete list of clubs, discos, organizations, Web sites, groups, saunas, gay-friendly restaurants, bookstores with gay titles, and even noted cruising areas. Though there is perhaps no way to "prove" this, on the street level, Singapore is probably the "cruisiest" city in Asia in terms of the sexually motivated and flirtatious eye contact between men. Complex codes governing the etiquette for casual pickups have included such visible cues as carrying a water bottle in a certain park, or sitting with a newspaper bundled under an arm while waiting outside a particular mass transit station. In many venues, the codes that govern contact are considerably less subtle, as any openly gay Singaporean will tell you. If the activities taking place in various locations around the island that are described in a range of Web sites are any indication, a great many men are figuring out ways to meet and have sex with other men.

For all the apparent freedom gay men enjoy on the street, however, there are many factors that continue to oppress them. For a start, there are the laws, which are positively draconian: Under Section 377 of Singapore's penal code, homosexual acts between males remain punishable by up to life imprisonment. Specifically, the law prohibits "carnal intercourse against the order of nature," which has traditionally been interpreted to mean sodomy and oral sex (Leong 14). Casting an even wider net is Section A of the code, which extends the category to include "any male person who, in public or private, commits, or abets the commission of, or procures or attempts to procure the commission by any male person of, any act of gross indecency with another male person" (Leong 14). This section of the act, which makes it illegal for two men to pick each other up, is used as the legal justification for the entrapment of gay men, with conviction bringing up to two years in prison. While these laws could be said to be holdovers from the Victorian era, when the colonizer feared that buggery (especially with the natives) would mean the end of the empire, it should be noted that Singapore's former colonizer decriminalized male homosexual activity between consenting adults back in 1967. Of course, given the fact that such laws remain on the books in many places throughout the world, the real issues are the extent to which these laws are enforced and the degree to which male homosexuals are subject to persecution and harassment. While no one is currently serving a prison term in Singapore for homosexual acts, gay men have consistently been singled out in police entrapment exercises and through police raids of bars and discos suspected of having a predominantly gay clientele. Entrapment of gay men by the police continues, and in one highly publicized entrapment exercise in 1998, a well-known entertainer was publicly "outed," making it clear that no one is beyond the reach of the law.[5] In spite of all of the best efforts by the police to keep men from yielding to sexual temptation, Singaporean men continue to find each other in parks, at mass transit stations, in shopping centers, in the corners of crowded discos, and even in the workplace.

Another factor affecting gay life in Singapore is the structure of a traditional Asian family, which would appear fundamentally at odds with the Western model of urban homosexuality that has emerged over the last hundred years. While emperors and high-powered men in the Chinese imperial court were apparently able to freely take on male lovers,[6] these pleasures were reserved primarily for the court world, where bloodlines were carefully guarded. Bret Hinsch's observations about male homosexuality in modern China have some relevance to contemporary Singapore, where the Chinese comprise the largest and most affluent ethnic group:

> In most societies, as the economy becomes more complex, social organization gradually realigns according to occupation and social class rather than kinship. China, however, has maintained kinship as the fundamental social force down to the present day. With a kinship-structured society has come the sometimes problematic combination of heterosexual marriage and homosexual romance. What this social organization prevented, and still prevents, was the emergence of a self-identified homosexual life-style independent of marriage, as with gays of the contemporary West. (19)

In a traditional Chinese context, the greatest shame one would bestow upon one's ancestors and parents is failing to continue the family line; thus the failure to procreate that would seem to accompany an exclusively gay male lifestyle is seen as constituting a fundamental threat to the continued existence of both the family and the state. Because male children continue to receive privileges and a status not accorded to female children, for a male to turn out to be openly gay would be regarded as a particularly insidious betrayal of family values in a traditional context. For the Singaporean man who wants to live an openly gay lifestyle, leaving one's family behind is often a requirement; yet given the stronger conflation of family and personal identity in Singapore than in the West, this course of action is difficult. Because the public acknowledgment of one's homosexuality would generally involve expulsion from the family as well as serious loss of face, it is far easier for many gay or bisexual Singaporean men to simply have sex on the side and retain the fiction of a marriage in the social sphere. Indeed, as the words of government minister Lim Swee Say suggest,[7] the government has no intention of softening its stand on homosexuality anytime soon: "If more Singaporeans end up embracing this sexual orientation openly, the foundation of the strong family, which is the core building block of Singapore 21,[8] would be weakened. This is why I feel it is better that we exercise great caution, be conservative, and stick to the basic concept of family and family values as much as we can, for as long as we can" (*Straits Times*, 6 June 2000). This statement, by a minister whose extensive portfolio includes information technology, virtually concedes that it is only a matter of time before an increasing number of Singaporeans come to accept and "embrace" this sexual orientation, as the final exhortation to the citizenry to stick to the basic concept of family values "for as long as we can" would seem to suggest. Minister Lim must be well aware that the Internet, more than any other single factor, is already transforming the lives of many Singaporean gay men by giving them immediate access to information on gay life both around the world and in their own backyard.

While the Internet is seemingly crammed with resources geared largely to Singaporean gay men, there are no officially sanctioned organizations that cater to the needs of the gay and lesbian community. Action for Aids (AFA), created in 1988 by a group of concerned physicians and citizens, is the closest thing one can find in Singapore to a gay organization, if only because the majority of individuals with HIV/AIDS are themselves gay males and bisexuals (Leong 21). While many of the outreach activities of this group point to its largely gay orientation, the group itself must continually walk a fine line between genuinely administering to the needs of those with HIV/AIDS and becoming an advocate for gay rights.[9] People Like Us (PLU), formed in 1993 as an informal group of gay, lesbian, and bisexual Singaporeans, is the only such organization that has attempted to obtain recognition as a legally authorized society. The group's 1997 attempt to obtain legal recognition was denied, even after appeals up to the level of the prime minister. No reasons for refusing the application of the group were given at any stage in the application or appeal process.[10] When Alex Au, a leader of the defunct PLU, attempted to secure a permit from the police to hold a public forum on "the role of gays and lesbians within Singapore 21" in May 2000, his application was denied five days before the start of the event. The written denial from the police made reference to the penal code and echoed Lee's rhetoric on CNN as well as previous statements by government ministers: "The Police cannot allow the holding of this forum which will advance and legitimize the cause of homosexuals in Singapore. The mainstream moral values of Singaporeans are conservative, and the Penal Code has provisions against certain homosexual practices. It will therefore be contrary to the public interest to grant a public entertainment license" (People Like Us). Thus not only are there no legally sanctioned organizations for gays and lesbians in Singapore, but it is not legal to even publicly discuss the matter in a civic forum.

Housing policies also work against the long-term survival of gay and lesbian relationships in that they make it difficult for single people to live on their own. Even if two same-sex partners were to set up a joint household, they would not be able to own property unless one of the individuals was relatively rich; the affordable housing offered by the government in the form of new flats in HDB (Housing Development Board) estates goes to married couples first; a single person is eligible only for the older, less desirable flats offered through the resale market, and then only when he or she has reached the age of thirty-five.[11] Prices for private flats are astronomical, leaving only the small rental market, which is also tightly controlled. Thus even living with another person of the same sex prior to the age of thirty-five is difficult indeed.

Given the continuing reality of police entrapment, the impossibility of creating communities through legally permissible organizations, and the extraordinary factors that work against the creation of households, it seems miraculous that homosexuality survives in Singapore at all. The reason it does has little to do with Western or Asian values and is instead more closely tied to the process of modernization and economic development; in virtually every society with a visible gay male community, the social construct of homosexual has emerged only after a society has become industrialized, urbanized, and relatively affluent. While most scholars would tend to agree that homosexual *behavior* has always existed, current scholarship would tend to suggest that the self-identifying concept of homosexuality is much newer indeed, emerging only at the end of the nineteenth century in some of the larger cities in Europe.[12] Singaporean leaders may not want to acknowledge it, but an increasing number of people will begin to identify themselves as homosexual or bisexual just as soon as they have education, wealth, and a bit of free time on their hands. Along with the "gracious society" and the "Singapore 21" plan that Singaporean politicians invoke in their vision of Singapore's future will come an increasing number of people who identify themselves as homosexuals, whether those in power like it or not.

If openly gay Singaporean men are few in number, then lesbians are all but invisible. In fact, lesbianism is not illegal, and no one has ever been arrested on such grounds (Leong 14). Apparently, Singaporean politicians have taken the Victorian view that sex between women is an impossibility. Following this heterosexist view, sexual expression requires the exchange of the phallus and penetration, marking male homosexuality as dangerous and subversive, while female homosexuality lacks the privileged signifying icon of the phallus. Not surprisingly, the comfortable fiction of two women together yearning for a male to "save" them from one another has traditionally fueled many a straight male fantasy, perhaps another reason (male) politicians have traditionally failed to see lesbianism as equal to the threat of male homosexuality. Leong Wai-Teng argues that in a Singaporean context, "silence, or the absence of discourse on lesbianism, is no better than the legal oppression of male homosexuality: it is repressive in itself by way of denying the existence of another form of human sexuality, thought and behavior" (14). Lesbians do exist in Singapore, of course, and the newspapers have on occasion even conducted modest campaigns to try to discourage "manly" behavior in school-age girls,[13] but they have never been targeted for persecution as male homosexuals have been. Possibly because of the lesser value attached to female sexuality and the perception that sex between women constitutes less of a threat to the state, in the 1990s it was honest portrayals of lesbians rather than gay men that first came to life on the Singaporean stage, a phenomenon that will be examined in greater detail later in the chapter.

Given its current squeaky-clean image, newcomers to Singapore are often surprised to discover that the country was once a world center for transvestism and transsexuality, with much of the activity centered in the narrow streets of the former Bugis Street, an area that was overtaken by urban development in the late 1970s. With the destruction of Bugis Street came an end to a Singaporean culture of men who chose to live as women, as well as men who underwent sex changes to become women. Until its closure in 2000, the only visible nod to the neighborhood's naughty past was the Boom Boom Room, a nightclub situated in the middle of the former Bugis Street district and owned by Dick Lee, the country's best-known pop star. Throughout the

1990s, Kumar, an outrageous drag queen with a viciously sharp tongue, performed regularly at the venue, delighting capacity audiences consisting mostly of younger people with his wit, his bawdy humor, his Malay and Hokkien expletives, and his penchant for embarrassing unsuspecting patrons. In the early 1990s, Kumar's show was routinely one of the hottest tickets in Singapore, and getting in to see his act often proved difficult indeed.

In 1995, a sudden change in the "Licensing Conditions" for performers issued by the Public Entertainment Licensing Unit (PELU) threatened to bring the curtain down on all drag acts. Yet even though the new regulations clearly stated that "female impersonators should not be allowed" (Nusantara), authorities appear to have routinely turned a blind eye to male-to-female drag onstage, provided the performers did not foreground their sexual identity in any way. The desexing of drag is an odd and seemingly impossible achievement, especially since, as Judith Butler observes, "drag is subversive to the extent that it reflects imitative structure by which hegemonic gender is itself produced and disputes heterosexuality's claim on naturalness and originality" (*Bodies That Matter* 125). Yet it would appear that the survival of drag on the Singaporean stage throughout the 1990s was predicated largely on Kumar's ability to steer clear of the subject of his own sexuality. Indeed, his act, though raunchy, tough, and absolutely hilarious, was always directed outward, toward the audience, and very rarely back toward himself. Unlike most American drag acts, which foreground the overtly sexual identity of the performer in a way that radically "destabilizes heterosexuality's claim on naturalness," Kumar came across as an outrageous entertainer who happened to be in drag.[14]

A similar situation existed on Singaporean television, where male-to-female drag was "officially" banned in 1994. According to an unnamed Singapore Broadcasting Corporation (SBC)[15] spokesperson quoted in the newspaper at the time, gender-bending acts had offended some members of the public: "The point made is that in Asian society, cross-dressing is a form of deviant behavior and should not be encouraged, particularly on SBC-produced shows for the family" (Foo). A more likely explanation for the ban was that political pressure had been brought to bear on SBC in the wake of a parliamentary "debate" in which MPs expressed the view that too many shows on SBC were "promoting undesirable values." Just as chewing gum was made illegal because an individual at the top of the party apparatus found it annoying,[16] the social contract governing drag could be altered in the wake of a single "debate" on the subject in Parliament.

During a brief window up to May 1994, a number of gender-bending characters appeared on television, including a male dressed up as a middle-aged Malay woman who went by the name of Bibik Belachan. Attired in the traditional wraparound skirt or *kebaya*, Bibik was frequently seen on television variety shows brandishing a local variety of squash known as a *brinjal* while announcing that she was on the lookout for a good man. The sexual connotations of Bibik's act were apparently clear to even the dullest of government hacks: it seemed that Bibik had a bit of a fetish for this stiff, dildo-shaped vegetable that provided a welcome surrogate for the sexual appendages of actual men. Surprisingly, one cross-dresser was allowed to continue to appear on television: a feisty old Chinese granny named Liang Po Po enacted by Jack Neo. However, Liang was admonished for past indiscretions and instructed to clean up her act and present only "a fresh, healthy image that is tasteful and generally approved." The *Straits Times* went on to note that henceforth "she will not be as saucy and will instead promote family values and neighborliness" (Foo). Thus Liang Po Po, formerly the mean-spirited old granny from hell, was co-opted as yet another tool in the government's social campaigns; too popular to drop from the air, the granny in drag was simply brought into the fold. Still, the public loved Liang Po Po, and Neo's granny character emerged as one of the most popular, endearing, and long-lived characters in Singapore television history; she still appeared as a regular on the hit show *Comedy Night* even at the end of the decade.

The same fundamental disjunction between government policies and social realities where gays and lesbians are concerned has played itself out on the Singaporean stage in the 1990s. Just when it appeared that a significant opening was taking place, the government would clamp down, at one point going so far as to completely proscribe a performance form that was deemed too political. Following the same pattern that emerged in the earlier discussion about society at large, representations of transvestism and transsexuality have been generally been regarded as permissible; plays with lesbian characters have invited no response from the government; and plays with gay male characters or themes have consistently generated the greatest controversy and brought the strongest and sharpest responses from the authorities. The sometimes erratic and volatile responses of the government to the queer male subject onstage is a strong testament to the power of theater. Lest Singapore's experience be seen as unique, it is perhaps worth remembering that photos of black penises and performances by queer artists and unruly women who dealt with subjects such as rape so threatened many of the old white men in the U.S. Congress that they sought to end federal funding for the arts, a crusade that continues to this day.[17] Singapore's battle over the sexual outsider onstage has been waged both publicly, where public pronouncements and carefully managed "debates" have repeatedly stirred the issue up, and privately, as artists have sought accommodation with the system by internalizing censorship. What follows is a largely chronological account of the journey that gay men, lesbians, transsexuals, and transgendered people have made across the Singaporean stage from the time that they first appeared in plays by Singaporeans, in the late 1980s, to the mid-1990s, when a major controversy over queer-themed performance art considerably dampened the ability of artists to deal openly with gay male themes.

The history of gays and lesbians on the Singaporean stage begins in earnest in 1988,[18] when two new plays that dealt with AIDS were scheduled for April performances, an event that was coproduced by the Ministry of Community Development and TheatreWorks. The double bill was to include Chay Yew's *Ten Little Indians* and Eleanor Wong's *Jackson on a Jaunt*. Singapore-born Chay Yew[19] based his first professionally produced play on his experiences working as an AIDS social service volunteer in Los Angeles (Holmberg). His *Ten Little Indians* focused on the relationship between a gay AIDS volunteer and his straight male client, while Wong's play featured a gay yuppie who was given a false-positive diagnosis for the AIDS virus in a hospital mixup. One month before the plays were to open, the ministry withdrew its support for both plays. The ministry's cultural affairs director, Ng Yew Kang, condemned both plays: "Homosexuality is portrayed as a natural and acceptable form of sexuality in the play. My ministry will not want to be a joint presenter of the play in its present form. This is in line with the Government's campaign against AIDS and homosexuality is one of its main causes. Homosexuality in Singapore is objectionable" (Yaw). The minister's comments foreground an often cited objection that would affect the staging of the gay male throughout the next decade: the real crime is not so much the staging of homosexuality as its representation as a "natural and acceptable form of sexuality." Therein lies the rub. As long as gay male sexuality is sidelined or relatively incidental, it seems to steer clear of the nebulous "out-of-bounds markers"[20] established by the government, but once it is presented as normal or natural, it becomes objectionable.

Following the ministry's withdrawal of support for the plays, both playwrights were told that if they made suitable changes to their respective scripts, the ministry would renew its support. In a newspaper account, Wong observed that "the ministry doesn't want him [the protagonist] portrayed as a sympathetic gay. It wants the gay character straightened." Wong categorically refused to make the recommended changes proposed by the ministry, noting that changing the script would mean that "the play won't have the same impact" (Yaw). According to Yew, the ministry wanted him to change the character of the gay volunteer worker to that of a woman. He refused, citing the importance of not compromising his "artistic integrity," adding that the play "should be staged as it is now or not at all" (Yaw). In the end, both play-wrights did in fact make alterations to the works, and they were produced the following year by TheatreWorks, without ministry support, under the title *Safe Sex*. That both plays were ultimately staged may have had some-thing to do with the pragmatic style and negotiating skills of TheatreWorks's then new artistic director, Ong Keng Sen, who had taken over from Lim Siau Chong during the intervening period. Yew altered the gay social worker char-acter by making him less "straight-acting" and more effeminate (Yew, tele-phone interview), and renamed the play *As If He Hears*, while Wong appar-ently made changes to her character Jackson, as her cryptic remarks in the program for the event suggest: "This *Jackson* is somewhat different from his prematurely terminated brother/father(?). . . . So, are you going to meet the real *Jackson* tonight? The most interesting, funny, thought-provoking meaningful *Jackson*? I have tried my best to ensure that. But we can't be sure, can we? And that's the price we pay for 'protection'" (TheatreWorks, program for *Safe Sex*). Wong's comments, written from New York, where the former deputy public prosecutor was working for an American law firm, made it abundantly clear that Jackson had indeed been "straightened" against her will. Yew recalls that this experience, coming early in his development as a playwright, taught him "how to write subtext," noting that the controversy generated by the play was even reported upon overseas, giving him wide ex-posure that was ultimately "good for his career," at least outside Singapore (Yew, telephone interview).

By 1990, the general artistic climate in Singapore had begun to shift, due in part to the seemingly liberal tone set by the country's new prime minister, Goh Chok Tong. One of the recurring tropes in Goh's rhetoric from his first years in office was the assertion that Singapore was now beginning its "sec-ond lap," a period in which the workaholism of the past could be relaxed slightly and attention could finally be paid to developing the country's cul-tural resources. Having successfully emerged from the recession of the mid-1980s, the country was seemingly faced with a long, prosperous future, one in which people could now take a bit more time the enjoy "the finer things in life." In 1990 the government also created an infrastructure for the arts virtually overnight, something that had significant repercussions for the kind of representations that would be possible onstage. The National Arts Council (NAC) came into being, and two established theater companies were given subsidized homes in flexible, black-box theater spaces: TheatreWorks moved into its permanent home in the historical, leafy, park setting of Fort Canning, while the Practice Theatre Ensemble, under the direction of playwright Kuo Pao Kun, moved into a centrally located former electrical substation, dubbed, appropriately enough, the Substation.

The same year, David Henry Hwang's *M. Butterfly* came to Singapore. Hwang's play, a reworking of the Madame Butterfly story, was inspired by a short newspaper article the playwright read about a French diplomat who maintained a twenty-year relationship with a male Chinese opera actor who specialized in female roles. The diplomat, who throughout that period labored under the false impression that his lover was a woman, faced charges of espionage back in Paris when it was revealed that the actor was also a communist spy. Produced as part of the 1990 Singapore Arts Festival and presented by TheatreWorks, the play was directed by Malaysian director Krishen Jit and featured Singaporean actor Ivan Heng in the role of Chinese opera actor Song Liling. Hwang's play is rich in sexual ambiguities, an element that has been foregrounded in some productions and deemphasized in others: Did Gallimard know that his Butterfly was a man, or are we to believe that one man could have sex with another without noticing that the object of his affections was equipped with male genitals? Just as the real-life Gallimard's sexuality is never wholly pinned down, Hwang's stage creation raises more questions than are resolutely answered. The fact that Song is taken to be a woman rather than a man may have made what might have otherwise been a controversial subject palatable to the authorities. The play was already a huge international hit by the time it reached Singapore; thus, when it was added to the 1990 arts festival program, it was too late for anyone to raise serious objections to the play's content.

Not surprisingly, advance press on the play failed to acknowledge the ambiguous sexuality of Gallimard and Song, instead focusing on a brief moment where the script demands that Song drop his briefs in a moment of truth. Given that the play was to be presented at a government-run arts festival, the question in everyone's minds was whether or not the nudity would be expunged from the play. The answer came just few days before the play was to

Ivan Heng as Song Liling and David Foster as Gallimard in David Henry Hwang's M. Butterfly, *staged by Krishen Jit and Christine Lim for TheatreWorks as part of the 1990 Singapore Arts Festival. This production paved the way for a number of works that brought sexual minorities onto the Singaporean stage. Photo courtesy of TheatreWorks.*

be cast when Robert Iau, a member of the festival's steering committee, held a press briefing at which he announced that the play would be staged "intact." He observed, "The play will be staged as written by David Hwang. Whatever that's required by the play will be staged. We are not going to be squeamish about it" (*Straits Times*, 21 March 1990). Accounts of the audition process that followed a few days later continued to focus on the nudity, rather than the sexuality of the play's central characters. One prospective actor predicted that Singaporean audiences would be "intrigued" by the nudity, adding, "It'll definitely be the talk of the town" (Ong Soh Chin, "M Butterfly role"). Such a prediction proved prescient indeed: the production was sold out even before opening night.

In retrospect, *M. Butterfly* was a landmark play, opening the door for trans-vestite characters to appear on the Singaporean stage. If foreign works with such characters could be presented at the country's premier arts festival, then there was clearly no sound reason to justify banning domestic plays with characters of a similar persuasion. More important, the ambiguities of Gallimard and Song's relationship may have encouraged Singaporean playwrights to test the limits of acceptability—the fabled "out-of-bounds markers"—by creating characters who were more clearly identifiable as lesbian or gay.

Between 1991 and 1993, a number of plays with lesbian and gay themes were produced out of the creative ferment of TheatreWorks's Writers' Laboratory. This workshop placed emerging Singaporean English-language playwrights under the tutelage of a more established playwright. The first staged work by a Singaporean playwright that dealt openly with lesbian sexuality was Ovidia Yu's monologue *Marrying*, which received a staged reading under the auspices of the first Writers' Lab in June 1991. This production was also noteworthy for having been cosponsored by Singapore Press Holdings, which, while not a government agency per se, is the publisher of Singapore's daily newspapers; thus, by 1991, the government was at least tacitly permitting playwrights to experiment with lesbian themes.

Fortnight Theatre 1991, sponsored by the Ministry of Information and the Arts (MITA), presented two plays that pushed the boundaries of expression even further. Ovidia Yu's *Imagine*, staged by Action Theatre, focused on a dead writer's failed relationships with her Caucasian husband, her lesbian lover, and her husband's best friend. *Straits Times* critic Hannah Pandian noted that while Yu's "characters have wandered far from stereotype," she observed there were "lingering overtones" of the butch/femme dynamic in the characterization of the "artistic-little-girl-lost" that was contrasted with a brittle, "butch" older woman (Pandian, review of *Imagine* and *The Joust*). In a country that fails to openly acknowledge lesbianism, it seems remarkable indeed that a newspaper critic could both recognize and comment upon seemingly well established lesbian stereotypes.

Also chosen by the ministry for presentation at the festival was *Akka* (Elder Sister), a short Tamil-language play that focused on a transvestite prostitute who reveals her story to an investigative reporter. *Akka* received notoriety when the coauthor who was to alternate the role of the transvestite with the play's other author/actor dropped out at the last moment when his mother threatened to kill herself by jumping off a block of flats if her son's name appeared again in the newspapers (Pandian, "Turning the Tide"). In an extended commentary following the production of the play, local theater critic Hannah Pandian observed that the mother's hysterical reaction to her cross-dressing son's appearance onstage was mirrored by the audience response to the event: "Last Sunday night, the Tamil-speaking audience was nervous, giggly and even openly appalled to see a male actor play a transsexual prostitute" (Pandian, "Turning the Tide"). The irony, argues Pandian, is that many traditional Indian performance forms feature male actors "dragging" in female roles. The contrasting audience reactions to the two disparate categories of female impersonations may have little to do with "drag" and more to do with a cultural and religious context which demands that certain traditional forms be enacted only by men; whereas a man playing a woman in a traditional *kathakali* performance is participating in an ancient cultural tradition, an actor playing a contemporary, real-life transvestite prostitute is embodying a cultural taboo. Perhaps more surprising than the audience reaction to the play was the response of Uma Rajan, a Tamil-speaking community leader on the board of the National Arts Council. Dr. Rajan stated publicly that she was "very proud that a good Tamil play has been performed for non-Tamil speakers," adding, "and I especially respect the young boy for being bold enough to put together a play like this" (Pandian, "Turning the Tide"). Her praise for a play that features a sexual outlaw stands in sharp contrast to the categorical condemnation of homosexuality by the cultural affairs director just a few years earlier, suggesting that those in government with oversight of the arts were far from presenting a united front on the issue.

The boundaries of permissibility were stretched even further in 1992, when three staged readings and seven fully realized productions of plays with gay, lesbian, transvestite, or transsexual characters or themes were presented.[21] Though all of these plays might seem rather tame by the standards of lesbian and gay playwriting in the United States, Australia, or England, they represent significant benchmarks in the representation of the sexual Other on the Singaporean stage. The two most significant plays in the field that year were Russell Heng's *Lest the Demons Get to Me* and Michael Chiang's *Private Parts*, both of which focused on society's treatment of transsexuals. The TheatreWorks productions of these two works proved to be huge hits with Singaporean audiences. Even though both plays appeared to focus on the challenges faced by transsexuals, the choices confronted by the characters in both plays had resonance for gays and lesbians as well.

Heng's play *Lest the Demons Get to Me*, written in 1986, was originally to have been presented at the Arts Festival Fringe in 1988, but the Ministry of

Kim (enacted by Jeremiah Choy), the Bugis Street prostitute, in act 1 of Russell Heng's Lest the Demons Get to Me. Directed by William Teo for TheatreWorks's Theatre Carnival on the Hill, 1992. Photo courtesy of TheatreWorks.

Community Development failed to approve it, "saying that perhaps the theme of transvestism and transsexuality was not suitable for the event" (Pandian, "High Drama at Fort Canning"). When the racy foreign import *M. Butterfly* was staged in 1990, Heng recalls that at the time "the thought did strike me that a foreign playwright was given more rights than I have" (Pandian, "High Drama at Fort Canning"). A year after the success of *M. Butterfly* unconsciously extended the boundaries of permissibility, TheatreWorks offered a public reading of Heng's *Lest the Demons Get to Me*, followed by a fully mounted staging of the work in April 1992. Heng's play features a transvestite prostitute named Kim who has been squirreling money away for a sex change. When Kim reappears in act 2, she has become a "real woman," telling her sister the good news that on her new identity card, "in the blank

Kim, as she appears in act 2 of Lest the Demons Get to Me, *after her sex change. Photo courtesy of TheatreWorks.*

space for sex, [a] capital 'F' for female" appears (40). As the play opens, Kim informs us that this is "the final night of Bugis Street" (29), linking her to a seamier, seedier Singapore that by the early 1990s had already achieved mythical status, especially as most younger people had never known a Singapore where the sex trade was quite so openly displayed before an international audience.[22] Kim's story is told through her own comments directly addressed to the audience, in "real time," and through her interactions with a range of offstage characters in reenactments of significant moments from her past. Rather than focusing on the glory days of Bugis Street, the play hones in on Kim's estranged relationship with her family and a married lover who keeps his life so strictly compartmentalized that he only calls her from public phones, contributing to Kim's surprisingly closeted and closed-off life, in spite of her flamboyant nature and seemingly tough exterior.

While Heng's play would appear to be very much Kim's story, its themes also have relevance to the lives of gay and lesbian Singaporeans. When Kim laments the fact that she and her married lover cannot live the sort of open life that others take for granted, she could be speaking for almost any gay or lesbian Singaporean involved in an same-sex intimate relationship. Furthermore, the details about Kim's character—her education at the London School of Economics, her knowledge of high culture, her keen eye for grammatical errors—suggest that she is not entirely the person she represents in the play, a point not lost on theater critic Pandian, who observed that "Heng flogs the point that Kim is not prostitute material" (Pandian, review of Lest the Demons Get to Me). Surely a prostitute with these attributes who could "pass" as Kim seems able to would have the wherewithal to ply her trade in the more upscale hotels of Orchard Road[23] rather than in the midst of the then vanishing Bugis Street transvestite ghetto. Playwright Heng himself acknowledges that his play is "not about transvestism. It's about honesty" (Pandian, "High Drama at Fort Canning"), suggesting that he too recognizes that Kim's transvestism is a device for touching on larger truths. Heng also reveals that Kim's secretive lover Chuck (who, significantly, is not seen onstage) is based on a well-known Singaporean: "If I divulged Chuck's profession, everyone would recognize him in Singapore" (Pandian, "High Drama at Fort Canning"). In Singapore, where relatively few men are comfortable labeling themselves as gay, a married, closeted character such as Chuck would probably be more recognizable to audiences than any openly gay character.[24]

The other play that effectively nudged the closet doors open a fraction farther was Michael Chiang's Private Parts, commissioned by the National Arts Council for the Singapore Arts Festival and staged by TheatreWorks under the direction of Ong Keng Sen. Chiang has a reputation for being the Singaporean Neil Simon, with a similar gift for pitching the audience a rapid succession of comic one-liners, except that his plays' settings and situations are unique to Singapore rather than New York. Thus it must have come as a surprise to many who expected to see another lighthearted comic romp when the raucously campy opening sequence, which featured a Singaporean transvestite version of the Supremes, rapidly veered off in a more serious direction. Subsequent scenes focused on a "nonsexual" love affair that develops between a male television show presenter and a transvestite named Mirabella, who, like Kim in Lest the Demons Get to Me, undergoes a sex-change operation during the course of the play. The male presenter is conveniently made impotent, thanks to a wayward golf ball that strikes him in the groin, thus making it possible for two actors played by males to have an intimate, though "nonsexual," relationship. Once again, the codes that govern the relationship between the ostensibly "straight" man and the transsexual point toward a homosexual relationship while simultaneously denying its existence. The presenter, Warren Lee, has an unsympathetic girlfriend who dumps him, presumably because he is no longer able to maintain an erection after the accident. When enacted onstage, it seems instead as if Warren has gone cold toward his girlfriend once he realizes his stronger attraction for the transsexual, as the former male seems to offer him something that his girlfriend cannot. Even though Mirabella is no longer a male after the operation, but a functioning female, she is still *embodied* by a male actor, and she never develops fully into a believable female character. In the 1992 stage production, actor Lim Boon Pin's Mirabella seemed more like a male version of a woman, a substitute for the generic "sign" of woman, but not the real thing. When she places Warren's hand on her heart on the day before her sex change and says, "Here. Here is where it matters. This is the organ you should worry about" (Chiang, *Private Parts* 268), it is hard to see two genders onstage, especially inasmuch as the other unnamed organ is the penis. Because at this point in the play Warren's penis is not functioning properly and Mirabella is about to voluntarily part with hers, these two emasculated men can express their love for one another in a way that circumvents active homosexuality. Nevertheless, especially given the social and legal constraints that mitigate against the open expression of homosexuality in Singapore, at that moment, whether intended or not, Chiang's play becomes a moving plea for greater tolerance by the general public for same-sex relationships.

The envelope was pushed even further in the second half of the year, when openly gay male characters appeared in the plays *Another Tribe* and *Glass Roots (Don't Step on Them)*. Fong Yong Chin's Mandarin-language play *Another Tribe* broke new ground by depicting two men in a gay relationship; although the older man, a photojournalist, was married, the relationship between the men was presented as a given, not as something morally wrong. Even though the play would appear to have broken the cardinal rule prohibiting the positive portrayal of homosexuality, the authorities allowed it to proceed, perhaps because the play was to be performed in Mandarin, before a young and relatively small audience, instead of in English, a language that reaches a larger and more established theatergoing audience. Indeed, throughout the 1990s, the authorities have consistently demonstrated greater latitude with respect to depictions of gay men in Mandarin-language drama than in English-language works.[25]

In July, The Necessary Stage (TNS), a company noted for creating work with a social conscience, presented *Glass Roots (Don't Step on Them)*, a futuristic play set in an unnamed country with obvious parallels to Singapore where social engineering mandated the imprisonment of the old, the intellectually slow, and the sexually deviant. Among the prisoners were two gay men who, along with the others, decide to rebel against the repressive regime. While the playwright, Haresh Sharma, was quick to deny any link between the characters or events depicted onstage and contemporary Singapore, audience reactions to the production suggested that connections between the fictional future and the present were quickly established. Sharma and Alvin Tan, the two artistic leaders of the company, have long had to sidestep the question of the social relevance of the original work that has constituted the bulk of their repertory over the years. Because *any* social criticism can be construed as antigovernment, it is essential for groups to demonstrate that while they may be looking at social issues, they are not making "prescriptions." With regard to *Glass Roots*, Sharma trod a careful middle path when quoted by the press: "I'm concerned about how we tend to marginalize the little people. We're not telling people to overthrow the government, but rather, to stop being so high-handed and look around you. Ask yourselves; we may be an incredibly efficient, well-ordered society, but at what expense?" (C. Liew). Thus the work was framed as a plea for greater tolerance by individuals rather than a criticism of a regime that perpetuates that intolerance. The distinction between the two positions is critical in a Singaporean context.

In the same year that these breakthrough plays were staged, the censorship restrictions were widely reported to have been "relaxed." As noted in chapter 1, this apparent liberalization late in 1992 was in fact a double-edged proposition. While established theater companies such as TheatreWorks and The Necessary Stage were no longer required to submit each script to the Public Entertainment Licensing Unit (PELU) for advance approval, in practice, those same companies have had to incorporate their own censors into the creative process, guessing where the "out-of-bounds markers" might be, and invariably having to err on the side of caution.

Also working against any relaxation of the rules was a very carefully stage-managed "public debate" in the press over the extent to which sexual freedom and values perceived as Western should be accepted in Singapore. Not surprisingly, theater often provided a focus in the discussion of these values. Some of the commentaries and letters to the editor in the *Straits Times* condemned the sudden surge in the number of "deviant plays" in 1992, citing those mentioned above as well as a few others. In April, as TheatreWorks was staging three plays with homosexual overtones or transvestite characters

(*Three Fat Virgins Unassembled*, *Lest the Demons Get to Me*, and *Blood and Snow*), the senior minister of education, Tay Eng Soon, publicly advised young local playwrights to be "sensitive to the moral values and sentiments of the majority of Singaporeans." He continued: "Ours is still a traditional society which values what is private and personal and is not comfortable with public and explicit discussion of sexuality and what it considers as deviant values. By all means, let our 'cultural desert' bloom. But please let the blossoms be beautiful and wholesome and not be prickly pears or weeds!" (R. Lim). Given the ambiguous final recommendations of the Censorship Review Committee in October of the same year, Tay's comments foreshadow the clampdown on alternative sexuality onstage that took place in 1994 and 1995.

Similarly, *Straits Times* columnist Tan Tarn How, in an extended analysis of the new rules, cautioned against optimism, noting that "any play which examines Singapore's society critically would fall into one of the three categories—and would thus be deemed objectionable" ("Liberal Questions"). The three categories, as noted in chapter 1, are plays that are deemed to: (1) erode the core moral values of society; (2) subvert the nation's security and stability; or (3) create misunderstanding or conflict in Singapore's multiracial and multireligious society. Tan observes that among the works prohibited under the guidelines as framed "will include plays which are sympathetic to homosexuals, which call for a break from traditions, which question the Government and its policies, which reinterpret history radically, which expose racism. In other words, all plays which are political in the sense that they seek to change society" ("Liberal Questions"). In the wake of these new rules, it is hardly surprising that Singapore's established theater companies virtually stopped depicting homosexual males onstage,[26] while moving even farther away from any kind of presentation of contemporary social issues that could be deemed to be in any way critical of actual government policy.

At the same time that gay men were disappearing from the stages of the established theater companies, the largely absent lesbian suddenly appeared, seemingly from nowhere, as a fully realized, three-dimensional human being. Eleanor Wong's *Mergers and Accusations*, staged by TheatreWorks in 1993, focuses on a successful Singaporean lawyer named Ellen who struggles to integrate her feelings for women into her complicated personal and professional life. In spite of the fact that Ellen is open about her lesbian identity with her closest friends, she finds herself relentlessly pursued by a quirky and unconventional male lawyer whose charms disarm her to the point where she agrees to marriage. Initially, the demands of her career and the emotional support provided by an understanding and accommodating husband enable her to keep her feelings toward women at bay. This changes one day when Lesley, a very "out" English lawyer, arrives to work with Ellen on a legal case. In a pivotal scene, Lesley confronts Ellen and attempts to force her to acknowledge feelings they both know they are experiencing. Lesley declares to Ellen, "No one can threaten you with the exposure of something you willingly disclose." Ellen counters with, "It's different here. I don't expect you to understand. . . . I've seen the mask of polite distaste come over the faces of people I thought were my friends enough to know that complete openness is not an option" (Wong, *Mergers and Accusations* 46). Even though Ellen and her husband separate by the play's end, it is left open as to whether or not Ellen will be capable of taking the next step: living openly with another woman as a couple. Indeed, most gays and lesbians would no doubt feel that "complete openness" is still not an option in Singapore.

Although advance publicity on the play made no mention of the "L word," there was nothing subdued about either the dialogue or the staging of the scenes featuring the two women. Not only does the couple speak openly about sexual desire; they also kiss onstage. By showing two lesbians interacting with one another as lesbians, Wong has gone further than any Singaporean playwright in presenting same-sex relationships in an honest and sympathetic light. The significance of this play was not lost on local critic Ng Sek Chow, who declared, "One must salute Wong for addressing an issue which has been locked up long enough. Thanks for burning down part of the closet door, Eleanor."

Wong subsequently wrote a sequel to the play entitled *Wills and Secession* in which Ellen, now living with Lesley in London, returns home to make arrangements for her aging father following her mother's death. The work takes the lesbian identity of the two women as a given and focuses largely on the issue of mortality, as Ellen comes to terms with Lesley's terminal illness. Lesley serves as a conduit for repairing Ellen's damaged relationship with her family, and by the end of the play Ellen has reached a higher level of truth and integrity in her most vexing relationship—the one between herself and her religious sister. Thus the play is more about mortality and the fragile but fundamental bonds between siblings than it is about Ellen's identity as a lesbian. Though given an R(A) rating by the authorities—presumably because the work featured two openly lesbian women—there was nothing racy about either the play or the 1995 TheatreWorks production. In program for

TheatreWorks's 1995 production of Eleanor Wong's Wills and Secession *was staged on installation artist Susie Lingham's cool, abstract set, which featured 3,104 empty whiskey bottles. Directed by Ong Keng Sen at the Victoria Theatre. Left to right: Claire Wong (as Grace), Koh Joo Kim (Lesley), and Tan Kheng Hua (Ellen). Photo courtesy of TheatreWorks.*

the event, Wong noted that the play is about "family and faith. The F words that (to me, at least) make this an R(A) play" (TheatreWorks, program for *Wills and Secession*). A powerfully moving play, *Wills and Secession* represents a significant milestone where representations of lesbians on the Singaporean stage are concerned. Unfortunately, Wong, herself a successful lawyer, has since stopped writing for the stage (*Straits Times*, 2 January 2000), and it seems increasingly unlikely that other women would risk writing a play on a subject that is controversial by virtue of its relative invisibility.

As with *Mergers and Accusations*, the mature and confident handling of the lesbian identity of the play's central character was not stressed in the promotional materials connected with the play's production. Director Ong Keng Sen's comments in the program for *Wills and Secession* rationalize the choice of producing the play in a way that distances the company from any connection with the work's lesbian content: "The most wonderful theatre, the most wonderful expression has always been focusing on the marginal to give a picture of what's happening in society. From these marginal positions, we begin to get a vision of how that society is constructed and hence, we can critique it. We are agitated through the throwing of marginalized characters into our world. We are forced to re-examine our lives" (TheatreWorks, program for *Wills and Secession*). Thus the view from the "margins" is presented in order to serve the larger goal of leading the generic, presumably nonmarginal spectator—the "we" in Ong's commentary—farther down the path of self-actualization; the margins have value for what they can reveal to the center, not because they have any inherent worth. In a sense, Ong's commentary effectively takes the bite out of the play, which is a canny and perhaps necessary maneuver. Because the lesbian identity of the play's central character is a purely personal matter and the play does not lobby for change or present any fundamental criticism of society, it falls squarely within established censorship guidelines. The way in which the play was framed for public consumption by TheatreWorks mitigated the potential explosiveness of the play's content, neutralizing any possible perception that the play contains with it a radical social statement.

Gay male equivalents of Wong's fully realized lesbian characters are still absent from the Singaporean stage, possibly because representations of two gay men in a committed, intimate relationship are seen as more threatening to the social order than concretizing the relatively invisible phenomenon of lesbianism in Singapore. In the same season that they presented Wong's play, TheatreWorks had originally intended to produce the Singaporean premiere of Chay Yew's *A Language of Their Own*. Yew's play, which focuses on the lives of four gay men, three of whom are Asian American, was well received in New York, where Ong directed it for the renowned Public Theatre. Yew's play, like Wong's, takes homosexuality as a given, though unlike Wong's two plays, *A Language of Their Own* focuses virtually exclusively on the dynamics in same-sex relationships. Not surprisingly, unconditional approval was not granted for the production, and it was pulled from the season well into the year.[27] By way of contrast, Wong's *Wills and Secession* was staged the same year in the Jubilee Hall at the Raffles Hotel, a highly visible and upscale venue, with a cast that included two of Singapore's best-known actresses, Tan Kheng Hua and Claire Wong.

As we have seen, concerted efforts have been made to unlink sexual politics from theater in Singapore, an absurd proposition as it is within the very nature of theater to represent and question all social phenomenon, making it impossible for any healthy theater environment to exist without even the possibility of actively considering the political. The final example in this chapter, drawn from the experience of Singapore's performance artists, demonstrates the perils of mixing sex with politics, especially when the sex being alluded to is sex between men. In some respects, the Singaporean government's reaction to performance art mirrors the response of those legislators in the U.S. Congress who were successful in disqualifying the form from federal financial support at virtually the same time. Were it possible for the likes of the powerful U.S. Senator Jesse Helms to ban all performance art, there is no doubt that he would have attempted to do so. In Singapore, however, the government *does* have the power to ban or heavily circumscribe an entire form of artistic expression, even one with a rich history and one that has contributed so much to the evolution of contemporary theater practice throughout the world. That the form briefly thrived in Singapore in the early 1990s is nothing short of miraculous.

As with the performance art fiasco in the U.S. Congress, the political and public response to the performance works that were singled out for criticism in Singapore had little connection with the actual performed work. Moments from the work of two performance artists were wrenched from their context and sensationalized by the press, while the entire performance piece, and, indeed, the form itself, was resoundingly condemned by people who had not even witnessed the work. But unlike the situation in the United States, where running afoul of the government will generally only cost an artist his or her funding, in Singapore, the two young performance artists who bore the brunt of the attacks were banned from "all future public performances." Not only was the work itself lost in the public "debate" over the subject of performance art, but the fundamental issues that motivated the creation of the work were rarely mentioned by anyone either in public or in private.

The event that everyone seemed to want to forget about took place in 1993, when twelve men were nabbed in an antigay operation in Tanjong Rhu, a known gay cruising area. As was the case in previous arrests of this type,[28] good-looking, young police officers known as "pretty police" were dispatched to entrap the men. The names, ages, and occupations of the arrested men were reported in the press, along with graphic descriptions of the encounter. Singapore's more sensationalistic, tabloid-style newspapers — *The New Paper*, *Lianhe Wanbao*, and the *Shin Min Daily News* — even went so far as to publish photos taken at the scene, leading to speculation that the police and the government-run media were jointly orchestrating these "media events" (Leong 15–16). In a description of what transpired published in *Straits Times*, one of the accused was said of have "chatted up a special constable before proceeding to caress his buttock and chest." Another accused man stated that "the guy [an officer] had approached me and smiled, so I walked over to chit-chat with him." He maintained that the officer then suggested that they go into the undergrowth to have sex. Once physical contact was made, each man was arrested and charged with "outraging their victim's modesty" (*Straits Times*, 23 November 1993), a quaint, Victorian-era phrase that basically denotes touching someone's genitals without their consent. The occupations of the arrested men ranged from butcher to Singapore Broadcasting Corporation producer. Of the twelve arrested, six pleaded guilty immediately, receiving sentences ranging from two to six months in jail. All were given three strokes of the rattan cane, a beating that results in permanent scarring of the buttocks.

In response to both the entrapment exercise and the sensationalistic treatment of this and other gay-related news stories by the press, two performers, Joseph Ng and Shannon Tham, created performance pieces that the government clearly found threatening to the dominant order. Ng and Tham's works were presented in the context of a twelve-hour New Year's Eve event that included numerous other performances, literary readings, and live music. This event, like the week-long arts festival of which it was but a part, was organized by The Artists Village and 5th Passage Artists Ltd. and held in their gallery space in the Parkway Parade Shopping Centre on 31 December 1993. Created in 1991, 5th Passage had a successful history of mounting installations and sponsoring performance work.

Ng's work was described at length by critic Lee Weng Choy in an article that appeared in the same unpublished 1994 edition of *Commentary* that contained Sanjay Krishnan's insights into the Forum Theatre controversy. Because Lee's description of the two works that were at the center of the controversy provides the only documentation of what actually transpired, his firsthand account of Ng's performance piece bears reprinting here, especially as few in Singapore have had access to this information.

Ng began the performance by arranging a three-dimensional installation in front of the audience: an arc composed of twelve tiles, and upon each he placed a block of white tofu and a plastic packet of red paint. This represented the twelve men arrested for alleged homosexual solicitation. The installation took over five minutes to complete, and it was like the laying of items before a ritual for mourning the dead. Its simplicity belied its effectiveness; the delicate texture of the tofu was accentuated by its minimal presentation on the tiles.

Ng was dressed in a black robe worn over black swimming trunks. Placed on the floor near him were three small rotan canes tied together as one. He read out loud random remarks from *The Straits Times* report of the arrest. Then he stood, and with the cane performed a dance for several minutes. He swirled the cane in the air; his body was at times highly tensed and then relaxed; he crouched down and shuffled, tapping the cane on the floor. When Ng finished the dance he came forward before the tiles. He said that he was now going to cane before delivering a blow. The tofu splattered, the plastic packets burst.

After finishing the twelfth, Ng returned to the center of the arc and said that some people cut their hair as a sign of silent protest. He stood up, took off his robe and walked to the far end of the performance space. With his back toward the audience he lowered his trunks and for about a minute did something the audience could not see. He returned forward to the tiles and placed in front what one realized to be pubic hair—in a sense completing his installation. Ng borrowed a cigarette from someone in the audience, smoked a few puffs, then extinguished it into his own shoulder, saying that maybe a silent protest isn't enough. The performance ended, the audience applauded, Ng asked some people to help him clear up. (63, 65)

Ng's sensitive and complex performance piece was reported to the general public as the work of a pornographer who had the audacity to cut off his pubic hair and call it art. The "debate" that ensued focused on whether the simple act of cutting pubic hair was, in fact, art, rather than considering the wider frame from which that single act derived its power and meaning. The situation for Ng was much more critical however, as he was to face criminal charges for public indecency even though—as Lee's firsthand account suggests—his back was to the audience when he snipped hair from the offending follicles.

The other performance that evening that caused offense, by artist Shannon Tham, was, according to the *Straits Times*, done "to protest at what he called unfair reporting of the Fifth Passage's screening of a censored videotape of a movie featuring homosexuality" (Tan Hsueh Yun). During the course of Tham's piece he burned a copy of the *New Paper*, the newspaper that ran the story, and then drank a glass of water containing the ashes, before vomiting into a trash can. On Monday, 3 January, that same newspaper ran a cover story on the performances of Ng and Tham under the headline "Pub(l)ic Protest," initiating a round of widespread condemnations of the two works. Among the accompanying photos was one of Tham burning a page of the *New Paper*. To my knowledge, none of the many people who came forth to condemn the works actually saw them.

The reaction of the government was swift and decisive. The sponsoring organization was told that they would no longer be able to gain approval to present works without fixed scripts. They were also barred by the National Arts Council from receiving any grant or financial assistance in the future. Iris Tan Khee Wan, the founder of the group and the organizer of the event, was prosecuted for providing public entertainment without a license; though the group in fact had a license, they continued to perform after midnight on 31 December, after their license had technically expired.[29] Artist Ng eventually pled guilty to the charge of committing an obscene act in public, a course of action that was clearly the path of least resistance. In addition, both young artists at the center of the "controversy" were barred from any future public performances.

As for the genre of performance art, a combined statement from the Ministries of Home Affairs and Information and the Arts declared, "Organizers of scriptless public performances must provide a synopsis when they apply for a public entertainment license. If approved, they will have to put down a security deposit" (Koh Buck Song, "Performance Arts Shows Axed"). Forthcoming performance art events sponsored by Artists Village, United World College, and the Nanyang Academy of Fine Arts were all canceled. Another unfortunate and probably unintended consequence of the restrictions placed on the form was defining performance art, a form whose beauty lies in its utter undefinability. Koh Buck Song provided a brief definition of the form that unfortunately stuck: "a spontaneous and scriptless presentation, with artists sometimes using their bodies to make a statement" ("Performance Arts Shows Axed"). In fact, what Koh is describing is what the "happening" had turned into by the mid-1960s in the United States, when it began to be used to denote virtually any unconventional, spontaneous activities, many of which were associated with the protest movements of the time. Very rarely is performance art ever "spontaneous" as it is practiced anywhere in the world; in fact, even when performance art events were wordless, they were often characterized by a very rigorous internal structure.

Not only did the prohibitions result in a de facto ban on all performance art, but the more serious consequence of the controversy was to put a damper on the artistic expression of an opinion on any subject that the government regarded as wholly within their proper sphere and thus not open for public discussion. The treatment of gay men by the press and the justice system was clearly one subject that fell outside the "out-of-bounds markers." *Straits Times* columnist Koh Buck Song articulates a position on the matter that is probably close to the government's:

> Such incipient pressure on the gay issue is more than what the authorities are comfortable with at the moment. The 1992 Censorship Review Committee chaired by Professor Tommy Koh had decided that, much as the committee accepted that homosexuals should not be persecuted, expressions that glorify homosexuality or agitate for its acceptance should continue not to be allowed because the act itself was illegal and such controls were consistent with the majority view. It seems unlikely that this position will change significantly in the years to come. ("Liberalising the Arts")

As long as newspaper accounts alone form the basis for the public's perception of the event, many Singaporeans would probably tend to agree with Koh Buck Song that the acts of these two performance artists were closer to political protest than to art. In Western democracies, most governments would probably be loath to attempt to draw a rigid line between politics and art; in Singapore, however, even many university students seem to accept that such a line is necessary in order to ensure domestic harmony.

Journalist and playwright Tan Tarn How, who himself has known what it means to test the limits of official tolerance,[30] had this to say about the effect of the crackdown in the self-censored edition of *Commentary*: "If society is a tree, and its fringes are the leaves at the tree's outermost reaches, then trimming the fringe, where the youngest, tenderest leaves grow nearest to the light, can only stunt the growth of the Centre. That is how you get the little bonsais — pretty but rather poor imitations of the real thing. . . . For if you think a bit more about it, what appears at first to be a fringe issue will slowly strike you as being at the root of the very kind of society that we are" ("Pruning the Bonsai" 70). Tan concludes that the affair, along with the so-called Marxist conspiracy that took place at roughly the same time, "is yet another shackle placed on freedom of expression," as well as "more specifically a far-reaching stricture on art." Rather than seeing performance art as a "fringe" activity, he cautioned his restricted readership to see the government's harsh response "as history being made" ("Pruning the Bonsai" 71). Indeed, if the performance art controversy in Singapore proves anything, it demonstrates the proposition that the fringe can control the center, as Singaporean theater artists have subsequently internalized a censor that makes sensitive, realistic portrayals of gay men too "political" to touch. Given the possibility that a playwright or theater company could stage a work so offensive to the government that they could be denied the right to stage work in the future, many gay male playwrights, actors, and directors in Singapore have decided to keep one foot firmly planted in the closet.

In the long run, however, the government is fighting a losing battle, as the June 2000 comments of minister Lim Swee Say cited earlier in the chapter suggest. At best, the government can only hold out for "as long as we can." Barring extreme repression of gay men and lesbians, which is highly unlikely due to the potential economic fallout that would probably follow, an increasing number of Singaporeans are likely to identify themselves as gay or lesbian. In the short term, however, the government will probably continue to deny the applications of gay and lesbian groups to meet and organize, as they did in May 2000. Ultimately, the forces behind the emergence of gay and lesbian identities cannot be stopped, as Dennis Altman observes: "The significant aspect of the contemporary globalization of capitalism is the growth of affluence in many countries and the corresponding greater freedom for individual choice it makes possible. Affluence, education, and awareness of other possibilities are all prerequisites for the adoption of new forms of identity, and the spread of these conditions will increase the extent to which gay identities develop beyond their base in liberal Western societies" ("Rupture or Continuity?" 87–88). The Internet revolution makes it impossible for even the most zealous of government censors to prevent the circulation of information on emerging gay identities in Singapore.[31] While this electronic meeting place is still largely restricted to affluent, educated, largely ethnic Chinese Singaporeans, this pattern of gay and lesbian identities being formed initially by the elite is by no means unique to Singapore; indeed, in Hong Kong and Taiwan, as well as in virtually every "liberal" Western country where concepts of gay and lesbian sexualities have emerged, the affluent and educated, which generally come from most advantaged ethnic group in a particular society, constitute the group that "comes out" first, eventually followed by the less favored minorities and those less blessed with the advantages of wealth and education. Ultimately, gays and lesbians in Singapore will increasingly demand recognition and even services, as Gerard Sullivan and Laurence Wai-Teng Leong argue:

As Singapore advances economically, cries for freedom (individual lifestyle choices, demand for political voices and input to public policy) and pressures for development of gay and lesbian social services will develop. The more educated, knowledgeable and articulate the population, and the more financially independent (all brought about by economic development), the more gay men and lesbians will choose or defend their respective lifestyles and demand the kinds of social services that have long been neglected and suppressed by an authoritarian state. (9)

While such a hopeful vision for the future is probably inevitable, in the nearer term, the government can still heavily restrict the means by which gays and lesbians can express themselves. This, then, is perhaps the most tragic loss: not that Singaporean gay and lesbian identities will never fully emerge but, rather, that the long road that will lead to the full expression of those identities will not be advanced and explored in any significant manner by Singaporean theater artists. To lose the ability to create gay and lesbian themed art is to lose an important component of Singaporean identity and to silence a rich and deep wellspring of artistic expression.

7

Singapore, whose name derives from the Sanskrit *singa
pura*, or "Lion City," is rapidly positioning itself to become
the "City of Festivals." The religious and cultural celebrations that extend from mid-November to mid-February
provide a virtual nonstop festival, including a tropical Christ-
mas, the calendar New Year, Chinese New Year, and the Muslim celebration Hari Raya Puasa, which marks the end of Ra-
madan. The Singapore Tourism Board (STB) links all four
events and packages them collectively as "Celebration Singapore," promoting the period on their Web site[1] as "the best
time to visit *New Asia–Singapore*." Singapore's festival strategy is part of its self-promotion as the embodiment of the
"New Asia," which has come to mean an Asia that is prosperous, confident, affluent, modern, multicultural, culturally
vibrant, open to the West but secure in its Asian identity. A
relatively endless succession of festivals is one way to market
the city to an overseas audience as a safe, interesting, and
colorful tourist destination, as the STB's proclaims on their
New Asia Web site: "New Asia–Singapore's cultural diversity
gives Singaporeans more reason to celebrate festivals and
events than perhaps any other place in the world. Combine
these with all the international sporting and competitions
and special events dedicated to the arts and you'll begin
to wonder if every day in Singapore isn't cause for some
celebration." Indeed, virtually every day of the year sees a
celebration or festival of some sort, and many of them over-
lap. This chapter will examine a number of key festivals, in-

cluding the oldest of the major festivals, the Singapore Arts Festival,[2] and consider the ways in which these festivals both shape and reflect the culture.

Given Singapore's international reputation as a site of culinary excellence, it should come as no surprise that the country aggressively markets its annual food festival overseas. Organized by the STB and held annually since 1994, the Singapore Food Festival extends over an entire month and showcases the wide range of Asian and Western cuisines that are available in the country. Singapore's affluence enables it to attract top European and American chefs, and when these chefs are added to the country's own complement of Singaporeans accomplished in every conceivable Asian cuisine, the result is easy access to superior food from the tremendous array of traditions from around the world. Even the most finicky of "foodies" cannot fail to be impressed by the sheer availability of food in Singapore, with even the humble "hawker stall" in the outdoor "hawker centers"[3] serving up fare that is both nutritious and appetizing. Events associated with the festival include demonstrations, cooking workshops, restaurant promotions, and food tours to a number of eating areas, the Singaporean equivalent of the "pub crawl."

Most major festivals, apart from the Singapore International Film Festival and the country's signature food festival, are centered around performance activities. One such event, the Chinese Cultural Festival, is offered every other year and in 2000 featured over 150 events extending over four weeks in February and March. The festival offers a wide range of activities, including Chinese Crosstalk, which stresses verbal sparring in Mandarin; performances by Singaporean Chinese opera groups; spoken drama in Mandarin; and performances by Chinese orchestral groups. An outgrowth of "Chinese Cultural Month," first offered in 1990, the festival endeavors to bring greater awareness of Chinese cultural traditions to the many ethnic Chinese Singaporeans who are English-educated and largely cut off from the culture of their grandparents. The comments of one teenage Taiwanese student studying in Singapore provide a model response to the festival: "I think I actually became more 'Chinese' after I came to Singapore," she said, adding, "There are conscious efforts to promote Chinese culture in this country, especially in my school" (*Straits Times*, 13 February 1998). While the largely government-owned newspaper monopoly, Singapore Press Holdings (SPH), serves as the festival's primary organizer,[4] it does not target the Malay or Indian communities in a similar manner for cultural rejuvenation. As noted in chapter 3, this is largely because younger, increasingly affluent, English-educated ethnic-

Chinese Singaporeans seem to be regarded as most "at risk" when it comes to adopting Western values.

In a sense, this festival is not intended to compete with the larger Arts Festival held later in the year, as the comments of SPH executive Lim Huang Chiang suggest: "Unlike the Arts Festival which goes for quality, we aim for quantity. A lot of events held at the community centers, for example, are small in scale" (*Straits Times*, 13 February 1998). Oddly enough, when the festival grew in size a few years later, the same executive proclaimed, "It is quality we want, not quantity" (Tee). The apparently contradictory statements may reflect the organizer's increasing circumspection with regard to the sensibilities of the largely amateur Singaporean groups presenting at the festival — groups that may have felt slighted by the earlier statement. Nevertheless, the thrust of the festival clearly seems to be toward involving the greatest number of Chinese Singaporeans as participants and observers, and while quality can always be said to be important, the work is largely presented by individuals who do not make a full-time living pursuing the arts. So in this respect, Lim's prior comments are probably more consistent with the overall goals and objectives of the event.

When Prime Minister Goh declared in his 1999 National Day rally speech that "people laugh at us for promoting fun so seriously" (*Straits Times*, 22 August), his comments might have served as a tag line for the Singapore International Comedy Festival, produced since 1998 by Arts Management Associates, with funding from the STB. Since unscripted performance is illegal and overt criticism of the government is not permitted in a performance context, it is not surprising that the vast majority of the high-profile comedy acts come from overseas, where performers are unlikely to know much about Singapore aside from its reputation as a clean and green tropical paradise. Established comedy groups from the United States, Canada, and the United Kingdom, most of whom seem to have already won awards and significant accolades in their home country, perform in a number of venues over a three-week period in March and April, following the Chinese Cultural Festival but before the Arts Festival.

One of the more surprising performance festivals to appear in Singapore in the 1990s was the Singapore River Buskers' Festival, created in 1997 and largely centered around the popular street-level shopping and dining area that runs along the Singapore River from Clarke Quay to Riverside Point. Ironically, street busking had to be legalized prior to the festival, as it had previously been banned. In order to keep it from "degenerating" into a form of "disguised begging," the NAC initially drew up guidelines that set the following conditions on the form: first, buskers were prohibited from interacting with the audience; second, after collecting enough to cover their basic costs, buskers were required to donate the money they earned to arts or charity groups; and finally, they were to audition for a license that granted them the right to perform (Dhaliwal). Many key members of the arts community spoke up publicly, concerned that these restrictions might undermine the spontaneity that is required for successful street theater. Most roundly criticized the controls as too harsh or even ridiculous; one critic, the artistic director of a well-known theater troupe, mused, "How does one audition a snake charmer? Make sure his snakes are well-groomed and do not run away?" (Dhaliwal). Not surprisingly, the *Straits Times* concluded its story on the new regulations with a restatement of the government's position by an authority with overseas academic training: "Mr. George Chua, 29, an executive in a non-profit organization who did a thesis on buskers for his master's in sociology in London, said starting off with certain controls would help Singaporeans get used to busking and also set certain standards" (Dhaliwal). Thus the unknown "executive" from an unnamed organization, cloaked in the authority vested in him by virtue of an overseas graduate degree, was used to justify the heavy-handedness of the government. Given the role of the press in promoting government policies, one can only assume that Mr. Chua's justification for tough controls over busking were the best defense the government was capable of mustering.

Bearing in mind the existence of these restrictions, the buskers appearing in the first so-called Busker Festival were not really buskers at all but, rather, paid outdoor performers who presented their work at approved sites without interacting with their audience. Potential buskers would presumably also be subject to the following additional licensing conditions for performing arts groups that are mandated by PELU (Public Entertainment Licensing Unit) and that have been in effect since 1 July 1995:

1. Performers should not make any vulgar gestures, actions or remarks during their performance.
2. Performers should not be scantily attired.
3. Performers should not step down from the stage. They should not mingle with the audience in any way during their performance or while dressed in costumes.

4. No audience [*sic*] should be invited onto the stage.
5. Female impersonators should not be allowed to participate/perform.
6. Dancing by the audience is not allowed.
7. The organizer/licensee shall stop the show at the instruction of the Police.
8. Only performers who are approved by the Licensing Officers are allowed.
9. Only songs that are approved by the Licensing Officers are allowed.
10. The organizer/licensee shall provide sufficient security guards.
11. No pyrotechnics is allowed [*sic*], unless it is approved by the Licensing Officer. (Nusantara)

The mind boggles in the face of such restrictions. An enterprising busker might do well to attempt combining all of the restrictions into a single act: No doubt a shirtless male performer in drag eating fire while singing unapproved profane songs and inviting the audience onstage to dance would prove itself quite a popular act. The organizer of the first Busker Festival expressed the hope that the festival would someday become the "the largest of its kind in the world" (*Straits Times*, 5 October 1997). In the years since the first festival, the government has apparently backed down from the strong stand it took in 1997, no doubt at least in part because the acts are largely imported from Europe, Canada, and the United States and highly unlikely to cause civil unrest. The "New Asia–Singapore" Web site entices visitors by offering the November festival as an adjunct to a river dining experience: "Let the street comedians tickle your funny bone while you dine alfresco by the river." With busking so carefully regulated and controlled, it is highly unlikely that any Singaporean will be making a full-time living at it anytime soon.

As noted in chapter 1, the PAP government in the mid-1980s announced plans to turn Singapore into a "culturally vibrant society" by 1999 (Lau 2). In 1997, when that goal was felt to be within reach, the Ministry of Information and the Arts (MITA) pledged its commitment to make Singapore "a renaissance city of information, culture and the arts in the 21st century" (*Straits Times*, 1 June 1997).[5] At the end of the millennium Singapore's ruling elite moved beyond the desire to simply create a "culturally vibrant society" to the more impressive-sounding goal of instigating a "renaissance," citing three factors that would advance that goal: the further development of the Singapore Arts Festival and its transformation from an annual into a biennial event; the completion of the two largest auditoriums in the Esplanade–Theatres by the Bay; and the promotion of responsible Internet usage (*Straits Times*, 1 June 1997). The more elusive sources from which this "renaissance" was to be created were not mentioned in the press at the time; only the apparatus to carry it out—the "hardware"—was identified. That information and the arts continue to be linked formally through a common ministry is hardly surprising, given the discourse of the state, which has consistently linked the arts with other industries to be developed. Indeed, a 1989 government report by the Advisory Council on Culture and the Arts[6] noted at the outset that "the arts can enhance our reputation and generate a high perceived value for our products and services world-wide" (12). Even the section devoted to the way the arts contribute to "quality of life" relates their value back into economic terms: "Knowledge and appreciation of the arts and of our heritage can provide the means to upgrade our standard of living" (11).

Given that many Singaporeans believe the government can do anything it sets its mind to, the comment of one arts patron probably summed up how the commitment to creating a renaissance was met with by the general public: "In Singapore, we take our cue from the government. If it focuses on the arts in a big way, it will go a long way in encouraging private individuals" (Tong). Those working in the arts were a little more circumspect. Michael Field, an arts dean at LaSalle-SIA College of the Arts in Singapore, went so far as to argue, "There is nothing to revive. . . . What the government means when it says Renaissance, I think, is the creation of a situation that is conducive to the arts." As an expatriate Australian, Field may have felt freer to express what others in the arts community might have been thinking when he added: "Right now, Singapore is far too pragmatic to be a Renaissance city. . . . Idealism and creativity will not happen overnight through legislation." Countering Field's cautionary comments was the optimism of Liew Chin Choy, the former director of arts programs for the Singapore Arts Festival: "The government is known for its persistence in getting things done. It is a bold vision but I believe we'll get there somehow" (Tong).

At the center of the "somehow" in Liew's statement has been the ambitious, ever-expanding Singapore Arts Festival. From its humble beginnings in 1977 as a community-based arts project, the festival has become Singapore's premier cultural event, with a multi-million-dollar budget, tens of thousands of festivalgoers, and as many as a hundred groups presenting a wide range of theater, music, dance, and interdisciplinary works over a month-long period in May and June. Prior to 1999, the festival was held in alternate years with the smaller, more regionally focused Festival of Asian Performing Arts. Once the two festivals were combined, Asian work was no longer relatively marginalized, and the annual festival increased its international stature to the point where it now attracts numerous foreign journalists and festival directors from overseas.

By providing significant sponsorship as well as the organizational apparatus required to run the Singapore Arts Festival, the National Arts Council is contributing to three significant longer-term economic objectives frequently cited by the government as essential for success in the twenty-first century: *(1) The festival contributes to the further growth of tourism and the development of Singapore as a regional arts center.* As Minister George Yeo observes, "Because the arts industry serves the region, those who live near the hub enjoy a facility which they otherwise could not have. As with everything in Singapore, we get more than what we would as a city-state of three million people because we serve, maybe, 300 million" (Oorjitham, "Why Art Cannot Be Like Hothouse Flowers"). *(2) The festival makes the city a more attractive place in which to invest, signaling its emergence as a "world-class" city, while also making the city a desirable place for expatriates with specialized skills and education to live.* A consistent theme sounded by Prime Minister Goh from the late 1990s has been the necessity of attracting talented expatriates to Singapore to support an expanding economy. *(3) The festival and the promotion of the arts in all sectors of society encourages Singaporeans to recognize the value of creative thinking, a skill that has been identified by the government as absolutely essential for Singapore's long-term success in a rapidly changing global marketplace that increasingly requires the ability to respond quickly and creatively to new challenges.*[7] The cool, pragmatic arguments in support of the arts used by Singapore's government could be put to good use in Western nations such as the United States, where, as in Singapore, the content of the art is repeatedly held up to scrutiny by politicians; whereas in the United States, the federal government simply chooses to provide minuscule support for the arts, especially for theater, in Singapore the government provides considerable financial support while taking on the responsibility of policing content. The Singapore Arts Festival, however, has generally assisted in expanding the boundaries of artistic expression, especially inasmuch as it has been responsible for importing some of the most demanding and challenging work seen by Singaporean audiences.

While the festival has in many respects been a major success for Singapore's policy makers and for the enhancement of the country's international image, much of the criticism leveled at it by Singaporean artists and patrons has remained remarkably consistent over the years. Their comments reflect the fact that the festival, administered and run by the National Arts Council (NAC), is very much the creation of the government, and consistent with its goals. Rather than using an external framework to evaluate the festival, something Western commentators are frequently condemned for doing, I will rely on the NAC's own stated policy objectives with regard to the event. The following festival objectives were provided by the NAC's Liew Chin Choy, the former director of arts programs, who was responsible for overseeing the festival until it became an annual event in 1999:

1. Provide an occasion for Singaporeans to celebrate the arts.
2. Create an arts event of high standard and visibility to promote wide-spread interest in and awareness of the arts.
3. Present mainstream, experimental and avant-garde works of the highest artistic standard by Singaporean and international artistes.
4. Aid the development of local talent and encourage new local productions through commissioning works for the Festival.
5. Facilitate exchange of skills and experiences between invited foreign artists and local performers through workshops, masterclasses, lectures and other training activities.
6. Increase the knowledge, understanding and practice of the arts among Singaporeans.
7. Develop Singapore as an international centre for the arts and enhance the attractiveness of Singapore for both visitors and residents.

Using these objectives, and relying on artists' comments and relevant examples from contributing productions, in the following paragraphs I offer a broad analysis of the festival as a whole rather than a detailed view of a particular festival.[8] A picture of a festival emerges that reflects some of the same fundamental tensions that continue to exist wherever politics and culture meet.

(1) *Provide an occasion for Singaporeans to celebrate the arts.* The festival features numerous fringe events and a range of free performance activities in shopping centers, housing estates, parks, and public places, all of which further the visibility of the event and serve to create new audiences for the arts. A 1994 survey suggested that almost 14 percent of festival audiences

were composed of people who had not attended any arts event in the preceding twelve months, while almost 29 percent of those attending had never been to an arts festival before (Koh Buck Song, "New Survey"). Prior to 1999, the festival began with a massive opening parade down Orchard Road, the fashionable shopping thoroughfare that is arguably the real heart and soul of consumer-driven Singapore. The parade, which organizers estimated was viewed by some 70,000 people in 1996 (*Straits Times*, 28 May 1996), was eliminated when the festival became an annual event. Similarly, the number of activities in the "fringe" program was seriously curtailed, probably in an effort to make the festival more cost-effective, especially inasmuch as many of the imported fringe events were relatively costly to import and yielded little if any revenue. In the wake of the 2000 Festival, there were complaints that the more informal performance events scheduled at Festival Village, an open-air venue in centrally situated Fort Canning, had been seriously cut back, creating an atmosphere that was "like a variety show for tourists" (*Straits Times*, 28 June 2000).

One thing the festival lacks that has been a subject of discussion for some time is a convenient and accessible venue to obtain information on the festival, grab a cup of coffee, and generally just hang out and meet other people before or after the various events. Malaysian theater director Kristen Jit argued in 1994 that this was one of festival's shortcomings. Some festivals, he observed, generate their own newsletter, which results in a dialogue "that's one of the deepest parts of the festival." By way of contrast with the Singapore festival, he recalled the atmosphere at the Tenth Cairo International Theatre Festival, where theater practitioners and fans freely mingled and exchanged views after the shows, creating both "a social and an intellectual event." By contrast, he found the atmosphere at the Singapore festival "terribly distant, even mechanical" (personal interview). The only official "watering hole," no longer in use, was an expensive, trendy restaurant, not exactly the most inviting or affordable venue for people who wish to mingle with other artists. By choosing a pricey restaurant rather than an informal meeting area, the administrators have followed the high-consumption model, looking to the bottom line and corporate tie-ins rather than considering how this choice has the potential to work against their own goals, which call for the celebration and development of a festival community.

(2) Create an arts event of high standard and visibility to promote widespread interest in and awareness of the arts. The overall standard of the festival has

also been a subject to which critics are drawn, and most of the criticism revolves around the issue of the festival's lack of artistic direction. While many of the individual events programmed are clearly of the highest international standards, especially to the extent that they are often drawn from other major festivals,[9] there is no overall vision for the festival, as programming decisions are made by the NAC's director of arts programs[10] and standing committees. Unlike most other major international festivals, Singapore's has no artistic director, resulting in a situation in which, according to one prominent arts professional, "You may have all world-class acts, but without clear artistic direction, it becomes like a buffet table. In the end, we do not know what we are eating" (Oon, "An Asian Buffet"). The buffet table analogy is an apt one, especially as one of the longest-running campaigns in the press has been to alter the *kiasu* behavior of Singaporeans at the buffet table, where they have been repeatedly admonished by the government for their lack of common courtesy as they pile on extra helpings of the most expensive items, with no apparent regard for the others following them in the line. The festival itself has been seen as a kind of international "buffet table" even by Singaporean and Malaysian artists who have had their work shown there repeatedly. Theatre director Krishen Jit, a longtime festival participant, observes that one of the problems with the event is that programming "choices are made relative to what are perceived as prestigious international companies." Jit argues that by bringing in what he terms "international art objects," Singapore is able to demonstrate that it is a nation with an "international art image." Singaporean playwright Kuo Pao Kun agrees. He believes that the NAC's programming decisions reflect their tendency to "just shop around for programs that are perceived as successful internationally or at other festivals" (telephone interview). In spite of this continuing criticism, primarily coming from within the arts community itself, there is no indication that the NAC has any intention of changing the way that programming decisions are made.[11]

The media resources of the state are used extensively to help generate a celebratory feel for the festival. Press coverage is extensive: every major performance event is reviewed and given advance coverage. In addition, numerous wrap-up pieces are published by journalists, analyzing the festival from every conceivable angle, from lighthearted ("best and worst") to weightier and more lengthy pieces of analysis. In addition, the Web site for the festival is extensive, easy-to-use, eye-catching, and even replete with video clips of upcoming events. Few festivals anywhere are fortunate enough to benefit

For all of the poison ink spilled by Singaporean critics over TheatreWorks's Desdemona, *the visual side of the intercultural production was stunning. Conceived and directed by Ong Keng Sen and written by Japanese playwright Rio Kishida, the production featured video/installation art by Matthew Ngui (Singapore/ Australia) and Park Hwa Young (Korea). Set design by Justin Hill (Australia/Singapore) and lighting design by Scott Zielinski (USA). The work premiered at the Telstra Adelaide Festival 2000. Photo courtesy of TheatreWorks.*

from this kind of exposure in the press, and while criticism of the festival as an event is generally relatively tame and typically takes the form of suggestions in a post mortem context, the comments of individual reviewers can be quite scathing, even downright nasty, when it comes to evaluating work that is perceived to be lacking. For instance, one of the reviewers of Theatre-Works's production of *Desdemona* at the 2000 festival pulled out all the stops in her poison-pen review of that company's avant-garde reworking of Shakespeare's *Othello*: "Shakespeare has survived some 400-odd years of tinkering, editing and deconstruction. But in TheatreWorks's director Ong Keng Sen, Shakespeare's ever-malleable text has finally met its match. . . . The entire production was creaking under the weight of its multiple, portentous, politically correct issues. . . . It is a postmodern con-job perpetuated by theatregoers' unwillingness to look uncultured in the face of artistic flim-flamming" (Ong Sor Fern).

Such harsh criticism of theater in the English-speaking world, once common in the larger theater markets such as New York and London, is now relatively rare, at least in part because of the fledgling status of theater as well as the widely acknowledged power such reviews have to drive away audiences and prematurely bring down the curtain on a new production. No such concerns seem to be evident in Singapore, one of the few places where one can still find reviews written by critics who seem to take genuine delight in trashing a show. Of all of the sins that seem to motivate a negative review, the sin of displaying artistic pretensions seems to be the most grave, a phenomenon which, depending on your point of view, is either a sign of Singapore's punitive culture or its willingness to call a spade a spade.

(3) Present mainstream, experimental and avant-garde works of the highest artistic standard by Singaporean and international artists. The NAC has demonstrated a strong commitment to this goal, consistently programming a balance between mainstream and what might be termed experimental or avant-garde works. Of the ten major theater events in the 2000 festival, for instance, fully half fell outside the category of mainstream theater, including the controversial Singaporean production of the NAC-commissioned *Desdemona*, which so enraged one arts administrator that his comments became legendary; Phan Ming Yen apparently stormed out of the Victoria Theatre muttering, "The greatest piece of shit I've seen on stage," as the door to the orchestra section slammed shut behind him (Oon, "Lessons"). Equally criticized was the world premiere of Robert Wilson's *Hot Water*, a multimedia work based on Franz Liszt's Twelve Transcendental Etudes performed by Tzimon Barto that was plagued with tremendous technical difficulties on opening night. A *Straits Times* editor wrote that he was so bored by the show he "couldn't wait to get out" of the theater (Oon, "Lessons"), prompting one to wonder if Wilson will ever consent to bringing another of his works to Singapore. The mean-spirited comments of some critics and private individuals in responding to both works suggest that the public may need a certain amount of education to prepare them for performances that cross artistic boundaries. As dance choreographer Angela Liong observed, "'I think some people here tend to be too clever and cynical and dismiss too quickly anything that baffles them ever so slightly. Most people tackle a performance like an exam, they want to get the "right answers." A performance does not communicate in such a way'" (Oon, "Lessons").

While it may well be that Wilson's *Hot Water* was not one of his more successful creations, it should be noted that the audiences for his work, though international, are relatively small in scale. When Wilson's work comes to Los Angeles, a metropolitan area with many times the population of Singapore, only a few thousand people see his operatic and multimedia spectacles. Unlike the United States and Europe, Singapore does not yet possess a sizable audience with decades of experience witnessing this type of demanding work. Much to their credit, the NAC has continually retained their commitment to such challenging programming, even when it meets with hostile responses from the audience and critics. The reason the commitment has held steady perhaps owes less to the love of arts bureaucrats for the avant-garde than it does to the realities of the marketplace. As the chairman of the NAC, Liu Thai Ker, noted in the wake of the 2000 festival, the future will see "more multi-media and multi-genre productions, the current trend adopted by festival around the world" (Oon, "Lessons"). The unspoken assumption seems to be that if Singapore is going to join the ranks of the world's great festivals, it needs to program work that segments of the audience may not yet be fully prepared to accept.

Wilson's *Hot Water* and TheatreWorks's *Desdemona* join a long list of productions that have challenged audience sensibilities. Krishen Jit recalls that audiences found the 1986 performance of the Merce Cunningham Dance Company "completely inaccessible" (personal interview). Yet a mere eight years later, the 1992 productions *Macbeth* and *Medea* by Japan's Ninagawa Company were apparently met with relative enthusiasm, so much so that my theater students in Singapore consistently held up these two productions as models that set the standards to which they aspired. Unlike Cunningham's relatively formalistic approach to modern dance, director Yukio Ninagawa tells a recognizable story, even a Western one, while relying upon strong visual images and a performance style that fuses Japanese and Western traditions. The 1994 festival production of the Warsaw Studio Theatre's *Pilgrims and Exiles*, a wordless meditation and lament on the political and social history of the Polish nation, built upon Ninagawa's legacy by providing Singaporean audiences with an opportunity to see a Western company working in a similar vein. Without words and with only the rawest of visual components —burlap sacks, shreds of cloth, pulley, antiquated sewing machines—the group created a series of complex and arresting stage pictures using stylized movements and punctuated by human-generated rhythms that demanded a visceral as much as an intellectual response. Subsequent interviews with the members of the Polish troupe revealed that the only reason they had never performed in the United States was due to the high cost of the work, which featured twenty-three performers, making it too expensive for U.S. art festivals. In this instance, the NAC's commitment to bringing in experimental work proved financially costly, especially in that the work was among the more poorly attended of the high-profile works staged that year. In this instance, the NAC cannot be accused of not being willing to put their money behind their principles.

(4) Aid the development of local talent and encourage new local productions through commissioning works for the Festival. The development of Singaporean work through the festival has been a touchy subject for Singaporean artists, especially given the size and scale of the event and its potential to overshadow the artistic offerings of local companies. Playwright and director Kuo Pao Kun has argued that the "attention drawn to the festival in proportion to the availability of people, money and groups is too large," adding that "by allocating so much money to festivals year-round you [the NAC] are effectively dominating the theatre scene" (telephone interview). In addition, he notes that Singaporean theater companies typically contribute their major work of the year to the festival; thus the festival dominates their programming decisions every other year (telephone interview). Even a cursory glance through the festival offerings of the 1990s suggests that Singaporean groups consistently program their largest, most ambitious works so that they fall within the purview of the festival. Clearly, there is no prospect of actually competing with the festival for attention. Kuo himself has benefited enormously from the scale of attention and publicity lavished on the festival; perhaps his most impressive English-language play of the decade, *Descendants of the Eunuch Admiral*, premiered at the 1995 Festival of Asian Performing Arts in a production staged by Ong Keng Sen of TheatreWorks. The play subsequently toured internationally to the Cairo International Theatre Festival and was later remounted in Mandarin. Indeed, Kuo's play, as noted in chapter 4, was probably the most trenchant political and social allegory ever written about contemporary Singapore. That it was produced as part of a government-run arts festival could be seen as proof that Singapore is a far less oppressive country than many in West might wish to believe. On the other hand, one could argue that by failing to acknowledge that Kuo's play was in part an allegory about oppression, the government's tacit sanctioning of this play diffused its political significance.[12] Once again, as was the case with theatrical censorship, the sword cuts both ways. Kuo's work was also advanced at

the 2000 festival when his two mid-1980s plays, *The Coffin Is Too Big for the Hole* and *No Parking on Odd Days*, were given major revivals in four separate, fully mounted productions in English, Mandarin, Malay, and Tamil. Now widely considered classics of the Singaporean stage, Kuo's two plays broke considerable ground in the uptight Singapore of the 1980s by showing the ordinary citizen at odds with the impersonal bureaucracy of the state.

Of all of Singapore's theater companies, TheatreWorks has most frequently been given a place at the festival table, offering up fare both mainstream and experimental. The company staged two huge hits at the 1990 and 1992 festivals—the Singapore premiere of *M. Butterfly* and the transgendered musical *Private Parts*, respectively. The sexually titillating nature of these two shows, both of which mess with gender in ways that had previously been considered too daring for the stage, may well have accounted for much of their appeal with Singaporean audiences. As noted in the previous chapter, *M. Butterfly* broke considerable new ground with its difficult themes, which dance around the possibility of homosexuality without actually naming it; Jit recalls that following the success of the production, the "Singaporean government congratulated itself on being able to do it" (personal interview). Less popular with audiences, however, have been TheatreWorks's festival offerings that tackle historical issues (Lloyd Fernando's *Scorpion Orchid*, 1994; Kuo's *Descendants of the Eunuch Admiral*, 1995) as well as works that require the audience to accept a more free-form, associative principle of dramatic organization (*Desdemona*, 2000). That the NAC has provided financial assistance to relatively unpopular work supports former festival head Liew's observation that "if the festival was organized as a purely commercial concern, then it doesn't make sense to support local work" (personal interview). Nevertheless, by providing financial assistance to the one company that has already demonstrated its ability to put Singapore on the international theater map by virtue of its overseas productions directed by Ong Keng Sen,[13] there is a sense in which the NAC is "banking" on TheatreWorks's ability to bring Singapore future returns.

(5) Facilitate exchange of skills and experiences between invited foreign artists and local performers through workshops, masterclasses, lectures and other training activities. Festivals can also provide an opportunity for Singapore's practitioners to rub shoulders with and work alongside international artists, resulting in an exchange of ideas and skills that can assist in the cross-fertilization of the arts both in Singapore and overseas. Arts administrator and technician

Ganesh Kalyanam believes that this has been one of the greatest spin-offs from the event, noting that the "impact of the festival has been quite positive, not just in terms of training, but also in terms of attitude," and adding that the opportunity to work alongside foreign artists has helped instill a "sense of professionalism" in Singaporean artists and technicians (personal interview). While many administrators and technicians have obtained experience working with artists from overseas, the same is not true for Singaporean performers. Apart from TheatreWorks's international collaborations, the vast majority of festival productions have failed to provide other theater artists with similar opportunities to cross international boundaries. Similarly, the relative absence of workshops, master classes, and lectures may have been largely responsible for the ongoing problem with festival audiences, which are often dismissive of difficult or unconventional work. Alvin Tan of The Necessary Stage argues that challenging work requires "rigorous follow-up: Academic discourse, critical essays in the media and public forums to bring together opinions from all quarters" (Oon, "Lessons"), suggesting that the critical infrastructure required to build a fully conscious theater in Singapore is not yet present.

(6) *Increase the knowledge, understanding and practice of the arts among Singaporeans.* Twenty-five years ago, notes Krishen Jit, Singaporean theater was polarized between expatriate drama clubs and an amateur, fledgling English-language drama scene insecure about its place on the stage. The festival, which took off in the 1980s, "started creating an audience for [English-language] theatre in Singapore" (personal interview). If the success of the event is "measured by attendance," as the NAC's Liew has asserted (personal interview), then the sheer number of people who attend ticketed festival events—a fairly steady 85,000 in the decade from 1986 to 1996[14]—is statistically significant, given the size of Singapore's population. By offering additional free events in the HDB heartlands where the majority of Singaporeans live[15] and in public spaces, the organizers hope to build an audience that will ultimately pay to experience the arts. In addition to increasing audience numbers, the NAC also hopes to raise the level of sophistication among Singaporean audiences on the most fundamental level. Following a number of well-publicized incidents of shockingly rude cell-phone behavior at the 1998 festival,[16] immediately prior to the 1999 festival an extensive article on "festival dos and don'ts" appeared in the *Straits Times*. In addition to talking on the phone, the long list of unacceptable theater behavior included reading the

newspaper during a performance; clapping between movements of a symphony; leaving early; taking flash photographs; failing to restrain unruly children; and arriving late, but with great aplomb, "a la Princess Diana" in an effort to "stun the rest of Singapore's arty elite with your cultured aura" (Tan Shzr Ee). Interestingly enough, the cell-phone outbreak took place after a year-long courtesy campaign on the proper use of mobile phones. With an entire year of television commercials demonstrating the courteous use of pagers and cell phones, supplemented by specially commissioned mass transit and phone cards as well as billboards underscoring the same message, the government's nineteenth annual National Courtesy Campaign was apparently less than successful,[17] requiring a brief refresher course courtesy of the press.

The commitment to programming not only mainstream but also experimental and avant-garde work, as noted previously, is also part of a larger strategy for audience development. In 1994 Liew spoke of the NAC's commitment to "consciously inject some experimental and avant-garde items" into the festival so that over time "we are slowly changing audience taste" (personal interview), a strategy that does not seem to have wavered in the years that have followed. Not only critics but also audiences have also been occasionally hostile to work that challenges their sensibilities. Liew points out that many individuals walked out in the middle of the 1994 arts festival performance by eighty-eight-year-old Kazuo Ohno, the "Father of Butoh" and a living legend. In spite of Ohno's fame, some Singaporeans slept through the performance, while the Straits Times dubbed it the "most abstract performance" of the festival, adding that "the dancers moved around in [sic] such 'intense inwardness' that audiences were sucked into an intellectual black hole" (Phan, "Tougher Challenges").

Equally perplexing to audiences was the Mabou Mines's production of The Bribe at the 1994 festival, a work that was characterized by self-referential rapid-fire bursts of jazz-inflected poetry that wove its wild and wicked threads around themes that only a hip New York performance art audience could possibly have understood. As the Mabou Mines actors slithered, leapt, and flew across the stage, Singaporeans reacted with bewilderment, prompting Mabou Mines stalwart Ruth Maleczech to admit that her actors were demoralized by the lack of any appreciable audience response to their work (personal interview). The review in the Straits Times seemed to lament not being able to reduce this multilayered and complex work to a simple narrative-driven scenario revolving around a visit by the tax man (Phan, review of The

Bribe), suggesting that the reviewer invested way too much energy in attempting to pin a narrative down on this playfully open-ended work. Perhaps the problems surrounding the public reaction to Mabou Mines could have been avoided if the NAC had simply picked another piece that the company had offered to perform,[18] instead of choosing such a dense, distinctly New York work. While it seems fair to argue that perhaps the NAC could have made a more effective choice, they should still be given credit for demonstrating a willingness to showcase challenging work, sometimes at great expense, even when the audience is not yet prepared to fully accept such work.[19]

(7) Develop Singapore as an international center for the arts and enhance the attractiveness of Singapore for both visitors and residents. As the "premier cultural event in Singapore," according to former festival director Liew, the Singapore Arts Festival is also a commercial endeavor. But in fact, most festivals are. The festivals that proliferated throughout Australasia in the 1980s and 1990s from Singapore to Hong Kong, Perth to Adelaide, and Sydney to Wellington all rely heavily on work that has been proven to be commercially successful elsewhere. However, unlike in the West, where artists and even arts bureaucracies have historically gone to great lengths to demonstrate their lack of complicity with market forces, in Singapore this connection is widely acknowledged. In an age of global capitalism, the only defense for supporting any form of human activity increasingly seems to be its contribution to the bottom line; only recently have defenders of the arts in the United States picked up on this strategy, arguing, quite correctly, that the arts do indeed generate money and jobs. As if to demonstrate the truth of this proposition, a whole new category of tourism has been created—or, rather, finally acknowledged—in the West: cultural tourism. Thus in this respect, one can argue that Singapore seems to have understood the economic value of the arts before it was widely acknowledged elsewhere. Ultimately, however, the development of an arts scene needs more than money; on a fundamental level, it requires sensitive, inquiring minds, a willingness to take risks, and the capacity for self-reflection and self-criticism, factors that are not yet fully present in Singapore.

Interestingly enough, when a Western country with the same size population as Singapore produced its own biennial arts festival, one that exceeded the size and scale of Singapore's festival, the *Straits Times* regarded the festival as a manifestation of "shoestring culture" (Chua Huck Cheng). The New

Zealand International Festival of the Arts, held in Wellington, a city that is a mere fraction of the size of Singapore, was characterized as "having to make do on a budget of NZ$10 million (S$9.7 million)." Apparently the writer was willing to overlook the fact that Singapore's then most recent festival had operated on a much smaller budget of S$6.63 million (*Straits Times*, 1 July 1996), while the then forthcoming 1998 festival was operating on S$7.8 million (*Straits Times*, 1 April 1998), still less than the "shoestring" New Zealand festival. Similarly, when the lead theater critic for the *Straits Times* went to Edinburgh in 1999, she found the festival "overrated," adding, "If the Edinburgh Festival Fringe is anything to go by, Singapore theatre is generally more experimental than the British. In fact, there are probably more spinning performers and flashing video screens per capita on this little island than anywhere else" (Oon, "Don't Sniff"). The superficiality of Oon's observations speak for themselves, as the underlying assumption seems to be that video technology and gimmicks are all that is required for "experimental" theater. While commentators in the West are often accused by the Singaporean government of denigrating Singapore's accomplishments, in this instance at least it would appear that Singaporeans are just as willing to knock some of the achievements of the West through misrepresentation.

As I flew into Singapore for the first time in 1992, I happened upon an article in the Singapore Airlines in-flight magazine which speculated that Singapore's Arts Festival had the potential to turn the city into the "Edinburgh of the East" (Kuan). Singapore is perhaps not alone in wanting to be the equal of Edinburgh, as critic Oon's comments suggest, though it may well be the only country with the chutzpah to admit the extent of its aspirations. Still, the Edinburgh Festival is what it is not because it buys the best of what the world has to offer but because it is a place where the best (and sometimes the worst) of world theater battle it out side by side in venues ranging from the funky to the elegant all over the city; as such, it is a place where work is seen for the first time in front of an international audience, not where it ends up five to ten years later. Edinburgh was not created from the top down; rather, it sprang up from the ground because the conditions that reward and recognize artistic excellence were and continue to be present. In the absence of such conditions it seems unlikely that Singapore will realize its dream of becoming the "Edinburgh of the East" anytime soon.

Singaporean students being interviewed for admission into
the Theatre Studies program at the National University of
Singapore in the 1990s routinely cited their love of American
and European musicals as the principal reason they were interested in studying theater at the university level. Among
the most frequently mentioned and lavishly praised musicals were *Les Misérables*, *Cats*, *Sound of Music*, and *Phantom of
the Opera*. Thus for many of my Singaporean (and largely
ethnic-Chinese) theater students, their ideas about the craft
of acting were more fully embodied by the Australian actor
playing Frankenfurter in the touring production of *Rocky
Horror* or actress playing the waiflike Cosette in *Les Misérables* than by an actor playing the *qingyi* (virtuous young
woman) or *xiaosheng* (scholar lover) roles in Chinese opera.

When asked specifically about Chinese opera, a form with
many regional varieties that is regularly presented in Singapore in three major Chinese dialects (Hokkien, Cantonese,
Teochew) as well as Mandarin, most admitted they had never
seen it apart from the ubiquitous street theater performances at festival times that coincide with the Chinese lunar
calendar. Few expressed any interest at all in the form, while
most of those who had seen productions by professional
companies went accompanied by an older female relative
(an "auntie") who dragged them along, often against their
will. Among the reasons students voiced for their lack of enthusiasm for the form were its linguistic inaccessibility and
its general lack of hip-ness. Many younger people cannot

fully understand the dialects that their "aunties" may speak as a first language, making the form seem doubly remote and foreign. For most of them, Chinese opera was regarded as a quaint, old-fashioned form with little relevance to their lives.

In spite of the Singapore government's "Speak Mandarin" campaign, the aggressive marketing of so-called Asian values, and the biennial Chinese Cultural Festival, the theatrical form most widely embraced by the greatest number of Singaporeans is not the Chinese opera but, rather, the Western-style musical. By the early 1990s, the major international tours of the Cameron Mackintosh organization routinely took in Singapore as a destination, and the nation's cultural czars came to see the country as a potential regional center for productions of these blockbuster hits. Even in the aftermath of the financial crisis of the late 1990s, which witnessed sharp declines in the value of neighboring currencies, the well-heeled from Kuala Lumpur, Bangkok, and Jakarta continue to fly into Singapore for a weekend of musicals and shopping. As the regional economies continue to regain lost ground while Singapore leads the pack, the government is still banking on the musical; the largest houses appropriate for the international tours of musicals and other high-profile events are the key components of the new Esplanade arts center.

In addition to imported work, which remains extraordinarily popular and lucrative, Singapore has developed a significant body of indigenous musicals over the course of the last decade. The Singaporean most associated with the rise of this phenomenon is Dick Lee, the pan-Asian pop star and prolific composer and lyricist who has been largely responsible for the indigenization of the genre. Relying on the basic form and structure of the Western musical, Lee has created a string of highly popular works on Singaporean themes that range from his fellow citizens' obsession with food (*Fried Rice Paradise*) to censorship (*Mortal Sins*) to his homage to Cantonese melodrama and 1960s Singapore (*Beauty World*). Many of his most popular works and greatest critical successes were created in partnership with other writers, notably Singaporean playwright Michael Chiang, and staged by TheatreWorks. By 1995 the Singapore *Straits Times* confidently declared that "the home-grown musical is the closest thing around to a uniquely Singaporean theatre form" (Lee Yin Luen). In the decade that followed Lee and Chiang's *Beauty World*, the form took off: Singapore's press proudly heralded each new Lee musical as bringing them one step closer to the biggest, most coveted prize, namely success on Broadway or the West End.

In terms of scale, the watershed Singaporean musical was Lee's 1992

Beauty World,
*Michael Chiang
and Dick Lee's paean
to Cantonese melo-
drama in the 1960s.
Revival production
staged by Theatre-
Works for President's
Star Charity, 1998.*

work, *Nagraland.* Backed with Japanese money—at least a third of which came from the economic giant Mitsubishi—the S$6.4 million production opened in Japan, where up to 70 percent of the 20,000 tickets on sale were snapped up well in advance of the show's opening. No Singaporean produc-tion had previously generated this much financial support from overseas, and, not surprisingly, advance press on the work focused on its impressive budget and its potential for success abroad. The *Singapore Sunday Times* noted optimistically that Lee and his Japanese producer "hope to eventually stage *Nagraland* on Broadway, in London's West End and even Paris" (Goh, "Not a Singaporean Musical"). After London and New York, what is left but Paris, where a Singaporean success would place the country squarely on the map of world culture. Lee's manager articulated the marketing strategy for

The S$6.4 million production of Nagraland, written and composed by Dick Lee and directed by Krishen Jit, opened in Japan and was the first major Singaporean musical to set itself up for international export. While it never "made it" to Broadway or the West End, the work's Asian theme and aesthetics garnered large and supportive audiences both at home and in Japan, where Lee was regarded as a pop superstar. Costumes by Yang Derong. Photo courtesy of Music and Movement.

the show: "We're selling *Nagraland* not as a Singapore musical but as an Asian event" (Goh, "Not a Singaporean Musical"). Given Lee's history as a writer of Singapore-based musicals, this switch to staging an "Asian event" is significant: while a Singaporean musical might not have the potential to succeed internationally, a musical that is seen to represent a more generic "Orient" has a shot at the global—or, rather, the Western—market. Not surprisingly, the *Sunday Times* reporter concluded her story with the observation that "the stakes are high but the prize—of international fame as well as success—is worth the plunge" (Goh, "Mad Chinaman").

Lee's pop-star status in Japan largely guaranteed the musical's success there, as fans eagerly awaited the opportunity to see their icon in his first "dramatic" role. Adding to the appeal of the musical in Singapore was a core artistic team that included many of the "who's who" of the Asian entertainment world. Lee was joined onstage by his wife at the time, Jacintha Abishe-ganaden, Singapore's most popular female vocalist, as well as Japanese rock star Kazufumi Miyazawa of the rock group The Boom, while Krishen Jit, one of the region's best-known directors, staged the work with his wife, Marion D'Cruz, a well-known choreographer.

Nagraland, written and composed by Lee, was in many ways designed from the ground up to be a hit, complete with musical numbers that owed more to Broadway and the West End than to Singapore or Beijing. The story, observed one local reviewer, was, "like the smash Broadway musical *The King and I*—the old 'Far East' repackaged" (Bachtiar).[1] The "legend" invented by Lee that served as the starting point for the work was fashioned to sound as if it were taken from one of the great epic poems such as the *Ramayana*. In Lee's mythical story, the daughter of the ruler of the universe falls in love with a mortal warrior, ultimately becoming pregnant by him. This so enrages the father that he promptly kills the warrior and banishes his daughter to the island of Nagraland, where she gives birth to a new race, the Naga people. In the contemporary story that is picked up in the musical, Lee enacts a journal-ist from an Asian metropolis who is driven to Nagraland by a series of haunt-ing dreams. He arrives just in time for a coup d'état and promptly falls in love with an orphan of uncertain parentage (played by Filipino Judith Banal), whose character merges with that of the legendary fallen princess. Lee's char-acter, in turn, blends into that of the legendary warrior. Their initial en-counter is responsible for some of the most unfortunate lines of the musical, including the journalist's query to the young orphan: "You may find this strange, but I feel I know you from somewhere before."[2]

At the heart of the work was the enactment of the conflict between tradi-tional and contemporary values. Like Rendra's play, *The Struggle of the Naga Tribe*, which may have been a source of inspiration for *Nagraland*, Lee's mu-sical looks at the immense gulf between affluent city-dwelling Asians and those eking out a subsistence existence from the land across the Straits in nearby Indonesia. Lee's remarks in the program for the event underscored his intent: "*Nagraland* speaks of the need to become this New Asian—one who, recognizing the importance of tradition, adapts and applies its teach-ings to the present and accepts the changes. For only when we see ourselves in a new way, will the rest of the world do the same" (Music and Movement). Lee's comments suggest that the motivating force behind the creation of the musical was not so much the relevance it might have for an Asian audience member but what it communicates to "the rest of the world" about the "New

Asian." Director Jit, also citing the Asianness of the musical, declared, "What you are therefore witnessing tonight is a unique moment in world theatre" (Music and Movement). Clearly, both Lee and Jit saw the work not as another "Instant Asia" presentation—or, worse, as an Asian *King and I*—but as a uniquely cross-cultural creation, a "real" Asian musical by and performed by actual Asians. Believing that Asians had laid claim to a Western form and indigenized it, *Nagraland*'s creators and producers no doubt hoped it could offer an antidote to the stereotypes unwittingly reinforced by the then recent hits *M. Butterfly* and *Miss Saigon*.

The work relied on a visual and dance style that conflated elements of Balinese and Javanese cultures, with a sprinkling of Thai and other Asian influences. The costume designer, Yang Derong, was a well-known fashion designer, whose work in Paris and Japan relies heavily on Asian design elements for inspiration. The traditional sarong, worn by many of the male dancers in the company, was worn hiked up and gathered in the middle of the chest, exposing considerable flesh and allowing for an expressive range of movement that was bolder and more open than traditional costuming would have permitted. Similarly, Marion D'Cruz's choreography had a pan-Asian feel; while it relied upon the general shapes and outlines of Javanese and Balinese dance, it also reflected the influence of modern (Western) dance. In one of the work's most exciting scenes, the residents of Nagraland enacted the story of their creation myth before a tourist audience, employing traditional dance movements in a riotous, energetic manner, while wielding brightly colored, oversized *wayang kulit* puppets that cast giant shadows on the screens at the back of the stage.

While D'Cruz's choreography was responsible for some of the work's most memorable moments, it also contributed to the pan-Asian feel of the musical. Indeed, one reviewer characterized the work as an "MTV-Ramayana," observing that "everything is thrown in and the performers look like they have only a surface understanding of the intricate complexity of the borrowed ancient forms" (Bachtiar). Interestingly enough, the reviewer offered these comments up not so much as criticism but as backhanded praise for the work, adding that this conflation of elements was "what makes *Nagraland* honest." Her concluding remarks are fascinating for what they suggest about the relationship many Singaporeans have to Asian cultures: "The newly aware Singaporean is now tired of pressing his nose against the glass window of Western culture, but he is not familiar enough with his own heritage to take it in undiluted. So, while *Nagraland* may be slick and shallow, it remains the best pop-fusion of East and West that Singapore can offer. Tradition and MTV, remixed" (Bachtiar). The reviewer seems to unquestioningly accept the notion that Singaporeans can only take their "heritage" in a form made palatable by the trappings of Western culture. Cultural studies critic Rey Chow's observations on Western attempts to extrapolate an "authentic native" from works of art can also be applied to this context, suggesting that Chow's construct is tied as much to economic development as it is to culture. Building upon Walter Benjamin's work "Art in the Age of Mechanical Reproduction," Chow writes that the way we perceive the "native" in art can be transferred to the way we construct our view of other human beings in "real" life:

> Once we do that, we see that in our fascination with the "authentic native," we are actually engaged in a search for the equivalent of the aura even while our search processes themselves take us farther and farther away from that "original" point of identification. Although we act like good communists who dream of finding and serving the "real people," we actually live and work like dirty capitalists accustomed to switching channels constantly. As we keep switching channels and browsing through different "local" cultures, we produce an infinite number of "natives," all with predictably automaton-like features that do not so much de-universalize Western hegemony as they confirm its protean capacity of infinite displacement. The "authentic" native, like the aura in a kind of *mise en abîme*, keeps receding from our grasp. ("Where Have All the Natives Gone?" 135–36)

Nagraland offers images of an imaginary "authentic" native inhabiting a familiar but fictive pan-Asian environment that is arguably closer to the construct of an exotic, generic "primitive" Asia shared by most English-speaking, educated Singaporean theatergoers than any "real" image of an actual native might be. The easily digested, MTV version of the native proposed by Singaporean critic Bachtiar is remarkably close to Chow's suggestion that individuals in wealthy Western countries (and, I would argue, wealthy Asian countries as well) have the luxury of "channel surfing" through local cultures, creating an "infinite" number of natives, while infinitely displacing the original.

The melding of Asian cultures in *Nagraland* also brings to mind critic Rustom Bharucha's warning about artistic products that reflect a "global indifference to the *context* of specific cultures, and of non-western cultures in particular" ("Somebody's Other" 206). Bharucha's criticism of intercultural works in a Western context would here seem to be applicable to Singapore as well; indeed, Singaporeans seem every bit as capable of engaging in the same kind of wholesale plundering of the "riches of the East" in their search for artistic inspiration as many Western artists are. Rather than dividing the world into the camps of cultural victim and victimizer, it might be more sensible to examine the economic basis of this cultural exchange, especially given the rhetoric of the Singaporean government, which clearly situates the arts as yet another industry in need of development. Instead of casting Singaporean artists in the appropriator role generally reserved for the big, bad West, it is more useful to see their ability to assemble and manipulate the cultural products of nearby Asian cultures as something that stems from their economically privileged position relative to their neighbors.

Another issue relevant to the case of *Nagraland* is the degree of exploitation — if any — in the creation of a kind of pan-Asian mode of expression and new pan-Asian mythology. Even Bharucha, one of the harshest critics of some intercultural work, admits that what he is in fact advocating "is not a closed-doors policy, but an attitude of critical openness, a greater sensitivity to the ethics involved in translating and transporting other cultures, and a renewed respect of cultural self-sufficiencies in an age of globalization, where there is a tendency to homogenize the particularities of cultures, if not obliterate them altogether" ("Somebody's Other" 208). Will productions such as *Nagraland* "homogenize the particularities of cultures"? To some extent they may, but as the *Straits Times* critic observes, this homogenization is the reality of life for many in contemporary Singapore. Instead of homogenization, it may be that pan-Asian work such as *Nagraland* is instead a reflection of the fact that, as Said has observed, "no one today is purely *one* thing. Labels like Indian, or woman, or Muslim, or American are not more than starting-points, which if followed into actual experience for only a moment are quickly left behind. . . . Yet just as human beings make their own history, they also make their cultures and ethnic identities" (*Culture and Imperialism* 336). It is no coincidence that *Nagraland* was staged in the three Asian settings where identity is the most challenged and stimulated by both modernization and Western forms of cultural expression: namely Japan, Hong Kong, and Singapore. In spite of its shortcomings, it is hard to imagine a Western-created musical based on an invented pan-Asian myth with the resonance, accuracy, and contact with the host cultures expressed in *Nagraland*. Setting aside the problems with the Singapore production, the work may in fact have been "too Asian" to make it to the West End or Broadway. Certainly far more brazenly appropriative and misleading representations of Asia staged by Western theater artists have met with great critical acclaim.

One of the primary criticisms leveled against Singaporean musicals in general and this production of *Nagraland* in particular was the unevenness of the singing. While singers like Lee and Abisheganaden can be counted upon to deliver performances of a high professional standard, they often end up sharing the stage with relatively inexperienced or even first-time singers. Singaporean critic Ida Bachtiar wrote that Lim Kay Siu, a dynamic Singaporean stage actor who played the important role of dragon king in *Nagraland*, "could hardly carry a tune," but added apologetically, "his forceful presence, however, more than made up for that" ("Surface-Deep"). Bachtiar was not exercising the poison pen; in fact, Lim was dreadful, as were a number of the supporting voices. However, this is hardly surprising, given the absence of a training academy or institution in Singapore at which people can receive training in musical theater. One company, Singapore Repertory Theatre (SRT), began to remedy this situation in the mid-1990s by bringing in Asian actors from Broadway and the West End and paying them professional wages to appear in their productions, including a number of splashy musicals. In 1993, at a time when TheatreWorks, the country's most professionally minded company, was paying actors an average of $50 a week, SRT artistic director Tony Petito gave voice to a sentiment that most people in the Singaporean theater community instinctively knew to be true: "Until we can offer full-time payment, it is unrealistic for people who are working all day to come in at night after work and do first class acting" (*Straits Times*, 28 September 1993).

The following year, SRT brought in one of Singapore's best-known expatriate actors, Glen Goei—who played Song Liling in the London production of *M. Butterfly*—to direct Philippines-born actress Lea Salonga in Stephen Sondheim's *Into the Woods*. Solanga, who played the role of Kim in *Miss Saigon* on both the West End and Broadway, had won numerous awards for the role, including the 1991 Tony Award for Best Actress in a Musical. SRT's strategy has been to cast professional Asian actors from overseas in most of the lead roles, while filling out the remaining parts with Singaporeans. Petito observes that "there is a much wider choice of people in the U.S. to choose from, and the professional caliber of some of them was just that little bit higher there." One Singaporean actor who appeared in SRT's 1996 production of the musical *Sing to the Dawn* noted that while she "did wonder why

Asian American actress June Angela as Somsri (the mother) and pop star Dick Lee as Somchai (the father) in the 1996 production of Sing to the Dawn by the Singapore Repertory Theatre. Based on a book by Ho Minfong, with music by Dick Lee and lyrics by Stephen Clark. Set by Francis O'Connor and costumes by Tan Hong Chye. Photo courtesy of Singapore Repertory Theatre.

actors had to be recruited from abroad—as soon as I heard them sing, I understood why" (Ho Minfong). Indeed, without the benefit of professional training, it hardly seems fair to compare Singaporean singers to Western-trained ones appearing in a theatrical form that remains fundamentally a Western one.

SRT's greatest artistic success to date was arguably its 1996 production of *Sing to the Dawn*, based on a children's book by Ho Minfong, a Singaporean writer living in the United States, with music by Dick Lee and words by English lyricist Stephen Clark. Ho's story revolves around a Thai girl named Dawan who wins a scholarship that provides her with the opportunity to leave her impoverished village for further studies in Bangkok. For a girl to win a scholarship that had previously gone only to boys comes as a shock to everyone in her family, especially as her brother, who had been favored to win, was the runner-up; Dawan's parents, assuming that the son would be the recipient of the award, had already made plans to marry their daughter off to a rich local boy, thus ensuring what they felt would be a bright future for both children. The story's straightforward, simple truths combined with its contemporary relevance made it a natural for musical theater, while Singaporean critics suggested that the work's success was partly due to Lee's decision to use a lyricist, leaving him free to write music that many felt was among the best of his career (Zach; Tsang, review of *Sing to the Dawn*). *Sing to the Dawn*'s accessible and timely story, combined with Lee's soaring melodies and Clark's lyrics, make it perhaps the best candidate to date for success on Broadway or the West End.

The same could not be said however, for *Mortal Sins*, a Lee/Chiang collaboration about "the stripper and the censor." While the *Straits Times* heralded the big-budget event as marking a "watershed in Singapore musicals" (Koh Boon Pin, review of *Mortal Sins*), in many ways it represented the dangers of trying too hard to challenge a relatively conservative art form. Chiang, responsible for the lyrics and book, and Lee, writing the music, were joined by TheatreWorks artistic director Ong Keng Sen and choreographer Najip Ali, the same creative team responsible for the popular 1960s retro musical *Beauty World*. In sharp contrast with Lee and Chiang's breezy earlier work, this musical tackled a thorny but relevant issue affecting all artists: censorship. The *South China Morning Post* acclaimed the work to the extent that it "tests official tolerance," even though, according to director Ong, "by the end of the play it is obvious that censorship is not the issue any more" (Heath).

In the musical, Lee's wife, Jacintha Abisheganaden, took on the role of Jackie Atria, the newly appointed "chief censor" of Singapore, who pledges to put a stop to the "moral sins" that threaten to "destroy our Asian values" (TheatreWorks, video of *Mortal Sins*). On the night of her thirty-sixth birthday, the nerdy, palpably spinsterish Jackie dreams herself into a parallel universe inhabited by a young striptease queen, Rosie (played by Wendy Kweh), who entertains nightly at the Eden Nightclub. As scenes alternate between the year of the encounter with Rosie (1960) and the present (1996), Atria and Rosie become friends in an indistinct, liminal world. Ultimately Atria learns to break down some of her emotional reserve, while Rosie begins to assert her own dreams and desires more fully. Rather than evoking a kind of kitschy nostalgia that characterized the earlier *Beauty World*, which was set in a similar environment, *Mortal Sins* showed a darker vision of the 1960s in which women such as Rosie were at the mercy of men and unscrupulous madams, or *mama-sans*.

Striptease queen Rosie (on left, played by Wendy Kweh) and "Chief Censor" Jackie Atria (Jacintha Abisheganaden) share confidences in Dick Lee and Michael Chiang's Mortal Sins. *Directed by Ong Keng Sen for TheatreWorks at the Victoria Theatre, 1995. Set by Myung Hee Cho and costumes by Tan Woon Chor. Photo courtesy of TheatreWorks.*

While one of the show's musical numbers does provide a critique of the values of corporatist Singapore, the work's ultimate trajectory moves in a more conservative direction. As the musical opens, censor Jackie condemns the forthcoming visit of a Japanese dance troupe at the Festival of Asian Performing Arts for its use of nudity.[3] The nudity of the dancers becomes Jackie's battle cry, setting us up for a climactic scene at the top of act 2, when we actually witness a public performance by the offending troupe. Encased in body suits, the dance troupe engaged in a stereotypically "arty" soft-core pornographic display that featured mock copulation and a generous display of vibrating tongues. Bad pornographic dance was staged in the name of high art (i.e., a festival offering), ultimately undermining any sympathy that most audience members would have for practitioners of new art forms; if the censors protect us from such blatantly sexual, unimaginative work, then the theatergoer might be highly disposed to argue for the continuation of theatrical censorship. Najip Ali's unthinking choreography unfortunately played right into the hands of those who would argue for the necessity of controls over the arts. In this sense, director Ong was quite right in asserting that censorship "is not the issue anymore" (Heath).

The suggestion in the press, both in Singapore and overseas, that the work somehow challenged the limits of official tolerance is quite misleading. While Jackie the censor is no role model in the first act of the play, her characterization is so extreme as to be laughable and, as such, both she—and by extension her actions—are rendered harmless; one would be hard-pressed to connect her character with any real-life censor, especially as there is no such thing as a "chief censor" in Singapore.[4] By the end of the musical Jackie is transformed into a caring, loving woman owing to her contact with Rosie, while the former stripper, whose face is disfigured by a possessive *mama-san*, dies in a hospice without making contact with her old friend from an alternate reality. The musical also features a pelvis-grinding strip-tease from Rosie in act 1 that one reviewer felt presented "some views normally reserved for husbands and gynecologists" (Heath). Thus a musical praised for pushing the boundaries of expression combined a bit of flesh and salaciousness for the straight male consumers with a relatively mild critique of consumerism and corporate values. While the character of Jackie the censor is extreme and ridiculous, the puerile and gross sexuality of the work she championed against (i.e., the "arty" Japanese troupe) suggests that perhaps censorship is a necessary evil.

While Lee is the most prolific writer of the Singapore-themed musical, others have tried their hand at the task, among them a creative team of six responsible for the book, lyrics, and music in the 1993 production of *Bugis Street*. The process behind the creation of this work embodied one of the most disturbing and counterproductive trends to emerge in the 1990s where the musical in Singapore is concerned: namely, the tendency to assemble an artistic team from the top down, meting out roles to those who are believed to have competence in a particular area rather than working on the much harder task of creating the conditions that enable artists to come together without the heavy-handed intervention of a profit-driven producing organization. Produced independently by Andy Lim, Pacific Theatricals, and a publishing company, *Bugis Street* brought together a diverse and unwieldy artistic team, including not one but two lyricists, who, curiously enough, both had MBAS from UCLA, facts that were listed in the program along with their respective occupations: research manager for an investment firm and managing director of a communications company. One of the lyricists noted in his biography that while pursuing his MBA, he was awarded a fellowship "for being among the top two percent in a class of 400" (Pacific Theatricals), as if to suggest that his academic success ensured that his lyrics would also be placed in the top 2 percent.

Joining the dueling MBAS from UCLA was scriptwriter Koh Buck Song, who also wrote the novel on which the musical was based. As one of the county's leading conservative columnists, who consistently articulates a position that is in lock-step with government policy, Koh would probably be the last person anyone would suspect capable of penning a paean to the legendary Bugis Street of old. As noted in chapter 6, this infamous street, devoured by the central commercial core of Singapore in the late 1970s, has become a kind of sticking point for all that was slightly bawdy and "bad" in old Singapore, embodying the excesses of the past, which included prostitution, gangsterism, and crime. The backdrop of numerous plays, among which the most significant are Ivan Heng's *Lest the Demons Get to Me* and Michael Chiang and Dick Lee's *Private Parts*, Bugis Street represents all that has been lost in the modernization of Singapore: the messiness, anarchy, freedom, surging energy, and wild confluence of people from all over Southeast Asia and the world who regularly converged on this little area in search of food, money, titillation, entertainment, and, most of all, sex.

It bears noting that Singapore's few remaining inner-city neighborhoods with vestiges of their original character have been largely transformed into centers for the consumption of various goods and services: the old shop houses along Boat Quay are now given over to outdoor dining along the Singapore River, while the Bugis Street area is being transformed into a major commercially driven entertainment center with large theaters and cinemas built on the former sites of hawker stalls, dingy bars, and cathouses. In central Singapore, only Chinatown and Little India retain much of their former character, though this is largely due to both their attractiveness to foreign tourists and their function as important focal points for segments of the two respective ethnic groups that require access to the specialized goods and services available in these two areas. Thus the continued existence of Chinatown and Little India is due largely to commercial rather than sentimental or historical considerations. In such an environment, the power of the old Bugis Street continues to haunt and attract many Singaporeans.

The theme of *Bugis Street*—the search for one's roots—became an ongoing cliché in 1990s Singaporean theater. Leila Florentino, a Filipino actress who had played the female lead in the Broadway production of *Miss Saigon*, took the role of Mei-li, a young women who spent her early years living near Bugis Street but who subsequently grew up largely in England and America. As the musical opens, Mei-li returns to Bugis Street as an urban renewal officer who is to clear the area of hawkers, pimps, and prostitutes, a task that is complicated when she falls in love with a good-hearted, principled young man named Siong-Wei who runs a drinks stall. Ultimately the character of Bugis Street is lost in the name of progress, and Mei-li is left doubting who she is and where she fits in.

Advance press for the work focused largely on the amount of money (S$40,000 to $50,000) being spent on a special effect: a rainfall that was to be used for a brief moment in the play in which Mei-li and Siong-Wei are left alone on stage as it begins to shower. Also described in painstaking detail was the process whereby the play's star transvestite — played by a woman, in an irony unobserved in the press — was to be hanged at a climactic moment. The *Straits Times* account noted that as "Rosie falls, dust will fly, the lights will dim and the haunting strains of Rosie's signature tune, 'Tears for Pay,' will be heard. The audience will observe the panic and pain on Rosie's face as her life slowly expires" (Rasina). When ultimately staged before an audience, Rosie's demise was considerably less dramatic, especially in that during the ensuing rehearsal process the staging was apparently altered so that Rosie's death involved a leap from a balcony into an unseen position behind the stage rather than the more dramatic onstage hanging promised in the advance press. As for the "panic and pain" that was to be evident on Rosie's face, this was indeed difficult to observe, as the actress plunged to her stage death so rapidly that scrutinizing her face for the subtleties of emotion was all but impossible. This production, more than most Singaporean musicals featuring casts of mixed ability, lost more than it gained from Florentino's onstage presence because no one else in the cast, aside from the male-to-female transsexual enacted by Singaporean pop singer Christina Ong, reached her level of skill and professionalism. Cobbled together from the top down, the production of *Bugis Street* had rough seams that were visible to the audience.

Private arts entrepreneurs can hardly be faulted, however, for engaging in this kind of artistic engineering when the government — through the National Arts Council (NAC) — has encouraged the application of this technocratic spirit to the arts. Because of the potential for huge financial rewards and the prestige associated with "making it" on the West End or Broadway, no cultural terrain in Singapore has received more conscious engineering on the part of the government or prominent individuals in the arts community than the Singaporean musical. As the government races to complete the new arts center, artistic teams have come together in a cookie-cutter fashion, with artists carving out their territories and carrying their artistic tasks through to completion much as they might do while working on a committee report. Perhaps no single cultural event in Singapore's history reflects this technocratic spirit at work more fully than the 1997 Singapore Lyric Opera[5] production of the country's first opera in English, *Bunga Mawar*, or "The Rose."

The team responsible for the event included four of the Singapore art world's most established leading lights, all of them Cultural Medallion winners. As noted in chapter 2, this award, given out annually, is bestowed by the NAC upon Singaporean artists in all fields who are deemed to have made significant contributions to the country's cultural life. The award-winning team behind *Bunga Mawar* included its composer, Leong Yoon Pin; the lyricist and book writer Edwin Thumboo, a distinguished poet and academic; and even the conductor[6] and producer[7] of the opera. Only the director, Australian Hugh Halliday, came from outside that elite circle.

As a Singaporean first, the show received considerable advance publicity that, once again, sidestepped questions of artistry and focused largely on the individuals behind the event, as if their stature were sufficient to ensure that the work would be an artistic success. The chair of the opera company, Leow Siak Fah, who also appeared in the production in a principal role, spoke of how a Singaporean opera had long been in the cards: "Very soon after being formed, we decided it would be part of our [company's] agenda" (Seah, "How Idea for an Opera"). The comments of composer Leong build on Leow's suggestion that creating the opera was a no-nonsense, nuts-and-bolts operation: "Where the musical inspiration is concerned it comes in the course of planning and working out the details. . . . As one works on it, inspiration will come" (Television Corporation of Singapore). No doubt Leong's comments were deeply reassuring for the arts funders to hear, as they seem to suggest that for the artist, the process of creation simply requires one to "get on with it."

The statements of the artistic collaborators both before and after the event are fascinating for what they suggest about the process. In the words of lyricist Thumboo, "You mustn't create too many problems for your composer because your composer too has wings. He must soar himself" (Television Corporation of Singapore 1997). According to the *Straits Times*, both Thumboo and Leong "trusted the other to do what he was good at," a point underscored by Thumboo, who asserted, "I didn't have to lean across his musical shoulders and he didn't have to lean over my rhyming ones" (Seah, "How Idea for an Opera"). Thumboo's remarks suggest two artistic egos working largely in isolation and failing to communicate with one another, a point corroborated by the press, which noted that he handed the lyrics over to Leong "in two big chunks." The production-oriented nature of the enterprise was further signaled by the newspaper's observation that it took Thumboo three years to write the whole libretto, "although he admitted that it could have been six months if he had applied himself" (Seah, "How Idea for an Opera"). As with the publicity and packaging of *Bugis Street*, the artistic collaborators for this event are framed as technically proficient, hard-working people who are capable of "delivering the goods" — to use a well-worn Singaporean phrase — in record time. While the *Straits Times* gives the impression that Thumboo could have written equally inspiring lyrics in a pinch if necessary, Leong's postshow comments suggest that writing appropriate music is little different from plotting out the benefits of a new policy decision.

As for the work itself, the opera's plot and thematic concerns could not have been in greater accord with the social policies of the ruling PAP had the work actually been written by government ministers. While the plot would seem to reinscribe the old boy-gets-girl-in-the-end scenario, the work was primarily concerned with attempts to find a balance between the traditional, supposedly family-centered values of old, and the money-driven reality of contemporary Singapore. Set in the present era, the opera focuses on two young lovers from different social backgrounds who wish to marry. While the young man, Andre, comes from a newly moneyed family, Siok Imm, the young woman he falls in love with, is relatively poor, though she hails from a more distinguished and refined Peranakan[8] background. Andre's father, the quintessential no-nonsense self-made man, refuses to grant his consent to the union, as he feels that his son should marry someone of the same economic class. Andre lashes back at his intransigent father, while the softer, less confrontational Siok Imm encourages Andre to reconcile with him, even if it means sacrificing their relationship. Thumboo's lyrics express her belief in the importance of filial piety: "Without his blessing we cannot find happiness, fulfillment."[9] She pleads with Andre to "apologize" to his father, ultimately sending him off with the words, "Much as I love you, for your sake and your family's, please go." As if this point needed to be underscored, she repeats this mantra thrice, lest the message be lost to the audience. Significantly, we later discover that Siok Imm is an honors student in philosophy at the university, a choice of study that is referred to as a "soft option" by many university students in Singapore due to the perception that it represents an easier course of study than others. Siok Imm is shown to embody the best of both old and new values; while she is educated and thoroughly modern in some respects, she also has great respect for her elders and, in spite of her training in philosophy, does not seem to question any fundamental teachings that have been passed on down to her.

Ultimately Andre's father comes to his senses and realizes that he has been overly harsh toward his son, saving the young man from the task of apologizing. In a climactic moment at the end of the first act, the father comes home to a house now devoid of both wife and son, presumably after a hard day's work. While pouring himself a drink of hard liquor—an act that itself denotes economic success in a Singaporean context—he sings, "It's great to be alone, I'm sure." As the reassuring "I'm sure" leads us to expect, his conscience soon interrupts his monologue of self-satisfaction, prompting him to query, "Am I a good man. Am I bad? What sort of husband, what sort of dad?" Organ music intervenes, as does a chorus of heavenly voices, while the father, now visibly alarmed, wonders, "Who are you who speak to me and make me shake from head to toe. I am afraid to speculate, to think or see if it be friend or foe." An apparition of his family appears on the veranda, and as he runs toward them to the strains of spooky organ music, they suddenly vanish. Now transformed, he concludes, "I've been selfish, stubborn, blind. Your voice has restored my inner spirit. The voice was right. I'll make amends." The scene concludes with a happy ditty, punctuated by crashing cymbals. Thus restoration occurs halfway through the piece, setting us up for a second act of equal length in which amends are made and all the rituals of filial piety are played out, seemingly in real time.

The anchor of the work and the living embodiment of traditional values is Siok Imm's grandmother, whose very name—Granny—suggests that she represents far more than a single individual. Dressed in traditional Peranakan attire, Granny rules her family as the proud, strong matriarch, offering advice to her children and all the while projecting warmth and love for her family. Standing beneath a portrait of an old Nyonya[10] ancestor, Granny laments, "Time changes too fast, too much. Life is always on the move," adding, "Many certainties no longer prove of any value to the young." The suggestion seems to be that it may be too late for Granny to change with the times; thus Siok Imm's position as the one who can integrate the old with the new is reinforced.

The musical's "subplot" involves Granny's son, Siok Imm's Uncle Jack, who provides the work's comic relief with his wayward disposition and roving eye for the women. He makes his first appearance in a fashionable striped jacket, sporting a Casanova-like pencil mustache, singing, "I'm happy to be single. See the way I live. Choose with whom to mingle. No need to take and give," adding, somewhat ominously, "You spin and spin and spin around and come at last to a giddy end, and come at last to a giddy end." Like that of Andre's father, the impending fall of Siok Imm's uncle is transparent to the audience from the moment we first see and hear him. Similarly, he too is transformed midway through the work as he realizes that he is "haunted" by the face of Siok Imm's perpetually knitting auntie (shades of Madame LaFarge in *Tale of Two Cities*), with whom he has always been secretly in love. He laments, "Something curious is spinning in me. I find no joy about the town as her face has been beginning to haunt me with smiles and frowns. There's some deep psychology at work for a love I had but never knew that makes me see I'm the jerk, that she's sweet and not the shrew." In the stage production, on the word *shrew* he resolutely put down his ever-present can of Singapore-brewed Anchor beer, as if to further signal his complete transformation from a beer-swilling, chain-smoking, womanizing man-about-town into a loving family man. The program states that "incidentally, if not already a 'goner,' Jack is in serious danger of losing his freedom," adding, somewhat ominously, "But that is another story" (Singapore Lyric Theatre). Thus we are set up for a future opera on the perils of singlehood.

As a piece of social propaganda, the work is amazingly complete and approaches the ideological intensity of the operas created in China during the Cultural Revolution, which were designed to teach the right moral lessons. The costuming and staging of the opera reinforced its moral dimension and underscored the message of acceptance and harmony embedded in the work. At the all-important meeting of the two families in the second act, Andre's father and Granny occupy the two high-backed Chinese-style chairs placed in positions of honor at the center of the stage, while the guests gather to pay their respects to the two icons of old and new Singapore. Andre's father, the hardworking patriarch who has contributed to the economic success of modern Singapore, is attired in a sharp business suit, while Granny is dressed in elaborate and formal traditional Peranakan attire. Reinforced visually is the notion that these two symbols of Singapore have spawned successors such as Siok Imm and Andre, who are capable of integrating the best of both traditions.

The structure of the work, unlike most opera, saves the climax and recon-ciliation not for the end of the work but for fully half of the piece; the entire second act of the opera is taken up with a series of happy, joyous encounters between the two families and their friends, while extras include a few token Indians in nonspeaking roles, as if to make a passing nod in the direction of a multiracial Singapore. Malays are notable by their absence, a factor that may reflect their position in society as economically disadvantaged and thus unlikely to be interested in or involved with a high-culture activity such as opera.

Musically, the work was very much in the tradition of nineteenth-century Western grand opera, with a series of duets and arias punctuated by vast choral numbers. The National Opera and Ballet of China Orchestra, noted for its expertise in the area of Western grand opera, was flown to Singapore to play for the opera's short season. The accessibility of the music was re-marked upon by cast member Nancy Yuen, the Hong Kong soprano who played Siok Imm: "It's not what people have in mind of contemporary music being atonal and funny-sounding and strange. It is basically very romantic music and very easy to listen to" (Seah, "How Idea for an Opera"). Though the *Straits Times* prepared audience members for a work that "drew influ-ences from regions such as China, Malaysia and Indonesia, giving it an Asian flavor" (Seah, "How Idea for an Opera"), this "flavor" was not much in evidence in the completed work. The critic from Singapore's *Business Times* criticized both the lyrics and the music, comparing the musical unfavorably with that of a popular Singaporean television sitcom, asserting that "the li-bretto rehashed every old joke, and due to the largely uninspired score, left us with *Under One Roof*[11] plus a couple of arias" (*Straits Times*, 15 August 1997). By contrast, the *Straits Times* critic praised the opera's libretto for "its deftness of versification, the sentiments often witty and always operatically poetic" (*Straits Times*, 15 August 1997). The opera was ultimately shown on Singaporean television in August 1997, along with four other works that also appeared under the aegis of that year's Festival of Asian Performing Arts, reaching a much wider audience in one evening than it would have during its two-day run at the Victoria Theatre.

Ultimately the legacy of *Bunga Mawar* may be not its rather limited artistic success but instead, as Said has put it, the work's "power to block other nar-ratives from forming" (*Culture and Imperialism* xiii). If, as former NAC chair Tommy Koh enthused on opening night, "this [opera] is a milestone in our musical history" (Television Corporation of Singapore), then opera in Singapore is poised to be a virtually perfect mirror of state-sanctioned discourse. By "banking" on the musical and, to a lesser extent, opera, through corporate and government support and by assembling artistic teams from the top down, Singapore may be setting itself up for artistic self-sabotage, creating works that adhere to a formula but that, quite frankly, lack soul. While lyricist Thumboo argues that "all art forms have the capacity for being indigenized, not so much in terms of structure, but in terms of its theme and contents" (Seah, "How Idea for an Opera"), the rather self-conscious way some Singaporean artists and producers have come together to demonstrate the truth of this proposition may ultimately undermine the stated goal of "indigenization." The case of the Singaporean musical would seem to suggest that art cannot be created simply by putting the right people on the job and using the structure of a Western form to create art.

On the other hand, some of the delightful, locally relevant operas of Dick Lee and Michael Chiang may be too culturally specific for a Western audience to appreciate, unversed as they are with anything other than the thin veneer of Asian culture. Given that most Broadway theatergoers are likely to believe that Singapore is now a part of mainland China after the 1997 "handover," it seems highly unlikely that a farmer from Iowa or a receptionist from Hoboken would appreciate the take on Cantonese melodrama that underlies Lee and Chiang's *Beauty World*. Some artists have asserted that if there is any possibility of communicating across cultures, it can only be achieved through an honest, thorough examination of that which is culturally *very, very* particular. However, it may be that these specifics communicate only if they have *some* cultural resonance for your audience. Thus, the wait for the "Great Singaporean Musical" to appear on the "Great White Way" may be a long one, as the conditions affecting both the creation of the musical in Singapore and its reception in the West may well represent the limitations of cultural expression in the age of global capitalism.

The 1996 Australasian tour of producer Michael Edgley's $4 million *Aida* received considerable attention throughout the region.[1] Boasting a cast of over one thousand, the Singapore production featured animals from the Singapore Zoo; a 200-ton, 65-by-45-meter set; and a huge central pyramid that nearly grazed the ceiling of the cavernous Singapore Indoor Stadium. According to Singapore's *Straits Times*, producer Edgley chose to begin the international tour in Singapore because "with its Global City of the Arts initiative, [it] is determined to be a pivotal arts capital." Echoing the rhetoric of Singapore's arts administrators, who are anything if not determined, he added, "No other city in my experience has such a powerful will to success in its pursuit of excellence" (Koh Boon Pin, "Pyramids"). The press held up the size and scale of the production as proof of Singapore's cultural greatness, while Edgley's glowing comments about the arts infrastructure provided confirmation that the country's arts policies were on the right track.

The choice of *Aida* is in itself significant, as this opera more than any other could be said to constitute the archetypal high-culture "Instant Asia" show. In *Culture and Imperialism*, Edward Said singles out *Aida* as one of the monumental works of Western culture that effectively "otherizes" Asia as the exotic East. He observes, "As a visual, musical, and theatrical spectacle, *Aida* does a great many things for and in European culture, one of which is to confirm the Orient as an essentially exotic, distant, and antique place in which Europeans can mount certain shows of force" (*Culture and Imperialism* 112). Indeed, given its cavalcade of soldiers, prisoners, guards, jugglers, dancers, court attendants, and priests, the key protagonists of *Aida*—the enslaved Ethiopian princess and the commander of the conquering Egyptian army—are almost lost in the visual splendor and human vastness of the work. Said argues that even though the story is set in North Africa, *Aida* has historically represented a kind of generic Orient to the Western audience: the pageantry and exoticism that characterizes this fictitious Orient reflects a vision of the East as a place of mystery and strangeness that is also present in many of the "masterpieces" of Western high culture. Thus *Aida* could be seen as yet another work that contributed to the Western view of Asia as a kind of monolithic Other, a sticking place for all that is exciting, different, sensuous, exotic, and—though unknowable—ultimately yielding and conquerable.

Certainly Singaporeans have every right to patronize an expensive[2] high-culture event such as *Aida*, just as Western operagoers do. The case of *Aida* is raised as an illustration on a grand scale of how a Western culturally generated view of Asia as a place of mysticism and exoticism can meet with an enthusiastic reception in an Asian country. Of course, the view of Asia offered in *Aida* is not one of a specific country or even of any of the three largest cultures that constitute contemporary Singapore (Chinese, Malay, Indian); instead the opera materializes a fictional, imaginative realm that reflects Western mythologizing about the idea of the Orient rather than the reality of any actual place. Thus the "cultured," educated, English-speaking Singaporean operagoers watching *Aida* share with their Western counterparts a willingness to enter into this fiction of a generic Orient.

To some extent, for the Singaporean theater practitioner working in English, social, political, and economic forces have all collectively contributed to an internalization of this Western gaze of a monolithic East, complicating and even derailing existing models of interculturalism. While many models of intercultural theater practice have been proposed, perhaps the broadest and most useful definition at this stage is the one proposed in 1996 by Patrice Pavis: "In the strictest sense, this [intercultural theater] creates hybrid forms drawing upon more or less conscious and voluntary mixing of performance traditions traceable to distinct cultural areas" (8). In Singapore's case, the concepts of "host" and "target" culture in an intercultural exchange, which Pavis proposed in the early 1990s,[3] can be radically undermined, notably when the Asian source culture is partially or largely derived from a view that others (e.g., Westerners) have of Asia. No theater company in Singapore better illustrates this complex subversion of the intercultural model than the ten-year-old company Asia in Theatre Research Centre.[4] Company founder William Teo has modeled his group quite consciously upon the intercultural work of Ariane Mnouchkine's Théâtre du Soleil and Peter Brook's Paris-based International Center for Theatre Research. The ways in which Teo's company have absorbed the Asian-influenced aesthetic of these two significant Western theater practitioners provides a vivid illustration of cultural studies critic Rey Chow's observation that "what confronts the Western scholar is the discomforting fact that the natives are no longer staying in their frames" (*Writing Diaspora* 28).

Teo's observations on the origin of his company suggest a spiritual affinity with the work of Jerzy Grotowski: "I wanted a study group. . . . We wanted to answer some big questions, like: What is theatre, and why must we have theatre?" (Tsang, "If It's a Good Piece of Art"). Similarly, his choice of dramatic material reflects a preference for works that cross cultural boundaries. He selects a play because "it is something that touches or moves me. I don't have a favorite style. Just a story to tell" (Ibid.). Among the works presented by the company are a range of Western and Asian canonical texts, including *Medea*, *Macbeth*, Brecht's *Mother Courage*, Lorca's *House of Bernada Alba*, an adaptation of the Yüan dynasty classic *Chang Boils the Sea*, Herman Hesse's *Siddhartha*, and *The Conference of the Birds*, a play based on the ancient Persian poem that was initially staged by Peter Brook.

By choosing to call itself Asia in Theatre Research, the group signals its intention to focus on the task of uncovering the "Asia" inherent in the category of "theater," a quest that has preoccupied many avant-garde Western theater artists throughout the century. The inclusion of the word *research* in the group's name reflects their commitment to in-depth and experiential research, which has taken company members to other Asian countries. "Theatre research" also brought members of the group to Paris, where they visited Peter Brook's company at the cavernous Bouffes du Nord and Mnouchkine's company at the Cartoucherie, an abandoned factory on the outskirts of Paris.

Over the last two decades, Mnouchkine's Théâtre du Soleil has developed a reputation for staging the works of Shakespeare using a range of Asian theatrical conventions and forms; they relied on Kabuki and Noh theater in their productions of *Richard II* and *Henry IV, Pt. I*, while employing the Indian traditions of Sanskrit drama and Kathakali in their version of *Twelfth Night*. Mnouchkine's productions of Shakespeare place his plays in a mythic dimension, a world where stylized gesture and ritual replaces psychologically motivated acting. In her discussion of the group's work with *Richard III*, Mnouchkine observes: "We wanted to make Asian theatre a voyage of research, simply because Western theatre offers little in this way, and because realism has started to bore me" (96). According to Mnouchkine, this "research" component is a search for fundamentals: "As far as I am concerned, the origin of theatre and my source is Asia. The West has led us towards realism, and Shakespeare is not realist. For actors who want to be explorers, the Asian tradition can be a base to work from. In Asia, the theatre seems to have stopped today, but traditions which die can give life to something elsewhere" (96). Adrian Kiernander observes that Mnouchkine traveled through Japan and Indonesia before the founding of the Théâtre du Soleil in 1964 (94), a trip that Mnouchkine remembers as "a bit hippie style" (95). Thus Mnouchkine's observations about Asian theater would appear to stem largely from her experience as a young backpacker traveling through a few Asian countries four decades ago. That her impressions were formed so long ago may explain her surprising ignorance of the incredible richness and diversity of performance in Asia today. Indeed, for Mnouchkine to assert that theater in Asia has "stopped" is not only culturally arrogant; it also suggests that she is ill-informed.

Perhaps the most striking feature of Mnouchkine's Orientalist discourse, however, is her tendency to make sweeping statements that are expressed as if they are true of Asian culture in its many manifestations from India to Japan. Mnouchkine elaborates on Antonin Artaud's[5] dictum "The theatre is Oriental" (Mnouchkine 95), observing, "I know what he meant. From Asia comes what is specific to theatre, which is the perpetual metaphor which the actors produce—when they are capable of producing it. That is what we do: try to understand the metaphors that an actor can make use of" (97). Like Artaud, Mnouchkine uses rhetoric which suggests that Asian theater is somehow closer to the source of a kind of prelinguistic knowledge, unfettered by the dead end of Western realism, thus providing Western actors with a new base from which to work. She adds, "I found in Asia such beauty in things, in gestures, a simple ceremonial quality which seems to be indispensable in the theatre. In Asia there is a perpetual formalization of every action" (97). As Rustom Bharucha has argued, interculturalism in this instance might be viewed as having been "born out of a certain ennui, a reaction to aridity and the subsequent search for new sources of energy, vitality and sensuality through the importation of 'rejuvenating raw materials'" ("A

View from India" 207). What Mnouchkine seems unconcerned with is the context from which the cultural borrowings of Noh, Kabuki, and Kathakali derive their meanings, a vexing point for a critic such as Bharucha, who has written extensively of "how non-western cultures have been encapsulated into the alluring Other of the Orient" ("Somebody's Other" 206). In such instances, context is rendered unimportant as the "raw materials" of the East are reworked by the creative geniuses of the West.[6]

Similarly, Teo's other source of inspiration, Peter Brook, has come under fire for ignoring the Indian cultural context in his production of the epic poem *The Mahabharata*. Brook's staging of the "poetical of mankind," which toured to six countries in 1987–88, was acclaimed by many Western critics but viewed more circumspectly by Indian critics such as Rustom Bharucha, who argued, "If Brook truly believes that The Epic is universal, then his representation should not exclude or trivialize Indian culture, as I believe it does. One cannot agree with the premise that '*The Mahabharata* is Indian but it is universal.' The 'but' is misleading. *The Mahabharata*, I would counter, is universal *because* it is Indian. One cannot separate the culture from the text" ("A View from India" 231).[7] Bharucha argues that Brook's reduction of a complex, multilayered religious and philosophical epic into a tight, narrative-driven story accessible to Western audiences results in a *Mahabharata* that has little to do with India, thus undermining the supposed universality inherent in the work.

Given the fierce criticism leveled against Mnouchkine and Brook for appropriating random aspects of Asian culture, it is noteworthy that an Asian group would hold the work of these practitioners in such high regard. The connection between Teo's group and the theater practices of Brook and Mnouchkine was furthered in 1992 when Georges Bigot, one of the leading actors from Mnouchkine's Théâtre du Soleil, conducted a month-long, hundred-hour workshop with company actors in preparation for their 1993 production of *Macbeth*. Bigot, known for his portrayal of Prince Norodom Sihanouk in *The Terrible but Unfinished History of Norodom Sihanouk, King of Cambodia*, and his Richard II, came to Singapore courtesy of the French government. This cultural connection was underscored by an introductory message in the program from the French embassy's cultural counselor, which cited Bigot's visit as an example of France's support for the arts in Singapore and added, "Rest assured that this will certainly not be the last time that leading French dramatic and performing personalities will be brought in to assist in the promotion of the arts in Singapore" (Asia in Theatre). The phrase "promotion of the arts" is revealing, as it suggests that the project was not about creation so much as it was about selling a cultural image.

Bigot makes his subject position abundantly clear in an extended statement that was also printed in the program: "My inspiration comes from here, from the east." He laments the lack of interest in Asian traditions that he finds "here"—meaning here in the "East"—and observes, "We learnt the art of theatre from here, whereas they [i.e., Asians] take inspiration from the caricature of Western theatre, mimicking the psychology and the realism" (Asia in Theatre). Bigot's comments reflect the continuing tendency on the part of many Western theater practitioners going back to Artaud to see all of Asia as a single entity that constitutes a monolithic Other. Given the Théâtre du Soleil's history of merely quoting the visual referents of the Asian forms they have borrowed, one wonders what he means when he suggests that "we"—meaning avant-garde Western practitioners like himself—"learnt the art of theatre *here*." While his comments might lead one to believe that he had in fact apprenticed with Asian theater practitioners "here" in Asia, he means nothing of the sort. The Théâtre du Soleil learned the Asian art of theater largely at home, in the Cartoucherie on the outskirts of Paris, and not in situ from masters of any of the vast array of Asian performance forms.

His dismissal of acting "here" in Asia as "mimicking the psychology and the realism" of Western theater is equally perplexing; where, specifically, is the "Asia" of which he speaks? Is he talking about acting in Mandarin-language historical soap operas on Singaporean television? Acting in Thai *likay* performances? Or acting in a Chinese-language version of *Death of a Salesman* staged in Shanghai? That Bigot fails to understand that Asian versions of stage realism may constitute something other than "caricature" or "mimicry" is significant, as it reflects an unwillingness to look at what this Western form might mean when applied to another cultural context with performance traditions and styles of acting that differ from those of the West. Furthermore, what he may perceive as clumsy attempts at expressing "realism" and "psychology" might be read completely differently by a rice farmer in West Sumatra, an English-educated Singaporean, or a noodle seller in Hong Kong. In his condemnation of Western acting, Bigot also contributes to the recurring trope that the theatrical avant-garde in the West has been repeating for about one hundred years now: namely, the insistence that realism is killing the theater, when in fact a great deal of performance in the West throughout the twentieth century involved radical departures from classic realism. Reactions against realism began the moment the form took hold i the West, and they haven't stopped coming—at least not yet.

Bigot concludes this section of his narrative by declaring, "I'm trying t(bring back some of what I've learnt here," and he adds, "You have riches here, you have a sense of theatre" (Asia in Theatre). Like Artaud, whose life was changed after witnessing a Balinese cultural show at the 1931 Exposition Coloniale in Paris, Bigot seems besotted by the exoticism of the East. What distinguishes him from Artaud, however, is that he is not content merely to use a very particular Asian performance tradition as a source of inspiration, but that he is willing and able to claim to be returning the "riches" of the East to their home. Putting aside the amazing cultural imperialism implicit in such a claim, the ultimately irony may well be that Singapore is perhaps the most highly manufactured place in all of Asia; creatively engineered by the English as a center for shipping operations in Southeast Asia, Singapore everywhere bears the imprint and the legacy of a city-state that was created for the benefit of its colonial masters. In virtually no sense at all did traditional Asian forms actually originate in Singapore; they merely ended up there. Thus Bigot's declaration that he is "bringing back" what he has learnt "here" makes little sense literally; instead his comment reflects a remarkable ability to conflate all of the East as a site of wisdom and knowledge.

Given the "Instant Asia" feel that Singapore aggressively markets overseas to potential Western tourists, it is perhaps not surprising that a Westerner might believe himself capable of guiding Singaporeans back to their Asian roots. The comments of actors who participated in the workshop further reinforce Bigot's position as Asian theater guru. One actor, who characterizes Bigot as a "theatre genius," writes that "various research [sic], with Chinese opera actors for example, has helped the troupe assemble ideas, simultaneously giving our work an Asian allure" (Asia in Theatre). While it should be noted that the actor who made these remarks was Caucasian, her uncritical acceptance of the language of exoticism and consumerism is quite telling. Chinese opera, a category of performance that includes a wide range of cultural expressions in a huge range of dialects, is seemingly reduced to a commodity that can provide a work of Western dramatic literature with a kind of "Asian allure." Thus Asia has been made alluring to an Asian audience, an audience that sees the Asian part of its own identity as having a kind of "otherness." In this case, the Other would appear to have "otherized" itself.

All of the extended commentaries contained in the program for the event were in fact written by Caucasian actors, further distancing Asian Singapore-ans from the process. Expatriate American actor Christina Sergeant's obser-vations on the workshop describe how Bigot taught them to create their char-acters externally, by encouraging them to put to creative use "a rack full of oversized, body disguising costumes and make-up laid out in front of lighted mirrors" (Asia in Theatre). She recalls how he would occasionally admonish them for not being "well dressed" when they devised costumes that were not both aesthetic *and* practical and notes that he would "rechannel" their "desire to get weird and wacky with white face and black eyeliner" by encouraging them to "[use] the make-up simply and economically to better project our characters." Bigot apparently also ingrained in them what he termed "the lit-tle laws of theatre," which in Sergeant's commentary are reduced to apho-risms such as "Listen to the other characters on stage," "Move, then talk," and "Play in the present" (Asia in Theatre). Oddly enough, the first and last of these "little laws" sound more like American method-acting mantras than guides to "avant-garde" acting.

Bigot's comments, as well as the statements made in the program by the actors themselves, place the French actor in the role of theatrical guru. In the early 1990s, it was not unusual for theatrical guru status to be claimed by a Singaporean artist who had taken a short workshop with a Western "mas-ter" and returned home to impart undigested bits and pieces of the master guru's technique to students who were equally hungry for new approaches to theater but equally short on time. More commonly, however, this pattern still prevails in the West, where it is often Asian forms that are the focus of these abbreviated workshops. Pavis speaks of the problems associated with gurus and the market value attached to an association with a particular theater artist or approach: "So each individual, and sometimes each micro-group, has at its disposal a series of (de)formative experiences, patiently acquired from the relevant masters; the sum of these, often mannered and exotic, be-comes their calling card. Moreover such acquisition sometimes degenerates into an exchange of cultural stereotypes, for metatheatrical amusement" (*Intercultural Performance Reader* 15). In Bigot's case, a Western guru would appear to have played his exotic Asian "calling card" before an Asian group, thus ultimately succeeding in exoticizing Asia for Asians.

An account of the rehearsal process for *Macbeth*, also contained in the pro-gram, makes it very clear that the production "was to be in the same style as that of Georges and the Théâtre du Soleil—facing front, for the audience, realistic but not naturalistic." That the term *realistic* was used to characterize the style of the production seems a bit at odds with Bigot's earlier disparagement of both psychology and realism. Nevertheless, there can be no doubt that the production very much reflected the working methods and visual style of the Théâtre du Soleil. A lengthy rehearsal process of six months preceded the final staging of the work, during which time all actors had the opportunity to play any part they wished. Final casting occurred only halfway through the rehearsal process. As with the Théâtre du Soleil, gestural patterns that reflected a fundamental emotional core for the character were developed during rehearsal and integrated into the action of the play; these gestural patterns, though all within the realm of ordinary human movement, were often pressed beyond the limits of realistic acting. In addition, actors went on outings to Chinese opera and *wayang kulit* performances and to a farm where they witnessed the ritual slaughter of chickens for dinner, to "get a taste of killing" (Asia in Theatre).[8]

While most of the group remained in Singapore rehearsing, Teo and a few company members went to India in search of "props and inspiration" (Asia in Theatre). Given that Indians constitute Singapore's third largest ethnic group and that the city's "Little India" is one of the most culturally vibrant neighborhoods on the island, one might imagine that an overseas venture to India would have been superfluous. Perhaps because Singapore's Indian community is largely South Indian and Tamil-speaking, they were bypassed in favor of the culture of India's northern regions. The account of the group's "passage to India" (entitled, interestingly enough, "Passage Through India") reads a bit like the travelogue of a Western backpacker in search of enlightenment. It begins, "We built our journey around the full moon in November," and proceeds to describe a number of encounters with a range of spiritual practices, including the annual Pushkar fair, a pilgrimage that brings hundreds of thousands of Hindu pilgrims to a sacred lake near the city of Jaipur (Asia in Theatre). Another site the group visited was an ashram outside of Agra that was started by the founder of the Krisha consciousness movement, as well as the North Indian city of Dharamsala, the home of the Dalai Lama and a world center for Tibetan Buddhism. Nowhere in the account of the group's pilgrimage to these holy sites is there any indication of the ways in which their experiences had an impact on the production they went there to research. Indeed, there was very little that was identifiably Indian in the final production of the play, apart from a generic overlay of Indianness in some of the costuming and makeup worn by the performers. As with the Théâtre du Soleil, the fullness of the costumes and some of the fabrics used suggested India, but they did not reproduce or engage with any one tradition within the culture.

The venue in which *Macbeth* was staged bears some similarities to Mnouchkine's Cartoucherie, a former munitions factory that the group initially occupied by squatting. Illegal occupation was not required to obtain a similar venue in Singapore, however. In 1992, with the help of Singapore's National Arts Council and the Urban Redevelopment Association (URA), Teo's group moved into an unoccupied warehouse on the banks of the Singapore River on Merbau Road. The first production in that space was the Brook-inspired work *Conference of the Birds*. Like Mnouchkine's Cartoucherie, the warehouse remained fundamentally a found space, complete with rough-hewn walls, moss, and bare floors. For the group's production of *Macbeth*, approximately half of the space was used as a public area and green room in which the actors and performers were free to mix before and after the show, while the other half was given over to the auditorium and stage. In the context of Singapore, where most theaters for English-language plays are air-conditioned and absolutely modern, Teo's choice of a warehouse space was quite unconventional indeed.

Teo's commitment to using "new, raw actors, not necessarily the best ones," resulted in a production with a diverse cast, many of whom lacked significant stage experience (Asia in Theatre). The cast was also quite international, prompting some critics to complain that the range of accents in the show was bewildering; the country's best-known theater critic at the time, Hannah Pandian, found the "Scottish" accent of the young actor playing Banquo quite incomprehensible, an observation that many in the theater community found amusing, given that the actor playing the role, Jean-Marc Favre, speaks with a very heavy French accent, both on- and offstage. Those who followed the reception that Brook's *Mahabharata* received will recall that the range of Englishes spoken in his production was also a source of contention. Because Teo is less concerned with classical oration than the physicality and visual dimension of the work, the final production was fast-paced and highly physical, full of regimented, stylized gestures and movement patterns, presentational and visually striking. The elaborate costuming and vaguely Kabuki-style makeup provided a sharp contrast with the roughness of the physical environment for the play, while the proximity of the actors to the audience—and the spectators to one another—coupled with the heat and relatively primitive conditions inside the theater contributed to a sense of heightened emotion and tension. In short, those who saw this *Macbeth* are not likely to easily forget it. As with Peter Brook's *Mahabharata*, many clearly found it thrilling theater in spite of the many problems associated with the nature of the intercultural exchange. Negative criticism of the show seemed to center largely around the way in which language was used by the cast members; because some had no acting experience, and only a few had any prior experience dealing with classical language, it is hardly surprising that lovers of verse found the production somewhat lacking.

For his part, Teo would probably not care about such criticism. Indeed, for him the process is all-important. One of his former students recalls how Teo repeatedly made the point in rehearsal that "the performance is the dessert. It is not essential" (Smith). Like the Théâtre du Soleil, Teo's group has had the luxury of a long rehearsal process; unlike Mnouchkine's company, however, no one in the group—including Teo—makes a full-time living as a theater artist. In fact, Teo's source of income derives largely from his popular hair salon on fashionable Orchard Road, at the very center of Singapore's consumer empire. It should be noted that Teo once lived in Paris, and it was there that he developed a taste for the work of the Théâtre du Soleil. Like Mnouchkine and Bigot, he states of his group that "our ideas and our point of departure comes from the ancient traditions found in Asia" (Asia in Theatre). While Teo's staging of *Macbeth* was exciting, visually stimulating theater, to some extent wrapping Shakespeare's text in an overlay of ancient generic "Asianness" absolves the creators of the work from having to ask fundamental questions about the play's content and its potential relevance for contemporary Singaporean audiences. For all of the extensive program notes about process, nowhere in the program did anyone ask, much less answer, the "why" questions that would seem to be at the core of any kind of dramaturgical practice: "Why this play?" "Why here in Singapore?" "Why stage it now?" To ignore these questions suggests that a search for pan-Asian truths in theater has the potential to take one farther and farther away from contemporary social and political realities.

As for the interculturalism of the production, the end result, while certainly attractive to the eye, comes closer to what Pavis terms "cultural collage" than to intercultural theater. Productions that consciously or unconsciously follow such a model "do not pretend to understand a civilization, and they choose their forms and techniques without regard for their ethnological function in their home cultures" (Pavis, *Intercultural Performance Reader* 9). Taking this distinction a step farther, Christopher Balme puts forth a model of theatrical exoticism that he applies to Western appropriations of Asian

ıltures, though it also seems relevant in this context: "Exoticism involves
e use of indigenous cultural texts purely for their surface appeal, but
with no regard to their original cultural semantics. They mean little else
than their alterity; they are no longer texts in the semiotic sense, but merely
signs, floating signifiers of otherness" (5). Indeed, while the entire production seemed vaguely Other in a sort of Asian way, it failed to connect on any
level with the actual source of any of those borrowings. As with Mnouchkine
and Brook's work, the "source" cultures are merely grist for the artistic mill.
One of the problems with such work is that though cultural theorists desper-
ately want to discount it for its lack of cultural integrity, most theatergoers in
wealthy countries are deeply drawn to this eclectic visual and performance
style, perhaps because it is consistent with the channel-surfing world of constantly and endlessly changing visual stimuli in which they live.

By the end of the 1990s, however, the Singaporean company known internationally for its aggressively intercultural work was not Asia in Theatre
Research but rather TheatreWorks, primarily due to two large-scale international collaborations directed by Ong Keng Sen, *Lear* (1997) and *Desdemona* (1999). Of the two, thus far *Lear* has the most significant track record
in terms of the sheer number of productions, having toured extensively to
festivals in Asia, Australia, and Europe. Given the ambitious scale of the
work, the originating force behind the production was of necessity money;
over S\$2 million was initially provided by the Japan Foundation (Oon, "A
Cheaper Lear"). Faced with the mandate to "bring to Japanese audiences new
Asian plays that transcend national styles and forms," Yuki Hara, an arts administrator with the foundation, decided to pair Ong with Japanese feminist
playwright Rio Kishida to create "a new Asian drama based on a Shake-
spearean play that could be universal in outlook" (Kwan). As we shall see, the
writer's use of the word *universal* is not unthinking, especially inasmuch as
this *Lear* was positioned very much as a reflection of a pan-Asian vision.

Based loosely on Shakespeare's *King Lear*, the production brought together
twenty-five performers from six Asian countries for an extensive rehearsal
period that resulted in a work that contained a number of distinct Asian performance traditions, while also layering on elements of contemporary staging and electronic music. Unlike much intercultural work, where the source
traditions are significantly altered in the process of creating the work, Ong
made the decision to rely principally on artists who were masters of forms
that ranged from Beijing Opera and Japanese Noh to Indonesian Pencak
Silat, a performance/martial arts form, and to have them perform intact

Produced by the Japan Foundation Asian Center, Lear toured internationally from 1997 to 1999 with Noh actor Naohiko Umewaka (left) in the title role and Beijing Opera star Jiang Qi Hu (pictured) as the eldest sister. The production brought together TheatreWorks's director, Ong Keng Sen, and Japanese feminist playwright Rio Kishida. Production designer: Justin Hill. Photo by Herick Lau.

within each of those traditions. Thus Beijing opera star Jiang Qi Hu, playing the role of the eldest sister, sang to her father, Noh actor Naohiko Umewaka, in the highly inflected Mandarin of her tradition, while Umewaka responded in Japanese using the characteristic vocal utterances of a Noh actor. Throughout the duration of the play, the actors preserved the integrity of their respective performance forms, using the appropriate gestural and movement patterns as well as the language appropriate to the form, resulting in a linguistic mix that included Japanese, Chinese, English, Thai, Malay, and Bahasa Indonesian. While in the abstract, the idea of creating a coherent work using actors from such diverse traditions would seem to be an impossible task, one of the successes of the production was the creation of a purposeful sense of overall unity, for which significant credit must be given to Ong, now widely considered one of Asia's leading theater directors on the world stage.

A Singaporean newspaper account that trumpeted the success of the venture with the headline "Ong's Lear Takes Tokyo by Storm" also contained

TheatreWorks's artistic director, Ong Keng Sen, is the country's best-known director internationally, in large measure due to his intercultural productions Lear *(1997–99) and* Desdemona *(2000) and his successful staging of Chay Yew's* A Language of Their Own *at the New York Public Theatre (1995). Photo courtesy of TheatreWorks.*

the more ambivalent comments of Yuji Odajima, regarded as one of Japan's leading theater critics. Odajima raises some interesting issues with regard to TheatreWorks's *Lear* that can be applied to other works where attempts are made to retain the integrity of each individual performance form: "We have a symphony where everyone is working together. I would have liked to see a violin concerto instead. Since there were so many theatrical styles and languages on stage, I had expected more tension, more chaos. In that sense, I cannot call the performance a huge success. But it is certainly a very successful step toward more of this kind of theatre" (Kwan). If "intercultural" implies a kind of reciprocity between elements and some kind of synthesis in the final artistic product, then TheatreWorks's recent production of *Lear* falls outside that category and lies instead in the realm of the "cross-cultural," where the cultural currents are placed together in the same stream but each element retains its distinct identity. Throughout the extended press accounts of a work that constitutes Singapore's most singularly ambitious work to date to cross cultural divides, the "why" question was again nowhere in evidence. Apart from the fact that one is *able* to create such theater, what is the *point* of creating it? Even Odajima's comments about the show representing a "very successful step toward more of this kind of theatre" do not question the value or use of the exercise. One of the problems with basing a theater practice largely on cross-cultural borrowings, or, in Teo's case, on the search for sources, roots, or authenticity, is that the finished work can easily become so detached from its home culture that it never fundamentally engages with the world as lived in and experienced by those who form the audience for the work.

For his part, Ong, in an interview broadcast on Japanese television, argued that this way of working provides a model for "negotiating between cultures," adding that "the production is not exotic. It is not an Orientalist production. I think that the production is very much an honest reflection of Asia by Asians. . . . It's quite an honest depiction of our feelings about being Asians" (Nippon Hoso Kyokai). While the range of Asian cultures represented in the project would seem to support this argument, it is noteworthy that Ong's vision of an Asia that retains cultural difference is a very Singaporean one, especially inasmuch as his government continues to work very aggressively to promote an image of itself as the epitome of the "new Asia" both at home and abroad, as noted in chapter 7. Ien Ang and Jon Stratton set out the cultural territory quite succinctly:

> Singapore is presented as the representative *par excellence* of this "new
> Asia," precisely because it harbors within its borders three ancient Asian
> civilizations, museumized, memorialized and memorized for their con-
> tributions to human greatness independent of European civilization. It
> is in this way that the Singaporean state mobilizes the figure of the "new
> Asian" to legitimize and strengthen its cultural nationalist agenda: a
> new, modern "Asianness" is promoted through the construction of the
> "West" as Other, and which, in its self-Orientalizing, Occidentalist oppo-
> sition to Westernness, mirrors the West's persistent neo-Orientalist
> othering of modern Asia. (190)

As *Lear* is the ultimate artistic expression of the state-supported project of the "new Asia," it is perhaps not surprising that the play became Singapore's major cultural export at the end of the millennium, proposing, as it does, a way of packaging Asian cultures that preserves its fundamental Asianness by recognizing cultural boundaries instead of constantly attempting to bridge them. However, what is distinctly Asian that cuts through the individual cultural expressions in the work is less clear, in spite of Ong's program notes, which suggest that the older daughter, trapped by an oppressive patriarchy, serves a "symbolic representation of new Asia" (Oon, "A Cheaper Lear"). Given that the older daughter is responsible for the murders of her sister, her lover, her father, and her father's loyal attendant, a host of problems arise, not the least of which is that the bloodthirsty daughter, though forgiven at the end by an ur-mother figure, is closer to the stereotype of the evil Empress Woo than to an image of an empowered, self-actualized new Asia. And finally, there also remains the thorny problem of gender: by being marked as female, this vision of the new Asia embodied by the elder sister plays into all of the old Orientalist stereotypes that mark the "East" as feminine.

Indeed, intercultural and cross-cultural work does not necessarily impart insights into cultures that are any more deep and meaningful than those offered by yet another reprise of the gargantuan grand opera *Aida*. In spite of the "authentic" pedigree of the cultural assemblages in some inter- and cross-cultural work, it is not merely their placement on stage but, rather, the context and politics of their embodiment that give them life in a new cultural context. Without context, the offerings are merely there for public consumption by the rich in the world's richest nations. David Savran's comments about the implications of the consumption model in American theater can also be applied to Singapore, or, for that matter, any wealthy, capitalist nation: "For the liberal pluralist, America is less a melting pot than a smorgasbord. He or she takes pride in the ability to *consume* cultural difference—now understood as a commodity, a source of boundless pleasure, an expression of an exoticized Other. And yet, for him or her, access to and participation in so-called minority cultures is entirely consumerist" (220). As inter-/multi-/cross-culturalism becomes increasingly the basis for theater practice throughout the developed world both East and West, it is important to question the ultimate value of this practice and ask who ultimately is served by it. Consumers in rich countries such as Singapore, Japan, Australia, Canada, the United States, and the European nations are increasingly offered a continuous buffet of cultural salads that rearrange and reconstitute cultures both foreign and domestic, "authentic" and syncretic, while they remain no closer to actual engagement with the big, bad Other—even when the Other may be themselves.

The news story that brought Singapore the greatest international attention during the 1990s was not the economic downturn at the end of the decade and Singapore's rapid recovery, or the PAP government's continuing and dogged pursuit of political foes, but, rather, the caning of an American teenager's bare buttocks by the Singaporean government. In 1994, Michael Fay, a senior at Singapore's American School, was convicted of spray-painting eighteen cars and of possessing stolen property that consisted largely of road signs. For this offense, he ultimately served four months in prison and received four strokes from a rattan cane. Though Fay carried out the illegal acts with fellow classmates — some of whom were also convicted — he alone received the lion's share of the press both at home and abroad and remained at the center of the controversy. The incident itself, Fay's punishment and the range of responses it generated, as well as the single play that touches on the event — *Six of the Best* — bring together virtually all of the key strands in this book, including the debate over values as well as issues of ethnicity, culture, and national identity.

From the Singapore government's point of view, the case of Michael Fay became the ultimate litmus test in the defense of so-called Asian values, as they asserted that Singapore had every right to draw up its own laws and enforce them. For Americans or any group of foreigners to critique Singapore's laws, they argued, constituted an arrogant imposition of "Western values" on an Asian nation. The law in question that enabled the government to administer the cane on Fay's backside dates back to the 1960s and was originally implemented to discourage anti-PAP political graffiti. Under the terms of the law, caning is mandated in situations where an "indelible substance" is used on someone's property (Wallace, "Ohio Youth to Be Flogged"), and though young people had in fact been caned for vandalism in the past, they had not been caned for spray-painting automobiles or private property. Rumor had it that Fay had made the mistake of spray-painting an automobile belonging to a prominent government official; in Tan Tarn How's play that touches on the subject, the suggestion is made that Fay had spray-painted a late-model Mercedes belonging to the permanent secretary for home affairs (TheatreWorks, video of *Six of the Best*).

Newspapers outside of Singapore were quick to report that "caning" is really a euphemism for flogging, as the moistened rattan cane that pierces the flesh of the victims leaves permanent scars on their buttocks. Press accounts in the West also noted that the punishment is administered by a specialist in the technique and that the flogging not only results in loss of blood but it is often so painful that the victim is rendered unconscious by the blows of the cane. The *Los Angeles Times* printed a photograph credited to Singapore's *New Paper* that showed such an "expert" flogging the raised behind of a dummy strapped to a frame (Wallace, "Singapore"), providing a graphic image of the punishment for the benefit of American readers. Yet even as much of the U.S. press rushed to condemn the punishment as "barbaric," other Americans went on record supporting Singapore's harsh penalties; some even argued that similar laws should be adopted in the United States in order to discourage juvenile delinquency.

While the relative severity of the sentence concerned many, two of the most influential and outspoken American newspapers, the *New York Times* and the *Los Angeles Times*, raised additional concerns relating to the rule of law in Singapore. Philip Shenon of the *New York Times* argued that Fay's "confession" was obtained only after Fay was subjected to physical and mental torture at the hands of Singapore's police. Among the techniques employed was the ubiquitous "air-con room," an ice-cold interrogation room in which the subject is held until he confesses. According to Fay, his police interrogators told him, "We will beat you and put you into the air-con room" (Shenon). Fay's description of the use of the "air-con room" bears striking similarities to some of the previously cited accounts of this ominous procedure: "You strip down to your underwear, take a freezing cold shower, go into a small air-con room . . . and the police investigators whip you with this stick which looks broken" (Shenon). According to Francis Seow, the former solicitor general of Singapore who is now a prominent dissident,[1] the air-con room is "so cold that even the interrogators cannot stand it, and they often have to leave the room, leaving you inside." Seow asserted that he was held repeatedly in the room during his seventy-two-day detention in 1988 and that it left him with "cold rashes" across his body (Seow 143).[2] It seems unlikely that an American teenager would be capable of fabricating such a similar story unless it had some basis in reality.

For many, the real issue became not Singapore's right to enforce its own laws but, rather, the rule of law in Singapore. Further articles in American newspapers pointed out that individuals suspected of criminal activity could be held indefinitely by the Singaporean police and that the accused has no right to silence when being interrogated by the police. Lee Kuan Yew himself provided the justification for these extraordinary legal measures over thirty years ago: "When a state of increasing disorder and defiance of authority cannot be checked by the rules then existing, new and sometimes drastic rules have to be forged to maintain order so that the law can continue to govern human relations. The alternative is to surrender order to chaos and anarchy" (Wallace, "Singapore"). Lee's argument, which may have had application to Singapore in the late 1950s and early 1960s, when the country was rife with gangs, plagued by domestic disturbances, and facing an increasingly dangerous regional situation, would appear largely irrelevant in a country as law-abiding and tranquil as Singapore has been for the last three decades. Critics of Singapore's justice system have argued that the country's draconian laws are less important for the maintenance of domestic harmony than they are for stifling dissent.

Countering the argument that strict sentences necessarily serve as a deterrent for crime, Stan Sesser argued in the New York Times that "if the Singapore argument made sense, Rio de Janeiro, where teen-age robbers are frequently killed by the police, would be a much safer city than Stockholm, where criminals are coddled with social services. Yet the opposite is true." He concludes, "What makes one country safe and another violent has far less to do with the severity of punishment than with the extent to which people are alienated from society. Singapore is free of violent crime and graffiti not because of the cane but because its authoritarian Government has otherwise minimized discontent and instilled an ethos of obedience that goes beyond fear of punishment" ("Singapore, the Orwellian Isle").

Charles Wallace of the *Los Angeles Times* used statistics to drive this point home in an Asian context, comparing Singapore's 1993 crime statistics with those of Hong Kong, "whose residents are also [predominantly] Chinese but which imposes neither the death penalty nor caning." While in Singapore, there were "58 murders, 80 rapes, 1,008 robberies and 3,162 car thefts, . . . with a population nearly double that of Singapore, Hong Kong last year recorded 86 homicides, 103 rapes and 22 armed robberies involving firearms." While he conceded that "nonviolent crimes such as burglary were more common" in Hong Kong ("Singapore"), when adjustments are made for population size, Singapore would appear to be marginally more dangerous than Hong Kong when it comes to violent crime.

While some "liberal" Western critics were raising concerns about the rule of law in Singapore and criticizing the harshness of the sentence Fay received, others were busy reading Francis Fukuyama's *The End of History and the Last Man* (1992), which advanced the argument that with the collapse of the former Soviet Union, Western-style democracy and capitalism had won, bringing an end not so much to history but to a history characterized by huge ideological fissures. In an article published the same year as the book, Fukuyama asserted that Singapore's "soft-authoritarian" model was poised to become the "competitor to Western liberal democracy" ("Asia's Soft-Authoritarian Alternative" 60). Picking up on that theme the following year, *Time* magazine ran a major story on Singapore that asked the question, "Is Singapore a Model for the West?" (Branegan 36). The article's author quotes a Western analyst who enthuses: "Fortune 500 companies love it here because the government runs the country the way AT&T would" (Branegan 37). Even in the wake of the Asian currency crisis of the late 1990s, Singapore is still widely admired and much copied. As the one economy in the region that emerged first from the economic storm, Singapore's reputation as a country that is "getting it right" was enhanced by the relative severity of the economic woes that confronted its neighbors. In the aftermath of the Michael Fay controversy in the mid-1990s, Singapore is both respected and criticized: admired for its perceived "successes" in the areas of crime control and economic development, and feared by civil libertarians who worry that the Singapore "model" may be adopted elsewhere in order to provide a quick fix to complex domestic problems.

Even as Singapore took center stage internationally over the Michael Fay incident, for a number of years Singaporean theater artists remained silent about the controversy. Here was a story with all of the hallmarks of a gripping drama or TV movie: a good-looking, white American male teenager goes on an adolescent car-tagging, license-swapping, and sign-stealing rampage with some of his spoiled rich-kid expatriate buddies from the elite American School and is not only caught, sentenced, and caned but also finds himself at the center of an international incident in which the president of the United States intervenes to plea for a reduction in his sentence. Instead of focusing on the issues raised by the press with respect to the incident, Tan Tarn How's *Six of the Best* was offered as a play about racism in Singapore. However, for all the play's efforts to get to the heart of a taboo subject, its real success is in reinscribing the values of the state with regard to ethnic and cultural difference, a trope repeatedly used by Singapore's leaders to justify policies of social and state control. In Singapore difference has become the basis on which an individual's self and national identity rests; a citizen is Singaporean to the extent that he exists within one of the four prescribed categories of CMIO: Chinese, Malay, Indian, Other. Tan's play provides an appropriate concluding frame in that it repositions the core issues of national identity and political control in ways that may not be entirely conscious, a reflection of the PAP's ultimate success in creating a concept of what it means to be Singaporean in the social sphere.

Though written in 1994, Tan Tarn How's play *Six of the Best* was first produced two years after the Fay controversy. Given the intense domestic and international interest in the caning of a young Caucasian's bottom, it is hardly surprising that the only Singaporean play that made considerable use of the controversy also received extensive attention by the press, not only in the West but also in other Asian countries. According to TheatreWorks, the company that produced the play in 1996, ten newspapers and wire agencies contacted the group during the run of the show, including the *New York Times*, the *Toronto Globe*, the *West Australian*, the *Philippine Star*, and the *Pioneer* from New Delhi (*Straits Times*, 7 June 1996). In their comments to the press, both the playwright and Ong Keng Sen, the director of the Theatre-Works production, made it clear that the play was not "about" the flogging of Michael Fay but, rather, merely used the event as the starting point for an exploration of racism in contemporary Singapore. Tan observes: "I pride myself in not being a racist, yet I found myself, and other people who professed they were not racist, reacting to the case in a visceral, sometimes rather unpleasant manner" (*Straits Times*, 19 April 1996). Ong is even more direct: "Anyone who says he's not a racist is lying to himself" (Phua Mei Pin).

Set in the Singapore offices of a prosperous, upscale, American-based advertising agency on the day Fay's sentence was passed down, Tan's play brings together six employees who represent "six of the best" in the sense that they have all made it to the top of Singapore's socioeconomic heap. The mix includes four Singaporeans (two ethnic Chinese males, one ethnic Chinese female, and one Malay male, who is gay) and two expatriate males (one American, one British, the latter also gay). The TheatreWorks production, which contains material not present in the original draft of the play,[3] goes to great lengths to demonstrate that racism cuts both ways; indeed, at a number of points the contemporary action of the play is interrupted by scenes in which the racism of the colonial era is recalled, one of the most graphic and disturbing of which involves the highly stylized rape and murder of an English woman by an angry Chinese man.

In a parallel moment where similar feelings of anger and powerlessness overpower an individual, Huat, one of the Singaporean Chinese men who works for the advertising firm, accuses his coworkers of "sucking up to the whites," provoking both his boss and his coworkers with racist, vulgar language (Tan Tarn How, unpublished script of *Six of the Best* 40). In an exchange that would shock theater audiences virtually anywhere, Huat, now overcome by a frenzy of hate, verbally assaults his coworker Peter in Hokkien. The playwright's English translation follows:

> *Huat:* Have you ever tasted a white cunt?
> *Peter:* I don't want to talk about it.
> *Huat:* I have.
> *Peter:* Huat. I don't really want to hear this.
> *Huat:* In Amsterdam. I made it a point. Once in a lifetime. Cheap too.
> Too loose though. (40)

Sex is reduced to body parts, the taking of power, and the trading of stereotypes, riffs entirely consistent with the Fay controversy in that the epicenter of the media coverage was the act of flogging a bare, white butt by an Asian, not the consistent and accepted practice of Singaporeans flogging other Asians. The fact that it was a white rear being cut into with the rattan cane meant that Asians and Caucasians had to acknowledge thorny and disturbing questions relating to sex, power, and the relative values they attach to their respective bodies. Just as the act of flogging is both violent and laden with overtones of sexual submission, these same forces threaten the relations between the "races" in Tan's fictional ad agency. Huat's hateful outburst is partly in response to *ang mo*[4] Jim's successful conquest of coworker Peter's girlfriend, a copywriter who is the only female in a male preserve.

Sexuality crosses the racial divide again with the two remaining male office workers, the very English Neville and Sam, a Malay Singaporean, who are revealed to be lovers. In a nightmarish dream sequence, Sam defends himself against charges of being both a homosexual and a "banana," a derogatory term used to denote an Asian who is yellow on the outside but culturally white on the inside. When Sam is asked to identify his last five lovers and the names are all Anglo-Saxon and male, it is clear that he is both a legal criminal (under section 377 of the Criminal Code) and a cultural one by offering his body to the enemy. As the nightmare continues, he angrily turns on fellow office worker Cherie, demanding to know if Jim, her American lover, is "well-endowed" (TheatreWorks, video of *Six of the Best*). She responds, "Of course," reinforcing old stereotypes about penis size while simultaneously marking herself as the stereotypical "Sarong Party Girl"[5] who dates and has sex with Western expatriate men in return for money and status.

Yet by merely presenting racism and not commenting upon it, there is a danger that the play served as a vehicle for reinscribing the worst stereotypes relating to race, gender, sex, and cultural insensitivity. Jim, the self-centered, sex-starved American boss, attempts to have sex with Cherie at work, moments after their coworkers leave the office. He persists, asserting, "This is *my* office," and when rebuffed by Cherie, who refuses to be treated as property, he behaves like a spoiled, sulking child, reinforcing the image of the sex-obsessed Caucasian used to getting his way with Asian women. His understanding of Singaporean culture is equally shallow and stereotypical: "I didn't have to learn the intricacies of another culture when I came to Singapore. . . . The Singapore dream and the American dream, they play to the same tune: rags to riches." Peter adds the rhyming tag line, "and shag the bitches" (TheatreWorks, video of *Six of the Best*), further reinforcing the view of the Caucasian as a sexual predator.

The character of "never-reveal Neville" similarly reinscribes the stereotype of the remote Englishman. As Peter observes: "The enigmatic English. That's why they write so many great novels and plays—it's all an attempt to understand themselves, work it out in words" (Tan Tarn How, unpublished script of *Six of the Best* 19). Indeed, the actor originally engaged to play Neville dropped out as rehearsals were getting under way because he found "he could not identify with the indifferent character" (Phua Mei Pin). The

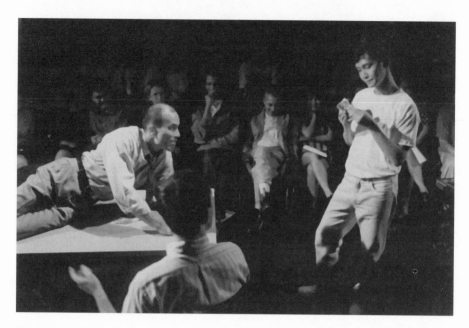

Tan Tan How's Six of the Best *uses the Michael Fay incident as a backdrop for an exploration of racism in Singapore. Directed by Ong Keng Sen for TheatreWorks, 1996. Left to right: Peter (Lim Yu-Beng), Neville (Peter Hodgson), and Huat (Koh Boon Pin). Production designer: Nicky Percival. Photo by Tharm Sook Wai.*

actor playing Jim also voiced his ambivalence about the ultimate impact of the production:

> My concern, then as now, is whether or not the play would be more
> divisive or helpful. . . . At the end of the day, I think raising the issue
> of racism in public is helpful, assuming that a lot of people would have
> had these thoughts. The danger is that people will not think or feel hard
> enough. Will they look at the character I play and say, "That's exactly how
> those bastards are?" Or will ang mohs look at the character of Huat and
> think, "Is that what's behind every Chinese face?" (*Straits Times,* 7 June
> 1996)

While exposing racism may require one to represent racism through the articulation of actual racist attitudes and beliefs, the problem remains that simply presenting a series of snapshots of racism in action has the potential to reinforce a racist belief system. Any art form that takes on racism as a subject has an obligation to make the audience "think or feel hard enough" to cut through surface realities and force the spectator to confront the cultural underpinnings of racism. By using the Fay episode as a mere backdrop for an exploration of racism, the play also successfully avoids having to deal with any of the many legal and political issues that were raised by caning, in effect neutralizing what could have constituted an inquiry into the complexities behind a highly charged political event. Given Singapore's sociopolitical climate and a legal framework that effectively preempts any kind of freewheeling public discussion of political matters, it is hardly surprising that perhaps Singapore's most "political" playwright would wisely choose to skirt this territory.

It is no accident that Singapore's first major play to deal openly with racism completely avoided the ways racism can manifest itself between the country's three largest ethnic groups: Chinese, Malay, and Indian. For a start, dealing with intra-Singaporean racism in the theater is illegal, as noted in chapter 1; plays that have the potential to "create misunderstanding or conflict in our multiracial and multireligious society" are specifically prohibited under the 1992 censorship guidelines. While the creation of a firm cultural identity tied to ethnicity has been a cornerstone of the government's social policy for at least two decades,[6] official rhetoric that acknowledges the continued existence of racism in Singapore is notable by its absence. Interestingly enough, one of the plays that resulted in the ban on Forum Theater, as noted in chapter 2, focused on parental disapproval of a relationship between a young Indian man and a Chinese woman. Rather than acknowledging racism and seeking to overcome it, as The Necessary Stage attempted to do with their 1993 production of *Mixed Blessings*, the government has instead repeatedly used the specter of ethnic "chauvinism" as one of the bogeymen capable of bringing the country down. While an exploration of racism between Asians and Caucasians is certainly appropriate for a play that grows from the debate over the punishment meted out to Michael Fay, it is important to note the absence of attempts to stage other, more statistically significant forms of racism that may exist in Singapore.

Tan's play begins and ends by giving voice to the most controversial person in the entire process: a nameless character referred to in the script as "The Flogger." The opening lines of the play, while clearly intended as a statement of the flogger's philosophy that guide and justify his practice, provide an unintended metaphor for three discernible historical stages in the development and articulation of the PAP's role in Singapore's social, political, and cultural life. His words, seen through this lens, take on an additional layer of meaning: "In the rotan [rattan cane], there is the *technique*, the *effect* and the *philosophy*. I used to be interested in the *technique*, then later it was the *effect* that fascinated me, but now it's the *philosophy*" (TheatreWorks, video of *Six of the Best*, italics mine). From the mid-1950s to 1965, the PAP under Lee Kuan Yew developed the *technique* of political and social control, emerging from a once fractured political field as the country's preeminent power. The period from full independence in 1965 to Goh's accession to the top job in 1990 was characterized by social experimentation, as the PAP tried a range of options and paid close attention to the *effects* of the policies, while fine-tuning the techniques in ways that would ensure their continuing hold on political power. The final period, from 1990 to the present, has witnessed the articulation and international dissemination of a *philosophy* of governance by the country's top leaders, wrapped in the cloth of "Asian values." While this tripartite structure is not meant to imply that sinister motives are behind the PAP's rule of modern Singapore (I genuinely do believe that compared to most autocratic regimes they honestly think they act consistently in ways that are in the best interests of the majority of Singaporeans), the fact remains that the PAP is one of the modern world's best examples of a political party that has done more than simply hold onto power; as I have argued throughout this book, through a succession of carefully crafted policies implemented over a number of decades, they have completely transformed a country and a culture in a manner so profound that Singapore now constitutes an important case study into the long-term effects of a government's political and social controls over its citizens.

From 1956, as Singapore moved toward independence from Great Britain, until 1965, when the brief and ill-fated union with Malaysia came to an end, the PAP pursued a series of politically motivated alliances that served to consolidate its power over the state apparatus. As previously noted, Lee's alliance with Singapore's communists was an important element in his rise to power. After purging the leftist elements from the party and setting up a cadre system in the early 1960s that was controlled from the top,[7] Lee effectively furthered the split with Chinese-speaking radicals by lobbying to join the Malaysian Federation. According to Lee Siew Choh, a left-leaning member of Singapore's Parliament in the early 1960s, Lee "accepted Malaya without consulting the PAP rank and file" (Sesser, *Lands of Charm and Cruelty* 21). As Stan Sesser points out in his detailed account of political life in Singapore, "Some Singaporeans speculate that another element could have been involved in his decision to join with Malaya: the possibility that Lee Kuan Yew might someday preside over the Malaysian Federation himself" (*Lands of Charm and Cruelty* 21). Apparently many in Malaysia, then under the leadership of Tunku Abdul Rahman, also viewed Lee's growing power with concern: it was only after the PAP contested seats in the Malaysian Parliament and won one that the relationship rapidly deteriorated. In August 1965, Rahman expelled Singapore from the federation, stating that the only alternative was to take "repressive measures" against the country, an action that began Singapore's life as a fully independent nation.

Upon independence in 1965, the state apparatus was solidly in the hands of the PAP under Lee's leadership, and a series of policies were instituted that ushered in and coincided with a period of rapid economic growth. The PAP leadership became increasingly concerned with managing the *effects* of their choices during this period and therefore implemented a plethora of state-mandated policies in the financial, social, and educational sectors. As Lee observed in his 1986 National Day speech only a few years before handing over the reigns of power to a younger generation, these controls were necessary to build Singapore:

> I am often accused of interfering in the private lives of citizens. Yet, if I did not, had not I done that, we wouldn't be here today. And I say without the slightest remorse, that we wouldn't be here, we would not have made economic progress, if we had not intervened on very personal matters — who your neighbor is, how you live, the noise you make, how you spit, or what language you use. We decide what is right. Never mind what the people think. That's another problem. (*Straits Times*, 20 April 1987)

No one can accuse Lee of not showing his true colors; he freely admits that it is within the scope of government to intervene in all aspects of the lives of its citizens. In 1994, when Singapore's best-known novelist, Catherine Lim, published an article in the *Straits Times* that was critical of Prime Minister Goh's style of leadership, Lee used the opportunity to counter with an ominous description of the techniques he would use to bring down those who opposed him: "I would isolate the leaders, the trouble-makers, get them exposed, cut them down to size, ridicule them, so that everybody understands that it's not such a clever thing to do. Governing does not mean just being pleasant. If you want a pleasant result, just as with children, you cannot just be pleasant and nice" (Wrage 44). Indeed, the story of the rise and rise of the PAP is one of unwavering adherence to that strategy. That the citizens of the state are likened to "children" is also appropriate for a country that has earned the nickname "The Nanny State."

From 1990, when Goh Chok Tong became prime minister, to the present, Singapore's ruling PAP has moved into a third developmental phase, in which the articulation of a *philosophy* has gone hand in hand with continuing political repression. Lee Kuan Yew's comments in his memoirs about the Japanese occupation of Singapore during World War II seem oddly prescient: "The third and final stage, which they [the Japanese] would have achieved if they had been given time, was to get us to accept them as our new masters as part of the natural order of things. Morality and fairness were irrelevant. They had won. They were on top and in command. We had to praise their gods, extol their culture and emulate their behavior" (77–78). Once the techniques of social control have been perfected, the ongoing process of naturalizing the values emanating from the top has come to rely on what the PAP leaders term "Asian values." As noted in chapter 1, the justification given by Prime Minister Goh for the 1997 libel suits against opposition politicians Tan Liang Hong and J. B. Jeyaretnam was that because Singapore is a Confucian society, its leaders are obligated to respond vigorously to any attack on their integrity: "We are a different society. In Singapore, we believe that leaders must be honorable men, gentlemen or *junzi*, and if our integrity is attacked, we defend it" (*Singapore Straits Times*, 20 August 1997). Apparently Confucian values justified the record S$8.1 million in damages initially awarded[8] to PAP leaders in their successful libel suit against Worker's Party candidate Tang.

At one point in the trial of Jeyaretnam, Goh became so incensed by George Carman's rhetoric that he indicated that he would sue the Queen's Counsel if he repeated some of his assertions outside the courtroom. Carman argued that rather than forming a constituent element in a philosophy of Asian values, Goh's use of the courts to pursue political opponents was motivated by the desire to maintain PAP supremacy. Making his case against the PAP government, Carman stated: "I suggest that you and Mr. Lee Kuan Yew, you learning from him, being a willing and able apprentice, have learned to play the system in this way: First you pay lip service of having the full rights of a democracy—with freedom of speech, independence of the judiciary, freedom of the press and freedom of opposition. But there comes a point where you adapt that for your own purpose in Singapore to stay in power and to stifle opposition" (*Straits Times*, 20 August 1997). Interestingly enough, Carman's comments mirror accusations Lee Kuan Yew leveled against the

British in the Legislative Assembly when he rose to condemn their repressive political actions in 1956:

> I'm told [repression] is like making love — it's always easier the second
> time. The first time there may be pangs of conscience, a sense of guilt.
> But once embarked on this course, with constant repetition, you get more
> and more brazen in the attack and in the scope of the attack. All you have
> to do is to dissolve organizations and societies and banish or detain the
> key political workers in these societies. Then, miraculously, everything is
> tranquil on the surface. Then an intimidated press and the government-
> controlled radio together can regularly sing your praises, and slowly and
> steadily the people are made to forget the evil things that have already
> been done. Or if these things are referred to again they're conveniently
> distorted and distorted with impunity, because there will be no opposition
> to contradict. (Qtd. in Seow 173)

As articulate a critic as Carman was of the PAP, the words of the senior minister, uttered while a young man and rising political star, lay out even more explicitly the very path pursued by the PAP as they captured and maintained a tight hold upon the country's political apparatus over the course the last four decades of the twentieth century. In the wake of the Jeyaretnam trial, the 1998 U.S. State Department *Country Report on Human Rights in Singapore* concluded, "The Government stepped up its intimidation of the opposition in 1997, an election year. After the election, PAP leaders filed a number of potentially ruinous defamation suits against opposition parties and their leaders. The ruling party's continued use of the judicial system for political purposes highlights concerns about the independence of the judiciary in cases that affected members of the opposition, or that had political implications" (U.S. Government 1998). While the actions of the Singaporean government in 1997 would seem to leave little doubt that the PAP's articulation of and adherence to so-called Asian values is little more than an attempt to justify "authoritarianism lite" in the political and social spheres, their government is not without its supporters, including many in the West, as the various reactions to the Michael Fay episode suggested. Like the Flogger in *Six of the Best*, the government of Singapore has perfected the technique of social and political control, has carefully monitored its effects, and is now in the process of articulating a philosophy to justify its continuing lock on political power.

Given the fact that so many obviously see through the PAP's attempts to manipulate its citizens and its judiciary, why does a tiny nation of 3 million with no natural resources matter in the global scheme of things? As Stephen Wrage observes, Singapore "matters . . . to the extent to which it is a model in the rest of Asia. It is a pioneer in the technology of social control, and its methods are being attentively studied by visiting teams from Beijing, Jakarta, Hanoi, Bangkok and elsewhere" (45). Singapore also matters because many politicians and citizens in the developed world have grown weary of dealing with the scale and complexity of their own social ills and are eagerly looking for other political, social, and economic models to embrace. To suggest that Singapore provides a model for any country other than Singapore is to over-look the ways in which its system grew out of a very specific set of political, cultural, and historical conditions and to disregard the manner in which the Singapore model functions on its home turf. Just as the "Japanese business model" was embraced by American businessmen in the early 1980s only until it proved itself deeply flawed even on its home territory, so will any attempt to embrace a "system" and transplant it wholesale to another cultural and political context ultimately prove to be a doomed proposition.

Politicians and corporate business interests throughout the developed world have come to rely increasingly on the "invisible hand" of market forces as the touchstone for a new world order, rather than turning to governmental or intergovernmental organizations for leadership or regulatory solutions to a range of social, political, and economic crises that continue to disrupt and impoverish much of the world's population. Ironically, Singapore is seen as a model "open economy," in spite of the fact that its economy, though open to the world, is virtually owned and directed by the state, a fact that many of the greatest international corporate champions of the Singapore model fail to re-alize. Indeed, in many respects Singapore is as close to a socialist country as one can find among the world's wealthy nations, given the degree of state control over key assets.[9] What saves Singapore from the dreaded epithet of "socialism," however, is that the country is run along the authoritarian lines of a well-run corporation, with power centralized at the top and a web of underlings who efficiently carry out their orders. As long as those orders contribute to the betterment of the greatest number, for many, their legiti-macy is assured. Thus Singapore has won its hard-earned reputation as Sin-gapore, Inc., a regional capitalist nexus, and it is likely to continue to serve as an Asian home for an ever-increasing number of multinational corporations in the years ahead.

With the increasingly free flow of capital between nations and an increased willingness to surrender individual agency to the machinations of the marketplace, the distinct possibility exists that all of the developed world is going to become a lot more like Singapore than many in the West might suspect. As Terry Eagleton queries, "Might not the anarchy of the marketplace necessarily breed an authoritarian state? Might not the forms of instrumental reason needed to control a hostile environment also be used to shackle and suppress human beings themselves?" (*Illusions of Postmodernism* 62–63). Eagleton's suggestion that authoritarianism works hand in hand with market forces in advanced capitalistic societies also applies to Singapore:

> It is a striking feature of advanced capitalist societies that they are both libertarian and authoritarian, hedonistic and repressive, multiple and monolithic. And the reason for this is not hard to find. The logic of the marketplace is one of pleasure and plurality, of the ephemeral and discontinuous, of some great decentered network of desire of which individuals seem the mere fleeting effects. Yet to hold all this potential anarchy in place requires strong foundations and a firm political framework. The more market forces threaten to subvert all stability, the more stridently one will need to insist upon traditional values. (*Illusions of Postmodernism* 32)

There is a strong sense in which individuals in advanced capitalist societies have been reduced to what Eagleton terms "empty receptacles of desire" (*Illusions of Postmodernism* 88), defined by their consumption patterns and cast adrift in a world in which politics has been eradicated as a relic from a time when people still believed in historical narratives. Replacing the tyranny of the narrative is an endlessly deconstructed reality characterized by discontinuity and the free play (or free fall, depending on your point of view) of signifiers divorced from *any* objective reality, undermining individual agency to the point that authoritarian models seem more "natural" in this new world order than participatory ones. The art of theater, too, can take on this glossy surface, endlessly displacing meaning to the point where it no longer engages with the culture and politics of a people. In fact, it is in the long-term best interests of the state to nurture and support artistic products that tap into endless niche markets that encourage consumption and fragmentation. Thus, the more "advanced" theater becomes in Singapore, the more it may ultimately disengage from the social and political life of the nation.

One of the most visible of all the social engineering campaigns aggressively supported by the government at the dawn of a new millennium is that of encouraging a relatively docile population to take initiatives. This campaign would seem to run counter to a culture in which citizens have been programmed to believe, as opposition leader Jeyaretnam observes, that they should "leave everything to us [the PAP] and we will give you what is good for you" (Loh). Peter Carey argues that the PAP has created "a system which has treated people as units of production rather than as human beings. Class, race, gender, religion, all have been used as tools in Singapore's social class experiment which has resulted in the increasing disempowerment of the ethnic minorities (Malays and Indians), the creation of a docile Chinese working-class, the political emasculation of the professional elite, and one of the highest suicide rates in Asia" (ix). The passivity of Singapore's citizens and their unwillingness to speak out and take risks has been at the core of a number of government-initiated campaigns, and there can be little doubt that the push toward developing the arts, in addition to its other merits, is part of a larger strategy to encourage Singaporeans to think laterally. The "chicken rice" analogy from chapter 1 used by Minister for Trade and Industry BG George Yeo is worth recalling: once a country has reached the point where it can no longer produce goods more cheaply than low-wage countries, value can only be added by making the product more aesthetically appealing, like selling the same chicken rice dish, only in more attractive surroundings. Enter the arts and the creative spirit, which can be harnessed to add that value to goods, a lesson Yeo apparently learned while apprenticing for the hugely important job of running the state economy while serving as minister for information and the arts. What the PAP fails to understand is that initiative and creativity cannot be manufactured according to some formula; they can only exist where the ground has been carefully nurtured and where individuals feel free to express themselves openly and without fear. In this respect the PAP may ultimately be working against its own long-term objectives; by choosing "who your neighbor is, how you live, the noise you make, how you spit, or what language you use," the government has denied its citizens the opportunity to develop as free-thinking human beings, thus possibly undermining long-term economic growth.[10]

As the ground on which culture is negotiated and creativity is expressed, theater is fundamental for Singapore's future. Recognizing the importance of the creative arts, Singapore has put more money into the arts than any country in the region, and theater has received significant funding. However, as noted earlier, the lion's share of the funding is designated for the construction of the S$595 million Esplanade arts center, not for direct support of theater companies.[11] When asked by an *Asiaweek* correspondent if the arts can "be nurtured the same way that Singapore developed its economy," George Yeo, then minister for information and the arts, articulated a position wholly consistent with past rhetoric:

> Visiting foreign troupes are like cut flowers from Europe and Japan. They add to the ambiance but what we want is a variety of local blooms which we supplement with foreign cuts. We are gardeners. The climate we have to accept as given. We can improve the soil. Occasionally we do some pruning and spraying but the plants have natures of their own, which we have to work with. It's a light-handed approach. Sometimes we try a plant we think will grow well but it doesn't take root, so we try a different combination. (Oorjitham, "Why Art Cannot Be Like Hothouse Flowers")

Yeo's placid and lovely images of floral artistry obscure the fact that it is the very stern hand of the PAP that does the planting, pruning, and spraying. With his talk of "foreign" and "local blooms" and "improving the soil," Yeo fails to grasp that gardening is the worst possible analogy for the development of the arts: whereas a garden is created by an individual who seeks to tame nature and impose his or her vision on the landscape, the arts are not the product of a singular vision; rather, they spring out of the cultural landscape of a nation in a way that reflects its diversity, its contradictions, and its complexity.

This book set out to examine Singaporean theater as a cultural phenomenon that operates by a set of rules and parameters that are distinctly Singaporean; by looking at the wider context in which Singaporean theater functions, it is my hope that this work has revealed more about the implications of the Singapore "model" than could be uncovered by even the most careful and detailed analysis of economic projections and crime statistics. I hope that this work will not be seen as a case of Singapore-bashing but, rather, as an extension of my love for the country and my deep and abiding concern for its future. My personal wish both for Singaporeans and theater practitioners there is that someday soon the government will come out of crisis mode and allow the richness, diversity, and promise of Singapore to shine through.

Notes

Introduction

1. Singapore's main island is 42 kilometers (26 miles) from east to west and nearly 23 kilometers (14 miles) at its widest north-south point. With its offshore islands, Singapore's total land area is 647.5 square kilometers. Singapore has 3.2 million citizens and permanent residents, though there are 3.9 million in the country when one adds the sizable population of imported workers (Source: Singapore Government, *Singapore 1999*).

2. Depending on whose statistics one turns to, by most measures Singapore's per capita wealth surpasses even Hong Kong's. *Asiaweek* puts Singapore's GDP figure at US$27,740, clearly ahead of Hong Kong's US$21,830. By contrast, Taiwan comes in at US$17,495, and Singapore's immediate neighbor to the north, Malaysia, at US$7,370 (Source: *Asiaweek* Web site, 21 July 2000).

3. I don't know whether I can lay claim to this term or not, but it certainly seems an appropriate one in an age of global capitalism characterized by endless branding in all areas of consumption, including matters of ideology and political organization.

4. I will use the terms *Western society* and *the West* throughout the book as they are generally used, to denote Europe, the United States, Canada, Australia, and New Zealand.

5. Lest I be branded a Marxist on my next trip to Singapore, I must hasten to add that though I read Marxists such as Terry Eagleton and admire their considered, careful, and colorful use of language and their concern with the blood-and-guts realities of this world, this does not mean that I myself am one. While it will be very clear that I am a critic of the consequences of global capitalism, which impoverish many while they enrich relatively few on the global scale, this does not mean that I am calling for anyone to overthrow Singapore's institutions. I am very much a gradualist and would not be writing this book if this were not the case.

1: Setting the Stage

1. Some useful articles that examine the phenomenon of "soft authoritarianism" are: Denny Roy, "Singapore, China"; Clark D. Neher, "Asian Style Democracy"; Douglas Sikorski, "Effective Government in Singapore"; and Kim Dae Jung, "Is Culture Des-

tiny." A number of full-length books have appeared on the subject, notably Michael R. J. Vatikiotis's *Political Change in Southeast Asia* and David Brown's *The State and Ethnic Politics in South-East Asia*. For Singaporean responses to Western criticism of the Singapore model, see Kishore Mahbubani, *Can Asians Think*, and Chua Beng-Huat, "'Asian-Values' Discourse and the Resurrection of the Social." As Singapore's representative to the United Nations, Mahbubani emerged in the 1990s as one of the leading proponents of the Singaporean position, which he wraps in the flag of pan-Asian values. By contrast, Chua's article examines the structure of Singaporean society from a sociological perspective, noting how freely aspects of socialism have been grafted onto a system that is regarded by much of the Western world as fiercely capitalistic.

2. Indeed, the praises of the Singapore model flow from within Asia as well. No less than the Chinese *People's Daily* has singled out the Singapore-developed Suzhou Industrial Park (SIP) as one of the greatest successes for a development model of this type, crediting the "Singapore experience" and the Singaporean government for creating "a conducive environment for investments by focusing on service." Presumably in contrast with the old communist model, "the Singapore Government does not interfere with the operations of the firms. It also works at not adding to the cost burdens of companies, and companies are responsible for their own survival" (*Straits Times*, 23 October 1998).

3. The U.S. ambassador to Singapore underscored this point while the crisis was still under way, noting that "in future, Singapore will have the opportunity to help restructure the region's financial architecture" (*Straits Times*, 17 October 1998). Singapore's leadership roles within regional and global organizations in the aftermath of the crisis suggest that his prediction is wholly accurate.

4. Singapore's per capita GDP of US$27,740 exceeds Britain's US$20,890, while their GNP figures are within US$2,000 of one another (Source: *Asiaweek* Web site, 21 July 2000).

5. Singaporean linguists consistently use the term *dialect* to characterize the variants of Chinese spoken in Singapore, a practice that I shall follow throughout this book. While the most common dialects used (Hokkien, Teochew, Cantonese, Hakka) share the same written script as Mandarin, they are pronounced quite differently and in that respect are not merely regional accents, especially inasmuch as Cantonese, for example, is the lingua franca of the region of southern China that includes Hong Kong. Ethnic Chinese are strongly encouraged to abandon using the dialects in favor of Mandarin, a phenomenon with important cultural, economic, and political implications that will be discussed in chapter 3.

6. All parenthetical references to the *Straits Times* denote the *Singapore Straits Times*, not Malaysia's *New Straits Times*. Unless marked with a page number, *Straits Times* news stories after April 1996 are from the *Singapore Straits Times/Asia One* Web site, which archives stories for up to one week after their first appearance. For the sake of simplicity, the precise address for each individual news story is not listed. News stories that appear on the Web site can also be found in the same form in the hard copy of the newspaper. The newspaper's Web site address is http://straitstimes.asia1.com.sg/.

7. The younger Lee, often referred to simply as BG Lee, was given the rank of Brigadier General (Reservists) some three months before he left the military for political life in 1984. Born in 1952, BG Lee is a decade younger than Goh Chok Tong (b. 1941).

8. James Minchin, writing in 1986, referred to the younger Lee at that time as the "crown prince of Singapore" (20). A few years after Goh took on the top job, BG Lee was diagnosed with colon cancer, and though he has subsequently made a complete recovery, his illness may have been at least partially responsible for his decision to step out of the limelight for a few years.

9. Early in 2000, Goh signaled his intention to step down after the 2002 general elections, adding, "But it does not mean the day after the elections. I mean, if I win, and people want me, I could stay on for a little while" (*Straits Times*, 18 April 2000). Less than a year later, he reversed his earlier pledge and placed 2007 as the deadline for the handover of the government to BG Lee Hsien Loong (*Straits Times*, 24 January 2001).

10. In the aftermath of the 1997 election, which saw the PAP obliterate the last remaining vestiges of viable opposition in Singapore, Goh and the PAP hierarchy won defamation suits lodged against two Worker's Party candidates, Tang Liang Hong, and longtime opposition voice J. B. Jeyaretnam. Such suits, which will be discussed in greater detail later in the chapter, have been used to systematically silence opposition over the course of the last two decades. Goh has showed just as strong an interest in this form of political bloodletting as his predecessor Lee. Similarly, when well-known Singaporean novelist Catherine Lim suggested in a newspaper column published in the *Straits Times* in November 1994 that Goh had retreated from his earlier commitment to "consultation and consensus," Goh responded by arguing that those who try to undermine the authority of the government can expect a "very, very hard blow from the Government in return," adding, "You can't just criticize without expecting us to reply to you in the same manner which you have attacked us. If you land a blow on our jaw, you must expect a counter-blow on your solar plexus" (*Straits Times*, 24 January 1995).

11. The HDB is Singapore's Housing Development Board, the government authority that builds and regulates the housing estates in which 86 percent of all Singaporeans live (Singapore Government, *Singapore 1999*).

12. Hokkien is the most popular of the southern Chinese dialects spoken in Singapore. Though the government has strongly encouraged ethnic Chinese to speak Mandarin, Hokkien remains closer to the cultural roots of a great many Singaporeans.

13. A government publication notes that Singapore's judiciary was "ranked number four in the world in the administration of justice" by the International Institute for Management Development, with a score of "8.31 out of ten," placing the republic "higher than many developed countries such as the United States, Switzerland, Australia and Japan" (*Singapore Bulletin*, July 1996). The country's gleaming, clean, and efficient Changi Airport is repeatedly voted the "world's best" by the London-based *Business Traveller*, while the Hong Kong–based Political and Economic Risk Consultancy (PERC) rates Singapore, Hong Kong, and Japan as the only three countries in

Asia with "satisfactory corporate governance systems, giving Singapore the highest rating with a '2' (where the low scores are the best) whereas Japan rated a '4' and China languished at the bottom with an '8.22'" (*Straits Times*, 25 June 2000).

14. At the time of its creation, the NAC's objectives were set out as follows: "(1) to harness the support and contributions of all Singaporeans to promote an artistically vibrant society; (2) to promote the appreciation and practice of the arts among Singaporeans; (3) to nurture artistic and creative talent in Singapore; (4) to provide and manage performing, exhibition and related facilities for the arts; (5) to promote Singaporean arts and artists overseas; (6) to attract to Singapore a wide range of international artistic talents and events; (7) to create a partnership between the artistic community, the private sector and Government in the promotion of the arts" (Lau 3).

15. This figure was reported in the *Straits Times* on 19 June 2000.

16. The first phase of the center, initially scheduled for completion in 2001, was to see the construction of the two largest indoor theaters (a Lyric Theatre seating 2,000 and a Concert Hall 1,800), and an outdoor amphitheater and *wayang* pavilion to be utilized for traditional performance. The smaller venues, which were more likely to host Singaporean work, were to be built at a later date, creating anxiety on the part of some theater practitioners that the center would function merely as a "road house" for high-profile musicals and international shows. During the economic crisis of the late 1990s, the government scaled back their initial plans, canceling the construction of the three smaller venues and replacing them with two 200-seat studios that were originally planned as rehearsal spaces, ostensibly for large-cast shows and musicals. Also cut was the *wayang* pavilion, which was replaced with a number of flexible outdoor venues. Thus the fears expressed privately by some Singaporean theater artists earlier in the decade appear to have been realized; the center is far more likely to provide a home to high-profile international work than act as a base for Singaporean theater.

17. In the years since 1996, the term *software* has been largely replaced with *heartware*, which has come to denote the touchy-feely, thinking-outside-the-box approach to problem solving.

18. This phrase is often used in Singapore to denote subjects in the arts and humanities. "Soft" also typically conveys a pejorative sense that these subjects are easier and less substantive than "hard" subjects such as science or business.

19. As of July 2000, new Honda Accords with the smallest engine (2.0 liters) were selling for S$133,888, according to the Automobile Association of Singapore Web site <www.aas.com.sg/>.The number of vehicles on the road is strictly regulated by the government, with high fees levied not only for importing vehicles, but for the right to continue to own and operate them. These rights, known as Certificates of Entitlement, or COES, were selling for S$33,000, a record low, in August 2000. Without these controls, it seems safe to assume that Singapore's roads would be choked with traffic.

20. After four years of running the Substation, in July 2000 Sasitharan left for a position as codirector (with Kuo Pao Kun) of the Practice Performing Arts School. Codirectors Lee Weng Choy and Audrey Wong took over the operation of the Substation.

21. In 1994 ministerial salaries in Singapore became tied to compensation packages in private industry. As a result of this reassessment, Prime Minister Goh's salary was increased to US$797,000, nearly four times what President Clinton earned at that time. Similarly, cabinet ministers' salaries were increased to US$535,000, compared to US$148,000 in the United States (Wallace, "Pay Raise Plan"). In the aftermath of the Asian financial crisis during which Singapore's economy grew 0.4 percent while other nearby countries witnessed significant contractions, Prime Minister Goh called for further increases, including an across-the-board pay raise of 13 percent for civil servants. His salary, linked to the median income of the top eight earners in six leading professions, was raised to S$1.94 million, or US$1.1 million at then-prevailing exchange rates (*Straits Times*, 1 July 2000). The justification for high salaries in the civil service has consistently been that financial incentives are the only way to ensure that the best and brightest minds join the government.

22. The January/February 1995 issue of *Foreign Affairs* contained an article by Mahbubani entitled "The Pacific Way," in which he put forth the Singaporean government's position as if it represented a model that is being uniformly adopted throughout all of Asia. Mahbubani's article prompted a response from Christopher Lingle, an academic who had recently fled Singapore in order to avoid prosecution for libel in Singapore's courts. Lingle sought to expose the self-serving nature of Mahbubani's argument and entitled his article appearing in the May/June 1995 issue of the same journal, "The Propaganda Way." Mahbubani's 1998 book, *Can Asians Think*, has already been cited. Mahbubani's stand would appear to have moderated more recently, however, as his comments delivered to the Royal Society of Arts/BBC's World Lecture 2000 Series in London would suggest. He argues for a more balanced position, noting that, "the 21st century will be fundamentally different from the 19th and 20th centuries. By the end of the century, we will return—in terms of balance of civilizations [east and west]—to the world we saw somewhere between AD 1000 and 1500" (*Straits Times*, 18 June 2000).

23. Singapore's ethnic breakdown is Chinese (77.2 percent); Malay (14.1 percent); Indian (7.4 percent); other (1.3 percent).

24. For a playful and spirited defense of communitarianism that removes it from an East/West context, see Daniel Bell's *Communitarianism and Its Critics*.

25. The "five pillars" of *Pancasila* are: monotheism, humanitarianism, national unity, representative democracy, and social justice.

26. As the highest-polling "loser" in the January 1997 general election, Jeyaretnam's Worker's Party was entitled to a seat reserved for the nominal "opposition" in Parliament. This scheme kicks in only when fewer than three opposition candidates are successful in their bid to obtain office. As only two non-PAP candidates were victorious in that election, Jeyaretnam was eligible to take up a seat on behalf of the district in which the opposition was the highest-polling loser. These Non-Constituency MPs are paid less than ordinary MPs and are prohibited from voting on constitutional amendments or budgetary matters. The other two opposition seats were won directly by opposition candidates, no mean feat given that residents of losing districts are

penalized by not having their government-brokered HDB (Housing Development Board) flats upgraded in a timely manner. This penalty is widely known before the election, and PAP candidates make no secret of the fact that citizens in their districts will benefit from a more pleasant living environment as well as more rapidly escalating home values should they chose to reelect the ruling party. In the January 1997 election, the PAP won 81 out of 83 seats. So chilling is the power of the PAP on dissent that a majority of seats in that election were uncontested; only 36 were challenged, while no opposition candidate ran for the remaining 47 spots.

27. The initial judgment against Tang totaled S$8.075 million, with a full S$2.3 million awarded to Lee Kuan Yew and S$1.4 going to Prime Minister Goh (*Straits Times*, 30 May 1997), though it was ultimately reduced to S$3.63 million on appeal (*Straits Times*, 2 February 1998). Tang was ultimately declared bankrupt in the Singaporean High Court in February 1998 (*Straits Times*, 7 February 1998), rendering him unfit for political office in the future.

28. On appeal in 1998, Goh succeeded in raising the damage award against Jeyaretnam to half of the amount initially requested as well as full legal costs. According to the U.S. State Department's *Singapore Country Report on Human Rights Practices for 1999*, "Goh also began bankruptcy proceedings against Jeyaretnam that would have dissolved the WP and deprived Jeyaretnam of his parliamentary seat, but suspended them while Jeyaretnam was making payments. The remaining defamation suits against Jeyaretnam still were pending at year's [1999] end."

29. After almost a decade of running the Ministry of Information and the Arts, in 1999 Yeo was appointed minister of trade and industry, a move that places him at the top of the country's most important ministry. That his technocratic spirit was first applied so successfully to the arts seems entirely appropriate given the government's view of the arts as yet another industry to be developed.

30. Writers in the West on both the Right and the Left rose to condemn the *International Herald Tribune* for caving in to the demands of the Singaporean government. In the *American Journalism Review*, Debra Durocher notes that "instead of fighting, the titan owner of the Paris-based International Herald Tribune, the New York Times Co. and the Washington Post Co. meekly accepted the punishment" (11). Similarly, in the *National Review*, Donald Kirk asserted that "if awards were given to newspapers for cowardice under fire, a major contender for 1994 would be the *International Herald Tribune*" (26). In the years that have followed, however, Singapore has continued to serve as an important base for Western journalists covering Asia. In a move that will no doubt be followed by other important media operations, the BBC in February 2000 announced its intention to move their Asian regional headquarters to Singapore (*Straits Times*, 29 February 2000).

31. It bears noting that in the years since Takashimaya has been open, its "cultural programs" have consisted largely of glitzy fashion shows and visits by singers and teen idols that attract legions of screaming, free-spending teens into the shopping center. Thus the so-called arts have been very effective in promoting commercial interests at Takashimaya.

1. The major parties contesting the 1959 election were the People's Action Party (PAP), the Liberal Socialist Party (LP), the Singapore People's Alliance (SPA), and the United Malays' National Organization (UMNO)/Malaysian Chinese Association (MCA).

2. Singaporean sociologist Chua Beng Huat argues quite convincingly that those caught up in the debate between Asian and Western values would do better to instead look at the specific economic and political choices made by Singapore's leaders that have favored the creation of a society that is both socialist and capitalist. For the full development of this thesis, see his 1999 article "'Asian-Values' Discourse and the Resurrection of the Social."

3. The Internal Security Act, a holdover from the period of British rule, allows for indefinite detentions for those deemed to represent a risk to the security of the state.

4. According to a government press statement released at the time, "these and other arrests have broken up a number of underground cells operated by the Malayan National Liberation Front (MNLF), a satellite of the MCP [Malaysian Communist Party], and by the Malayan People's Liberation League (MPLL), the political wing of the MCP (Marxist-Leninist) which broke away from the MCP in August 1974" (Stockwin 12).

5. Actors associated with Third Stage who were arrested in 1987 made similar claims of torture. Similarly, in 1994, the *New York Times* reported that the confession extracted from American teenager Michael Fay for spray-painting a number of automobiles came about only after he had been tortured by police (Shenon). The case of Faye will be examined in greater detail in chapter 10. The following year, in another high-profile case that is discussed in chapter 5, a number of people who had spoken to convicted Filipino maid Flor Contemplacion prior to her execution claimed that she too confessed only after being tortured by Singaporean police. According to one woman whom Contemplacion befriended while in jail, the maid was "forced by prison personnel to lie down inside a coffin lined with dry ice." Contemplacion's niece claimed that she had written her several letters "narrating her ordeal in the hands of prison personnel, including incidents when Contemplacion was forced to imbibe some sedatives and an incident when she was actually raped" (*Straits Times*, 10 April 1995).

6. For further documentation of abuses at the hands of the ISD, see the U.S. State Department's annual *Country Reports on Human Rights*; read the account of Francis Seow, Singapore's former solicitor general, in his book *To Catch a Tartar: A Dissident in Lee Kuan Yew's Prison*; or contact Amnesty International.

7. Francis Seow, who defended a number of the arrested individuals, observes, "There were reservations in the establishment itself that Lee and his government had overreacted in arresting the young professionals. Today, there is broad consensus that it was a bloody, knee-jerk action" (230).

8. While visiting two of the re-arrested individuals at the Whitley Detention Center in May 1988, lawyer Francis Seow was himself detained by the ISD until mid-July, when he signed a statement admitting that he was involved in a U.S. plot to influ-

ence domestic politics. Why the U.S. government, with its long history of fierce anti-communism, would support a communist or nominally left-leaning group of individuals over a friendly, relatively pro-Western government that helped create the conditions under which the U.S. could extend its economic and military influence in a key geopolitical region was never made clear by anyone, least of all Lee Kuan Yew himself. Seow's account of his experience in Lee's facility is quite hair-raising, as the following description of his experience attests: "I was made to stand in the middle of the room. I could scarcely make out a desk behind which there was a chair. I became uncomfortably aware of an air-conditioner blower duct directly above me on the ceiling, which directed a continuous and powerful cascade of wintry cold air down at the spot where, barefooted, I was made to stand. The floor was like a slab of ice that rapidly drained away the body's heat. I could not see any one; but I could sense the presence of several persons sheltering behind the anonymity of darkness, whose silhouettes assumed bizarre forms as they moved. As I stood there, someone shouted out with mock civility: "Oh, give him a chair to sit." A chair was thrust forward into the spotlight. I sat down and was momentarily thrown off my poise. The chair was unexpectedly low and wobbled precariously. It stood on three legs. The legs had been perversely sawn off to shorten them and its fourth leg sawn shorter than the rest of them. A sudden shift in weight could throw a person off his balance" (122–23). The book describes in detail other, less playful attempts to render inmates helpless and to remove their resolve to contest the charges against them. Seow makes it very clear that detainees were there only to sign confessions to crimes for which they had already been found guilty by the authorities.

9. Founded in Manila in 1967 in response to the lack of social and economic justice under the Marcos regime, PETA was an important regional disseminator of theater techniques designed to empower disenfranchised groups. See Eugène van Erven's book *The Playful Revolution: Theatre and Liberation in Asia* for information about PETA and theater working for social change in Asia.

10. The entry on Boal in the *Cambridge Guide to Theatre* states: "An inveterate experimenter and Marxist ideologue, Boal encountered problems with the Brazilian political situation. After a period of imprisonment, he sought exile in Argentina and other countries, where he continued to develop new forms of radical theatre such as the *teatro jornal*, a documentary drama based on current events (newspaper events), and the *teatro invisible*, which consists of staged performances in public places before unsuspecting audiences" (Banham 110). This characterization of Boal completely ignores his work over the last two decades, during which time he denounced his earlier experiments with *teatro invisible* as "dishonest" and came up with new forms such as Forum Theatre. In 1995 he was elected to Brazil's national legislature, where he practiced "Legislative Theatre" until recently. Though still left-leaning in his politics, he is now actively engaged in the political life of his country and is working within the system. The Cambridge entry is seriously flawed and demonstrates the danger that ill-informed Western scholars can create for artists around the world when reporters and writers turn to their publications for authority. Rather than conveying an accurate picture of Boal's work, the *Cambridge Guide* in this instance reflects an outdated,

twenty-year-old view of Boal's practice that provided the moral authority for placing two of Singapore's most promising young theater practitioners in grave danger.

11. The editor replied to the reader's letter with a question: "Is Miss Woon [the writer] suggesting that because she is convinced that there is nothing subversive about that particular technique [i.e. Forum Theater], then those on whom it was used, especially young students, need not be told about it?" (*Straits Times*, 16 February 1994). The implication seems to be that the technique has within it the potential for subversion, thus buttressing the government's position that the form needed to be banned.

12. Indeed, shortly after reading Soh's article on the morning of Saturday, 5 February, I phoned a number of expatriate theater colleagues in an attempt to see what kind of concerted response we might make as a group in defense of these two promising young theater artists. The consensus of my peers seemed to be that we would be seen as interfering Westerners if we raised our voices in protest. Later that evening a colleague of mine from the National University of Singapore met my partner at a party and greeted him with the words, "You know Bill's phone is tapped." The indirect way in which this threat was delivered back to me is typical of the way in which people are made to behave in ways that are sanctioned by the state. Whether or not my phone was actually tapped was in many ways irrelevant; what was important was that I understood that they had the *power* to tap my phone and to do far worse things. While I taught at the National University of Singapore, it was widely held that anyone teaching in areas that touched on politics—which would obviously include theater—had their phone conversations monitored and/or recorded by the Internal Security Department.

13. TNS's Haresh Sharma and Alvin Tan have brought a number of their productions overseas. Sharma has the distinction of being one of the few Singaporean playwrights with a single anthology devoted to his work (*This Chord and Others*).

3: Staging Identity and Nationhood

1. As noted in chapter 1, the precise ethnic breakdown is Chinese (77.2 percent); Malay (14.1 percent); Indian (7.4 percent); other (1.3 percent).

2. In a shift that suggests they are following Singapore's example, the government of Malaysia, which took another course by supporting the widespread use of Bahasa Melayu rather than English in the years after breaking with Singapore, has begun to change its language policies and now encourages the business and government elite to become competent English speakers.

3. Readers interested in finding out more about Singaporean theater in English prior to the 1990s should look at David Birch's "Singapore English Drama: A Historical Overview, 1958–1985."

4. *One Year Back Home* was written in 1978, but it took almost two years for Yeo to secure permission from the Ministry of Culture to have it produced. Objections presumably came from the political criticism embodied in the play, something that seems difficult to fathom twenty years on, as the character in the play who espouses the anti-PAP line is hardly written from an overwhelmingly sympathetic point of view.

5. Between its opening on 7 May and 29 June *Money No Enough* took in S$4.79 in

ticket sales (*Straits Times*, 29 June 1998), earning it a place on the list of the country's top ten box-office successes (*Straits Times*, 12 June 1998). The popularity of the film, most of which was in Hokkien, speaks volumes about how hungry Chinese Singaporeans are for movies that reflect the way many of them live and speak.

6. Linguist Mary W. J. Tay provides a more comprehensive definition of the two terms: "Code switching is generally considered to be intersentential whereas code mixing is intrasentential. Thus while code switching involves the embedding or mixing of words, phrases and sentences from two codes within the same speech event and across sentence boundaries, code mixing involves the embedding or mixing of various linguistic units, i.e. morphemes, words, phrases and clauses from two distinct grammatical systems or subsystems within the same sentence and the same speech situation" (408).

7. People identifying themselves as Peranakan are unique to Singapore and the east coast of peninsular Malaysia. When Chinese male laborers arrived in Singapore in the late eighteenth and early nineteenth centuries, they found few Chinese women with whom to intermarry. As a consequence, many men married Malay women, resulting in families that identified with both Chinese and Malay traditions. Many Peranakan people occupied important positions in the social and economic sphere in the years prior to independence, and as a group they were generally more Westernized than dialect-speaking Chinese or Malay Singaporeans. Their culture, unique to this region, is also responsible for the development of a type of fusion cuisine that continues to be very popular with both Singaporeans and overseas visitors.

8. More recently, a cross-dressed version of *Emily* enacted by Singaporean actor Ivan Heng and codirected by Malaysian director Krishen Jit hit the stage. From 1999 to 2001, this production was seen by audiences in Kuala Lumpur and Singapore as well as at festivals in Hong Kong, Sydney, Melbourne, Adelaide, Perth, Auckland, New York, Hamburg, Berlin, and Munich.

9. I am grateful to Robert Yeo for pointing out this particular section of the text in his unpublished paper "Singaporean Theatre in English: Knowing Where It Wants to Go," presented at the International Seminar on Southeast Asian Traditional Performing Arts, Universiti Sains Malaysia, Penang, Malaysia, 10–13 August 1992.

10. Ah Hoon is usually a female Chinese name.

11. *Botak* is "bald" in Malay. Thus Emily is hailing him, "Hey, bald one!"

12. *Chiak pah boey* means "Have you had your meal?" A similar greeting is commonly used in Malay.

13. *Chin ho, chin ho* means "Very good, very good."

14. Achar is a Malay dish of pickled and preserved vegetables, primarily long beans, pineapple, cucumber, and carrots in a sour and somewhat hot vinegary sauce.

15. *Tambi* is a mildly derisive term meaning Tamil/Indian "boy," used even when the "boy" is in fact a fully grown man. By using this term Emily asserts her position of class superiority over the Tamil spice merchant.

16. Kuo was born in 1939 in China's Hebei Province.

17. Lee Kuan Yew was once known as "Harry," especially in the years leading up to independence from England. Generally speaking, only individuals who have had a

very long, personal association with the man remember the time when he was called "Harry." People in this category are relatively few in number, as Lee has a history of alienating his former domestic political allies.

18. The play was produced by the National University of Singapore Society (NUSS).

19. Unless otherwise noted, all quotes are from the manuscript of the play provided by the author. Note that this analysis also utilizes the video record of the January 1992 production.

20. I am referring, of course, to Christopher Lingle, a university lecturer who was successfully sued by the government for writing these words about an unnamed Asian country and publishing them in the *International Herald Tribune*. Lingle writes about his ordeal in *Singapore's Authoritarian Capitalism: Asian Values, Free Market Illusions, and Political Dependency*.

21. In the English system, an ordinary university degree is obtainable after three years of full-time study. The "honors year" is devoted to in-depth study in a particular field and typically culminates with the writing of an honor's thesis in which the student is expected demonstrate mastery of a particular aspect of the discipline.

22. Francis Seow, Singapore's former solicitor general who ran afoul of Lee Kuan Yew in the late 1980s, had this to say about Lee's National Day speeches: "During the annual National day rally, the prime minister would characteristically deliver meandering speeches of Castro-length proportions, sermonizing while he spoke and blustering with the confidence of a man who was accustomed to a captive audience of cabinet ministers, members of Parliament, party members and supporters, senior members of grassroots organizations, the judiciary and members of the civil service, amongst many others. The docile media loyally serialized the speech over successive days. On one occasion, he spoke for as long as three hours" (26).

23. Goh's 1997 Rally Speech for National Day issued a further warning of the dangers inherent in multiracial Singapore: "History and geography made us a small island, in a strategic location, with 3 million people of different races, languages and religions. These are our material for building a nation. They will always make our survival a challenge. If we don't understand these basic facts, we will perish" (*Straits Times*, 18 August 1997).

24. For the music and lyrics to these songs, see the Web site from Singapore's Ministry of Information and the Arts <http://www.gov.sg/mita/songs.htm>.

25. That the heroic efforts of a single mother to care for her son would be one of the themes of the 1994 National Day musical is ironic given that Prime Minister Goh that year announced the government's intention to no longer permit single mothers to buy flats directly from the Housing Development Board. Single motherhood in fact became viewed as a social evil: Goh's National Day announcement of the policy change was followed up in the press by a series of articles on the perils of single motherhood. One true-confession-style article that appeared in the *Straits Times* was entitled "Single Mothers: The Stark Reality" (Ibrahim).

26. In May 1955 a strike against the Hock Lee Bus Company instigated by students and workers turned violent and resulted in a loss of lives (Turnbull 255).

27. In the concluding section of his 1997 speech, Goh observes, "My vision of

Singapore in the 21st Century is: a cohesive, vibrant, and prosperous country, founded on justice and equality, excellence and social mobility, discipline and graciousness. Citizens care for one another. The ablest commit themselves to lead. People of all races, from all walks of life, work together to make this our best home." Similarly, the 1994 National Day musical, *A River in Time*, concludes with the song "City of Mine," which links the past with a glorious present: "People came from many lands / joining heart and linking hands, / shaping a future for us all. / Common purpose, common bond / learning trust from all around, / giving whenever / and building together / striving for-ever-more; / Feel the pulse / feel the beat of Singapore, / You and I / we're the heart of Singapore, / Magic in the air surrounds us, / giving hope to all around us, / taking all our futures with us, / joining all of our lives; / Feel the drive / feel alive in Singapore, / Feel the pride / far and wide in Singapore, / Sense the spirit of elation, / the city lights and towers shine, / symbol of a vibrant nation, / city, oh city of mine / Singapure, Xin Jia Po, / Singapura, Sinjapur, / Singapura, Xin Jia Po, / Singapore" (Source: Official Programme for *A River in Time*, Singapore Indoor Stadium, 5–8 August 1994).

4: Commodifying and Subduing the Body

1. Portions of this chapter are based on my article "Commodifying and Subduing the Body on the Singaporean Stage."

2. All quotes from the play come from the unpublished manuscript of the production, which was provided by TheatreWorks.

3. Vast sums of money are spent on some of the annual productions staged by the university's halls of residence. Money is obtained through corporate sponsorship and the contributions of "old boys" and in some cases "old girls" who lived at those halls while at university. Given the competitiveness of Singaporeans, it is hardly surprising that the halls vie for the title of staging the most elaborate, most expensive works. In one hall of residence show staged while I taught at NUS, the lasers used in the production were rumored to have cost more than S$30,000. By contrast, my budget for a departmental production featuring theater studies majors was a few thousand dollars, much of which came in the form of in-kind contributions. The hall productions, while often characterized by lavish spectacle and staged at expensive venues, are generally marred by amateur acting. Few actors appearing in these productions have any training, and many of them have not appeared before on stage. Thus the entire exercise has nothing to do with quality and everything to do with a massive show of "face." Because virtually all of the country's top leaders in government and industry who did not go overseas for their university education were trained at NUS, the audience for these shows often includes many VIPs and top politicians. For many of them, this is their only annual encounter with theater, and there can be little doubt that it strongly colors their ideas of what the form is all about.

4. That both *Children of the Pear Garden* and *The Eye of History* should include tea-party scenes is fitting, especially given that afternoon tea is probably done better in Singapore than in England. Many of the country's largest hotels serve huge and elaborate spreads for afternoon tea. Upwardly mobile Singaporeans seem to take a great deal of pride in this imported tradition and are not shy in comparing the vastly superior array

of foods available at a Singaporean high tea to the relatively paltry fare offered at most hotels in England.

5. Shenton Way is a street in the heart of Singapore's high-rise financial district, comparable to America's Wall Street.

6. All quotes are taken from the video of the TheatreWorks production.

7. Kuo Jian Hong is playwright Kuo Pao Kun's daughter.

5: Constructing Gender

1. Fees were as low as S$388 a month for a Filipino maid in the early 1990s. In 1994, the government of the Philippines instituted a bond that the agencies hiring the maids were required to pay for every fifty Filipino maids they brought into Singapore. Suddenly, the monthly charges for a Filipino maid skyrocketed from a low of $388 to prices ranging from $998 to $1,600, a jarring change that brought about charges that the agencies were profiteering (see *Straits Times*, 10 November 1994). The bond was instituted by the Philippines to stem what they felt was the abuse of maids on the part of some Singaporean employers.

2. The statement by the Philippine presidential fact-finding commission, printed in full in the *Straits Times*, made an impassioned plea for the improvement of conditions affecting the lives of Filipinos overseas. "We cannot resurrect Flor Contemplacion, but she became the symbol of the liberation of our overseas contract workers from the trauma of poverty which forced them into migration and slavery. . . . We echo the message we have been hearing from the Filipino overseas contract workers employed as domestic helpers that their Singaporean employers generally treat them like machines and not as fellow human beings" (10 April 1995).

3. In 1996, as part of the Festival of New Writing sponsored by Singapore Press Holdings, the government-controlled print media corporation, Singapore's Theatre-Works presented five short plays that were inspired by the Flor Contemplacion controversy. The only one that has been turned into a full-length performance piece and staged is Chin Woon Ping's *From San Jose to San Jose*. Not surprisingly, Chin's piece has been performed not in Singapore but in the United States. The text is published in *(Post)colonial Stages: Critical and Creative Views on Drama, Theatre and Performance*, a volume edited by Helen Gilbert. Chin's work will be discussed in greater depth later in the chapter.

4. In one of the more sensationalistic cases involving a maid and her employers, in 1998 a mother and her teenaged son were jointly charged in district court with repeated abuse of their fifteen-year-old Indonesian maid. The *Straits Times* provides an account of the charges: "A teenaged maid told a district court yesterday that she was made to eat dog faeces twice because she did not clean up after her employer's dog quickly enough. Miss Hartati Ali Sodikun, 15, said that on one occasion, after she ate the dog poo and was almost sick, her employer's 13-year-old son asked her: 'Was it delicious?' She had to call him 'Boss Besar,' which means 'Big Boss' in Malay, and his five-year-old brother 'Boss Kecil' ('Small Boss'). Describing her four-month stay with the family, she said she had to sleep on old newspapers on the kitchen floor of her employer's luxury apartment. . . . She also said she was not given enough to eat.

Sometimes her only meal of the day comprised rice and tomato sauce" (3 February 1998).

5. When I heard of the play's basic premise, as a university educator I must admit that I too was concerned about the problematic relationship between a professor and a student seeking advice on how to snag an eligible man. Surely, I told myself, such a situation could only play itself out in the fantasy life of a middle-aged professor. I was proven wrong when shortly after seeing the play a colleague approached me privately and told me of an unsolicited counseling session with a young female student that mirrored the basic premise of Yeo's play so completely that I was forced to acknowledge that the social pressures on women to marry "at their level" were in fact so strong in Singapore that the play's starting point was an accurate reflection of reality.

6. Staged in April 1999 by the National University of Singapore Society (NUSS) as part of a double bill entitled *Double Dogs Second Chance*, Yeo's play was directed by Corrine Yeo, whose comments in the program notes suggest that she was well aware of the criticisms leveled at the play in the past: "Being the first woman director of a play previously labeled sexist, I asked, what would I contribute to this play that a man couldn't? The answer, I suspect, is perspective."

7. Because *Emily of Emerald Hill* was already examined in detail in chapter 3 for its rich use of language, Kon's work will not receive further consideration here. Sadly, Kon has virtually stopped writing for the theater, depleting the already limited number of women's voices present on the Singaporean stage.

8. Given the strong historical, political, and cultural ties between Singapore and peninsular Malaysia, to some extent Malaysia's "Straits Chinese" culture, particularly in the areas nearest to Singapore and extending through the large cities of their west coast, has much in common with Singaporean Chinese culture. *Straits Chinese culture* is a generally recognized term referring to those common cultural referents that cut through the administrative boundaries created by the English, which became permanent national boundaries in 1965.

9. As we shall see in chapter 8, TheatreWorks's 1995 production of *Mortal Sins*, a musical about censorship, reinscribed (though perhaps unwittingly) the values of the state, in spite of its use of time travel and other non-naturalistic devices.

10. For the full thrust of this argument, see Judith Butler's *Bodies That Matter*.

6: Queering the Stage

1. See the Singapore 21 Web site: <http://www.gov.sg/singapore21>.

2. The five key areas that provide the basis for the Singapore 21 campaign are: (1) Every Singaporean matters; (2) Strong families: Our foundation and our future; (3) Opportunities for all; (4) The Singaporean heartbeat; and (5) Active citizens: Making a difference to society. Source: Singapore 21 Web site <http://www.gov.sg.singapore21>.

3. This figure rose to 83 percent among those responding via the Internet. While Singaporeans are generally reticent when responding to questions relating to social policy, especially when asked on the street, it should be noted that those with access to the Internet are likely to be more affluent and highly educated, factors that everywhere seem to be related to an individual's ability to affirm the rights and gays and lesbians.

This survey was conducted privately by a group of concerned Singaporeans and was released to the international news media in May 2000. The complete results can be found on the PLU (People Like Us) Web site: <http://www.geocities.com/WestHollywood/3878/gls21.htm>.

4. Indeed, many of the vast Web sites devoted to gay and lesbian life in Singapore are accessed through U.S. servers such as Geocities, which enable individuals to create very large sites in webbed communities that link them with groups devoted to similar subjects or reflect related geographic areas.

5. It bears noting that police entrapment exercises are not uncommon in the United States, where undercover police have also arrested some high-profile individuals. In one such exercise in Los Angeles in April 1998, the police used decoy agents to entrap a man who turned out to be well-known singer and musician George Michael.

6. For a fascinating account of homosexuality in the Chinese imperial court, see Bret Hinsch's *Passions of the Cut Sleeve: The Male Homosexual Tradition in China.*

7. Lim Swee Say is minister of state for trade and industry and communications and information technology. His comments were published in an extensive statement that appeared on the *Straits Times* on 6 June 2000.

8. The second value embedded in the Singapore 21 campaign is that of creating "strong families." While the first one, "Every Singaporean matters," would appear to suggest that embracing diversity is important, the minister's statement makes it clear that he believes family to be the fundamental core value.

9. For a detailed account of the history and function of this group see Laurence Wai-Teng Leong's "Walking the Tightrope: The Role of Action for AIDS in the Provision of Social Services in Singapore."

10. See the PLU Web site, <http://www.geocities.com/WestHollywood/3878>, for a detailed account of the group's attempt to obtain legal recognition. One of the things that strikes the casual reader is the great thought and care that went into each of the submissions by PLU, while the government responses are curt, even threatening. The first response of the Registrar of Societies denying PLU's application reminds them of "the provisions in the law for the imposition of heavy penalties on organizers and members of unregistered societies. The organizers and members of 'People Like Us' should therefore cease all activities in connection with the society."

11. This policy, which essentially prevents single people from purchasing affordable new flats from the government, was announced by National Development Minister Lim Hng Kiang in March 1998. Singles had previously been permitted to pool their resources with another party and put their names on a list for flats under the Joint Singles Scheme (JSS). This scheme was eliminated, the minister said, "because the single will bring in another elderly single, a grandaunt or a relative, but there is no intention at all that the two will stay together" (*Straits Times*, 19 March 1998).

12. For an extensive analysis of how this general pattern emerged in the West, see the essays in Martin Duberman et al., eds., *Hidden from History: Reclaiming the Gay and Lesbian Past.* Though the articulation of a gay male identity will differ in Singapore, it seems highly likely that urbanization and wealth will also prove themselves to have been the principal requirements for the development of an independent gay

male identity in Singapore as well. Of course one can point to many "premodern" traditions among indigenous peoples where men lived as women, but these models are much closer to transvestism or even transsexuality than they are to modern male homosexuality in that they assume that men who desire other men—especially those seen as feminized or as the ones who serve as passive partners to a more masculine male—are simply born into the wrong bodies. Picking up on this strand, Dennis Altman observes, "To identify as homosexual without rejecting conventional assumptions about masculinity or femininity (as with today's 'macho' gay or 'lipstick lesbian' styles) is one of the distinguishing features of modern homosexuality" ("Rupture or Continuity?" 82).

13. One 1992 ad for an upcoming issue of Singapore's *Friday Weekly*, a Chinese-language newspaper for students, featured a candid-style photo of two young school-age women peering into a refrigerated dessert unit. The "femme" long-haired girl, wearing a school uniform, was shown leaning into the "butch" short-haired girl, attired in jeans, a button-down shirt, and shiny Doc Marten's, their bodies touching suggestively. The accompanying text read: "Schoolgirls were caught binding their breasts to make themselves more 'manly.' In another case, a tomboy had another girl on her lap. Tomboys can be seen hanging out with younger schoolgirls at places like Marina Square, Far East Shopping Centre and Wisma Atria [three popular shopping centers]. Is it normal for adolescent girls to be attracted to other girls? Why do girls turn to older lesbians for attention and love? Read *Friday Weekly* this week for a better understanding of this sexual problem." Thus the text expands upon the suggestive photo by playing into parents' fears that their child might fall prey to "older lesbians" while simultaneously problematizing a whole range of behaviors. The ad also has the potential to create a more paranoid atmosphere regarding same-sex attractions: not only does it name the places where suspected lesbians meet, but the candid shot of the two school-age women also reminds all young women that there is a danger of being caught on film—with a corresponding loss of face—simply by standing too near another woman in public.

14. Where traditional theater is concerned, cross-dressing in both directions is a standard feature in much Chinese opera, something the government has apparently chosen not to prohibit, as it would result in some of the most highly skilled and respected theater artists in Asia being banned from the Singaporean stage. In the context of Chinese opera, cross-dressing is not only sanctioned, but the skill and artistry behind it is recognized and even lauded. One of the country's 1997 Cultural Medallion winners was Lou Mee Wah, a well-known female Cantonese opera artist who specializes in playing male leads (Seah, "Male Impersonator, Author Recognised").

15. SBC was replaced by the Television Corporation of Singapore (TCS) in 1995.

16. The official reason for the banning of gum was that it created a public nuisance in that it was hard to remove from public conveyances such as the MRT.

17. I refer, of course, to the controversy that arose over the National Endowment for the Arts (NEA) funding for gallery displays of Robert Mapplethorpe's contested photographs. After politically motivated attacks on Mapplethorpe and *Piss Christ* artist Andres Serrano, U.S. politicians moved against the already fledgling field of perform-

ance art and, in 1990, defunded the so-called NEA Four: performance artists Holly Hughes, Tim Miller, John Fleck, and Karen Finley. Apart from Finley, the remaining artists are openly queer and deal with lesbian and gay issues in their work. Finley examines difficult terrain such as rape, using her body as a canvas on which to represent manifestations of female degradation. Thus she proved equally "pornographic," and her work was also defunded. In 1996, grants to individual performance artists were cut entirely from the NEA budget, effectively eliminating federal support for this category of work. Thus the "fringe" ultimately proved to be at the center of a national debate.

18. The segment that follows is based on my article "Sexual Minorities on the Singaporean Stage." An expanded version of that article, covering the period 1988–1998, is forthcoming from the Millennium Project in Singapore. This project seeks to commemorate the lives of Singapore's sexual minorities through the publication of a work that includes topics ranging from GLB (gay/lesbian/bisexual) theater to gay pride. The work, which is being published privately with all proceeds going to support community projects, will represent a landmark publication for Singapore. Unfortunately, circulation of the book will probably be quite limited, and it seems highly unlikely that the volume will be available in Singapore's bookstores.

19. Chay Yew's *Porcelain* (1992) and *A Language of Their Own* (1994) have been professionally produced in the United States and Britain, where they have garnered considerable critical acclaim. Yew has served as resident artist and director of the Asian Theatre Workshop at the Mark Taper Forum in Los Angeles since its founding in 1995.

20. "Out-of-bounds markers" (or, more simply, "OB markers") is the phrase used by both the government and the media to denote the limits of free expression. Apart from the clearly stated boundaries discussed in chapter 1, there exist more nebulous areas of expression, such as the depiction of sympathetic gay characters, that would also seem to be "out-of-bounds."

21. The plays I refer to are *Famous Five Go on an Adventure*, by Robin Loon, and *Vegetarian*, by Theresa Tan, both presented in January 1992 as part of the TheatreWorks Writer's Lab staged reading series. In April, TheatreWorks presented the following works: *Three Fat Virgins Unassembled*, by Ovidia Yu; *Lest the Demons Get to Me*, by Russell Heng; *Blood and Snow*, by Desmond Sim; and *Raw Material*, by Claire Tham. June and July saw productions of *Private Parts*, staged by TheatreWorks, and Haresh Sharma's *Glass Roots (Don't Step on Them)*, by The Necessary Stage. Finally, in October, Fong Yong Chin's Mandarin-language play, *Another Tribe*, was presented at the Substation, as was Lee Chee Keng's play *Life's Elsewhere*, presented under the auspices of the Singapore Press Holdings (SPH) Playwriting Studio.

22. Of course the sex trade thrives in Singapore, though it is less visible to tourists than it once was. Now largely restricted to certain districts, notably sections in Little India and the Geylang, prostitutes of all ages and ethnicities are available to service men in the nearby hotels and houses of prostitution. The more elegant and expensive prostitutes are more likely to be found in the upscale hotels and are thus harder to detect. The fact that prostitution on this scale continues in Singapore, along with the

apparent cooperation of the police, who allow these establishments to continue to exist, suggest that the government's pragmatic attitudes also extend to the private pleasures of the largely Singaporean and imported worker populations that frequent these sexual playgrounds. One particular red-light district in Little India, for instance, rivals similar neighborhoods in Amsterdam for its openness; the only real difference is that women are on display through open doorways rather than through the large glass windows found in the canal city. What distinguishes these red-light districts from the Bugis Street of old, however, is that they are not intended to be known or used by tourists. Indeed, few tourists would even know of the existence of these neighborhoods, and many Singaporeans are apparently unaware of them as well, in spite of their popularity with certain segments of the public.

23. Late on a Saturday night it is not that unusual to see transvestites on Orchard Road who cannot "pass" at all!

24. When I lived in Singapore, speculation about the sexual orientation of a number of well-known individuals, including government ministers, was common. The bottom line always seemed to be that as long as the individual in question kept their private life strictly out of the public eye, they would be permitted to retain their position and its attendant perks. This is not unlike the situation in the United States, where there are many well-known actors and pop stars who are widely acknowledged as gay or lesbian but who scrupulously avoid making any public pronouncements on the matter.

25. For instance, in 1997, PELU permitted William Wu to mount an independent, Mandarin-language production of his work *Crystal Boys*, which featured six gay male characters said to "represent the six broad types of homosexuals" according to "studies carried out by the [show's] producers" (*Straits Times*, 10 May 1997). Similarly, in 1999, Drama Box obtained permission to present a double bill in Mandarin that included a stage adaptation of well-known gay American writer Paul Monette's memoir *Borrowed Time*, a stirring and moving account of how he and his lover faced lives prematurely shortened by AIDS. While the *Straits Times* characterized the relationship between the actors playing the two lovers as "tender, if subdued" (14 September 1999), the key point is that the relationship itself is accepted as a given. Monette, a product of gay urban male culture in the United States, starts from a position of acceptance of homosexuality and presumes that any reader (and presumably any viewer, in this stage adaptation by the company) also accepts and understands the need for two men to create and sustain intimate relationships. By contrast, when a fledgling drama group applied for permission to stage American playwright Larry Kramer's groundbreaking early AIDS play, *The Normal Heart*, in English, they were guided by a set of restrictions that included "no same-sex kissing onstage, and no affiliations with any religious denominations, in the event that a same-sex wedding ceremony was to be portrayed." The reviewer noted that the producer's decision to present the play as a rigid, staged reading, rather than as a fluid play with physical contact between actors, "crystallized one of the themes of the play: that sometimes even after having found a voice, one still has to constantly shout to rise above the dominant oratory of one's oppressors" (*Straits Times*, 2 November 1999).

26. The larger, more established theater companies, which are given the greatest leeway with regard to the censorship requirements, also have the most to lose if they step outside the nebulous boundaries of acceptable public expression. Thus the vast majority of the plays produced in the second half of the 1990s with openly gay male characters have been staged not by the established theater companies but by smaller companies operating largely outside the structure of public and private support.

27. After dropping Yew's play from the season, TheatreWorks successfully staged another one of his plays, *Half Lives* (later reworked and renamed *Wonderland*), in 1997, despite the fact that it features a sympathetically drawn gay male character. Yet unlike *A Language of Their Own*, Yew's *Half Lives* dealt largely with a young gay man's relationship with his family and not with issues of sexual identity. Yew also notes that the government would have been happy with this play, as from their perspective "it was a damnation of American society": the Singaporean woman who emigrates to the U.S. becomes homeless, while her gay son turns to prostitution (telephone interview). Yew's contributions to American theater have been significant. It is difficult to quantify what the loss of creative talents such as his means for a small country like Singapore.

28. In a well-publicized prior incident in March 1992, eight arrests were made, and four men had their photos published in the newspaper. One of the four subsequently committed suicide (Leong 15).

29. After initially being acquitted in April 1994, organizer Tan, defended by opposition politician Philip Jeyaretnam, was fined $700 for providing entertainment without a license in August. Articles about Tan's trial appeared in the *Straits Times* on 21 April, 3 August, and 13 August 1994.

30. The published version of Tan Tarn How's 1993 play, *The Lady of Soul and Her Ultimate "S" Machine*, includes a "Diary of Censorship" that chronicles the long journey of the play toward ultimate approval by the Ministry of Information and the Arts (MITA) and the Public Entertainment and Licensing Unit (PELU). Tan's play, staged by TheatreWorks, took a heavily farcical look at the attempts of government bureaucrats to manufacture soul, thus taking on two sacred cows at once: bureaucrats *and* the heavy-handed efforts of the government to create something as elusive as a "Singaporean soul."

31. This is the conclusion of the *Los Angeles Times* as well, which backs up its assertion that Singapore "has quietly given up its efforts to control the Internet" with the observations of Deputy Prime Minister Lee Hsien Loong: "The 100 sites we monitor are purely symbolic. You can get around them in so many ways. . . . Any teenager who is well-informed will find out how to do it" (Iritani).

7: Festival Culture

1. For the Singapore Tourism Board's "New Asia" Web site, see <http://www.newasia-singapore.com/>.

2. Prior to 1999, the festival, which was held biannually, was known as the Singapore Festival of the Arts. In this and all subsequent references to the festival I shall use its current name, the Singapore Arts Festival.

3. Each "hawker stall" housed inside a "hawker center" specializes in a few items,

a holdover from the days when people pushed carts though the city and literally had to "hawk" their food, typically announcing their offerings by shouting out or singing an attention-grabbing jingle. This is different from Western-style food courts (which do exist in Singapore, though they're typically indoors), where a huge range of items—often of dubious quality since they were prepared hours earlier—are offered. By specializing, a hawker can prepare your food to order, resulting in much better quality at a price that is affordable even for ordinary working-class Singaporeans.

4. Technically, the Chinese Newspapers Division of SPH is the umbrella organization for the event.

5. The term *Renaissance City* is credited to Brigadier-General George Yeo, minister of information and the arts, who first used the term in a speech to launch the National Library Board's new logo in July 1996 (*Straits Times*, 29 August 1999).

6. This report made recommendations concerning future arts policies, including the recommendation that led to the creation of the National Arts Council. Most of the report's recommendations have been largely followed. I am grateful to Catherine Diamond for first bringing this report to my attention.

7. In 1997, the government formed a parliamentary committee to look at the ways in which the country's arts training institutions could further contribute to Singapore's economy. Announcing the formation of the committee, Deputy Prime Minister Tony Tan said: "In this information age, the spirit of creativity will be a key factor which will sharpen Singapore's competitive edge" (*Straits Times*, 4 June 1997). This theme has subsequently appeared in virtually all major public policy pronouncements, notably the National Day speeches of Prime Minister Goh.

8. For a detailed analysis that focuses almost entirely on the 1994 Singapore Arts Festival, see my article "Singapore's Festival of the Arts." Some of the information contained in that article is reorganized and subsumed by this chapter, though the discussion of a number of productions has been cut here.

9. I realize that here I am working against my own pledge not to use imported standards by which to judge the festival, but it seems abundantly clear that by "standards" in this context the NAC means international standards, especially inasmuch as the government relies chiefly on international organizations to validate claims of excellence in virtually every other field in which the government has a significant stake.

10. Since 1998, the director has been Goh Ching Lee. The prior director was Liew Chin Choy.

11. In response to the call for an artistic director for the festival following the 1999 Singapore Arts Festival, the NAC's director of program development, Goh Ching Lee, made it clear that such a change would not be forthcoming (*Straits Times*, 22 June 1999).

12. In a 1996 feature article in the *Far Eastern Economic Review*, Murray Hiebert points to several productions staged in the mid-1990s, among them Kuo's *Descendants of the Eunuch Admiral*, to argue that the authorities in Singapore have significantly relaxed their restrictions on theater over the course of the decade.

13. His NAC-sponsored *Desdemona* premiered at the Adelaide Festival in March 2000 before returning home to Singapore, while his production of *Lear*, which premiered in Japan in 1997, was presented at arts festivals in Asia, Australia, and Europe.

14. According to the NAC, the number of tickets sold at festivals are as follows: 1977: 6,328; 1978: 7,232; 1980: 20,000; 1982: 57,048; 1984: 40,367; 1986: 79,167; 1988: 88,875; 1990: 85,208; 1992: 104,365; 1994: 85,052; 1996: 82,064. Apart from the figure for 1996, which was reported in the *Straits Times* on 1 July 1996, all figures were provided by Liew Chin Choy, director of arts programming for the NAC.

15. Most Singaporeans own their own flats in housing estates built and run by a government agency, the Housing Development Board, or HDB.

16. The two 1998 festival productions highlighted in the press that were marred by inconsiderate phone users were the RSC's *Romeo and Juliet* and Kuo Pao Kun's *The Spirits Play*. According to the *Straits Times*, six cell phones went off during the opening night of the RSC production, prompting the NAC to record a reminder for theatergoers to switch off mobile phones and pagers before the performance. Yet the following night, in spite of the message, two cell phones went off (*Straits Times*, 26 June 1998). The press apparently stopped counting after the second night!

17. Articles decrying the inconsiderate use of cell phones continue to appear in the press on a regular basis. In one of the more bizarre legal cases involving cell-phone use, in January 2000 four young men were charged in a Singaporean district court with bashing a lawyer after he told one of them to stop carrying on a mobile-phone conversation in a cinema showing the Arnold Schwarzenegger movie *End of Days*. The four men, all full-time national servicemen, faced charges of causing grievous hurt for dislocating the shoulder of the lawyer, who was trying to watch the movie with his girlfriend (*Straits Times*, 8 January 2000). Stiff fines went into effect on 1 July 2000 for individuals talking on their cell phones while driving. First-time offenders face up to six months in jail, a S$1,000 fine, and twelve demerit points (*Straits Times*, 23 June 2000).

18. In a 29 June 1994 interview, Krishen Jit noted that Mabou Mines presented the NAC with a choice of works to present.

19. To my knowledge, the only other nation of a similar size that has taken a risk with expensive, relatively avant-garde work in the context of a festival is New Zealand. Their 1998 International Festival of the Arts featured Robert Lepage's seven-hour, fifteen-minute epic *Seven Streams of the River Ota*, widely regarded as one of the most important new pieces of theater to emerge in the 1990s.

8: The Great Singaporean Musical

1. It bears noting that *The King and I* is banned in Thailand for its racist and inaccurate portrayal of King Mongkut, who was in reality a highly educated former Buddhist monk who spoke half a dozen languages fluently, a far cry from the character created by Yul Brenner, who requires instruction by an English schoolmistress. When *Anna and the King* was released in 1999, it too was banned by the Thai Film Board for its historical inaccuracies and its disrespectful view of a much-revered king.

2. All quoted material is from the October 1992 production of *Nagraland* at Singapore's Kallang Theatre.

3. In an interesting historical parallel, in the 1980s it took the intervention of Singapore's cabinet to enable female dancers in a Senegalese troupe to perform barebreasted at the Singapore Arts Festival.

4. While theater is reviewed by civil servants working for an arm of the police

department, films are reviewed by a panel of highly placed individuals who sit on the Cinematograph Film Appeal Committee.

5. In 1999, the company changed its name to the Singapore Opera Company. For the sake of clarity, I will use the company's earlier name, the Singapore Lyric Opera, as it was the name of the company at the time *Bunga Mawar* was produced.

6. Lim Yau, then associate conductor of the Singapore Symphony Orchestra, was awarded the Cultural Medallion in 1990.

7. The producer was Choo Hwee Lim, who was awarded the Cultural Medallion in 1992.

8. Peranakan culture is discussed more fully in chapter 3. Essentially it is a unique blend of Straits Chinese and Malay culture that is found in Singapore and on the West Coast of Malaysia.

9. All quoted passages from the musical *Bunga Mawar* are taken from the video record of the June 1997 production created by the Television Corporation of Singapore for Television 12.

10. The term *Nyonya* is used to denote the woman in a Peranakan household, and the term *Baba* is used to denote her husband. *Nyonya* simply means "married woman" in Malay.

11. *Under One Roof* is a popular Singaporean sit-com about an "ordinary" family living in the HDB heartlands.

9: Interculturalism and the Big, Bad Other

1. Much of the first section of this chapter is based on my article "Interculturalism Derailed: The Case of Singapore."

2. Tickets to *Aida* cost S$70, $150, and $250.

3. See Patrice Pavis's *Theatre at the Crossroads of Culture*. Pavis has subsequently refined his model in the introduction to his *Intercultural Performance Reader*.

4. The original name of the company was Asia in Theatre Research Circus. The company's artistic director, William Teo, notes that "we called it a circus because we would rehearse in parks, at the beach, and we didn't know where we would perform" (Tsang, "If It's a Good Piece of Art"). In this chapter, the company will be referred to by the shorter "Asia in Theatre Research."

5. The Frenchman Antonin Artaud (1895–1948), after witnessing a performance of *legong* by a Balinese dance troupe at the 1931 Colonial Exposition in Paris, became so enamored with what he saw that he proposed a total break with the word-based Western theater tradition, going so far as to argue that the theater was like a plague that needed to infect the organism on a visceral level. He believed that the complex sign-systems he witnessed while watching Balinese dance were more closely linked to a deeper, more spiritual, archetypal reality than Western drama was. Like many Western artists of his day who had little sustained and meaningful exposure to other cultures, on the basis of this single experience, he assumed his "reading" of Balinese dance was by extension also true for all of Asian performance. Artaud's writings on theater, collected in 1938 to form *The Theatre and Its Double*, became a virtual bible for many avant-garde Western theater practitioners from midcentury until the late 1970s,

unintentionally reinforcing Orientalist notions about a generic Asia with great depth and mystery capable of rescuing Western artists from the tyranny of logos and linear thinking. I would argue that Mnouchkine is in many respects the inheritor of this tradition, which was still strong when she began her theater practice.

6. Another articulate early critic of intercultural theater practice at the hands of Western artists was Daryl Chin, whose 1989 article "Interculturalism, Postmodernism, Pluralism" is much cited.

7. For the substance of Bharucha's argument, refer to his "A View from India"; "Somebody's Other: Disorientations in the Cultural Politics of Our Times"; and "Peter Brook's *Mahabharata*: A View from India," in *Theatre and the World: Performance and the Politics of Culture*.

8. Literally "performance/show leather," in Bahasa Indonesian and Malay, *wayang kulit* is the generic term for the shadow puppetry traditions of Indonesia and Malaysia. One of the few full-time professional *dalangs* (or master puppeteers) in peninsular Malaysia is Pak Hamzah Awang Amat, who has performed frequently in Singapore. No Singaporean makes a living performing in this tradition.

10: Conclusion

1. Seow, also mentioned in chapter 2, is generally referred to as a "fugitive lawyer" in the Singaporean press. It seems remarkable indeed that a "criminal" could have made it to the top of the legal profession in squeaky-clean Singapore.

2. The U.S. State Department's 1997 *Singapore Country Report on Human Rights Practices* observed that "there have been credible reports in past years of police mistreatment of detainees. Reliable reports indicate that police have sometimes employed sleep deprivation or interrogation of detainees in very cold rooms where the prisoners may be stripped of their clothes and doused with water. In 1993, the last year for which statistics are available, of the 94 complaints of police abuse investigated, 14 were substantiated."

3. Unless otherwise noted, all quotes are from the unpublished script of *Six of the Best*, dated 14–30 April 1994, provided by TheatreWorks. In addition to the script, extensive use was made of the video of the original production.

4. As noted in chapter 4, *ang mo* is Hokkien for "orange hair," a derisive term used for all Caucasians.

5. The "Sarong Party Girl," or "SPG," is a well-known archetype in Singapore. Action Theatre's 1997 production of Pek Siok Lian's *Mail Order Brides and Other Oriental Take-aways* featured four stereotypes of single women in Singapore: the Filipino maid, the Thai prostitute, the China bride, and the SPG (Teo Pau Lin).

6. While policies in housing have encouraged the breakup of ethnic enclaves, policies such as the introduction of "Moral Education" into the educational system in 1981 have encouraged difference based primarily on an individual's ethnicity to be activated and developed. When "Moral Education" was introduced as an O-level subject in the schools for students fifteen to sixteen years of age, they were given a choice between the following: Bible Knowledge, Hindu Studies, Sikh Studies, and Confucian Ethics. What generated the most attention at the time, however, was that eight Chinese schol-

ars were brought in from overseas (seven from the United States) to devise the Confucian Ethics curriculum (C. J. W.-L. Wee 155), a move consistent with the government's concern that the Chinese represent the single group most at risk when it comes to the encroachment of "Western values."

7. Lee cites the hierarchical structure of the Catholic Church as the Western equivalent of the PAP oligarchy: "The Pope chooses the cardinals and the cardinals elect the Pope" (T. J. S. George 45).

8. In an unprecedented move, prompted no doubt by international concern about the integrity of Singapore's judiciary, the Court of Appeal reduced the judgment against Tang to S$3.63 million in November 1997 (*Straits Times*, 2 February 1998).

9. Christopher Tremewan notes that in Singapore the state is "the exclusive or major provider of infrastructure (utilities, communications, media, industrial estates, port and airport services) and of social services (housing, health, and education). . . . It is the country's largest employer, it sets wage levels, regulates labor supply and controls all unions. It holds approximately 75 per cent of the land and has the power to take the rest" (2). In addition, Singapore's system of compulsory savings through the Central Provident Fund (CPF) requires fixed contributions from every employer and citizen. Free marketeers argue that the vast sums the government invests for its citizens would be better invested by private individuals, while others, more interested in the long-term social welfare of the greatest number (and I would count myself in this camp), feel that the CPF system has merit, even if it does enable the government to essentially play with other people's money and prop up government-owned industries. But as Singapore's government has demonstrated greater skill at investing than I possess, I shall leave the ultimate verdict to the political economists, who are perhaps in a better position to judge the merits of the system.

10. Chris Lingle, in his book *Singapore's Authoritarian Capitalism*, reaches such a conclusion. By contrast, Joseph Tamney, in *The Struggle over Singapore's Soul*, argues that "countries such as Singapore will be more successful than countries such as the United States. This is true for several reasons. First, Singapore's dominant ideology assumes a merciless world society, and this ideology effectively shapes public policies. Second, Singaporeans are more willing than Westerners to live in accord with conservatism because the Singaporeans are less affected by either libertarianism or the counterculture" (201). Unlike Lingle, Tamney generally fails to consider the links between creativity, risk taking, and entrepreneurial initiative.

11. By way of contrast, in 1996 Singaporean theater companies received S$1.2 million in rental subsidies and S$2.4 million in grants (Seno and Oorjitham), which is significantly less than 1 percent of the money being spent on the massive arts edifice.

Works Cited

Ahmad, Aijaz. *In Theory: Classes, Nations, Literatures.* London: Verso, 1992.

Altman, Dennis. "The New World of 'Gay Asia.'" *Asian and Pacific Inscriptions: Identities, Ethnicities, Nationalities.* Ed. Suvendrini Perera. Spec. issue of *Meridian* 14.2 (1995): 121–38.

——. "Rupture or Continuity? The Internationalization of Gay Identities." *Social Text* 48, vol. 14.3 (Fall 1996): 77–94.

Ang, Ien, and Jon Stratton. "Straddling East and West: Singapore's Paradoxical Search for National Identity." *Asian and Pacific Inscriptions: Identities, Ethnicities, Nationalities.* Ed. Suvendrini Perera. Spec. issue of *Meridian* 14.2 (1995): 179–92.

Appiah, Kwame Anthony. "Is the Post- in Postmodernism the Post- in Postcolonial?" *Contemporary Postcolonial Theory.* Ed. Padmini Mongia. London: Arnold, 1996. 55–71.

Asia in Theatre Research Circus. Program for *The Tragedy of Macbeth.* Merbau Road Warehouses, Singapore, March/April 1993.

Asiaweek. Web site <www.cnn.com/ASIANOW/asiaweek/>, July 2000.

Aston, Elaine. *An Introduction to Feminism and Theatre.* London: Routledge, 1995.

Austin, Gayle. *Feminist Theories for Dramatic Criticism.* Ann Arbor: University of Michigan Press, 1990.

Automobile Association of Singapore. Web site <www.aas.com.sg/>, August 2000.

Bachtiar, Ida. "Surface-Deep but It Shines." *Singapore Straits Times* 23 September 1992: Life Sec., 3.

Balme, Christopher. *Decolonizing the Stage: Theatrical Syncretism and Post-Colonial Drama.* Oxford: Clarendon Press, 1999.

Banham, Martin, ed. *The Cambridge Guide to Theatre.* Cambridge: Cambridge UP, 1995.

Ban Kah Choon et al., eds. *Imaging Singapore.* Singapore: Times Academic Press, 1992. 320–61.

Baratham, Gopal. *A Candle or the Sun.* London: Serpent's Tail, 1991.

Bell, Daniel. *Communitarianism and Its Critics.* Oxford: Clarendon Press, 1993.

Bellows, Thomas. "Singapore in 1988: The Transition Moves Forward." *Asian Survey* 29.2 (February 1989): 145–53.

——. "Singapore in 1989: Progress in a Search for Roots." *Asian Survey* 30.2 (February 1990): 201–9.

Bennett, Susan. *Theatre Audiences: A Theory of Production and Reception.* London: Routledge, 1990.

Bhabha, Homi K. "Introduction: Narrating the Nation." *Nation and Narration.* Ed. Homi K. Bhabha. London: Routledge, 1990. 1–7.

Bharucha, Rustom. "Negotiating the 'River': Intercultural Interactions and Interventions." *Drama Review* 41.3 (Fall 1997): 31–38.

——. "Somebody's Other: Disorientations in the Cultural Politics of our Times." *The Intercultural Performance Reader.* Ed. Patrice Pavis. London: Routledge, 1996. 196–212.

——. *Theatre and the World: Performance and the Politics of Culture.* London: Routledge, 1990.

——. "A View from India." *Peter Brook and the Mahabharata: Critical Perspectives.* Ed. D. Williams. London: Routledge, 1991. 228–52.

Birch, David. "Singapore English Drama: A Historical Overview 1958–1985." *Nine Lives: Ten Years of Singapore Theatre, 1987–1997.* Ed. Sanjay Krishnan. Singapore: The Necessary Stage, 1997. 22–52.

——. "Staging Crises: Media and Citizenship." *Singapore Changes Guard: Social, Political and Economic Directions in the 1990s.* Ed. Garry Rodan. New York: Longman Cheshire, 1993. 72–83.

Boal, Augusto. *Games for Actors and Non-Actors.* London: Routledge, 1992.

Boehmer, Elleke. *Colonial and Postcolonial Literature.* New York: Oxford UP, 1995.

Brandon, James, ed. *The Cambridge Guide to Asian Theatre.* Cambridge: Cambridge UP, 1993.

Branegan, Jay. "Is Singapore a Model for the West?" *Time* 18 January 1993: 36–37.

Brown, David. "The Corporatist Management of Ethnicity in Contemporary Singapore." *Singapore Changes Guard: Social, Political and Economic Directions in the 1990s.* Ed. Garry Rodan. New York: St. Martin's Press, 1993. 16–33.

——. *The State and Ethnic Politics in South-East Asia.* London: Routledge, 1994.

Butler, Judith. *Bodies That Matter.* New York: Routledge, 1993.

——. "Performative Acts and Gender Constitution: An Essay in Phenomenology and Feminist Theory." *Performing Feminisms: Feminist Critical Theory and Theatre.* Ed. Sue-Ellen Case. Baltimore: Johns Hopkins UP, 1990. 270–82.

Carey, Peter. "Foreword." *The Political Economy of Social Control in Singapore.* By Christopher Tremewan. London: Macmillan, 1994.

Case, Sue-Ellen. *Feminism and Theatre.* New York: Methuen, 1988.

——. "From Split Subject to Split Britches." *Feminine Focus.* Ed. E. Brater. New York: Oxford UP, 1989. 126–46.

——, ed. *Performing Feminisms: Feminist Critical Theory and Theatre.* Baltimore: Johns Hopkins UP, 1990.

Catherall, Sarah. "The Price of Fleeting Fame." *New Zealand Herald* 17 February 1998: E3.

Césaire, Aimé. "From Discourse on Colonialism." *Postcolonial Criticism.* Ed. Bart

Moore-Gilbert, Gareth Stanton, and Willy Maley. London: Addison Wesley Longman, 1997. 73–90.

Chan Heng Chee. "Singapore in 1985: Managing Political Transition and Economic Recession." *Asian Survey* 26.2 (February 1986): 158–67.

Chay Yew. *Porcelain and a Language of Their Own*. New York: Grove Press, 1997.

Chee Soon Juan. *Dare to Change: An Alternative Vision for Singapore*. Singapore: Singapore Democratic Party, 1994.

Chew, Melanie. "Human Rights in Singapore: Perceptions and Problems." *Asian Survey* 34.11 (November 1994): 933–48.

Chiang, Michael. *Private Parts. Private Parts and Other Play Things*. By Chiang. Singapore: Landmark Books, 1994. 222–95.

Chin, Daryl. "Interculturalism, Postmodernism, Pluralism." *Performing Arts Journal* 33/34 (1989): 163–75.

Chin Soo Fang. "It's Strictly Beautiful People for New NUS Play." *Straits Times* 6 September 1995: Life Sec. 6.

Chin Woon Ping. *Details Cannot Body Wants*. 1992. Manuscript provided by author.

——. "From San Jose to San Jose." *(Post)colonial Stages: Critical and Creative Views on Drama, Theatre and Performance*. Ed. Helen Gilbert. West Yorkshire: Dangaroo Press, 1999. 253–59.

——, ed. *Playful Phoenix: Women Write for the Singapore Stage*. Singapore: TheatreWorks, 1996.

Chow, Rey. "Where Have All the Natives Gone?" *Contemporary Postcolonial Theory*. Ed. Padmini Mongia. London: Arnold, 1996. 122–46.

——. *Writing Diaspora: Tactics of Intervention in Contemporary Cultural Studies*. Bloomington: Indiana UP, 1993.

Christian, Barbara. "The Race for Theory." *Contemporary Postcolonial Theory*. Ed. Padmini Mongia. London: Arnold, 1996. 148–57.

Chua Beng Huat. "'Asian-Values' Discourse and the Resurrection of the Social." *Positions: East Asia Cultures Critique* 7.2 (1999): 573–92.

——. "Beyond Formal Strictures: Democratisation in Singapore." *Asia Studies Review* 17.1 (July 1993): 99–106.

Chua Huck Cheng. "Shoestring Culture at Wellington Arts Festival." *Singapore Straits Times* Web site, 28 February 1998.

Clammer, John. "Deconstructing Values: The Establishment of a National Ideology and Its Implications for Singapore's Political Future." *Singapore Changes Guard: Social, Political and Economic Directions in the 1990s*. Ed. Garry Rodan. New York: St. Martin's Press, 1993. 34–51.

Devan, Janadas. "Blind and Irrational Fears Should Not Be Allowed to Fester." *Singapore Straits Times* 8 November 1994: 7.

——. "Why the US Is Not Dying — Yet." *Singapore Straits Times* 23 September 1994: 6.

Dhaliwal, Rav. "Many Fear Control May Kill Spontaneity." *Straits Times* Web site, 5 October 1997.

Dolan, Jill. *The Feminist Spectator as Critic*. Ann Arbor: UMI Research Press, 1988.

Duberman, Martin et al., eds. *Hidden from History: Reclaiming the Gay and Lesbian Past*. New York: Penguin Books, 1989.

Durocher, Debra. "Times and Post Cos. Bow to Mighty Singapore." *American Journalism Review* 17.8 (1995): 11.

Eagleton, Terry. *The Illusions of Postmodernism*. Oxford: Blackwell Publishers Ltd., 1996.

——. *Literary Theory: An Introduction*. Minneapolis: University of Minnesota Press, 1983.

Elegant, Simon. "Unleashing the Lion's Pen." *Far Eastern Economic Review* 30 July 1992: 46–47.

Esslin, Martin. *The Field of Drama*. London: Methuen, 1987.

Fanon, Franz. *The Wretched of the Earth*. London: Macgibbon & Kee, 1965.

Fernandez, Warren. "Confucian Values Helped S'pore Prosper: SM Lee." *Singapore Straits Times* 6 October 1994: 1.

——. "Latest Figures Show Children of Grads Do Better in Exams." *Singapore Straits Times* 3 September 1994: 3.

Fernando, Lloyd. *Scorpion Orchid*. Kuala Lumpur: Heinemann Educational Books (Asia) Ltd., 1976.

——. *Scorpion Orchid*. 1994. Unpublished manuscript, TheatreWorks, Singapore.

Fong, Leslie. "Domestic Politics." *Singapore: The Year in Review, 1990*. Ed. Tan Teng Lang. Singapore: Times Academic Press, Institute of Policy Studies, 1990. 1–11.

Foo, Juniper. "SBC Bans Cross-Sex Acts, Except Liang Po Po." *Singapore Straits Times* 13 May 1994: Life Sec., 14.

Forte, Jeanie. "Realism, Narrative, and the Feminist Playwright — A Problem of Reception." *Modern Drama* 32.1 (1989): 115–27.

Foucault, Michel. *The History of Sexuality*. Trans. Robert Hurley, New York: Pantheon Books, 1978.

Freud, Sigmund. "Jokes and Their Relation to the Unconscious." 1905. Trans. James Strachey. *Dramatic Theory and Criticism*. Ed. Bernard Dukore. New York: Holt Rinehart and Winston, 1974. 831–36.

Fukuyama, Francis. "Asia's Soft-Authoritarian Alternative." *New Perspectives Quarterly* 9.2 (1992): 60–61.

——. *The End of History and the Last Man*. New York: Macmillan, 1992.

Gandhi, Leela. *Postcolonial Theory: A Critical Introduction*. New York: Columbia UP, 1998.

George, Cherian. "Banking on Yuppies to Sell Cool Groundbreaking Images." *Straits Times* Web site, 28 December 1999.

George, T. J. S. *Lee Kuan Yew's Singapore*. Singapore: Eastern Universities Press, 1984.

Gilbert, Helen, and Joanne Tompkins. *Post-Colonial Drama: Theory, Practice, Politics*. London: Routledge, 1996.

Gilbert, Helen, ed. *(Post)colonial Stages: Critical and Creative Views on Drama, Theatre and Performance*. West Yorkshire: Dangaroo Press, 1999.

Gillian Woon Mei Ching. Letter to the Editor. *Singapore Straits Times* 16 February 1994: 29.

Goh, Julia. "Mad Chinaman: Today Japan, Tomorrow Broadway." *Sunday (Straits) Times* 16 August 1992: Life Sec., 8.

———. "Not a Singaporean Musical but an Asian Event." *Sunday (Straits) Times* 16 August 1992: Life Sec., 8.

Goodman, Lizbeth. *Contemporary Feminist Theatres.* London: Routledge, 1993.

Gray, Denis D. "Critic, 86, Carries on Lonely Human-Rights Crusade in Singapore." *Seattle Times* 1 May 1994: A15.

Hall, D. G. E. *A History of South-East Asia.* 4th ed. London: Macmillan, 1981.

Han Fook Kwang. "When Smart Parents Lead to Smart Kids—And Fewer Smart People." *Singapore Straits Times* 3 September 1994: 33.

Heath, Ray. Review of *Mortal Sins*, Kallang Theatre, Singapore. *South China Morning Post* Web site, 11 November 1995, <http://business.scmp.com/Search/SearchArticles.asp>.

Heilbrunn, Jacob. "Yew Turn." *The New Republic* 9 December 1996: 20–21.

Heng Hiang Khng, Russell. *Lest the Demons Get to Me. Fat Virgins, Fast Cars and Asian Values: A Collection of Plays from TheatreWorks Writers" Lab.* Singapore: Singapore Press Holdings, 1993. 27–53.

Herbert, Patricia. "Nanny State Seeks Moral Mandate." *New Zealand Herald* 18 February 1998: 1.

Herrnstein, R. J. "Fewer Kids of Graduate Mums Could Lower Society's I.Q. Levels." *Straits Times* 3 September 1994: 35.

Hewison, Kevin, et al., eds. *Southeast Asia in the 1990s: Authoritarianism, Democracy and Capitalism.* St. Leonards, New South Wales, Australia: Allen and Unwin, 1993.

Hiebert, Murray. "Acting Up: Singapore's Playwrights Test the Government's Limits." *Far Eastern Economic Review* 21 November 1996: 62–63.

Hinsch, Bret. *Passions of the Cut Sleeve: The Male Homosexual Tradition in China.* Berkeley and Los Angeles: University of California Press, 1992.

Ho Kwon Ping. "Allegations of Torture." *Far Eastern Economic Review* 9 January 1976: 13–14.

———. "Countering the Communist 'Sinister Conspiracy.'" *Far Eastern Economic Review* 14 May 1976: 21–22.

———. "Singapore Students: End of the Lesson." *Far Eastern Economic Review* 17 September 1976: 8–11.

———. "Students Rally Again and Win the Day." *Far Eastern Economic Review* 5 March 1976: 18.

———. "When Language Is a Class Issue." *Far Eastern Economic Review* 19 November 1976: 22.

Holmberg, Judith. "AIDS Play Premiere in April." *Singapore Straits Times* 3 February 1988.

Ho Minfong. "Shedding Light on the SRT Backstage." *Straits Times* Web site, 30 May 1996.

Ho Sheo Be. "Dramatists Get Help from the Archives." *Singapore Sunday Times* 28 August 1994: Life Sec., 4.

Hwang, David Henry. *M. Butterfly.* New York: Penguin Books, 1988.

Ibrahim, Zuriadah. "Single Mothers: The Stark Reality." *Straits Times* 3 September 1994: 32.

Iritani, Evelyn. "Singapore Loosens Its Reins to Get Internet Economy Running." *Los Angeles Times* 23 July 2000: C1, C6.

Jackson, Adrian. "Introduction." *Games for Actors and Non-Actors*. By Augusto Boal. London: Routledge, 1992. xix–xxiv.

Jagose, Annamarie. *Queer Theory: An Introduction*. New York: New York UP, 1996.

Jameson, Fredric. *Postmodernism, or The Cultural Logic of Late Capitalism*. Durham, N.C.: Duke UP, 1991.

——. "Postmodernism and Consumer Society." *Postmodernism and Its Discontents*. Ed. E. Ann Kaplan. London: Verso, 1988. 13–29.

Jit, Krishen. "Modern Theatre in Singapore: A Preliminary Survey." *Tenggara* 23 (1989): 210–26.

——. Personal interview. 29 June 1994.

Jit, Krishen, and Ong Keng Sen. "Director's Notes." *Three Children*. By Leow Puay Tin. Singapore: NUS Theatre, Southeast Asian Play Series, 1992. viii–xv.

Kalyanam, Ganesh. Personal interview. 14 June 1994.

Kandiah, Thiru. "Audience and Form: Singaporean Plays in English." *Beyond the Footlights: New Play Scripts in Singapore Theatre*. NUS-Shell Short Plays Series, no. 6. Singapore: UniPress, 1994. 1–41.

Kaplan, E. Ann, ed. *Postmodernism and Its Discontents*. London: Verso, 1988.

Kiernander, Adrian. Introduction to Ariane Mnouchkine interviews, "The Theatre Is Oriental." *The Intercultural Performance Reader*. Ed. P. Pavis. London: Routledge, 1996. 93–94.

Kim Dae Jung. "Is Culture Destiny: The Myth of Asia's Anti-Democratic Values." *Foreign Affairs* 73.6 (November/December 1994): 189–194.

Kirk, Donald. "Sorry Performance." *National Review* 3 April 1995: 26, 28.

Koh, Tommy. Letter to the Editor. *Singapore Straits Times* 7 February 1994: 29.

——. "Singapore in 1990: Continuity and Change." *Singapore 1991*. Singapore: Ministry of Information and the Arts, 1991. 1–8.

Koh Boon Pin. "Castration and Corporate Ladder." *Singapore Straits Times* 6 June 1995: Life Sec., 3.

——. "Pyramids, 800 Homegrown Talents and Animals." *Singapore Straits Times* Web site, 22 May 1996.

——. Review of *Mortal Sins*, Kallang Theatre, Singapore. *Singapore Straits Times* 8 November 1995: Life Sec., 7

——. "What Was Delivered." *Singapore Straits Times* 11 September 1995: Life Sec., 3.

Koh Buck Song. "Liberalising the Arts Takes Time." *Singapore Straits Times* 8 February 1994: 4.

——. "New Survey to Gauge Festival Awareness to Be Carried Out." *Straits Times* Web site, 24 May 1996.

——. "Performance Arts Shows Axed." *Singapore Straits Times* 23 February 1994: Life Sec., 4.

Koh Tai Ann. "Commentary." *Singapore: The Year in Review, 1990*. Ed. Tan Teng Lang. Singapore: Times Academic Press, Institute of Policy Studies, 1990. 79–89.

———. "Culture and the Arts." *Management of Success: The Moulding of Modern Singapore.* Ed. Kernial Singh Sandhu and Paul Wheatley. Singapore: Institute of Southeast Asian Studies, 1989. 710–48.

Kon, S. *Emily of Emerald Hill.* Singapore: Macmillan, 1989.

Krishnan, Sanjay. "Waiting for Theatre." Unpublished edition of *Commentary* 12.1 (1994): 88–94.

Krugman, Paul. "The Myth of Asia's Miracle." *Foreign Affairs* 73.6 (1994): 62–78.

Kuan Yoke Kiew. "Spotlight on Singapore: Arts Fiesta." *Silver Kris* (June 1992): 21.

Kuo Pao Kun. "Between Two Worlds." *Nine Lives: Ten Years of Singapore Theatre, 1987–1997.* Ed. Sanjay Krishnan. Singapore: The Necessary Stage, 1997. 126–42.

———. *The Coffin Is Too Big for the Hole and Other Plays.* Singapore: Times Books International, 1990.

———. "Commentary." *Singapore: The Year in Review, 1990.* Ed. Tan Teng Lang. Singapore: Times Academic Press, Institute of Policy Studies, 1990. 69–78.

———. "Evolving an Identity: The Root Problem of Contemporary Singapore Theatre." Working Paper for the Seminar on the Performing Arts in Malaysia and Singapore, Universiti Sains Malaysia, Penang, 8–9 August 1992.

———. "Evolving Roles of Theatre: The Singapore Experience." Keynote Address at Australasian Drama Studies Conference, University of Western Australia Perth, 30 November 1993.

———. Interview with Janadas Devan. *Straits Times* Web site, 19 May 2000.

———. Telephone interview. 30 June 1994.

Kuttan, Sharaad. "Theatre and the Singaporean State." Unpublished academic exercise, Department of Sociology, National University of Singapore, 1988–89.

Kwan Weng Kin. "Ong's Lear Takes Tokyo by Storm." *Straits Times* Web site, 12 September 1997.

Lau, Wendy. "Role of the National Arts Council: The Singapore Experience." Paper presented at the SPAFA Training Course in Performing Arts in Southeast Asia, National University of Singapore, 3 February–1 March 1993.

Le Blond, Max. "Drama in Singapore: Towards an English Language Theatre." *Discharging the Canon: Cross-Cultural Readings in Literature.* Ed. Peter Hyland. Singapore: Singapore UP, 1986. 112–25.

Lee, Edwin. *Historic Buildings of Singapore.* Singapore: Preservation of Monuments Board, 1990.

Lee, Mary. "Marshall Lore." *Asia Magazine.* 17–19 June 1994. 8–11.

Lee Kuan Yew. *The Singapore Story: Memoirs of Lee Kuan Yew.* Singapore: Times Editions Ptd. Ltd., 1998.

Lee Lai To. "Singapore in 1986: Consolidation and Reorientation in a Recession." *Asian Survey* 27.2 (February 1987): 242–53.

———. "Singapore in 1987: Setting a New Agenda." *Asian Survey* 28.2 (February 1988): 202–12.

Lee Weng Choy. *Chronology of a Controversy.* Unpublished edition of *Commentary* 12.1 (1994): 59–68.

Lee Yin Luen. "The Singapore Musical: Singing Out Loud and Strong." *Singapore Straits Times* 21 October 1995: Life Sec., 6–7.

Leong, Laurence Wai-Teng. "Walking the Tightrope: The Role of Action for AIDS in the Provision of Social Services in Singapore." *Gays and Lesbians in Asia and the Pacific*. Ed. Gerard Sullivan and Laurence Wai-Teng Leong. Binghamton, N.Y.: Harrington Park Press, 1995. 11–30.

Leow Puay Tin. *Family. Playful Phoenix: Women Write for the Singapore Stage*. Ed. Chin Woon Ping. Singapore: TheatreWorks, 1996. 159–269.

———. *Three Children*. Singapore: NUS Theatre, Southeast Asian Play Series, 1992.

Li, Tania. *Malays in Singapore: Culture, Economy and Ideology*. Singapore: Oxford UP, 1989.

Liew, Cheryl. "Rebels with a Cause." *Singapore Business Times* 22 July 1992: 21.

Liew Chin Choy. Personal interview. 6 July 1994.

Lim, Charlotte. "What's She Been Up to Lately." *Singapore* (November 1992): 7.

Lim, Lydia. "$50m Boost for the Arts." *Singapore Straits Times* Web site, 10 March 2000.

Lim, Richard. "Criticise, but Don't Prescribe or Proscribe." *Singapore Straits Times* 2 August 1992: Life Sec., 8.

Lim Chor Pee. "Is Drama Non-Existent in Singapore?" *Temasek* 1 January 1964: 42–44.

Lingle, Christopher. "The Propaganda Way." *Foreign Affairs* 74.3 (May/June 1995): 193–96.

———. *Singapore's Authoritarian Capitalism: Asian Values, Free Market Illusions, and Political Dependency*. Fairfax, Va.: Locke Institute, 1996.

———. "The Smoke over Parts of Asia Obscures Some Profound Concerns." *International Herald Tribune* 7 October 1994.

Lo, Jackie. "Theatre in Singapore: An Interview with Kuo Pao Kun." *Australasian Drama Studies* 23 (October 1993): 135–46.

Locke, John. *Two Treatises of Government*. Ed. Peter Laslett. London: Cambridge UP, 1967.

Loh, Sharon. "Grow Up, Take Charge, and Be Counted." *Singapore Straits Times* Web site, 3 January 1997.

Macaw. "The Great Cultural Dessert." *Singapore* (March/April 1994): 26.

Mackerras, Colin. "Chinese Drama: A Historical Survey." Beijing: World Press, 1990.

Mahbubani, Kishore. *Can Asians Think*. Singapore: Times Editions Pte. Ltd., 1998.

———. "The Pacific Way." *Foreign Affairs* 74.1 (January/February 1995): 100–111.

Mahone, Sydné. "Introduction." *Moon Marked and Touched by Sun: Plays by African-American Women*. Ed. Sydné Mahone. New York: Theatre Communications Group, 1994. xiii–xxxiii.

Maleczech, Ruth. Personal interview. 10 June 1994.

Marshall, David. "Singapore's Struggle for Nationhood, 1945–1959." *Journal of Southeast Asian Studies* 1.2 (September 1970): 99–104.

Mauzy, Diane. "Leadership Succession in Singapore." *Asian Survey* 33.12 (December 1993): 1163–74.

——— "Singapore in 1995: Consolidating the Succession." *Asian Survey* 36.2 (1996): 117–22.

Means, Laurel. "The Role of the Writer in Today's Singapore." *Asian Survey* 34.11 (November 1994): 962–73.

Milne, R. S., and Diane Mauzy. *Singapore: The Legacy of Lee Kuan Yew*. Boulder: Westview Press, 1990.

Minchin, James. *No Man Is an Island: A Study of Singapore's Lee Kuan Yew*. Sydney: Allen & Unwin, 1986.

Mnouchkine, Ariane. "The Theatre Is Oriental." *The Intercultural Performance Reader*. Ed. P. Pavis. London: Routledge, 1996. 95–98.

Moh Hon Meng. *Single*. Singapore: NUS Theatre, 1991.

Mongia, Padmini, ed. *Contemporary Postcolonial Theory*. London: Arnold, 1996.

Moore-Gilbert, Bart, Gareth Stanton, and Willy Maley, eds. *Postcolonial Criticism*. London: Addison Wesley Longman, 1997.

Mukherjee, Arun P. "Whose Post-Colonialism and Whose Postmodernism." *World Literature Written in English* 30.2 (1990): 1–9.

Music and Movement and Promax. Program for *Nagraland*, Kallang Theatre, Singapore, October 1992.

Mutalib, Hussin. "Singapore in 1992: Regime Consolidation with a Twist." *Asian Survey* 33.2 (February 1993): 194–99.

——. "Singapore in 1993: Unresolved Agendas in an Eventful Year." *Asian Survey* 34.2 (February 1994): 127–32.

Nair, C. V. Devan. "Open Letter to Lee Kuan Yew." *Far Eastern Economic Review* 21 July 1988: 6–8.

National University of Singapore Society. Program for *Double Dogs Second Chance*. Guild House, Singapore, April 1999.

Neher, Clark. "Asian Style Democracy." *Asian Survey* 34.11 (November 1994): 949–61.

Newton, Christopher. Review of *Mortal Sins*, TheatreWorks, Singapore. *Theatre Journal* 48.3 (October 1996): 381–83.

Ng, Irene. "Do Gays Have a Place in Singapore." *Straits Times* Web site, 27 May 2000.

Ng Sek Chow. Review of *Mergers and Accusations*, TheatreWorks, Singapore. *Singapore Straits Times* 13 July 1993: Life Sec., 12.

Nippon Hoso Kyokai (NHK)/Japanese Broadcasting Service. Television broadcast of *Lear*, 1997. Bukamura Theatre, Tokyo.

Nusantara. Web site <http://www.nusantara.com/PELU.html>, November 2000.

Ong Chit Chung. "The 1959 Singapore General Election." *Journal of Southeast Asian Studies* 6.1 (March 1975): 61–86.

Ong Soh Chin. "M Butterfly Role: We Wouldn't Mind the Nudity, Say Hopefuls." *Singapore Straits Times* 24 March 1990: Life Sec., 3.

——. "Singapore's First R-rated Play." *Singapore Straits Times* 9 September 1992: Life Sec., 3.

Ong Sor Fern. "Moaning Desdemona." *Straits Times* Web site, 10 June 2000.

Oon, Clarissa. "An Asian Buffet, but What Are We Eating." *Straits Times* Web site, 22 June 1999.

——. "A Cheaper Lear: Pan-Asian Play." *Straits Times* Web site, 17 October 1998.

——. "Don't Sniff at Our Arts Fest." *Straits Times* Web site, 16 September 1999.

——. "Lessons from This Year's Arts Fest." *Straits Times* Web site, 28 June 2000.

Oorjitham, Santha. "Some Degree of Damage." *Asiaweek* Web site, 10 October 1997.

——. "Why Art Cannot Be Like Hothouse Flowers." *Asiaweek* Web site, 12 September 1997.

Osman, Ahmad. "Tang Liang Hong Declared a Bankrupt." *Straits Times* Web site, 7 February 1998.

——. "Two Human Rights Groups Here to Watch Jeya Case." *Straits Times* Web site, 17 August 1997.

Pacific Theatricals Pte. Ltd. and Magazines Inc. Pte. Ltd. Program for *Bugis Street*, Victoria Theatre, Singapore, March 1995.

Paglia, Camille. "Animal House: Camille Paglia Comments on the Sexual Politics of the Clinton White House." *Salon Magazine* Web site, 20 January 1998 <http://www.salon.com/people/col/pagl/>.

——. "Ninnies, Pedants, Tyrants and Other Academics." *New York Times Review of Books* 5 March 1991: Sec. 7, pp. 1, 29, 33.

——. *Vamps and Tramps*. New York: Viking, 1994.

Pakir, Anne. "Linguistic Alternants and Code Selection in Baba Malay." *World Englishes* 8.3 (1989): 379–88.

Pandian, Hannah. "High Drama at Fort Canning." *Singapore Straits Times* 3 April 1992: Life Sec., 3.

——. "1991: A Year of Singapore English Drama in Retrospect." *Singa* 23 (December 1991): 82–88.

——. Review of *Imagine* and *The Joust*, Drama Centre, Singapore. *Singapore Straits Times* 30 August 1991: Life Sec., 5.

——. Review of *Lest the Demons Get to Me*, TheatreWorks, Singapore. *Singapore Straits Times* 20 April 1992: Life Sec., 6.

——. Review of *Renewable Women*. *Singapore Straits Times* 14 September 1992: Life Sec., 3.

——. "Turning the Tide." *Singapore Straits Times* 31 August 1991: Life Sec., 12.

Pavis, Patrice. *Theatre at the Crossroads of Culture*. Trans. L. Kruger. London: Routledge, 1992.

——, ed. *The Intercultural Performance Reader*. London: Routledge, 1996.

People Like Us (PLU). Web site <http://www.geocities.com/WestHollywood/3878>, July 2000.

Perera, Suvendrini, ed. *Asian and Pacific Inscriptions: Identities, Ethnicities, Nationalities*. Spec. issue of *Meridian* 14.2 (1995).

Peterson, William. "Commodifying and Subduing the Body on the Singaporean Stage." *SPAN Journal* 42/43 (April/October 1996): 124–36.

——. "Foreword." *Second Chance: A Cross Cultural Theatre Casebook*. Singapore: TheatreWorks, 1996. 3–7.

——. "Interculturalism Derailed: The Case of Singapore." *Disorientations: Intercultural Theatre from an Australian Perspective*. Ed. Rachel Fensham and Peter Eckersall. Melbourne: Centre for Drama and Theatre Studies, Monash University, 1999. 83–96.

———. "Kuo Pao Kun." *Contemporary Dramatists*. Ed. Thomas Riggs. 6th ed. New York: St. James Press, 1999. 375–77.

———. "Sexual Minorities on the Singaporean Stage." *Australasian Drama Studies* 25 (October 1994): 61–72.

———. "Singapore's Festival of the Arts." *Asian Theatre Journal* 13.1 (Spring 1996): 112–24.

Phan Ming Yen. "$406,000 Not Enough." *Straits Times* 17 May 1994: Life Sec., 5.

———. Review of *The Bribe*, Mabou Mines, Drama Centre, Singapore. *Straits Times* 13 June 1994: Life Sec., 10.

———. "Surprises, and Some of Theatre's Best." *Straits Times* 11 July 1994: Life Sec., 8.

———. "Tougher Challenges for Arts Festival." *Straits Times* 11 July 1994: Life Sec., 8.

———. "Will Polish Play Be the Rave?" *Straits Times* 30 April 1994: Life Sec., 22.

Phua Mei Pin. "Play Looks at Racism by Getting under the Skin." *Straits Times* Web site, 2 May 1996.

Phua Siew Chye, and Lily Kong. "Ideology, Social Commentary and Resistance in Popular Music: A Case Study of Singapore." *Journal of Popular Culture* 30.1 (Spring 1996): 215–31.

Pieterse, Jan Nederveen, and Bhikhu Parekh. "Shifting Imaginaries: Decolonization, Internal Decolonization, Postcoloniality." *The Decolonization of Imagination*. Ed. Pieterse and Parekh. London: Zed Books Ltd., 1995. 5–15.

Precourt, Geoffrey, and Anne Faircloth. "Best Cities: Where the Living Is Easy." *Fortune* 11 November 1996: 126+.

PuruShotam, Nirmula. "Women and Knowledge/Power: Notes on the Singaporean Dilemma." *Imaging Singapore*. Ed. Ban Kah Choon et al. Singapore: Times Academic Press, 1992. 320–61.

Quah, Jon S. T. "Singapore in 1984: Leadership Transition in an Election Year." *Asian Survey* 25.2 (February 1985): 220–31.

Rajaratnam, S. "Singapore's Future Depends on Shared Memories, Collective Amnesia." *Singapore Straits Times* 20 June 1990: 33.

Rasina, Noh. "Special-Effects Firsts in Musical." *Singapore Straits Times* 14 December 1993: Life Sec., 6.

Renan, Ernest. *What Is a Nation?* Trans. Martin Thom. *Nation and Narration*. Ed. Homi K. Bhabha. London: Routledge, 1990. 8–22.

Rigg, Jonathan. "Singapore and the Recession of 1985." *Asian Survey* 28.3 (March 1988): 340–52.

Robinson, Geoffrey. "Human Rights in Southeast Asia: Rhetoric and Reality." *Southeast Asia in the New World Order: The Political Economy of a Dynamic Region*. Ed. David Wurfel and Ruce Burton. London: Macmillan, 1996. 74–99.

Rodan, Garry. "Elections without Representation: The Singapore Experience under the PAP." *The Politics of Elections in Southeast Asia*. Ed. R. H. Taylor. London: Cambridge UP, 1996. 61–89.

———. "Preserving the One-Party State in Contemporary Singapore." *Southeast Asia in the 1990s: Authoritarianism, Democracy and Capitalism*. Ed. Kevin Hewison et al. St. Leonards, New South Wales, Australia: Allen and Unwin, 1993. 77–108.

———, ed. *Singapore Changes Guard: Social, Political and Economic Directions in the 1990s*. New York: Longman Cheshire, 1993.

Roy, Denny. "Singapore, China, and the 'Soft Authoritarian' Challenge." *Asian Survey* 34.3 (March 1994): 231–42.

Said, Edward. *Culture and Imperialism*. New York: Alfred A Knopf, 1993.

———. *Orientalism*. New York: Vintage, 1979.

Savran, David. "Ambivalence, Utopia, and a Queer Sort of Materialism: How *Angels in America* Reconstructs the Nation." *Theatre Journal* 47.2 (1995): 207–27.

Schechner, Richard. *The Future of Ritual*. London: Routledge, 1993.

Scott, Margaret. "Behind Bars, Again: Claims of Torture Lead to the Re-arrest of Ex-detainees." *Far Eastern Economic Review* 28 April 1988: 15.

Seah, Lynn. "How Idea for an Opera Blossomed into the Rose." *Straits Times* Web site, 5 June 1997.

———. "Male Impersonator, Author Recognised." *Straits Times* Web site, 30 August 1997.

Seet, K. K. "Cultural Untranslatability as Dramatic Strategy: A Speculative Look at the Different Language Versions of Kuo Pao Kun's Plays." *Beyond the Footlights: New Play Scripts in Singapore Theatre*. NUS-Shell Short Plays Series, no. 6. Singapore: UniPress, 1994. 243–55.

———. Review of *Six of the Best*. *Theatre Journal* 49.2 (1997): 214–16.

Senkuttuvan, Arun. "Singapore Tightens the Reigns." *Far Eastern Economic Review* 5 December 1975: 12–13.

———. "A Student's Disappearance." *Far Eastern Economic Review* 14 November 1975: 24–25.

Seno, Alexandra A., and Santha Oorjitham. "Gaining Cultural Capital." *Asiaweek* Web site, 12 September 1997.

Seow, Francis T. *To Catch a Tartar: A Dissident in Lee Kuan Yew's Prison*. Monograph 42. New Haven, Conn.: Yale University Southeast Asia Studies, 1994.

Sesser, Stan. *The Lands of Charm and Cruelty*. New York: Vintage Books, 1993.

———. "Singapore, the Orwellian Isle." *New York Times* 30 April 1994: 23.

Sharma, Haresh. *Still Building*. Singapore: EPB Publishers Pte. Ltd., 1994.

———. *This Chord and Others*. Singapore: Minerva, 2000.

Shee Poon Kim. "Singapore in 1990: Continuity and Stability." *Asian Survey* 31.2 (February 1991): 172–78.

———. "Singapore in 1991: Endorsement of the New Administration." *Asian Survey* 32.2 (February 1992): 119–25.

Shenon, Philip. "Overlooked Question in Singapore Caning Debate: Is the Teen-Ager Guilty?" *New York Times* 17 April 1994: 110.

Sheridan, Greg. *Asian Values, Western Dreams: Understanding the New Asia*. St. Leonards, New South Wales, Australia: Allen and Unwin.

Sikorski, Douglas. "Effective Government in Singapore: Perspective of a Concerned American." *Asian Survey* 36.8 (August 1996): 818–32.

Singapore Broadcasting Corporation. "Face to Face" with President Ong Teng Cheong, aired on Channel 8, 24 October 1994.

Singapore Government. "Background Paper on Singapore Festival of the Arts."
National Arts Council, 30 July 1992.

——. Committee on the Performing Arts, "Report on the Performing Arts." 1988.

——. "Report of the Advisory Council on Culture and the Arts." 1989.

——. *A River in Time.* Official Program, National Trades Union Congress, Singapore
Indoor Stadium, 5–8 August 1994.

——. "Separation: Singapore's Independence on 9th August 1965." Singapore: Ministry of Culture, 1965.

——. *Singapore 1999.* Singapore: Ministry of Information and the Arts, 2000.

——. Singapore Tourism Board New Asia Web site <http://www.newasia-singapore.com/>, July 2000.

——. Web site for Singapore Food Festival <http://www.travel.com.sg/sog/eatout/foodfestival.html>, July 2000.

——. Web site for Singapore 21 <www.gov.sg/singapore21>, July 2000.

Singapore Lyric Theatre. Program for *Bunga Mawar.* Victoria Theatre, June 1997.

Singapore Straits Times (1996–2000) Asia One Web site <http://straitstimes.asia1.com.sg/>, 1996–2000.

Slemon, Stephen. "Unsettling the Empire: Resistance Theory for the Second World."
World Literature Written In English 30.2 (1990): 30–41.

Smith, Dane. Personal interview. Hamilton, New Zealand, 12 March 1997.

Soh, Felix. "Two Pioneers of Forum Theatre Trained at Marxist Workshops." *Singapore Straits Times* 5 February 1994: 3.

Spivak, Gayatri. *The Spivak Reader: Selected Works of Gayatri Chakravorty Spivak.* Ed.
Donna Landry and Gerald MacLean. New York: Routledge, 1996.

Stockwin, Harvey. "Lee Reveals His Ace in the Hole." *Far Eastern Economic Review*
11 June 1976: 12–16.

Sullivan, Gerard, and Laurence Wai-Teng Leong, eds. *Gays and Lesbians in Asia and
the Pacific.* Binghamton, N.Y.: Harrington Park Press, 1995.

Tamney, Joseph B. *The Struggle over Singapore's Soul: Western Modernization and Asian
Culture.* Berlin: Walter de Gruyter & Co., 1996.

Tan, Kaylene. *Children of the Pear Garden.* 1993. Unpublished manuscript of Eusoff
Hall production.

Tan, Sumiko. "59% of Male Grads Pick Graduate Wives." *Singapore Straits Times*
17 September 1994: 1.

Tan Bah Bah. "Many Little Things Endear the us to Me." *Singapore Straits Times*
23 September 1994: 4.

Tan Hsueh Yun. "'Art' Acts at Parkway Parade Vulgar and Distasteful: NAC." *Singapore Straits Times* 5 January 1994: 3.

Tan Shzr Ee. "If You Must, Snore in Tune: Festival Dos and Don'ts." *Straits Times*
Web site, 26 May 1999.

Tan Sung. "BG Yeo: Culture Important for Singapore." *Singapore Straits Times*
9 October 1993: 3.

Tan Tarn How. *The Lady of Soul and Her Ultimate "S" Machine.* Singapore: Sirius
Books, 1993.

——. "Liberal Questions." *Singapore Straits Times*, 22 October 1992: Life Sec., 3.

——. "Pruning the Bonsai." Unpublished edition of *Commentary* 12.1 (1994): 69–71.

——. Unpublished Script of *Six of the Best*. 14–30 April 1994.

Tay, Mary W. J. "Code Switching and Code Mixing as a Communicative Strategy in Multilingual Discourse." *World Englishes* 8.3 (1989): 407–17.

Tee Hun Ching. "Take Your Pick of 151 Events." *Straits Times* Web site, 19 February 2000.

Television Corporation of Singapore. Video of *Bunga Mawar*. 1997, produced by Singapore Television 12.

Teo Pau Lin. "Check Out Prostitute, Sarong Party Girl for Answers." *Singapore Straits Times* Web site, 3 July 1997.

TheatreWorks. Program for *Safe Sex*. 1989.

——. Program for *Wills and Secession*. Jubilee Hall, September 1995.

——. Video of *Descendants of the Eunuch Admiral*. Victoria Theatre, Singapore, June 1995.

——. Video of *Mortal Sins*. Kallang Theatre, Singapore, November 1995.

——. Video of *Six of the Best*. The Black Box, Singapore, May 1996.

Tong, Kelvin. "Show Me the Money: Renaissance City." *Straits Times* Web site, 29 August 1999.

Tremewan, Christopher. *The Political Economy of Social Control in Singapore*. London: Macmillan, 1994.

Tsang, Susan. "If It's a Good Piece of Art, I Cry." *Straits Times* Web site, 3 March 1997.

——. Review of *Sing to the Dawn*, Kallang Theatre, Singapore. *Singapore Straits Times* 31 May 1996: Life Sec., 3.

——. "20 Year Arts Dream Turning into Reality for Singapore." *Straits Times* Web site, 12 August 1996.

Turnbull, C. M. *A History of Singapore: 1819–1988*. Singapore: Oxford UP, 1989.

United States Government. *Singapore Country Report on Human Rights Practices for 1997*. U.S. State Department Web site, <www.state.gov/www/global/human rights/1997 hrp report/singapor.html>, November 1998.

——. *Singapore Country Report on Human Rights Practices for 1999*. U.S. State Department Web site, <www.state.gov/www/global/human rights/1997 hrp report/singapor.html>, July 2000.

Utopia. Web site <http://www.utopia-asia.com/tipssing.htm>, July 2000.

van Erven, Eugène. *The Playful Revolution: Theatre and Liberation in Asia*. Bloomington: Indiana UP, 1992.

Vatikiotis, Michael R. J. *Political Change in Southeast Asia: Trimming the Banyan Tree*. London: Routledge, 1996.

Wallace, Charles P. "Ohio Youth to Be Flogged in Singapore." *Los Angeles Times* 4 March 1994: A1, A12.

——. "Pay Raise Plan Gets a Rise out of Public." *Los Angeles Times* 3 December 1994: A2.

——. "Singapore: What Price Justice?" *Los Angeles Times* 2 April 1994: A1, A8.

Wee, C. J. W.-L. "Contending with Primordialism: The "Modern" Construction of Postcolonial Singapore." *Asian and Pacific Inscriptions: Identities, Ethnicities, Nationalities.* Ed. Suvendrini Perera. Spec. issue of *Meridian* 14.2 (1995): 139–60.

Wee, Vivienne. "The Ups and Downs of Women's Status in Singapore: A Chronology of Some Landmark Events, 1950–1987." *Commentary* 7.2–7.3 (1987): 5–12.

Williams, David, ed. *Brook and the Mahabharata: Critical Perspectives.* London: Routledge, 1991.

Wong, Eleanor. *Mergers and Accusations. Dirty Laundry, Mergers and Undercover: Plays from TheatreWorks" Writers" Lab.* Singapore: Singapore Press Holdings, 1995. 1–73.

——. *Wills and Secession Playful Phoenix: Women Write for the Singapore Stage.* Ed. Chin Woon Ping. Singapore: TheatreWorks, 1996. 83–158.

Worsley, Peter. *The Third World.* Chicago: U of Chicago P, 1964.

Wrage, Stephen D. "Singapore, a Model of Intimidation." *Nieman Reports* 49.4 (Winter 1995): 43–45.

Yaw Yan Chong. "Ministry Says 'No' to Play on Aids." *Singapore Straits Times* 16 March 1988: Life Sec., 3.

Yeo, Robert. *The Eye of History.* 1991. Manuscript provided by playwright.

——. *The Eye of History.* Video of National University of Singapore Society Production, Victoria Theatre, January 1992.

——. *One Year Back Home.* Manila: Solidarity Foundation, Inc., 1990.

——. "Singaporean Theatre in English: Knowing Where It Wants to Go." Paper presented at seminar on the performing arts in Malaysia and Singapore, Universiti Sains Malaysia, Penang, 8–9 August 1992.

——. "Survey: Drama in Singapore." *Singa* 16 June 1988: 57–63.

——. "Theatre and Censorship in Singapore." *Australasian Drama Studies* 25 (1994): 49–60.

Yeo, Robert, and Guy Sherborne. *Second Chance, A Cross Cultural Theatre Casebook.* Singapore: TheatreWorks, 1996.

Yew, Chay. *Porcelain and A Language of Their Own.* New York: Grove Press, 1997.

——. Telephone interview. 19 July 2000.

Yu, Ovidia. *A Woman in a Tree on the Hill. Playful Phoenix: Women Write for the Singapore Stage.* Ed. Chin Woon Ping. Singapore: TheatreWorks, 1996. 3–36.

Zach, Paul. "Time Lee's Efforts Dawn on Radio." *Singapore Straits Times* Web site, 24 May 1996.

Index

Abdul Kadir, Abdullah bin, 68–69, 73
Abisheganaden, Jacintha, 185, 191–92
Action for Aids (AFA), 133
Action Theatre, 58, 142
Aida, 203–4, 218, 258
Akka, 142
Ali, Najip, 191–93
Altman, Dennis, 158
American Express, 93
American School in Singapore, 219, 223
Amnesty International, 27, 38
Anchor Beer, 100
ang mo, 89, 225, 259
Angela, June, 190
Artaud, Antonin, 206, 209, 258–59
Artists Village, The, 154, 156
Arts Management Associates, 163
Asia in Theatre Research Center, 205–14, 258
Asian Festival of the Arts. *See* Festival of Asian Performing Arts
"asian values" in Singapore: as opposed to Western values, 1–2, 9–10, 20–28, 162–63, 191, 218, 219, 230; relative to other Asian countries, 107, 191–93. *See also* Confucian values; Lee Kuan Yew
Association of Women for Action and Research (AWARE), 103
attire: Chinese, 52; cross-dressing, 252; Malay, 52, 137

Au, Alex, 133–34
authoritarianism, Singapore-style, 1, 9, 20–28, 222
Automobile Association of Singapore, 224, 240
Awang Amat, Pak Hamzah, 259

Bachtiar, Ida, 187, 189
Balinese dance, 186, 209, 258
Balme, Christopher, 213–14
Banal, Judith, 185
Baratham, Gopal: *A Candle or the Sun*, 42–44
Barto, Tzimon, 172
Beauty World, 182, 183, 191
Beijing Opera, 214–15
Belachan, Bibik, 137
Bell, Daniel, 241
Benjamin Sheares Bridge, 77
Bhabha, Homi, 66–67
Bharucha, Rustom, 187–88, 206–7, 259
Bigot, Georges, 207–11, 213
Birch, David, 5, 33, 245
bisexual. *See* gay male; lesbians; People Like Us (PLU)
Blyton, Edith, 123
Boal, Augusto, 44–47, 244–45
body, 83–102; ambivalent, 83, 88–92; Asian, 101–2; as metaphor, 84, 96–100; Caucasian, 6, 85–88, 100–101; commodified, 83, 92–96;

body (*continued*): sexualized, 83–88, 100–101, 125, 224–25
Boehmer, Elleke, 124
Boom Boom Room, 135
Brecht, Bertolt, 120
Brecht Forum, 44
Brook, Peter, 205, 207, 212–14
Brown, David, 22
Bugis Street, 193–95
Bunga Mawar, 196–201, 258
Butler, Judith, 118, 127–28, 136, 250

Cairo International Theater Festival, 169, 174
Cambridge Guide to Theatre, 46, 244
caning, 220; and the flogger, 227–28
capitalism: implications of global capitalism, 1, 178, 232–35
Carman, George, 27, 230–31
Case, Sue-Ellen, 127
castration, 98
Catholic Church, 25–26, 39–40, 43. *See also* liberation theology
censorship, 28–30; dramatized, 191–93; "out-of-bounds markers," 142, 148, 157–58, 253; self-censorship, 108, 138, 255. *See also* Censorship Review Committee; Cinematograph Film Appeal Committee; Internet; libel suits; Public Entertainment Licensing Unit (PELU)
Censorship Review Committee, 29, 149, 157
Central Provident Fund (CPF), 260
Chan, Margaret, 61
Chang Boils the Sea, 205
Changi Airport, 77
Cheng, Vincent, 40
chewing gum ban, 136, 252
Chia Chor Leong, 57
Chiang, Michael, 182–83, 201; *Private Parts*, 143, 146–47, 175, 194, 253. *See also Mortal Sins*
Children of the Pear Garden, 88–92, 248
Chin, Daryl, 259

China: Cultural Revolution, 36, 199; homosexuality and the imperial court, 132, 251; Special Economic Zones, 74
Chinese Cultural Festival, 162–63, 182
Chinese Cultural Revolution, 36, 199
Chinese New Year, 161
Chinese opera, 4, 55, 89, 120, 162, 181–82, 199, 209, 211, 252
Chin Woon Ping, 115, 124; *Details Cannot Body Wants*, 124–28; *From San Jose to San Jose*, 249
Choo Hwee Lim, 258
Chow, Rey, 86, 91, 187, 205
Choy, Jeremiah, 144
Christianity in Singapore, 27
Chua Beng-Huat, 238
Cinematograph Film Appeal Committee, 257–58
Citibank, 101
City Hall, 77
Clark, Stephen, 190
Clinton, President William, 84
Close, Glenn, 93
colonization under British, 34, 51, 54, 85–89, 131, 209, 231
Commentary, 49, 154–55, 157
communism in Singapore, 34, 36
communitarianism, 241
Conference of the Birds, The, 205, 212
Confucian values, 9, 21–24, 27–28, 120–23, 128, 230, 260
Congress, U.S., 153
Contemplacion, Flor, 107, 243, 249
"courtesy campaigns," 15; cell phone behavior, 176–77, 257; Singapore Kindness Movement (SKM), 16. *See also kiasu*
crime and sentencing, 221–22
Cultural Medallion, 39, 196, 252
cultural tourism, 178

D'Cruz, Marion, 186
deconstruction, 8
defamation. *See* libel suits

dialects in Singapore, 58–66; Cantonese, 4, 51, 55, 64, 181, 238; code switching and mixing, 60–63, 246; Hakka, 55, 238; Hokkien, 4, 55, 59, 61, 64, 122–23, 136, 181, 224, 238–39 (*see also ang mo*); in film, 59–60; onstage, 60–66; Teochew, 4, 55, 64, 181, 238. *See also* Mandarin

Diamond, Catherine, 256

domestic workers. *See* maids, foreign

Double Dogs Second Chance, 250. *See* Yeo, Robert: *Second Chance*

Drama Box, 254

Duberman, Martin, 251

Eagleton, Terry, 233, 237

economy: financial crisis of late 1990s, 182, 222, 238; state controls, 232, 243, 260. *See also* Central Provident Fund (CPF)

Edgley, Michael, 203

Edinburgh Arts Festival, Edinburgh Festival Fringe, 117, 179

elections, 34, 36, 239, 243

Esplanade—Theatres on the Bay, 19, 166, 182, 234, 240

eunuchs, 96–100

Eusoff Hall, 89

family: and male homosexuality, 132–34; Straits Chinese, 121–23, 197

"Famous Five," 123–24, 253

Fanon, Franz, 10, 82, 124

Farquhar, Colonel R. J., 67

Favre, Jean-Marc, 212

Fay, Michael, 7, 21, 219–24, 226–27, 231, 243

feminism, 103–4, 124, 128; and theatrical realism, 115–16

Fernando, Lloyd, 85, 175. *See also Scorpion Orchid*

Festival of Asian Performing Arts, 96, 167, 174, 192, 200

Field, Michael, 166

5th Passage Artists, Ltd., 154

Florentino, Leila, 194–95

Fong Yong Chin: *Another Tribe*, 147, 253

Foreign Maids Scheme, 106

Fort Canning, 140, 169

Forte, Jeanie, 116

Fortnight Theater, 142

Forum Theatre. *See* Necessary Stage, The (TNS)

Freud, Sigmund, 91, 126–27

Fried Rice Paradise, 183

Fukuyama, Francis, 9; *The End of History and the Last Man*, 222

gay male: onstage, 30, 137–49, 253–55; police entrapment of gay men, 132, 134, 153–55, 251; rights, 130–32; section 377 of Criminal Code, 131, 225; social construction of male homosexuality, 134–35, 251–52. *See also* China: homosexuality and the imperial court; family: and male homosexuality; Internet: and the gay community; lesbians; People Like Us (PLU); performance art; transvestism and transsexuality

gender: as construct, 118, 126–28. *See also* Butler, Judith; gay male; lesbians; bisexual; transvestism and transsexuality

Gifted Education Program (GEP), 113

Gilbert, Helen, 249

Goei, Glen, 189

Goh, Michelle, 59

Goh Ching Lee, 256

Goh Chok Tong: accession, 13, 228; as liberalizing influence, 30, 139–40; leadership style, 16, 229; National Day Speeches, 52–53, 76, 79–81, 163, 247–48, 256; on dissent, 25, 239; on expatriates, 167; relationship with Lee Kuan Yew, 13–15, 72; salary, 20, 241; succession, 239; values, 23; vision for Singapore, 16–17. *See also* libel suits

Goh Lay Kuan, 35, 37–39, 49

Grotowski, Jerzy, 205

Halliday, Hugh, 196
Hampton, Christopher, 92–94, 100
Hara, Yuki, 214
Hari Raya Puasa, 161
hawker food, 162, 255–56
Helms, Senator Jesse, 153
Heng, Ivan, 140–41, 246
Heng, Russell: *Lest the Demons Get to Me*, 143–46, 149, 194, 253
Herrnstein, R. J., 112
Hill, Justin, 171, 215
Hock Lee Bus riots, 80, 247
Hodgson, Peter, 226
Ho Minfong, 190. *See also Sing to the Dawn*
Housing Development Board (HDB), 134, 176, 239, 242, 247, 257
housing policies for singles, 251
Huang, Nicholas, 107
human rights. *See also* Amnesty International; torture, allegations of; United States State Department
Hwang, David Henry, 140–41. *See also M. Butterfly*

Iau, Robert, 141
I Ching, 120
independence from Malaysia, 34, 228–29
Indians in Singapore: *bharata natyam*, 5; *kathak*, 5; Malayalam, 5; position of, 115, 162, 234; Tamil, 5, 12, 55, 59, 64, 142–43, 175, 211; values, 21
Indonesia, 23, 25
"Instant Asia," 209
intelligence level of population, 112–13
interculturalism, 6, 187–88, 203–18. *See also* Balme, Christopher; Bharucha, Rustom; Chin, Daryl; Pavis, Patrice
Internal Security Act, 35, 40, 243
Internal Security Department (ISD), 38, 243
International Center for Theatre Research, 205

International Commission of Jurists, 27
International Confucian Association. *See* Confucian values
International Herald Tribune, 28–29, 242, 247
International Women's Year, 105
Internet, 166: and censorship, 28, 255; and the gay community, 129–31, 133, 250–51

Japan Foundation, 214–15
Japanese occupation, 230
Javanese dance, 186
Jeyaretnam, J. B., 42, 241, 255; criticism of PAP, 234. *See also* libel suits
Jiang Qi Hu, 215
Jiang Qing, 36
Jit, Krishen, 85, 87–88, 119–20, 140–41, 184–86, 246; on Singapore Arts Festival, 169–70, 173, 176, 257. *See also Nagraland*
Jubilee Hall, 93–94

Kabuki, 212
Kallang Theater, 257
Kalyanam, Ganesh, 176
Kennedy, Adrienne, 118
Kennedy, President John F., 84
Khan, Ahmed Ali, 112
Khoo, Eric: *Mee Pok Man*, 59–60; *Money No Enough*, 59, 245–46; *12 Storeys*, 59
kiasu, 15, 170
Kim Dae Jung, 23, 237
King and I, The, 185, 257
Kishida, Rio, 171, 214–15. *See also* TheatreWorks: *Lear*
Kissinger, Henry, 84
Koh, Janice, 99
Koh, Leslie, 71
Koh, Tommy, 47–48, 157, 200–201
Koh Boon Pin, 95–96, 226
Koh Buck Song, 156–57, 194. *See also Bugis Street*
Koh Joo Kim, 151

Kok Heng Leun, 47–48

Kon, Stella, 115; *Emily of Emerald Hill*, 60–63, 246, 250

Kramer, Larry: *The Normal Heart*, 254

Krishnan, Sanjay, 49, 154

Kumar, 136

Kuo Jian Hong, 97, 99, 249

Kuo Pao Kun, 49, 53, 140, 170, 174, 240, 246; arrest and detention, 35–39; *The Coffin Is Too Big for the Hole*, 175; *Descendants of the Eunuch Admiral*, 64, 96–100, 174–75, 256; *Geylang People on the Net*, 64; *Lao Jiu*, 64–65; *Mama Looking for Her Cat*, 64; *No. Parking on Odd Days*, 175; on culture and identity, 53, 63–66, 82; *The Silly Little Girl and the Funny Old Tree*, 64; *Spirits Play, The*, 64, 257; *Sunset Rise*, 64. *See also* Cultural Medallion; Practice Performing Arts School; Worker's Theatre

Kweh, Wendy, 192

Lacan, Jacques, 126–27

language policy: Chinese, 34, 55; English, 34, 54–55; in Malaysia, 245; Speak Mandarin Campaign, 58, 182

LaSalle-SIA College of the Arts, 166

Law Society, 40

Le Blond, Max, 56–57, 60

Lee, Dick, 20, 135, 182–85, 193, 201. *See also Beauty World; Fried Rice Paradise; Mortal Sins; Nagraland; Sing to the Dawn*

Lee Chee Keng: *Life's Elsewhere*, 253

Lee Choo, 104

Lee Hsien Loong, BG, 13, 239, 255

Lee Kuan Yew: alliance with communists, 34, 228; cadre system, 228, 260; contributions of, 11; early years, 5; "Harry" Lee, 246–47; National Day speeches, 229, 247; on Asian values, 2, 9–10, 21–22; on homosexuality, 129–30; on Japanese occupation, 230; on opposition, 43, 229; on private lives of citizens, 229; on procreation, 41, 109, 112–13; on repression, 231; on rule of law, 221; on women, 105–6, 112; and Sir Thomas Stamford Raffles, 5, 66–76, 84; succession, 13, 66, 72. *See also* libel suits; "Marxist Conspiracy" of 1987; People's Action Party (PAP)

Lee Siew Choh, 228

Lee Weng Choy, 154–55, 240

Lee Yock Suan, 18

Leong Wai-Teng, Laurence, 135, 158–59

Leong Yoon Ping, 196–97

Leow Puay Tin, 115, 119–24; *Three Children*, 119–20, 122–24; *Family*, 119, 120–23, 128

Leow Siak Fah, 196

Lepage, Robert: *Seven Streams of the River Ota*, 257

lesbians: onstage, 137, 142, 149–52, 253; school-age, 252; visibility and the law, 135. *See also* gay male; Internet: and the gay community; People Like Us (PLU)

Les Liaisons Dangereuses, 92–96

Les Misérables, 181

Lewinsky, Monica, 84

Liang Po Po, 137

Lianhe Wanbao, 153

libel suits: against J. B. Jeyaretnam, 26–27, 230–31, 239, 242; against Christopher Lingle, 28–29, 247; against Tang Liang Hong, 26–28, 230–31, 239, 242, 260

Liberal Socialist Party, 243

liberation theology, 39–40, 108

Liew Chin Choy, 166, 168, 175–78, 257

Lim, Andy, 193. *See also Bugis Street*

Lim, Casey, 65

Lim, Catherine, 25, 229–30, 239

Lim, Christine, 111, 141

Lim Boon Pin, 147

Lim Chor Pee, 56

Lim Hng Kiang, 251
Lim Huang Chiang, 163
Lim Kay Siu, 189
Lim Siau Chong, 139
Lim Swee Say, 133, 158, 251
Lim Yau, 258
Lim Yew Hock, 34
Lim Yu-Beng, 226
Lingham, Susie, 151
Lingle, Christopher, 260. *See also* libel
  suits
Liu Thai Ker, 173
Locke, John, 24
Loon, Robin: *Famous Five Go on an
  Adventure*, 253
Los Angeles Times, 220
Lou Mee Wah, 252
Lum, Audrey, 94

M. Butterfly, 140–42, 144, 175
Mabou Mines: *The Bribe*, 177–78, 257
Mackintosh, Cameron, 182
Maga, Della, 107
Mahabharata, The, 207, 212–14
Mahbubani, Kishore, 21, 238, 241
maids, foreign, 106–8; abuse of, 249–50;
  from Indonesia, 106; from the Philip-
  pines, 106–7, 249; from Sri Lanka,
  106
Malacca, 119
Malayan National Liberation Front, 243
Malayan People's Liberation League,
  243
Malaysia: union and separation from,
  11–12, 34, 80, 228–29
Malaysian Chinese Association, 243
Malaysian Communist Party, 243
Malays in Singapore: *bangsawan*, 4;
  culture, 104, 137; language, 12, 55–57,
  59, 61–63, 136, 175; position of, 24,
  115, 162, 200, 234; values, 21; women
  and Chinese men, 246
Maleczech, Ruth, 177
Malkovich, John, 93

Mandarin: and culture, 4, 22, 55, 238;
  onstage, 63–64, 147, 162, 174, 175,
  181. *See also* language policy
Mark Taper Forum Asian Theater
  Workshop, 253
marriage, 250
Marshall, David, 12, 22, 33
"Marxist Conspiracy" of 1987, 39–44,
  107–8
McDonald's, 15
Merce Cunningham Dance Company,
  173
Merlion, 77–79, 84
Millennium Project, 253
Ming dynasty, 96–97, 100
Ministry of Communication and Infor-
  mation, 77
Ministry of Community Development,
  15, 41, 138, 143–44. *See also* "courtesy
  campaigns"
Ministry of Culture, 245
Ministry of Information and the Arts, 77,
  142, 165, 247, 255. *See also* "Renais-
  sance City"; Yeo, George, BG
Mitsubishi, 183
Miyazawa, Kazufumi, 185
Mnouchkine, Ariane, 205–7, 212–13, 259
Moh Hon Meng. *See Single*
Monette, Paul: *Borrowed Time*, 254
moral education, 259–60
Mortal Sins, 182, 191–93, 250
motherhood, 109–10, 113–15; single
  moms, 113
MRT (rapid transit), 92
Mukherjee, Arun, 83
multinational corporations, 10, 21, 55–56
musical theater, 6, 181–95, 201; created
  for Broadway and the West End,
  182–85, 189, 195, 201; National Day
  musicals, 79–81, 247–48. *See also
  Bugis Street*; Chiang, Michael; Lee,
  Dick; *Mortal Sins*; *Nagraland*; *Sing
  to the Dawn*; Sondheim, Stephen:
  Into the Woods

My Singapore, Our Future, 79
Myung Hee Cho, 192

Nagraland, 182–89, 257
Nanyang Academy of Fine Arts, 156
National Arts Council, 143, 195–96, 256;
    creation of, 17–18, 29, 140, 240, 256;
    guidelines for buskers, 164; and
    Singapore Arts Festival, 168, 172–73,
    175–78; sponsorship, 45–46, 146,
    156, 167, 175, 212, 256, 260. *See also*
    "Renaissance City"
National Courtesy Campaign. *See*
    "courtesy campaigns"
National Day, 6, 54, 76–81. *See also*
    musical theater: National Day
    musicals
National Endowment for the Arts and
    "NEA Four," 252–53
National Identity, 53–54, 71–72, 81–82,
    84, 219, 223
National Opera and Ballet of China
    Orchestra, 200
National University of Singapore, 28,
    43–44, 89, 245; residence hall pro-
    ductions, 248; Theatre Studies, 181.
    See also University of Singapore
    Students' Union
National University of Singapore Society
    (NUSS), 49, 71, 92, 94, 111, 126, 247,
    250
Necessary Stage, The (TNS), 58, 66, 148,
    245; Forum Theatre, 44–50, 154,
    227, 245; *Glass Roots (Don't Step on
    Them),* 147–48, 253; *Mixed Blessings,*
    45, 227. *See also* Sharma, Haresh;
    Tan, Alvin
Neher, Clark D., 237
neighborhoods: Boat Quay, 194; Bugis
    Street, 135, 145–46, 194–95; China-
    town, 54, 194; Geylang Serai, 54, 253;
    Little India, 54, 194, 211, 253–54;
    Shenton Way, 56, 249
Neo, Jack. *See* Liang Po Po

"New Asia," "New Asian," 3, 185–86,
    217–18; Web site, 161, 165
New Paper, 153, 156
New Straits Times, 238
New York Times, 220, 242
New Zealand International Festival of
    the Arts, 178–79, 257
Ng, Joe, 59
Ng, Joseph, 154–56
Ng, Rosita, 117
Ngui, Matthew, 171
Ng Yew Kang, 138
Ninagawa Company (Yukio Ninagawa),
    173
Noh, 214–15

O'Connor, Francis, 190
Odajima, Yuji, 216
Ohno, Kazuo, 177
Ong, Christina, 195
Ong Keng Sen, 99, 119–20, 139, 151–52,
    171, 174, 175, 215–16, 223; on inter-
    culturalism, 217; on value of history,
    65–66. *See also* Kuo Pao Kun: *Descen-
    dants of the Eunuch Admiral;* Theatre-
    Works: *Lear;* Leow Puay Tin: *Three
    Children; Mortal Sins;* Tan Tarn How:
    Six of the Best; TheatreWorks: *Des-
    demona*
Ong Teng Cheong, 52–53
Oon, Clarissa, 179
opera, 196–201
Opus Dei, 25–26. *See also* Catholic
    church
Orchard Road, 31, 94, 146, 169, 213,
    254

Pacific Theatricals, 193. *See also Bugis
    Street*
Paglia, Camille, 84
Pancasila, 23, 241
Pandian, Hannah, 142–43, 212
Panicker, Remesh, 111
Park Hwa Young, 171

Parliament, 37, 136; House, 67; Nomi-
nated Member of Parliament (NMP),
103; Non-Constituency MPs, 241
Pavis, Patrice, 204–5, 210, 213
Pek Siok Lian: *Mail Order Brides and
Other Oriental Take-aways*, 259
Pencak Silat, 214
People Like Us (PLU), 133–34, 251
People's Action Party (PAP); contribu-
tions, 2, 11–12; controlling terms
of debate, 40, 47–48, 98; creator of
Singaporean identity, 54, 223, 227–35;
Democratic Socialist Club (DSC), 37;
history of, 33; "old guard" and next
generation, 72; on social issues, 130;
on women's rights, 104–6; penalties
for opposition voters, 241–42; politi-
cal graffiti, 220. *See also* Lee Kuan
Yew; libel suits
Peranakan culture, 61–63, 104, 197–99,
246, 258
Percival, Nicky, 226
performance art, 153–58, 255
Perot, Ross, 1
Petito, Tony, 189
Pfeiffer, Michelle, 93
Phan Ming Yen, 172
Philippines: government of, 107
Philippines Educational Theatre Associa-
tion (PETA), 41, 244
Pieterse, Jan, and Bhikhu Parekh, 22, 52
postcolonial: decolonization, 52, 124;
identity, 66–76; theory, 74, 81, 83,
86–87, 91, 95
Practice Performing Arts School, 35, 240
Practice Theatre Ensemble, 140
press: Western, 242. *See also Lianhe
Wanbao; New Paper; Singapore Press
Holdings; Singapore Straits Times*
prostitution, 253–54
Public Entertainment Licensing Unit
(PELU), 29, 124–25, 136, 148, 255;
licensing conditions, 164–65
Public Theatre (New York), 152, 216

Quek, Kenneth, 94–95
qingyi, 181

R(A) ratings for theater, 93–94, 124–25,
150–51
racism onstage, 223–27
Raffles, Sir Thomas Stamford, 5, 11,
66–76, 84, 96
Raffles Hotel, 93
Rahman, Tunku Abdul, 229
Rajan, Uma, 143
Ramayana, 185
realism in acting, 208–211
Registrar of Societies, 251
"Renaissance City," 18–19, 165–166, 256
Renan, Ernest, 71–72, 75, 80
Rendra: *The Struggle of the Naga Tribe*,
185
River in Time, A, 79–81, 248
Rocky Horror, 181
Roy, Denny, 237
Royal Shakespeare Co. (RSC), 257

Said, Edward, 7, 10, 25–26, 81, 84, 200,
203–4
salaries, ministerial, 241
Salonga, Lea, 189
Sarong Party Girl, 225, 259
Sasitharan, T., 20, 57, 240
Savran, David, 218
Schneemann, Carolee, 124
Scorpion Orchid, 85–88, 175
Seet, K. K., 67, 71, 92–94, 100, 125–26
self-help organizations, 24
semiotics, 83
Seow, Francis, 41, 221, 243–44, 247, 259
Sesser, Stan, 221, 228–29
Shakespeare, William: *King Lear*, 214;
Macbeth, 205, 207–14; *Othello*, 171
Shanghai Philharmonic, 81
Sharma, Haresh, 44, 47–48, 66, 148, 245
Sharmeen, Farhana, 95
Shenon, Philip, 220
Sherborne, Guy, 111

Shields, Thomas, 27
Shin Min Daily News, 153
Sikorski, Douglas, 237
Sim, Desmond: *Blood and Snow*, 149, 253
Simon, Neil, 146
Singapore: model, 232–35, 238; statistics, 237–38, 241, 245; 21 Campaign, 129, 133, 250
Singapore Airlines, 77–78
Singapore Arts Festival, 6, 18, 140–41, 143, 146, 162–63, 166–79, 255–57
Singapore Broadcasting Corporation, 52, 136, 154, 252. *See also* Television Corporation of Singapore
Singapore Festival of the Arts. *See* Singapore Arts Festival
Singapore Food Festival, 162
Singapore Indoor Stadium, 203
Singapore International Comedy Festival, 163
Singapore International Film Festival, 162
Singapore Lyric Opera, 197, 258. *See also* *Bunga Mawar*
Singapore Opera Company. *See* Singapore Lyric Opera
Singapore People's Alliance, 243
Singapore Press Holdings, 28, 142, 162–63, 253, 256
Singapore Repertory Theater, 189. *See also* *Sing to the Dawn*
Singapore River Buskers' Festival, 163–65
Singapore Straits Times, 238
Singapore Tourism Board, 161–63, 255
Single, 110, 114–16
Singlish, 58–62
Sing to the Dawn, 189–91
Slemon, Stephen, 74
Social Development Unit (SDU), 109–11, 113
social engineering: initiative-taking, 233–34. *See also* "courtesy campaigns"
"soft" subjects, 240

software versus "heartware," 240
Soh, Felix, 44, 46–48
Soin, Kanwaljit, 103
Sondheim, Stephen: *Into the Woods*, 189
Stand Up for Singapore, 77
stereotypes, cultural, 90–92, 218, 225–26
sterilization, 109
Straits Chinese, 250. *See also* family: Straits Chinese; Peranakan culture
Straits Times. *See Singapore Straits Times; New Straits Times*
street theater, 181
Substation, The, 20, 126, 140, 240
Suzhou Industrial Park, 238

Takashimaya Shopping Center, 31, 242
Tamney, Joseph, 260
Tan, Alvin, 44, 47–48, 66, 148, 176, 245
Tan, Kaylene, 88–89. *See also Children of the Pear Garden*
Tan, Theresa: *Vegetarian*, 253
Tan, Tony, 19–20, 256
Tan Bee Leng, 112
Tan Ek, 38
Tang dynasty, 89, 92–93
Tang Fu Kuen, 89, 99
Tang Liang Hong. *See* libel suits
Tan Hong Chye, 190
Tanjong Rhu, 153
Tan Khee Wan, Iris, 156, 255
Tan Kheng Hua, 151
Tan Tarn How, 149, 157; *The Lady of Soul and Her Ultimate "S" Machine*, 255; *Six of the Best*, 219–20, 223–27, 231, 259
Tan Wah Piow, 36–37, 39
Tan Woon Chor, 192
Tay Eng Soon, 149
Television Corporation of Singapore, 258. *See also* Singapore Broadcasting Corporation
Teo, William, 144. *See also* Asia in Theatre Research Center

*Terrible but Unfinished History of Noro-
dom Sihanouk, King of Cambodia, The,*
207
Tham, Claire: *Raw Material,* 253
Tham, Shannon, 154–56
theater criticism in Singapore, 125–26,
172, 179
Théatre du Soleil, 205–13
TheatreWorks, 49, 58, 85, 96, 99, 117,
120, 138–49, 189, 248–49; *Desdemona,* 171–73, 175, 214, 216, 256; *Lear,*
214–18, 256; and the Singapore Arts
Festival, 175–76; Writer's Laboratory,
142, 253. *See also Beauty World*; Chiang, Michael: *Private Parts; Fried Rice
Paradise*; Heng, Russell: *Lest the
Demons Get to Me*; Hwang, David
Henry; Kuo Pao Kun: *Descendants of
the Eunuch Admiral*; Leow Puay Tin:
Three Children; Leow Puay Tin: *Fam-
ily; M. Butterfly; Mortal Sins; Nagra-
land; Scorpion Orchid*; Tan Tarn How:
Six of the Best; Wong, Eleanor: *Jackson
on a Jaunt*; Wong, Eleanor: *Mergers
and Accusations*; Wong, Eleanor:
Wills and Secession; Yew Chay: *As If
He Hears*; Yew Chay: *Half Lives*; Yew
Chay: *A Language of Their Own*; Yew
Chay: *Ten Little Indians*; Yu, Ovidia:
A Woman in a Tree on the Hill
Third Stage: arrests and detentions,
14, 40–42, 50, 243; *Corabella,* 41;
Esperanza, 41, 107–8; *Oh Singapore!,*
41
Thumboo, Edwin, 196–97, 201
Tiger Beer, 100–101
torture, allegations of, 38, 220–21, 243,
259
Townsend, Christopher, 70–71, 85,
87–88
transvestism and transsexuality, 135–36;
onstage, 137, 141–43. *See also* Chiang,
Michael: *Private Parts*; gay male;

Heng, Russell: *Lest the Demons Get to
Me; M. Butterfly*; neighborhoods:
Bugis Street
Tremewan, Christopher, 260

Umewaka, Naohiko, 215
Under One Roof, 258
United Malays' National Organization
(UMNO), 243
United States State Department: *Country
Report on Human Rights,* 231, 242–43,
259
United World College, 156
University of Malaya in Singapore, 85
University of Singapore Students' Union
(USSU), 36–37
Urban Redevelopment Association
(URA), 212

Vatikiotis, R. J., 238
Victoria Theatre, 67, 71, 85, 99, 151, 172,
192, 200
volunteerism, 24

Wallace, Charles, 222
Warsaw Studio Theatre: *Pilgrims and
Exiles,* 173–74
Washington Post, 242
Watson, Eric, 81
wayang kulit, 186, 211, 259
Western standards: Arthur Andersen, 17;
in arts, 182–89, 201, 256; in educa-
tion, 75, 247; judging the judiciary,
239–40
Whitley Detention Center, 38, 243
Wilson, Robert: *Hot Water,* 172–73
women in the workforce, 106–7
Women's Charter, 105
Wong, Audrey, 240
Wong, Claire, 151
Wong, Eleanor: *Jackson on a Jaunt,* 138;
Mergers and Accusations, 149–50; *Wills
and Secession,* 150–52

Wong Sing Keong, 107
Worker's Party (WP), 40, 230, 241. *See also* Jeyaretnam, J. B.
Worker's Theatre, 34–38
Wrage, Stephen, 232
Wu, William: *Crystal Boys*, 254

xiaosheng, 181

Yang Derong, 184, 186
Yeo, Corrine, 112
Yeo, George, BG, 28, 30–31, 167, 234–35, 242, 256
Yeo, Robert, 126, 246; *The Eye of History*, 66–76, 84–85, 116, 248; *One Year Back Home*, 56–57, 245; *Second Chance*, 110–12, 124. *See also* marriage
Yew, Chay: *As If He Hears*, 139; *Half Lives*, 255; *A Language of Their Own*, 152, 216, 253, 255; *Porcelain*, 253; *Ten Little Indians*, 138
Yu, Ovidia, 115, 124: *Imagine*, 142; *Marrying*, 142; *Three Fat Virgins Unassembled*, 149, 253; *A Woman in a Tree on the Hill*, 116–18, 128
Yuen, Nancy, 200

Zhenghe, Admiral (Admiral Cheng Ho), 96
Zielinski, Scott, 171

Library of Congress Cataloging-in-Publication Data

Peterson, William, 1956–
Theater and the politics of culture in contemporary Singapore /
William Peterson.
    p. cm.
Includes bibliographical references and index.
ISBN 0-8195-6471-0 (cloth : alk. paper) —
ISBN 0-8195-6472-9 (pbk. : alk. paper)
1. Theater—Political aspects—Singapore—History—20th century.
2. Theater and society—Singapore. 3. Politics and culture—
Singapore. 4. Singapore drama (English)—20th century—History
and criticism. 5. Singapore—Cultural policy. 6. Singapore—
Politics and government.

PN2960.S5 P48 2001
792'.095957—dc21   00-069598